CARNIVOROUS PLANTS
of the United States and Canada

CARNIVOROUS PLANTS

of the
United States
and Canada

SECOND EDITION

Donald E. Schnell

TIMBER PRESS
Portland, Oregon

Frontispiece: *Sarracenia flava* variety *rugelii*

First edition published in 1976 by John F. Blair.
Second edition published in 2002 by Timber Press.

Timber Press, Inc.
The Haseltine Building
133 S.W. Second Avenue, Suite 450
Portland, Oregon 97204, U.S.A.

Designed by Susan Applegate
Printed in Singapore

Library of Congress Cataloging-in-Publication Data

Schnell, Donald E., 1936–
    Carnivorous plants of the United States and Canada / Donald E. Schnell.—2nd ed.
        p. cm.
    Includes bibliographical references (p.).
    ISBN 0-88192-540-3
    1. Carnivorous plants—United States—Identification.
    2. Carnivorous plants—Canada—Identification.
    I. Title.

    QK917 .S36 202
    583'.75'0973—dc21

                                                        2001052528

To Brenda

CONTENTS

PREFACE

WHEN THE FIRST edition of this book was published in 1976, I had no idea that the response would be so positive. Apparently, there is both a keen interest in carnivorous seed plants and a great desire for knowledge about them. According to readers' comments, a concise work with easily understood descriptions and good illustrations filled a gap in the literature. Today, however, we understand much more about the classification, identification, physiology, and ecology of carnivorous seed plants. Also, I noticed areas that could benefit from lengthier discussions and more photographs and drawings. So, here is the second edition that some of you have been requesting.

I have again limited the book's scope to the green carnivorous seed plants. There are also interesting carnivorous fungi, which feed mainly on small roundworms (nematodes). These fungi are of some agricultural and horticultural interest because their nearly microscopic prey often cause damage to plant roots. However, the taxonomy of carnivorous fungi is still in disarray, and they require microscopy and growth on special culture media for adequate observation and study. For those interested in carnivorous fungi, two good review references with photographs and drawings are Maio (1958) and Pramer (1964).

Descriptions of the plants are intended to be sufficient for identification. I also present some additional interesting points. Readers requiring more detailed botanical descriptions for study or research purposes are referred especially to Diels (1906), Macfarlane (1908), Bell (1949), McDaniel (1966), Radford et al. (1968), Godfrey and Wooten (1981), and Taylor (1989, 1991).

Some of the most fascinating aspects of carnivorous plants relate, of course, to their biology—their mechanisms of entrapment, digestion, and absorption along with other factors such as growth, pollination, and reproduction. I discuss these factors more thoroughly than in the first edition. Again, readers desiring more physiological and anatomical details are referred to two general references, each with extensive bibliographies: Lloyd (1942) is good for all work and publications prior to 1940, and Juniper et al. (1989) cover material until 1987. These two works complement each other.

A major change in this edition is the elimination of the cultivation chapter. Instead, I present some general discussion of North American carnivorous plant horticulture in the introduction. Details for each genus and species are now included in the respective chapters. I feel this will make the horticultural comments for particular species more accessible. Also, the first edition had a section listing commercial sources, displays with public access, and various carnivorous plant clubs and societies. Because such entities and their addresses change, this information has not been included in this edition.

When reviewing the carnivorous plant literature, I often come across research results that contradict one another and observations that are contrary to my own and others with whom I have spoken. I have not been shy about presenting these contradictions. Rather than being a source of frustration to the reader, I hope these still-unanswered questions stimulate curiosity along with a realization that many definitive answers are not yet available. As a result, readers may even wish to undertake their own observations and simple research projects. Many enthusiasts who are not botanists have contributed greatly to our knowledge of these plants, particularly with field observations and experiences growing carnivorous plants.

Because one may encounter older names in the literature, I have included some pertinent nomenclature synonymy. For example, someone may come across an article from the 1940s, see *Sarracenia sledgei* listed, and wonder why I did not mention it in this book. I have—under the more appropriate scientific name *Sarracenia alata*. This edition also has a brief chapter on some North American species that have been proposed to be carnivorous plants. Most of these have failed various tests of what constitutes a carnivorous plant, however, and others require much more study. Perhaps some of these species should be placed in a new category, "paracarnivorous."

All photographs are by me unless otherwise indicated in the caption. Most of the photographs were taken in the field, but I have included some of cultivated material so that readers may see how the plants do when grown. Botanical artist David Kutt did the drawings throughout the book. Professor Daniel Krider of the Mathematics Department of Concord College in Athens, West Virginia, kindly worked up the location map computer program.

I thank the editors and production personnel at Timber Press for undertaking this project to begin with and then being so helpful and hardworking in bringing it to fruition. I must also express deepest appreciation and love for my constant field companion and wife, Brenda, who did not ask too often, "When are we going to take a real vacation?" Finally, I wish to thank all those who over the years have been bogging with me, taught me much, brought up interesting points and questions, and discussed our beloved plants seemingly ad infinitum—but there is always something else to say. The list of those people is too long to include here, and I would not want to offend by leaving someone out through oversight. Suffice it to say that you know who you are and I thank you.

CARNIVOROUS PLANTS:
An Introduction

G REEN PLANTS HAVE certain needs for growing, thriving, and reproducing. The well-known process of photosynthesis requires sunlight, water, and carbon dioxide. As a result of this process, green
plants produce oxygen; along with cyanobacteria, phytoplankton, and
algae, green plants are a source of this vital gas in the world. Many people
seldom realize, however, that plant cells, like all cells, need oxygen for respiration to use the sun's energy and produce carbon dioxide. Gardeners
are aware that plants must be able to absorb and use certain elements
supplied as minerals. Major mineral needs include nitrogen as soluble
ammonium or nitrates, phosphorus, and potassium. Many other elements
are required in minor quantities, such as iron, copper, boron, manganese,
magnesium, and calcium.

Gardeners and growers of houseplants are well aware of what happens
when these minerals are absent or depleted. In spite of plenty of sun,
water, carbon dioxide, and oxygen, such deprived plants wane and eventually move to the compost heap. Yet, as a group, plants are very tough
and we might even say determined. Through various strategies they can
overcome shortages and still thrive. For example, succulents in the desert
withstand very dry conditions by having the capacity to store water when
it does rain. Some plants produce chemicals that suppress competitors
to provide space around themselves. Plants also may compete by having
deeper root systems. Many plants grow and thrive in deep shade with

seemingly little exposure to sunlight and, in fact, die when exposed to direct sunlight. There are also plants that through various adaptations can survive in adverse, mineral-depleted situations. Some of these become more adept and efficient in absorbing what little mineral material may exist through their roots. Others obtain needed minerals by alternative strategies, one group of which is the carnivorous plants.

Imagine the following habitat—one that the average gardener might dread. We have a piece of land that is open and sunny. The soil is very sandy or may be replaced by a particular *Sphagnum* moss. Mixed with the sand or underlying the moss is a wet substance made up of partially degraded, dead plant material called peat. The peat is sterile and bereft of minerals, as is the sand or moss, and is quite acidic. Now we will add another problem: Our little plot of land is very wet, almost constantly wet to the point of muckiness, and even contains standing water—root-smothering wet. Gardeners might throw up their hands, listing what would need to be done with this plot to make it habitable to corn or roses. They may even say it is impossible. But this land has life if one looks closely. Many green plants make a fine living there, much to our gardeners' confusion, as they slap yet another mosquito or buzzing fly away. At least there seems to be abundant insect life over our plot of land.

Some of those plants growing in the seemingly soggy mire do better and work harder to absorb the scant minerals in their soil. Others get their minerals another way: from the buzzing, biting insects. Life forms have evolved over the millennia by being very adaptable. We will see how some of these plants fulfill their mineral and other needs by luring, trapping, and digesting insects and occasionally other animals. Meat eating is known as carnivory, a process usually relegated to animals but now clearly recognized in certain plants.

Carnivorous or Insectivorous?

Readers may become confused by these two terms describing the same group of plants. In early studies, it was noted that the plants' predominant prey items were insects, thus, this group of plants was called *insectivo-*

rous, or insect eating. This term was used for many years and, in fact, is still sometimes used. Since Lloyd's (1942) book, however, the term *carnivorous*, or meat eating, has become more appropriate because these plants trap and consume animals other than insects. For example, the aquatic genus *Utricularia* traps small water animals, as do members of the genera *Aldrovanda* and *Genlisea* elsewhere in the world. Furthermore, North American pitcher plants trap slugs, spiders, and even the odd tree frog skeleton has been found in their depths. Thus, *carnivorous* is more inclusive and is now the preferred term.

General Characteristics Related to Habitat

The following combination of characteristics generally describes carnivorous plants in their habitats, most specifically in North America. As a group, these factors are more or less an ideal that is seldom found in an individual plant. Although a species or genus may not have several of these features, they will have most of them. The list is useful to show an overall pattern in carnivorous plants. Some of the characteristics may describe noncarnivorous plants as well, but no other plant will likely fit the entire list.

1. Carnivorous plants are generally weak rooted, that is, there is a relatively small root system for the size of the plant. Some ecologists speak of cost-benefit models. In trade for the benefit of special adaptations for luring, trapping, and digesting prey, there must be a cost. Perhaps part of the cost of maintaining these specialized structures is decreased root mass, because valuable energy and materials are required to produce plant parts. In other words, carnivorous plants partially trade roots for highly specialized traps (Juniper et al. 1989). But there may be other reasons for weak root systems, including the nature of the soil or growth medium (see below).

2. Carnivorous plants are usually perennials, living for more than two years. There are several notable exceptions that I will discuss in the species chapters. Some of the perennials are rather short lived; others have

large, branching rhizomes or stolons that can form relatively large colonies.

3. Carnivorous plants usually are found in acidic soil habitats (calcifuges). Again, we will see that a few plants may adapt to either acidic or basic conditions, the latter sometimes with high levels of calcium. But, as a whole, most North American carnivorous plants grow in acidic habitats.

4. Carnivorous plants are usually not tolerant of competition from other plants. A location that was originally a fine carnivorous plant habitat may rather rapidly become inhospitable due to various changes, most prominently drainage or lack of fire. Other plants find the changed habitat more suitable and may literally crowd out carnivorous plants. Sometimes, carnivorous plants are outcompeted by other carnivorous plants or even nonsphagnous mosses.

5. Carnivorous plants are generally tolerant of low-nutrient soils, which, in the case of North American soils, are generally quite wet and usually acidic. Some carnivorous plants, such as some bladderworts, are aqueous and grow in acidic or basic waters. Occasionally, carnivorous-plant soils are neutral or basic, however, particularly in the Great Lakes fens (Schwintzer 1978; Schnell 1980a, 1982b; Crum 1988). The combination of acidity, abundant water, and rain results in nutrients that *do* enter the environment becoming soluble and literally being washed out. Thus, very low levels of nutrients remain. Roots of many noncarnivorous and some carnivorous plants do not absorb nutrients well in these very wet, acidic, and usually low-oxygen soils. Plants roots are stressed in such soils, and higher levels of hydrogen sulfide are also potentially toxic. However, absorption of nitrogen and phosphorus by carnivorous plant leaves seems to stimulate better root function with resulting better absorptive capabilities (Adamec 1997). In some lakes in upstate New York, polluted rain has acidified the waters to the degree that many water plants and fish find the habitat intolerable, resulting in strikingly clear blue lakes that are sterile. In an attempt to correct the acidity, some lakes have been limed with calcite to raise the pH. As this happens, *Sphagnum* mosses and the

carnivorous aqueous bladderworts *Utricularia geminiscapa* and *U. purpurea* have been markedly decreased or even extirpated, their acidic habitat having been destroyed (Weiher and Boylen 1994). These studies demonstrate the rather complex relationship between habitat and certain carnivorous plant species.

6. Nearly all North American carnivorous plants grow best in bright, full sunlight. Some plants may subsist in shaded locations but they become etiolated with poorly formed trap structures and they rarely flower.

7. Carnivorous plants are not only tolerant of frequent, low-temperature fires but actually become dependent on fire in certain habitats such as coastal plain savannas. Fires burn off duff (dead, dried plant material), which often smothers smaller plants and prevents seed germination. Fires also eliminate competing plants that are incapable of surviving conflagration. There is even evidence that fire enhances nutrient availability when rain leaches minerals from the ash (Gilliam 1988).

8. Carnivorous plants have the capacity to lure, trap, digest, and then absorb the digestive products from prey. The concept of luring prey has been brought into question with several well-recognized carnivorous plant species—some would appear to almost capture prey accidentally. This question and the nature of the digestive process will be discussed later in this chapter.

An interesting concept to consider is the relationship of carnivorous plant habitats to other habitats. Obviously, suitable carnivorous plant habitat as briefly described above is not wide ranging and may only be found in locations spanning a few meters to several hectares. These hospitable parcels of land are often surrounded by mesic (drier) areas; shaded, heavy shrub growth; swamp forest with constant surface water; or even beach and saltwater ocean. Clearly, the last is not suitable for carnivorous plant populations. The suitable areas may be thought of as islands, beyond the usual sense of islands in bodies of water (Whittaker 1998).

Island habitats are interesting from the viewpoint of their varying degrees of isolation from one another and how plants may pass from one suitable patch to another through a hostile environment. Migration may be accomplished either by seeds or plant parts capable of generating an entire plant (propagules) getting from one island to another. Seeds may be carried on birds' feet, for example, and propagules may pass from one location to another via water as a result of severe flooding, changes in stream courses, and other events.

The propagules brought from another habitat are often a limited sampling of a much larger gene pool. When the founders (as propagules moving from a larger habitat to another are called) interbreed, previously concealed gene combinations may arise. In the larger, original population, these repressed (or recessive) genes were mostly covered up or swamped by well-ordered genetic combinations that were adaptive to the old environment. But founders may have carried a significant number of these recessive genes to the new island habitat. Because there are so few founders, these genes are more likely to be expressed in sexual seed production in the new location. To be sure, many of these new gene combinations will be just as lethal in the new habitat, but in some cases they will not. These new genetic variations are of considerable importance in ecology and evolution. As I discuss the species in later chapters, some unusual variants of carnivorous plants in isolated habitats will be mentioned. Those readers interested in pursuing the nature of plant variation and adaptations may wish to look into the following, very readable works: Grant (1963), Bell (1967), and Whittaker (1998, ch. 5).

Must Carnivorous Plants Be Carnivorous?

This section title may seem to belabor what would seem obvious, but that may not necessarily be the case. Quite properly, scientists seek experimental proof of any hypothesis. When a scientist seems to find an answer, his or her work should be repeatable by another scientist. If it is not, the question then is still open unless errors in technique, experimental protocol, unwarranted assumptions, or other problems come to light. One of the most common problems I see in conflicting scientific reports is in the statistical handling of data. This usually comes up in very complex experiments and analyses when the scientist employs complex calculations to balance one probability against another or to compare data in an attempt to account for confounding factors and results. I find that the most useful work is that with the most direct and almost startlingly simple approach, a so-called elegant study.

Throughout the eighteenth century, several amateur and professional observers suspected that various examples of plants we now call carnivorous were indeed trapping prey and possibly digesting the victims for nourishment. Because the concept seemed so preposterous, the notion that insects were seeking refuge from foul weather in plants such as pitcher plants kept coming to the fore. From an anthropomorphic perspective, plants were supposedly so benign and genteel that they could not possibly partake of flesh.

However, Charles Darwin (1875), no stranger to tackling controversy, reported that plants did just that. In a series of detailed experiments with a sundew (*Drosera rotundifolia*), he showed that (1) the plants did indeed trap insects; (2) they were well adapted to that function; (3) some form of digestion occurred; and (4) the plants benefited by exhibiting enhanced growth. Darwin even described cellular changes microscopically in the plants incident to feeding.

Following in his father's footsteps, Francis Darwin (1878) proved with numerical results that feeding *Drosera rotundifolia* promoted flowering, numbers of maturing seed capsules, and total numbers and weight of seeds. He kept one set of plants unfed as controls and fed the test plants artificially with insects. The younger Darwin also described parallel, unpublished work done by others.

In spite of this, as late as the 1970s (Daubenmire 1974) some workers still felt that carnivory was at best an ancillary factor. Some of these studies suffered from being short term (many carnivorous genera such as *Sarracenia* have large rhizomes for several seasons' food storage). Others did not use controls or evaluate comparative plant vigor, flowering, seed set, quality and quantity of resulting seed, and so on. Some studies were done in axenic cultures, that is, pure, microorganism-free, agar gel culture media similar to what is used for tissue culture, or other sterile media.

Although these last experiments seem interesting, Gibson (1983), for instance, pointed out that they are essentially irrelevant because in nature the plants live in unsterile media in the company of other plants and animals. Gibson also showed that in nature carnivory accelerated the maturation of carnivorous plants, an important factor in seasonal and competitive situations. Plants and other organisms cannot be interpreted in isolation, but only as members of a larger ecological community.

I agree with those who conclude that carnivorous plants do indeed benefit from their unique adaptations by exhibiting more rapid and enhanced growth, more prolific flowering and seed set, and a better ability to maintain and even improve their competitive edge within their habitats. All sides of this argument are nicely reviewed in Juniper et al. (1989).

Trapping Mechanisms

As I have stated previously and will again emphasize, carnivorous plants must use photosynthesis for energy just as other green plants do, and they must employ nearly all the other pathways of plant metabolism as well. The main difference is that carnivorous plants obtain most of their major mineral needs from trapped prey rather than root absorption from rich soils. To trap animals, special adaptations have evolved.

The traps of carnivorous plants are all modified leaves. Reworking leaf morphology and physiology to lure, trap, digest, and absorb nutrients requires alterations that impinge on the efficiency of photosynthesis, mainly because of changes in surface shape and variation in coloration that masks or even replaces chlorophyll-containing cells. This is the primary reason for discussion of cost-benefit ratios.

Because of leaf modifications, the traps of many carnivorous plants are quite attractive and some people think that the trap leaves are flowers. Indeed, I have spoken with many rural people who had great stands of pitcher plants on their farmland and referred to them as "lilies." Some people have called me to their land to see pitcher plants only to proudly point out *Hexastylis* (wild ginger) with their little juglike flowers or even *Arisaema triphyllum* (jack-in-the-pulpit), in these cases confusing flowers with pitcher leaves. Flowers attract insects for pollination, and carnivorous plant leaves attract insects for a very different reason, but both are indeed attracting insects.

In the geographic area covered by this book, there are four major kinds of leaf traps to consider. There are one or two other kinds in other regions, and there are additional genera in the world for the kinds of traps listed below. However, I will confine my discussion to the traps and their examples in North America. There will be more detail given in the species chapters.

The Venus flytrap, *Dionaea muscipula,* growing in North Carolina. Note the open trap leaves, the brightly colored trap interior, and the fine teeth on the free margins of the trap leaves.

Closing Traps

These traps are present in one North American species, the quintessential carnivorous plant, the Venus flytrap (*Dionaea muscipula*). The leaf blade is modified into a bivalved (two-part) blade something like a book held open at about a 45° angle. The two parts of the blade are attached at the prominent midrib. When the trap is stimulated by suitable prey, the two halves snap together, trapping the prey between the walls and within the cagelike structure formed when the marginal teeth intermesh. This trap has two important broad features: an electrical sensory mechanism for detecting prey and movement stimulated by the electrical signals, both of which use energy.

Suction Traps

The traps of bladderworts (*Utricularia*) function in an aquatic environment. Although the entire plant is visible, especially when growing in masses, the individual traps are only a few millimeters across. In many North American species, these traps can barely be seen with the naked

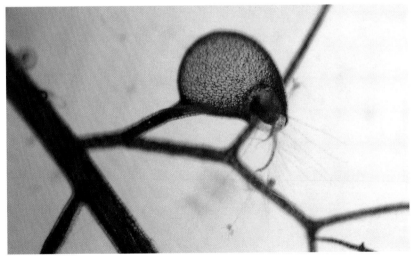

An aquatic trap of the bladderwort *Utricularia gibba*. This microscopic view shows the cellular structure of the trap wall. Note that the minute trap is affixed to a stalk (left) and the trap door with its guard and sensory hairs (right).

eye, yet, they are among the most complex and rapid traps known. The suction trap is a cavity structure filled with water and lined by specialized glands. The walls of the chamber tend to curve outward to maintain shape, but as a result of water evacuation (which requires energy) a negative pressure develops within and the walls of a set trap pinch inward, somewhat analogous to squeezing the bulb of a medicine dropper. At the free end of the structure is a trapdoor surrounded by protruding sensory hairs. When a small water animal swims by, it may stimulate a trigger hair. The door then opens inward and the negative interior pressure results in water and the hapless prey flowing in, at which point the trapdoor closes. All of this occurs so rapidly that the timing has not been accurately measured.

A sundew (*Drosera capillaris*) growing in South Carolina shows an example of an adhesive trap. Note the rosette of leaves, the paddle-shaped blades, and the stalked glands around the margins. On a fresh, dewy summer morning with the sun at the right angle, the plants glisten like an array of jewels.

Adhesive Traps

Species of North American sundews (*Drosera*) and butterworts (*Pingu-icula*) use adhesive traps. As their name implies, sundews are most obvious, with stalked glands on their leaf margins producing mucinous droplets that glisten in backlighting sun. The butterworts, with some very short-stalked glands, are a bit more subtle. Both groups depend on attracted prey becoming mired in the mucinous droplets. There is then some slow movement in most species: The sundew's stalked glands and often the leaf blade slowly fold inward to the center of the leaf, where the prey is held in the mire, whereas the flat leaves of the butterwort curl on the margins to form a shallow bowl. These movements take upward of thirty minutes to a few hours.

Pitfall Traps

The pitcher plants (*Sarracenia* and *Darlingtonia*) produce the largest of the carnivorous plant trap leaves, which are modified into tubes. Prey is

A butterwort (*Pinguicula caerulea*) growing in Florida also catches prey using an adhesive trap. Note the curved leaf margins. The trap leaf has short-stalked glands as well as minute, flat or sessile glands, which can be seen as glistening droplets in the photograph.

attracted to the tube margins by some combination of color, sweet nectar droplets, or fragrance. As the prey tries to reach into the pitcher for more nectar, the waxy inner walls cause a loss of footing and the prey tumbles in. Escape is discouraged by the waxy lining; downward pointing hairs in the depths of the pitcher, and the narrowness of the trap tube, which prevents effective flight. The tube is often topped by a lid or flap of leaf tissue, which usually arches over but, contrary to popular assumption, the lid never closes off the opening. When walking through a stand of pitcher plants, one frequently hears the frantic buzzing of insects trying to escape.

The pitcher plant *Sarracenia purpurea* subspecies *venosa* variety *venosa* growing in North Carolina. The tubular pitfall trap leaves are arrayed in a rosette. Note that in this species the flapped lid is erect. The downward pointing hairs on the inner surface of the lid encourage prey to move toward the pitcher opening.

How Traps Attract Prey

Little exacting work has been done on what actually causes prey to approach and land on a carnivorous plant leaf trap. There are many likely, anecdotal suggestions, some of which were alluded to in the previous section. Although some of these hypotheses may indeed be true, there has been slight rigid scientific confirmation of them.

Williams (1976) observed that as many flying insects landed on plants surrounding sundews as landed on the sundews themselves; Lichtner and Williams (1977) recorded a varied mixture of arthropods captured by *Dionaea muscipula*, as though there were no preference. However, Jones (1923) noted that single flies approaching Venus flytrap leaves were primarily attracted to the leaf trap margins, where there is a heavy secretion of nectar. In reading accounts of what is or is not trapped by carnivorous plants, I see possible variations depending on season, time of day, solar radiation versus clouds, other plants in the immediate area, and what insects are actually abroad. In fact, it is likely that carnivorous plants both actively lure and randomly catch insects. I will discuss a few factors that have been implicated in attracting prey to carnivorous plants. These attractive mechanisms may work in concert in various combinations for any particular species.

Fresh pitchers of *Sarracenia* plants have a sweet fragrance that is sufficiently strong to detect while walking among them (Slack 1979; Gibson 1983; personal observation). The question is whether these olfactory cues, which are pleasant to us humans, attract prey. Insects are sensitive to many aromatic chemicals, as evidenced by bees attracted to people wearing certain fragrances, biting insects being repelled by oils of citronella and eucalyptus, and the serpentine route of pollinators approaching fragrant flowers as though they were guiding in on the fragrance source. These olfactory attractions may either be instinctual or learned from experience with secondary rewards such as nectar associated with a certain fragrance (Juniper et al. 1989).

Some workers have proposed that putrefaction odors from decaying prey in traps (particularly pitcher plants, which have continuous trapping, digestion, and absorption) attract more prey. However, most prey is captured by a pitcher in the first few weeks after its maturation. Beyond that time, insect trapping is markedly decreased and it is at this later point that putrefaction is most intense (Fish and Hall 1978). We know from everyday observation that flies, for instance, are readily attracted to putrefying flesh, but this does not seem to be what is attracting insects to pitcher plants.

Nectar is a watery substance secreted by specialized plant glands that are associated with fragrances. Nectar is a reward for pollinators and has been called the "junk food of the plant kingdom" (Juniper et al. 1989). All North American carnivorous plants produce copious nectar, not only in their flowers for pollinators, but also from arrays of glands around the edges of and within traps. Insects consume nectar as a source of both water and energy (Vogel 1983). Nectar sugar is primarily fructose, but the liquid contains other components as well. There are probably amino acids (the building blocks of proteins), as evidenced by parallels with floral nectaries (Baker and Baker 1973) and the character of ultraviolet absorption of nectar on pitcher surfaces (Joel et al. 1985).

There is a possibility that some carnivorous plant nectars contain compounds that stun or anesthetize an insect so that it more readily slips into pitcher pools. I have noted that a drop of nectar from pitchers of the tropical genus *Nepenthes* has a sweet taste and in addition leaves that portion of my tongue numb for many minutes afterward. Another anecdote comes from D'Amato (1999), who was potting plants one day when he accidentally bumped a *Sarracenia flava* pitcher and it bent over with its top on the bench. Meaning to trim and pot the plant the next day, he left it over night. When he returned, he found that nectar from the tipped pitcher had dripped onto the bench top. Many ants had also arrived and were feeding on the fallen nectar drops, while many other ants lay apparently dead. As he watched, feeding ants lost control of their legs first and stumbled and fell. Then, control of antennae and mandibles was lost and the ants lay still. There was no evidence of recovery.

A compound called coniine has been extracted from rhizome and leaf tissues of the American pitcher plant *Sarracenia flava*, although Mody et al. (1976) did not report in what concentration the compound was found. Indeed, Lambert (1902) noted a "mouse-like" smell in *Sarracenia purpurea* pitchers, which he thought might be coniine. This chemical is an extremely toxic, liquid alkaloid first isolated from hemlock seeds; coniine was likely the principle component in the fatal hemlock juice Socrates consumed. As little as 200 mg of the compound is fatal to humans (Wertheim 1951). A dose of 100 ng causes partial paralysis in ants in as little as thirty seconds. The question of whether coniine will be found in leaf nectars and has any effect requires further work.

As an interesting aside, there is a proprietary liquid extract of roots of *Sarracenia purpurea* that is locally injected by physicians for the treatment of neuralgic pain. Some workers felt that the results were due to the presence of ammonium compounds in the extracts. However, the effects of the whole extract were much more prolonged and effective than pure ammonium salt solutions, suggesting a potentiating effect with some other undetermined compound in the extract (Bates 1943).

Insects may originally be attracted to nectar secretions by a combination of fragrance, associated gland and leaf colors, and glistening of the nectar droplets (Oliver 1944; Vogel 1983). However, eventually they seem to simply learn of the nectar's presence by experience. In the case of carnivorous plant trap leaf nectar, that may prove fatal.

Trap color may play an important role in luring prey, although a common mutation in pitcher plants (*Sarracenia*) that results in green pitchers without any red coloration does not seem to interfere with at least some prey capture (personal observation). Again, attractants must be considered in combination because the green pitchers still produce fragrance and nectar. Fish and Hall (1978) noted that in plants with red pigmentation, trapping reaches its peak when color is fully developed, but other attractants may also peak at that time. Trap leaves with red pigment (anthocyanins) achieve their brightest color in full sunlight. But there is some question of how attractive red pigments are to different insect species, compared to blue or yellow, which may be present and masked to our vision and still visible to insect vision. Apparently, however, in the California pitcher plant (*Darlingtonia*) the most insects can be found in pitchers with the deepest red color (Edwards 1876).

Joel et al. (1985) photographed ultraviolet color patterns in various carnivorous traps and noted absorption and reflectance patterns and apparent guides similar to flowers that lure insects for pollination. It is generally accepted that insects visualize strongly in the ultraviolet range, but as one might suspect, their vision seems to be more complex (see Kevan 1978, 1979). Insects may also incorporate significant portions of the visual range (in human terms) as well. According to Kevan, strict ultraviolet filter photography on black-and-white film may illuminate only a portion of the insect visual system. Systems using television cameras and multiple sequential color filters are awkward. A simple lighting system under which one can film insect visual system patterns with an ordinary camera and color film has been developed. The system contains an equal mixture of black-light fluorescent ultraviolet and ordinary daylight fluorescent lamps, the latter wrapped in blue and green cellophane to attenuate red illumination (McCrea and Levy 1983). This system provides direct photographs similar to what Kevan describes as insect color vision. Recently I have been experimenting with viewing plants through a Tiffen 47 deep blue photographic filter with some interesting preliminary results that seem to approach McCrea and Levy's.

So far, I have not mentioned specific attractive mechanisms in bladderworts (*Utricularia*). There is some weak evidence that special glands in the area of the trapdoor secrete chemicals that attract prey, which may also be attracted by the various bristles and hairs at the trap opening (Meyers and Strickler 1979). However, given the aqueous medium in which this trap exists and functions, random capture due to close contact between large numbers of suitable prey and the trap's trigger hairs is also very likely.

Carnivorous Plant Prey

Most studies of carnivorous plant prey have been confined to terrestrial species. Although insects predominate, spiders, slugs, and even the occasional tree frog have been trapped by North American pitcher plants (Lloyd 1942). Green tree frogs (*Hyla cinerea*) can occasionally be seen hanging just inside the mouths of tall pitcher plants during the day, their heads just protruding from the opening. The frogs intercept insect prey entering the pitchers, lured by the attractive features of the traps. Now and then, however, a frog skeleton is found among insect debris deep inside pitchers when they are opened—no doubt a fatal slip.

People have been opening carnivorous plant traps for years and enumerating the contents (Lloyd 1942; Juniper et al. 1989). Insects predominate and the diets are rather broad. Wray and Brimley (1943), for instance, found in *Sarracenia purpurea* pitchers insects of 14 orders and 150 families in addition to slugs and snails. Prey numbers and species tend to vary by location, relative dryness and wetness of habitat, latitude, time of day, and season—in other words, all those factors that might cause an insect population to vary in any location. Gibson (1983) postulated that recent fire may also be a factor because ants become more active after fire. Those who try to make too much of localized trap content studies, especially comparative studies, without comparing plants across the range, growing season, times of day (including night), and even different years (because of variance in rainfall and water tables) are doomed to erroneous conclusions. Researchers also must use window traps to see what flying insects are abroad before concluding anything about relative trapping by tall pitchers. Still, it is interesting and fun to make anecdotal records of what these plants are trapping. It is certainly an initiation rite of students being introduced to these plants.

I mentioned in the previous section that younger pitchers trap the majority of prey and that this peaks in about thirty days (Wolfe 1981). In fact, new pitcher leaves may trap up to 82% of the plant's total prey during that time period. Wolfe felt that this was due to some senescence of aging pitchers in such things as nectar production and possible olfactory cues.

Williams (1980) recorded Venus flytraps (*Dionaea muscipula*) in North Carolina to have captured mostly crawling or ground insects and arthropods, chiefly ants (30%), spiders (39%), and grasshoppers (10%). In spite of the common "flytrap" name, flies and mosquitoes were only 1–4% of the captured prey. Williams repeated these studies in that location during several seasons. However, Jones (1923) opened fifty traps in the Wilmington, North Carolina, area and counted a much higher proportion of winged insects. Apparently Jones's count was done once, and both he and Williams studied plants in only one location. I think we learn more from the variations in the counts and limited samplings than trying to reconcile the disparities in the two reports.

There have been studies to discern if prey are partitioned in the case of one or more species of sundew or pitcher plant growing in close proximity to one another, if not intermingled. This question stems largely from the ecological concept of niche, which basically states that organisms living in the same location cannot have a completely overlapping resource base. The niche concept is difficult to define, with definitions varying between botanists and zoologists as well as among general ecologists. Recently, an overly rigid concept of niche has been properly questioned (such as Stebbins 1977; Drury 1998; Whittaker 1998) in light of some interesting studies and observations that seem to contradict a rigid concept. These are beyond the scope of this book. However, two of the studies regarding carnivorous plants deserve mention.

Gibson (1983) concluded that there was competition between individual plants and across species for a limited supply of prey in any one bog. The author noted different insect counts in the traps of different species and space competition. Thus, taller pitcher plants such as *Sarracenia leucophylla* and *S. flava* compete for the same flying insects (assumed because of the height and general morphology of their pitchers), whereas, lower to the ground, *S. psittacina* and *S. purpurea* compete more with each other and sundews than with the taller plants. Window trapping of insects flying in the bog and counts of ground insects would have been useful controls in Gibson's study, especially when defining "limited prey" and estimating insect replacement rates. Because he noted faster maturation and more flowering of self-fed plants (some fresh pitchers of control plants were stopped with cotton plugs for the season), the partitioning of prey may prevent direct competition that might exclude one or more species. Gibson's paper should be read in its entirety for more details and arguments. There may be validity in the partition concept, but additional studies using more plant pairs, more bogs of varying composition, and different latitudes may be helpful. Such work should also assess species adaptation to specific habitats and characteristics of hybrids, particularly because these are so abundant in Gibson's study area.

Achterberg (1973) did a roughly similar study in the eastern Netherlands involving three common sundews, with the species often growing in the same bog. The species have traps at three different spatial levels, although *Drosera rotundifolia* and *D. anglica* are closer in height than the taller *D. intermedia*. Rather than fixed competition and partitioning of prey, Achterberg observed that varying wetness of habitat in bogs seemed to play a more important role. This wetness seemed to account for differences in what insects were abroad because the flying insects were those emerging from water, such as midges, and these were far fewer to absent in dryer habitats.

Other carnivorous plant enthusiasts and I constantly hear of people interested in growing these plants in their yards or on the windowsill to control insects. However, in numerical terms carnivorous plants are relatively inefficient trappers of insects. Although one may note that pitchers, for example, have excellent catches in their depths out in a bog, one also is acutely aware of the numbers of insects still about. The plants seem to catch enough to do very well, but they do not deplete overall insect numbers.

I can offer an anecdotal exception to the concept of poor trapping efficiency by *Sarracenia* pitcher plants. Each summer in central North Carolina, we had a terrible infestation of Japanese beetles (*Popillia japonica*). They did severe damage to fruit tree leaves, vegetables, and flowerbeds. I always noticed that pitchers of the white-topped pitcher plant (*S. leucophylla*), yellow pitcher plant (*S. flava*), and pale pitcher plant (*S. alata*) were brimming full of beetles. In *S. leucophylla*, in particular, the beetles were literally piled to the tops of the pitchers so that beetles could land on the writhing mass of their brethren and take flight again without difficulty. I often wondered how many tall pitcher plants I would have to grow to make a dent in the yearly infestation. I realized, however, that the situation would become similar to the commercial pheromone-baited traps sold to catch these beetles in that the pitchers might just attract more beetles from neighboring property.

Bladderworts (*Utricularia*) seem to do better at controlling insect populations. Ponds containing *U. minor* had significantly lower numbers of mosquito larvae and eggs than control ponds without the bladderworts (Angerilli and Beirne 1974). In California, Juniper et al. (1989) observed that in areas with ponds where *U. vulgaris* (= *U. macrorhiza*) was abundant there were far fewer mosquitoes.

There is one interesting incident recorded on a small British island near Norfolk (Oliver 1944). The island had a heavy growth of the sundew *Drosera anglica* and one afternoon the author noted that each plant had several white cabbage butterflies (*Pieris rapae*) adherent to their traps that were not there the day before. Furthermore, none of the butterflies were flying on the island. Apparently an unseen swarm had blown over the island from Europe, the swarm having been liberally sampled by the sundews before it passed on.

The Value of Prey and Its Digestion and Absorption

Insects, the predominant prey of most terrestrial carnivorous plants, are bundles of nutrition, and studies show that insects are nutritious and effective in promoting growth in carnivorous plants. When compared to unfed controls, sundews fed one fruit fly (*Drosophila melanogaster*) per week all show enhanced growth on soils with absent or decreased organic nitrogen (Chandler and Anderson 1976). In other genera, however, there are often different responses to various mineral sources and how they are administered. There seem to be two possible explanations for these results: either there were experimental errors (probably at least a few) or there is true variation among genera and even among groups of species in the same genus. It is remarkably interesting that different carnivorous plants use different sources of minerals within a habitat. We must then think not only of carnivorous plants in a functioning community of plants and animals, but also a community of carnivorous plants within a habitat.

One study indicated that *Sarracenia flava* plants absorbed significant quantities of nitrogen and phosphorus into their tissues from insects, but not calcium, magnesium, or potassium (Christensen 1976). In another study, an interesting possible effect on root activity was noted in the butterwort *Pinguicula vulgaris*. When fed insects alone or in combination with foliar fertilizer, the plants' leaf concentrations of nitrogen and phosphorus were greater than in the insects or fertilizers, suggesting that leaf feeding increased root absorption of what minerals were in the soil (Aldenius et al. 1983). Adamec et al. (1992) did a similar experiment with three species of sundew and Venus flytrap; they also showed greater uptake into the entire plant than was available in the feedings. They suggested the possibility of increased root growth with resulting increased absorbing capabilities or simply more efficient root activity.

Generally, prey is considered not to supply carnivorous plants with significant quantities of trace elements (Juniper et al. 1989). However, Sorenson and Jackson (1968) grew the aquatic bladderworts (*Utricularia*) in liquid media deficient in the trace elements magnesium and potassium. When the plants were fed a ciliate protozoan *Paramecium* species, their growth increased.

What happens when carnivorous plants are grown in nutrient-rich soils? In a nice summary paper, Roberts and Oosting (1958) discussed what was, even back then, a shrinking range for Venus flytrap in the Carolinas. Among other things, Roberts and Oosting did some transplant experiments and observed that plants moved into garden soils languished, few formed good trap leaves, flowering was rare, and many plants died. There were similar results when plants were potted up in houseplant potting soils. In both cases, some surviving plants revived nicely when planted in poor, coastal plain savanna soils and watered with distilled water.

Further south, in the Mississippi coastal plain, the soil at a location containing the pitcher plant *Sarracenia alata* was found to have sufficient nutrients to serve as agricultural soil, unusual in what was a thriving carnivorous plant habitat. Eleuterius and Jones (1969) applied agricultural fertilizer (6-6-12 NPK) in a typical growing field amount, and the pitcher plants declined, with smaller, fewer, and weaker pitcher leaves and less flowering. The pitcher plants responded similarly to the Venus flytraps, but the Mississippi location's soil was rich in the first place, which is unusual. It may have been interesting to see how other pitcher plant species would have responded in the unamended soil in the Mississippi location.

Carnivorous plants may benefit from material other than animal, for example, falling detritus. In one experiment, a butterwort (*Pinguicula*) was grown in a nutrient-poor agar medium in the laboratory. Some plants were fed with sprinklings of pine pollen, and these responded with better growth and more flowering (Harder and Zemlin 1968). Pollen grains have been noted to germinate on leaf glands of butterwort (Juniper at al. 1989). The resulting pollen tubes are far more tender than the grains and perhaps more digestible. The daily rain of material floating in the air may benefit other carnivorous species as well.

Prey captured by carnivorous plants is largely not ready for direct absorption into the plant. Except for possible excretions during the insect's struggle that may contain absorbable nutrients, proteins and other nitrogenous and phosphate compounds must be chemically broken down into smaller compounds that can be absorbed and used by the plant. Most difficult to break down is the insect's exoskeleton, which is something like a suit of armor. The exoskeleton is made up of a substance called chitin, a carbohydrate polymer.

To digest their prey, carnivorous plants produce watery solutions of chemicals called enzymes. Enzymes are relatively unstable proteins that help chemicals react with one another, particularly in aqueous media and at temperatures compatible with life. Many of the chemical reactions that enzymes drive to completion would take, for example, a great deal of heat, time, or caustic chemicals without enzymes. Enzymes are poorly characterized chemically and they are commonly named according to what they do. The suffix *-ase* in an enzyme's name roughly means that it helps break down the chemical compound indicate in the prefix. Thus, a protease helps reduce proteins to simpler nitrogenous compounds, a lipase reduces lipids (fats) to simpler substances, and so on.

So, we have a watery medium, various enzymes, and plenty of complex chemical compounds to work on. But remember the exoskeleton—how does the plant get to these proteins and other substrates? There is an enzyme called chitinase, but it apparently is not very effective. The key is in the armor joints: The insect must move, and flexibility calls for softer tissues at joints. Here enzymes can begin acting until the interior is penetrated. Also, some insects do not have their entire bodies covered with chitin; many insects have soft abdomens, for instance.

The next question is the source of the enzymes. These compounds either come from the plant itself or external sources. Carnivorous plant traps are often teaming with microorganisms (see Lindquist 1975), particularly in the cavities of pitcher plants and on the leaf surfaces of butterworts. One strategy for a microorganism to acquire nutrition is to secrete enzymes into its surroundings; complex chemicals are simplified, and the bacterium or fungus absorbs what it needs. Another indirect, external source of enzymes for carnivorous plants is in the digestive tract of another arthropod. Certain insect larvae are adapted to survive in traps and even feed on other trapped insects. They digest the eaten insects (often with enzymes secreted by specialized bacteria in their digestive tracts) and excrete simplified waste products that may contain nutrients absorbable by the carnivorous plant trap.

The internal source of enzymes is a specialized aggregate of cells called a gland. Most of the external leaf surface is covered by a tough, water-impermeable layer called the cuticle. This layer is absent in microscopic surface openings, called stomata, through which air is exchanged. (When one foliar feeds plants by spraying water-soluble fertilizer on the leaves, a now common gardening practice, the material is absorbed through the uncuticled stomata.) In some plants, carnivorous plants among them, there are aggregates of specialized glandular cells that also do not have or lose the cuticle on their surfaces and may transfer substances readily to the surface or aqueous environment.

Carnivorous plant leaf glands have several functions. In many plants, glands are capable of detecting when prey is present, either by absorbed excretions of the prey and/or by its movement. In some plants, glands secrete digestive juices containing enzymes. As digestion occurs, the glands become absorptive structures and take in the digested nutrients, which are carried throughout the plant by a vascular system. The chemical materials capable of initiating glandular secretion are usually active or partially ionized, including nitrates, ammonium ions, uric acid, and even sodium. Compounds such as egg albumin and urea produce little or no reaction (Robins 1976; Lichtner and Williams 1977). The chemistry of these digestive processes has been fairly well studied and may be reviewed in detail in Juniper et al. (1989).

On most carnivorous plant leaves, the glands are of two sorts. Stalked glands are at the tips of relatively long stalks, and sessile glands are set directly on the leaf surface. The stalked glands, particularly in sundews, are capable of bending, whereas the sessile glands are immobile. The stalked glands gradually move the struggling prey toward the center of the leaf; the prey becomes more entangled in additional stalked glands as it is moved in to the center, where sessile glands further entangle the prey through secretions of thick, tenacious mucilaginous material. In addition, many *Drosera* leaves bend inward, further fixing the prey in the center. You can mimic the stalked glands' movement by bringing the five fingers of one hand together at a point, then bending them toward the palm. Further folding of your hand is similar to the leaf's folding movement.

Sex in Bogs

The ultimate endpoint of green plant growth is reproduction, and carnivorous plants are no exception. The chief modes of reproduction in carnivorous plants are vegetative and sexual. The most important vegetative means in plants capable of this mode are budding and division of rhizomes with multiple budding points. Sexual reproductive is achieved through the production of flowers.

Flowers have stamens topped with anthers that produce pollen. Pollen grains must find their way to the flower pistil, where they are brushed or settle onto the sticky, sugary top of the pistil, called the stigma. The pollen grains germinate something like a seed: They form pollen tubes that grow down through the stalk (style) of the pistil to the bulging ovary at the bottom, where ova await fertilization from certain nuclei in the pollen tubes. Some flowers contain both stamens and pistils, some one or the other.

Ideally, sexual reproduction is most useful genetically if pollen from one plant is transferred to the stigma of another, that is, cross-pollination. Self-pollination is often prevented by genetic and other factors. When self-pollination does occur, it serves as a backup to ensure production of at least some seed even if there is no genetic crossing. With seeds, plants are able to produce new generations (annuals and biennials), increase the number of plants (perennials), or expand ranges (all three).

Pollen gets to stigmas through various avenues, including gravity, water, wind, and animals. Insects are the most important pollinators for most herbaceous plants and are drawn to their work by flowers' petal colors, fragrances, and nectar. But carnivorous plants' flowers grow with leaf traps, a significant risk for the insect pollinators.

There are several ways to reduce risk for these pollinators. One is for the flowers to mature at a different time than the trap leaves. Indeed, in many plants, especially pitcher plants, the flowers appear early in the season before the pitchers, or at least before the pitchers open, and insects can safely cross-pollinate the plants (Schnell 1976). The Venus flytrap (*Dionaea*) produces some trap leaves very early in the spring, but these are pressed to the ground and trap-leaf production temporarily ceases during flowering. A second way contact between pollinators and traps can be minimized is by spatial separation. Carnivorous plant flowers in North America are nearly all located atop very tall flower stalks (peduncles), which gets them into the air near flying pollinators and away from traps near the ground. (I empathize with Juniper et al. [1989], who commented on the difficulty of photographing flowering carnivorous plants due to focal plane problems, with the flower so far above the rest of the plant.) Another way to keep potential pollinators from traps is to produce flowers and traps in different media, such as in air and water. Bladderworts (*Utricularia*) are the best example of this. Species that grow in water send their flowering stalks into the air, and the water surface nicely separates the two.

Surprisingly, pollination mechanisms are not well understood in most carnivorous plants, as will become evident when I discuss the biology of individual plants in the main chapters. We understand the pollination of two *Sarracenia* pitcher plants very well and have extrapolated this knowledge to the other species of the genus. In butterworts (*Pinguicula*), we can see by the flower structure how it is pollinated, but we must confirm the identity of the pollinator. In North American sundews (*Drosera*), there is a mechanism that works to ensure at least self-pollination if there are no pollinators, but we have no idea what the pollinators usually are.

Carnivorous Plant Communities

Until this point, we have been looking at carnivorous plants from a very narrow viewpoint, as though they are the center of the habitat in which they grow and more or less voraciously take what they need. But all living things are part of a community. In spite of an important role, even certain animal and plant species called keystone species, because of their seeming predominance in the system, are far from domineering. Carnivorous plants do take from those in their community but also serve the community in many ways, some of which I will refer to here.

As older leaves of some carnivorous plants die back due to senescence or because the plants go dormant in autumn, they very likely have partially digested and absorbed materials in or on their leaf traps. This is especially true of the pitcher plants, which continuously trap, digest, and absorb prey, as opposed to the periodic activity in such plants as the Venus flytrap, sundews, and butterworts. As the pitchers dry up and fall to the ground and late autumn and winter rains come, the pitcher leaves begin to break down and the soluble portions of their contents can be leached into the ground for absorption by other plants. The deterioration of the leaf tissue itself provides compost on which microorganisms and other secondary and tertiary detritus consumers can work (Plummer 1963). This decomposition, along with periodic fires in certain habitats (see Carnivorous Plant Habitats), carries significant quantities of nutrients into the soil, which helps explain the rich panoply of species (although not often in large numbers) one often finds in these poor soils.

The leached materials may also include elements not primarily absorbed by carnivorous plants, but that were part of the insect masses in their traps and that may be useful to other plants through root absorption. Although these leached minerals and compounds are eventually depleted by rains, the burst of absorption by noncarnivorous plants in the community could result in storage for use in the growing season.

Some suggest (such as Juniper et al. 1989) that carnivorous plants are essentially doomed to destroy their habitat by supplying nutrients to originally poor soils; other plants grow and thus force out the poorly competing carnivorous plants. I think this is an extreme extrapolation of what is happening. For instance, the nature of the southeastern coastal plain sandy soils encourages further washout in continuing rains, which would then result in fewer nutrients for noncarnivorous plants if carnivorous plants were no longer part of the system. Other factors are likely at play in the continuing, rapid disappearance of wetland habitats able to support carnivorous plants, even where there seems to be no direct interference by people. These factors will be discussed in the final chapter.

Because carnivorous plants are green seed plants, their flowers supply pollen and nectar to the communities of various pollinators. Even the enticing nectar around the entrances of pitchers feeds potential prey who eat but do not fall into the traps.

The aquatic bladderworts (*Utricularia*) seem to be host to many organisms. Most are microscopic, rather complex water animals, called rotifers. These animals rest on a foot structure affixed to a solid surface while their cilia wave smaller creatures into their mouths. Under the microscope, the cilia look like rotating wheels, hence the name rotifers. These interesting animals often perch on the nontrigger bristles of *Utricularia* traps. They do no harm, and the plant supplies a place from which to capture food. Of course, the occasional hapless rotifer may touch the wrong bristle and fall prey.

As the warm, humid growing season goes on in pitcher plant habitats, the nectar secreted in the area of the trap mouth accumulates and often dries. These areas may immediately be colonized by sooty molds, their black stains present on nearly every tall pitcher mouth. Sooty molds are superficial, and their quantity, location, and growing habits are no problem for the plants, which supply a platform and some sugary nutrients.

Although it may seem strange, carnivorous plants are not immune to attack by pests, many of which are quite familiar to gardeners. Hard scales sometimes attack pitcher plants. Larry Mellichamp and I have noted mealy bugs covering the rhizomes of pitcher plants in some eastern North Carolina habitats. The infested locations are often stressed, usually by water depletion, but even so, the pests seem to do little harm to the plants in the short run. I see aphids on flower stalks of many butterworts each spring. Aphid infestations of emerging spring pitcher leaves can cause severe deformities of the leaves to the extent that they never mature or open properly.

Strangest of all are the insects whose life cycle is carried out within the pitcher or the rhizome of pitcher plants. Some of these insects are harmless to the plants, others do great harm. In the depths of pitchers, where there is a great deal of liquid and organic material in varying degrees of decomposition, a medium is created for insects inherently resistant to digestive enzymes and microbial action to live in their larval stages. Such little aquatic systems on or within plants are called phytotelms (Frank and Lounibos 1983), and animals that live in them have been called inquilines, although a few debate whether the exact definition of the term *inquiline* fits this particular situation (such as Juniper et al. 1989). However, I have frequently seen the term used in the sense I have just described in peer-reviewed journals published since 1989.

In addition to the capability of the larvae to survive enzymes and microbial action, the adult insects are able to enter and exit the pitchers at will with especially adapted footpads that do not slip on the pitcher's upper waxy lining. Whereas larvae of the moths *Exyra* and *Papaipema* do a great deal of damage, the larvae of the fly *Sarcophaga sarraceniae* and the mosquitoes *Wyeomyia smithii* and *W. haynei* seem harmless and may in fact contribute to pitcher plant nutrition by consuming small insects and converting them to a more usable manure. These specially adapted insect larvae are discussed more in the pitcher plant chapters.

These few examples illustrate that carnivorous plants not only take from their environment but also give something to the other inhabitants in return. There have been an increasing number of studies of carnivorous plants from the viewpoint of the whole ecosystem rather than just their carnivorous properties in a simplified consumer-prey relationship (for some examples, see Juniper et al. 1989).

Carnivorous Plant Habitats

I mentioned carnivorous plant habitats in a very general sense earlier in this chapter when I listed the characteristics of the plants. Now it is time to go into somewhat greater detail. This discussion does not cover all wetlands; I will be mentioning peatlands, sphagnum bogs, fens, seepage bogs, savannas, and a few others. Of course, we will not be concerned with tidal wetlands or even much with marshes and swamps. There may be peatland on the edges of marshes and swamps or small islands or hummocks of peat in them, but North American carnivorous plants, as a whole, are not directly associated with marshes and swamps per se. For definition purposes, I consider a marsh as a place with standing water that has mostly nonwoody water plants, rushes, reeds, and sedges growing in it. A swamp is a place with standing water and a good stand of water-tolerant trees growing in it.

There is a problem concerning what to call the particular wetlands of interest. Often, they are simply lumped into the term *bog*, but purists would argue that the term should be reserved for a particular kind of peatland. Yet, informally, those of us who go into the field to find and research carnivorous plants often speak of "bogtrotting" (an older term) or "bogging" for the activity, even though we may be in a fen (also known as a marly bog) or a savanna. All of this is closely related to the problem of classifying wetlands.

The classification of wetlands, particularly peatlands, has been in a state of flux for years. I have many books on my shelves and papers in my files in which the authors present a wetlands, bog, or peatlands classification. The problem is, most are different to varying degrees and there seems to be much animated argument back and forth in the authors' references one to the other. Those who wish to delve further into the mire of peatlands classification should refer to Deevey (1958), Pringle (1980), Larsen (1982), Johnson (1985), and Crum (1988), among others. Good luck to you.

I do not intend to get bogged down in the discussion and controversies. Granted, it is important work from a research standpoint, but it is often poorly accessible from a practical, everyday standpoint. Thus, I take the bull by the horns, risk ire from some wetlands experts, and say that for the purposes of this book I will speak very generally of carnivorous plant wetlands as bogs (although I will often specify special kinds of bogs). This very simplified habitat classification can be divided into five general categories: (1) bogs that are mainly sphagnous in character (including kettle bogs; some stream-associated bogs; and raised, flat, or hillside dip blanket bogs); (2) marl fens; (3) seepage bogs; (4) southern savannas; and (5) sinkholes. Actually, *Sphagnum* can be found to some degree in all of these peatland types, but it is predominant and the key growth medium for carnivorous plants in the first category.

In informal discussions, botanist Larry Mellichamp and I found that we agreed that North American carnivorous plants sites are more alike than they are different. Although at initial glance the locations appear to be quite different, nearly all fulfill the basic requirements as outlined earlier in this chapter. I now briefly describe particular characteristics of the habitat types outlined above.

Sphagnum

We are all acquainted with mosses, in general, but I must introduce one particular genus of mosses, *Sphagnum*. This moss nearly always grows in or near an abundant water supply. In those locations, *Sphagnum* often grows across huge areas, sometimes many square kilometers.

Sphagnum has some important and unique properties. It grows as fascicles of leaves on a central stalk that can attain a length of up to about 30 cm. The mature plant has no roots and, of course, no flowers. *Sphagnum* reproduces by vigorous vegetative budding and by production of spores, which behave like seeds. Microscopic examination of a leaf discloses a unique structure. The photosynthetic cells are narrow, elongate, and arranged end to end. Between these rows of living and functional cells are larger, empty cells, each with a large pore. These specialized cells fill with water so that a *Sphagnum* plant has a huge capacity for absorbing liquid (Stoutamire 1967; Crum 1988).

The cell walls have polyuronic acids on their surfaces. These acids function as ion exchange units, roughly parallel to how the resins in a water softener exchange calcium and magnesium in tap water for sodium. In this case, the living *Sphagnum* exchanges various aqueous ions for its hydrogen ions, which are acidic. The moss, then, is capable of releasing acid into the environment, which depresses the growth of many plants but encourages others, such as carnivorous plants. A study by Kilham (1982) indicates that, in addition to releasing hydrogen ions by cation exchange, organic acids also dissociate and release their hydrogen ions under certain circumstances; chemical reactions with sulfur com-

A close-up view of *Sphagnum*. The tightly packed heads, or capitula, are the actively growing portions; the stalk extends deeper down. Note the branching fascicles and their tiny leaves.

pounds produce sulfuric acid. Thus, *Sphagnum*'s acid production seems more complex than originally thought, and further research may yield more on this.

These functional properties of *Sphagnum* are most apparent in the living plant, where physiologic processes constantly renew them up to a certain point, barring some toxic event. The strands of living moss are like little renewable factories. When rewetted, even the commercially available dead and dried moss can exchange ions, although usually only for one round. Different species of *Sphagnum* are capable of greater or lesser degrees of acid production and living at different levels above water (Crum 1988; Daniels 1989).

Outside its habitat, *Sphagnum* has been put to some use by humans. Most commonly, horticulturists use it to wrap the root systems of trees, shrubs, and other plants for transport after sale, due to the moss's moisture-retention qualities. Of course, carnivorous plant enthusiasts use the moss for cultivation, and *Sphagnum* is used to some extent for other plants such as certain species of orchids. From the time of the American Civil War to just past World War I, *Sphagnum* was also used to dress open wounds because it had a great capacity for absorbing bodily fluids and blood and seemed to have some antiseptic properties (Crum 1988).

Many observers have a great deal of difficulty identifying *Sphagnum* beyond the genus level. Crum (1988) and McQueen (1990) are two excellent identification references that provide species' morphologic features, the general color and appearance of the species, and the level above water where they grow.

Sphagnous Carnivorous Plant Habitats in the North and the Appalachian Mountains

In the southern half to two-thirds of Canada, New England down through parts of New Jersey, across Pennsylvania, down the Appalachian chain, then back up to the Great Lakes, carnivorous plant habitats are mainly of two types: sphagnous and fen. Fens will be discussed in the next section. For the purposes of this book, sphagnous habitats are of three significant forms: kettlehole bogs, blanket bogs, and streamside and string bogs.

Kettlehole Bogs

Kettlehole or kettle bogs are products of the last ice age, with the Wisconsin ice sheet having receded about 10,000 years ago. As boulders were dragged along, some areas were excavated, leaving what essentially amounts to large potholes. As the chunks of ice that filled these holes melted, various sized lakes characterized by rather steep drop-offs resulted. Continued water feed was supplied by either streams passing through the lakes and/or springs beneath the water surface. When I have swum in these lakes (either on purpose or accidentally), I have often been aware of sudden changing temperature zones or even a water flow pressure while passing through or over spring outlets underwater.

At an unpredictable time and rate, many of these lakes begin to change character. Mats of sedges (*Carex*) and rushes and reeds extend their rhizomatous growth mat out from the shore onto the water surface. As these extend, other plants take advantage of the expanding habitat, including *Sphagnum* and small shrubs such as cranberries and blueberries (*Vaccinium*), Labrador tea (*Ledum groenlandicum*), bog rosemary (*Andromeda glaucophylla*), leatherleaf (*Chamaedaphne calyculata*), along with ferns and other bog plants. As the mat extends further out and becomes wider, remains of dying plants, including the dead deeper branches of *Sphagnum*, begin to accumulate beneath the surface. Breakdown of these plant remains is retarded because of the cold water temperatures, lack of water nutrients, and few microorganisms. The dead material gradually becomes peat, which gets deeper and extends out beneath the mat right behind its leading edge. Back at the original edge of the lake, the peat is deep enough to reach bottom, providing a more solid footing for larger shrubs and trees to begin to grow. Out further on the mat in full light, carnivorous plants may be found growing, particularly the northern pitcher plant (*Sarracenia purpurea* subspecies *purpurea*) and acid-tolerant sundews (*Drosera rotundifolia* and *D. intermedia*).

Over time, the mat may extend clear across the entire lake and enclose the last open water. Sometimes the central water opening remains for a period and is informally known as the eye. We now have a kettlehole bog. The waters in kettlehole bogs are either oligotrophic (poor in nutrients) or dystrophic (poor in nutrients and containing floating, particulate, dead plant matter). They are generally acidic, as is water obtained from squeezing the bog surface material. Although the details of how these bogs form may vary from place to place and even from bog to bog, these are the general principles. Actually, no two bogs are exactly alike, which is one more reason for difficulties in classification (Crum 1988).

Kettle bogs are also known as quaking bogs. When you walk (cautiously) out onto the mat and approach the thinner sections near the middle, you begin to notice that the mat is undulating up and down all around you, somewhat like a carpet floating on water, which it is, in a way. You may be tempted to experiment by alternating pressure from one foot to another or even jumping up and down to increase this strange sensation. You should do so at your own peril. It is possible to penetrate the surface and sink very suddenly to varying depths. Usually it is one leg soaked to the hip, but it can be worse. Needless to say, extricating oneself from the mat can be rather difficult. Luckily, I have never fallen through, but have been with companions who have. You should not explore a kettle bog alone, particularly if it is quaking, and the people involved should be some distance from one another to prevent excess weight concentration in one place. At least one person should have a coil of rope on their shoulder. Some have told of using snowshoes to spread their weight and lessen the chances of surface puncture, but as clumsy as I am and some others are with snowshoes, there may be an increased risk for accident.

Kettlehole bogs are most common in the Great Lakes states and provinces, but can be found on occasion anywhere in the broad area discussed in this section. These bogs are a truly interesting phenomenon; clearly, most are doomed to eventually become filled in with their own debris and covered in forest (Pringle 1980).

Blanket Bogs

We are less certain of the origin of blanket bogs. They form as sheets of *Sphagnum* over an area, which is usually composed of igneous rock or glacial gravel. These bogs are mainly ombrotrophic, that is, they seem to obtain all needed water and any nutrients through rain or snow. Therefore, blanket bogs are largely concentrated in coastal New England and up into the Maritime Provinces, but may also be found in other areas with appropriate geography and climate. The sheets of moss grow vertically and laterally with variable speed and tend to expand into adjacent areas. In Ireland, there are stories of such blankets covering over houses and sheds. Creeping or blanket bogs can form on flat land, on slopes, in valleys, up the sides of hills, or even at the tops of hills (Deevey 1958; Larsen 1982; Johnson 1985). Blanket bogs that are not expanding fast tend to develop a moat, or lagg, of water around their edges. (Such laggs may also be found at the margins of more advanced kettle bogs.)

Blanket bogs may become several meters deep. As the surface moss continues to grow up, the older mosses below slowly die and then break down into granular brown peat, but very slowly because of cool temperatures and lack of oxygen in the depths. Again, the dying vegetation and peat in the depths is rather acidic, as are the living surface mosses. As with kettle bogs, pitcher plants and sundews grow in blanket bogs.

Streamside and String Bogs

The final category of predominantly sphagnous bogs is little understood. A string bog is sometimes known as a ladder bog because, when viewed from above, there are alternating bands of *Sphagnum* bog in rather straight rows between rows of open water (flarks). These moss and water rows are of varying width, even within the same string bog. Several theories have been offered for how these systems form (see Crum 1988), but all seem to relate to the usual occurrence of right-angle strings on very slight slopes with a downhill water flow. Ladder bogs are more common in more northern boreal areas, although a few are present in the most northern of the Great Lakes states.

In some areas, streamside sphagnous systems may be related to the formation of ladder bogs. These streamside bogs range in size from less than a meter to more than a hectare. Basically, a well-established steam, creek, or even a small river may have sphagnous and peat bogs in places along its shore. In some cases, the bogs can be related to smaller shoreline streams or springs with slow water flow becoming streamside bogs. In other places, there are simply wider portions or small bays along a stream shore where water slows down so that a sphagnous deposit with underlying peat may form. These systems are most frequently found in the Appalachians. Indeed, I have a favorite series of sphagnous sites along a stream in Giles County about forty-five minutes from my home in southwestern Virginia.

Some Concluding Remarks on Sphagnous Systems

I have introduced *Sphagnum* moss and some of its interesting properties to you. There is ongoing active research on these mosses, and I encouraged you to review some of the references mentioned above for greater detail and more theoretical consideration.

Relatively smaller quantities of whole, surface *Sphagnum* are harvested for mainly horticultural purposes these days, whereas rather enormous amounts of the deeper peat mosses are mined, again chiefly for horticulture. This peat is used as an organic additive for heavy clay soils and to manufacture the very popular soilless planting mixes on the market. Peat mining can be a threat to existing bogs. In Europe peat mining has been all but discontinued due to decreasing numbers of bogs to mine and conservation restrictions to save what few bogs are left. In North America most peat is mined in Canada, although there have been smaller operations in the Great Lakes states and in eastern North Carolina.

In boreal and subarctic Canada there are huge deposits of peat in large bogs extending many kilometers. In the areas with trees, muskeg—large peatlands with thinly spaced trees and shrubs—forms. Further north, aerial views disclose the peculiar patterned peat formations typical of the region. In these places, the peat forms into large polygons surrounded by water, the polygons being of greatly variable size. These patterns are not entirely understood, but may be related to permafrost formation and freezing and thawing cycles (Crum 1988).

As a strand of *Sphagnum* grows (up to about 30 cm in length), the older end tends to die and become brown. This brown portion begins to break down very slowly into a less well-formed material of variable moss and other plant fragments that is peat, particularly brown *Sphagnum* peat. These peat layers may extend many meters deep, are of variable acidity, and are mostly water saturated with little oxygen present. These conditions, along with cold temperatures, inhibit further decay.

Peat seems to have antiseptic and preservative properties, although anaerobic (not requiring oxygen) organisms do live in its depths. Bodies of well-preserved animals and even humans have been recovered from peat. There is some evidence that in parts of northern Europe and the British Isles early humans used this property of peat to bury their dead, although occasional bound limbs suggest another, more sinister reason for interment. Large logs have also survived in peat bogs and apparently were extracted and used by early humans.

If you insert a shiny copper wire into a *Sphagnum* bog, you will find that at a depth of about 20 cm the wire will turn dark after a few minutes. You have tapped into the anaerobic level where microorganisms produce hydrogen sulfide, which you can detect as a rotten-egg smell when you turn up a good, deep handful of bog. Under these low-oxygen conditions, bacterial inhabitants are less able to produce soluble nitrates from decaying organic material, instead producing organic nitrogen compounds, which are less available to plant roots. Phosphorus is also less available for similar reasons. Iron is best utilized by plants in its chemically reduced, ferrous form, but in bogs iron is converted to the less available ferric form. In fact, this ferric form collects to the extent that mining peat for iron was once a thriving source of the mineral in colonial America. Iron also tends to combine with organic compounds that sometimes produce a partial slick on bog waters that may be mistaken for petroleum pollution.

The low levels of nutrients in bogs seem to be reflected in the plants that grow in them. Chemical analysis of many bog plants' leaves disclose that nutrient levels in these leaves are far lower than what is adequate for other plants, yet the bog plants thrive. Species of these wet, seemingly deprived areas live more efficiently. For one thing, many retain their leaves for two to four years instead of having a nutrient-wasting annual leaf drop. Also, when winter dormancy is coming on or when leaves are shed, nutrients are transported from the leaf tissues to the main stems, rhizomes, or roots (Crum 1988). Bog plants also seem to be more tolerant of higher levels of certain minerals. Levels of iron and manganese, for instance, are often higher in some bog soils and in the leaves of bog plants than what would be toxic for other plants.

One last interesting aspect of northern sphagnous bogs is the false-bottomed lake, which has fooled me a few times. Many glacial lakes are shallow and accumulate a great deal of mud over their sandy bottoms. Often, water and temperature conditions cause this mud to float in a sort of colloidal slurry. The result is that when you view the lake from the shore, there seems to be clear water about 2–15 cm deep over a mud bottom. However, when you step in, you sink up to your hip. In Michigan, this particular habitat is a favored place for the bladderwort *Utricularia resupinata* to grow. The vegetative and trapping portion of the plant seems adapted to the muddy slurry and the purple flowers appear above the water. Take care when you step in to photograph it.

Northern and mountain sphagnous bogs are truly wondrous places. Although some people focus on the wetness, the biting insects, and sometimes the poison oak, others of us adapt like the bog plants. Once we acquire a sense of what to avoid and what to ignore, we begin to share a great secret that eludes those who look at boggy areas as wasted places where you cannot swim, boat, or grow corn. The adaptation of bog plants to such a seemingly poor habitat demonstrates the elasticity and tenacity of life. Beside the carnivorous plants, grasses, sedges, reeds, and specialized shrubs, one finds precious jewels of orchids, trilliums, and many other wildflowers, as well as some unusual little animals. As I gingerly squish and slosh into a bog, I feel cooled air; smell the wet, mossy, peaty fragrances; and always have a sudden surge of exhilaration and refreshment, knowing that this is the way it is supposed to be. Bogs must be saved and savored. If we were all boggers, we would be richer for it.

In the Fen Country
For this section, I borrow a title from Ralph Vaughn Williams's tone poem, which to me sounds just like the fens look and feel. As with bogs, fens are defined, classified, and cross-classified in many debatable ways,

but in this book I will discuss the marl or alkaline fen. In the North, the best examples of marl fens are in the Great Lakes region, although scattered examples can be found into Quebec, northern Maine, and the Maritime Provinces (where they are often cobbles), and on the West Coast. A sort of fen area also exists in the Big Cypress Swamp in southwestern Florida, but, of course, it has a somewhat different structure and flora than those in the North.

The typical northern fen bog is a flat, open, sand-based expanse covered with a thin layer of peat and over which a shallow, broad sheet of water almost imperceptibly flows. The water comes from slow, limestone-based springs. Calcium and magnesium are dissolved in the water as bicarbonates, which precipitate out on exposure to the air. These calcium and magnesium carbonate particles affix to the peat as a flocculent, light material known as marl, thus the designation marl fen. Because it is alkaline, the floor of the fen has a somewhat greasy feel when rubbed between the fingers. The water in fens tends to run an even, shallow depth of 1–3 cm in the portion that supports carnivorous plants.

Most marl fens originate in either Great Lakes beach pools fed by springs or, somewhat inland, most commonly at the foot of a lakefront escarpment. Some exist even further inland and are associated with beaches along slow, shallow streams or on the margins of smaller lakes. Within or along the edges of some fens are deposits of weathered, smooth rocks seemingly pressed together in almost pavement form and sometimes known as a type of cobble. Some fens, particularly in the Maritime Provinces, are almost entirely stone.

A feature of marl fens is the sandy, sphagnous hummocks, or little islands, scattered over the surface. These vary from just a few centimeters to several meters across, with the larger ones supporting small shrubs, trees, and herbaceous plant life as well. Due to the *Sphagnum*, the hummocks above the water line are actually acidic, so there are two contrasting habitats within a few centimeters of each other. If not lake dunes, the edges of marl fens are northern woods. Between the open fen and the forest there is usually a band of *Sphagnum* habitat of variable width that supports acid-loving or acid-tolerant plants.

Analysis of fen waters discloses clear, odorless water with nearly neutral or slightly alkaline pH, rather high levels of calcium and magnesium, and very low levels of phosphate and nitrogen. Iron and copper levels are extremely low. The soils are predominantly sand with a pH of 8.0 (alkaline), a corresponding high level of calcium and magnesium, a surprisingly medium level of phosphate, and a very low nitrogen content (Schnell 1982b). These relatively high levels of salts—although still with low nitrogen levels—are rather unusual for a carnivorous plant medium, but some species grow very nicely in fens. In fact, some carnivorous plants are almost specifically adapted to growing in the marly fen soils, whereas

A typical northern marl fen in Ontario. The bottom is covered by a thin sheet of water. There are several little hummocks visible, and in the near distance is the sphagnous shoreline next to forest. Pitcher plants (*Sarracenia purpurea*) grow on the hummocks, although they may also grow in the marl itself.

others are capable of doing so as well as growing in sphagnous areas. Still other carnivorous species grow only on the acidic hummocks. The hummocks also support other plant groups such as orchids.

Most fens are surprisingly hospitable to visits. Generally, the dense sand substrate is quite close to the softer marl surface and provides solid footing. The water runoff sometimes forms a channel near an edge or between two larger hummocks—here the water may be deeper and the bottom softer, requiring caution. In the open fen on a clear, cool northern spring day with a light onshore breeze from the nearby lake, exploration is very pleasant and free of biting insects if you are past the black-fly season. However, passing through the woods to get to a fen can be battle between you and mosquitoes, so proper dress and precautions are required.

Fens are relatively fragile ecosystems; they are easy to abuse and bear their scars for prolonged periods. Continued or heavy foot traffic by groups of visitors can create path channels that disturb the delicate and vital water layer. One of my favorite fens had been pristine until the early 1990s, when one spring I saw unmistakable snowmobile tracks from the previous winter's activities. The riders had passed through and around the fen, no doubt because the tract was level and relatively free of trees. Ten years later, those tracks were still obvious. Many of the best remaining fens are kept secret by those who love and wish to protect them from abuse. Others that are officially preserved have boardwalks across them so that visitors may see and photograph these beautiful areas without disturbing them.

The greatest threats to northern fens are by destruction to do something else with the land. Fens are easily drained by creating channels through them, whereupon their life- and character-giving water is diverted to a roadside ditch or into a lake. People want lakeside cottages on beachfronts, and further inland there is a desire for farmland, housing developments, and shopping malls. Even if the fen itself is not directly attacked, adjustments to the nearby water table can be disastrous. Fortunately, conservation organizations are preserving some of the remaining fens for all of us.

I must also mention the fenlike stretches in the western Big Cypress Swamp just east of Naples, Florida. The marl flats are very similar to fens in structure but even larger. The little land islands, called hammocks, are mostly much larger than northern hummocks, with extensive growth of subtropical trees and shrubs. The hammocks are sand based, with little or no *Sphagnum* except for incidental patches. Soils in these southern Florida fens are very similar to the northern variety, with pH up to 8.0 (alkaline) and high levels of calcium and magnesium, but in this case elevated aluminum and potassium levels, only modest phosphates, and practically no nitrates. The hammocks are 97% sand with a slightly acidic pH of 6.3 and low to absent calcium and magnesium (Schnell 1980c). These areas, or prairies, extend for many kilometers. Some typical southern and disjunct tropical species of bladderwort (*Utricularia*) frequently grow in the water and the sandy edges of the hammocks, along with one southern butterwort (*Pinguicula pumila*). Fortunately, the Big Cypress Preserve is extensive and still growing.

Seepage Bogs

Seepage bogs are most common in the Appalachian Mountains and their foothills, the sandhills of the upper coastal plain, and west of the Continental Divide from northern California north into Alaska. These bogs are usually associated with artesian springs. Instead of the springs flowing boldly, however, they tend to seep through wet soil or muck across broad fronts, forming wet, boggy areas. Some of these areas are small, whereas others may extend for hectares and might be associated with multiple seeping springheads. Because such springs are usually found at the tops, along the sides, or at the bottoms of slopes, this accounts for the secondary name, seepslope bogs.

The soils of seepage bogs usually have a sand base but often with a great deal of grass and other herbaceous (rarely sphagnous) peat mixed in, resulting in a mucky consistency. The seepage bog is usually closely associated with forest. The size of the bog, with variable breaks in the shrub and tree canopy, helps determine what plants are able to grow in a seepage bog. Although there may be various sized patches of *Sphagnum* growing alongside or even in the bog, usually this is not the same as the typical northern *Sphagnum* bog. However, some seepage bogs may arise in a leveled, shallow basin and here they may adopt all the seeming characteristics of a *Sphagnum* bog. One such bog was very familiar to me when I lived in Iredell County, North Carolina, in the western piedmont of that state. When I moved there, the bog was shown to me by a retired history teacher who was locally renowned as a county historian and amateur naturalist. This bog was in dense scrub woods at the foot of a hill adjacent to a small stream. After battling through dense thicket, we came out into a very wet *Sphagnum* bog similar in character to the northern bogs well known to me but in this case watered by seeping springs at the

A seepage bog in Autauga County, Alabama. The sandy, wet seep is clearly seen on the left and bordering shrub to the back. The clumps of pitcher plants to the right are the federally endangered *Sarracenia rubra* subspecies *alabamensis*.

foot of the hill. There were two species of pitcher plant (*Sarracenia flava* and *S. purpurea*), their hybrid, and one sundew (*Drosera rotundifolia*) along with a bladderwort (*Utricularia gibba*) in an open, wet area near the center, just like the eye of a northern bog. Several orchid species also grew here. Unfortunately, I relate the sad, slow ending of the bog in this book's final chapter.

Seepage bogs appear to be decreasing at an alarming rate (Weakley and Schafale 1994). Some attribute their eventual overgrowth to natural succession, which in some cases may be true. Others mention suppression of regular natural fires that tend to keep advancing tree saplings and shrubs at bay. Although fires seem vital in maintaining savanna wetlands, in particular (see the next section), their value in more continuously wet areas such as seepage bogs and northern bogs is more doubtful except for the possible advantage of perimeter mesic growth suppression. Given seepage bogs' association with some degree of sloping, I feel they are most sensitive to falling water tables with springs shutting down, which is happening at a striking rate throughout seepage spring areas. Water tables are clearly dropping in a portion of Butterfly Valley in California, where a large reserve for the California pitcher plant (*Darlingtonia*) was established. Nearby housing development with well-water requirements has caused springs feeding the area to run dry along one margin. This historic habitat is now in danger (Rondeau 1995).

The Great Southern Savannas

Areas of the southeastern coastal plain are some of the richest locations for carnivorous plants in North America. To the north, the coastal plain extends into and includes Long Island, New York, and the rather well-known New Jersey Pine Barrens, which occupy the southern half of that state. The barrens are beloved by naturalists and have been well studied (such as Harshberger 1970; Forman 1979). To the west, the coastal plain extends into eastern Texas. Map 1 shows the limits of the coastal plain, which can be roughly divided into the Atlantic and Gulf coastal plains.

The coastal plain in the Southeast is demarcated from the more inland piedmont areas by an often-broad border known as the Fall Line. The origins and precise meaning of the term are somewhat clouded. Some say it is a series of points where the last waterfalls or rapids occur in rivers flowing to the Atlantic or Gulf of Mexico, with these points connected to form a line. Others say it refers to the line where the upland falls off onto the flatter coastal plain. In either event, the line is actually a rather broad boundary between the upland igneous base rock, overlying clay, and organic soils and the coastal sedimentary and limestone base with very sandy soils. Along the Fall Line, elevations become less extreme; streams and rivers become wide, slow, and meandering; and predominant vegetation changes from mainly deciduous to evergreen. The Fall Line is also the line of the greatest inland extent of the ocean in the late Cretaceous period.

Between the flatter coastal plain and the rolling piedmont are many so-called sandhill areas; these sandy elevations are ancient dunes now covered in vegetation. The upper parts of the hills are covered by a mesic to almost xeric growth of pines with underlying evergreen shrubs. The low areas between hills are more deciduous in vegetation character with many springs, seeps, and seepage bogs. These seepage bogs are common sites for carnivorous plants.

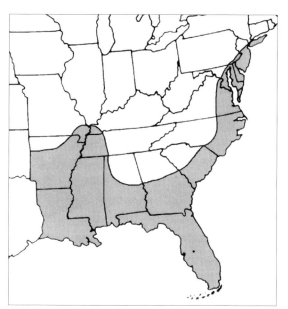

Map 1. The coastal plain is the shaded area of the map. It is delimited by the Fall Line, which runs roughly from the northeast to the southwest. See text for further discussion.

In addition to flatlands crossed by slow, wide streams with scattered swamps, there are mysterious structures known as the Carolina Bays on the coastal plain. Supposedly named because they often contain multiple species of evergreen shrubs that are collectively called bays, these are shallow, oval depressions with the ovals uniformly aligned northwest to southeast. The Carolina Bays are best appreciated from the air. They are surrounded by slightly raised ridges of sand, which are most pronounced on the southeast borders. The Carolina Bays vary in size from a few meters to several square kilometers. Several are filled with water and are the few natural lakes in the coastal plain. Most are filled with mixed peat and have a nearly impenetrable dense growth of broadleaf ericaceous evergreen shrubs. Carnivorous plants may be found at the margins of the bays, where there is some clearing.

The origin of the Carolina Bays is far from decided. There are many theories, including everything from takeoff locations for ancient alien spaceships to depressions left by whales swishing their tales when the ocean covered the area. The most likely theory seems to be that the bays are the result of meteor showers some 50,000 years ago. There do not seem to be foreign rock traces, but the meteors could have been dirty ice, as so many seem to be. Savage (1982) wrote an exhaustive and readable study of the possible origins of these depressions.

In addition to the slow rivers and streams, with their swamps and marshes, and the more-inland sandhills, with their seepage bogs, the coastal plain has particular kinds of extensive woodlands known as wet savannas, or simply savannas. Estimates indicate that only 2–5% of the original savannas remain due to woodcutting for commercial lumber and drainage and clearing for farmland. In these areas of mild winters and close proximity to the ocean beaches, retirement communities are a threat to savannas.

Savannas are very flat, expansive, sandy-peat areas with widely spaced pine trees beneath which grow sparse stands of shrubs and extensive sedges and grasses, with wiregrass or bunchgrass (*Aristida*) being particularly prominent. These plants form slightly raised, small, fountain-like tufts of growth that are difficult to walk on. The predominant coniferous trees are longleaf pine (*Pinus palustris*), loblolly pine (*P. taeda*), slash pine (*P. elliotii*), and pond pine (*P. serotina*). Savannas are often located on the borders of swamps, Carolina Bays, and riverine overruns. The trees are widely scattered with extensive openings due to several factors, among them the poor-quality soils and recurrent natural fires. These fires maintain the savanna's sparse character by getting rid of fallen vegetation and duff that would provide abundant fuel for less frequent but more intense fires. These infrequent, intense fires provide a flush of nutrients that are rapidly washed through the sandy soils by the area's heavy rains.

Savannas generally have a high water table, but there is seldom standing water due to excellent drainage through the peaty sand soils. Soil analyses from two widely separate sites (Brunswick County, North Carolina, and south-central Alabama) were remarkably similar, with pH averaging 4.0–4.6; low to absent primary nutrients (nitrates, phosphates, calcium, and magnesium); and prominently elevated levels of aluminum and iron, the former to levels toxic for many plants (Schnell 1978b; Murphy and Boyd 1999, respectively).

The water in small streams, ponds, and drainage ditches associated with dense shrub bogs (pocosins) and savannas has a rich tea color, but is normally quite clear. The color is due to leached tannic and humic acids —the same compounds that give coffee and tea their color—from peat and decomposing vegetation. The water is acidic, low in salts, and relatively sterile. In colonial times, ships' crews would bring water casks inland to collect from the streams because the water remained potable for a longer period of time aboard ship than did water from other sources.

Fire is very important in maintaining southern coastal plain savannas. Ideally, fires should occur no less than every three to five years. In early attempts by biologists to manage savannas, fires were started in winter to minimize damage to growing herbaceous plants. However, prior to human interference, it is clear that most natural fires were due to lightening, which is a summertime phenomenon. More recent management programs that set fires in the summer have been successful in spite of temporary herbaceous setback; the herbaceous plants resprouted and seemed no worse the wear the following season. Again, fires reduce accumulation of dry materials and supply a flush of nutrients, but also reduce competition for growing space by suppressing tree saplings and shrubs. Without fire, many savannas turn into dense shrub bogs, often called pocosins (although the latter term is also used for the shrub bogs in the Carolina Bays; Wells 1932; Richardson 1981). Because carnivorous plants are generally poor competitors, fire is clearly beneficial to them.

Plants have many strategies for surviving fire. For example, many carnivorous plants, such as pitcher plants and the Venus flytrap, have underground rhizomes that are not affected by the quick, cooler fires and can resprout from these protected rhizomes. Other plants rely on restarting from seeds. Certain pines do not shed seed until their cones open under the influence of fire. The pine trees of the savannas are largely fire resistant, longleaf pine (*Pinus palustris*) more so in this respect. However, logging has depleted longleaf pines severely and caused them to be replaced by greater numbers of loblolly pines (*P. taeda*), which are somewhat less fire resistant; still, a good number of longleaf pines survive along with slash pines (*P. elliotii*). Unfortunately, fire suppression has high priority with the forestry industry, which views drained and planted savannas from a productivity standpoint rather than as natural ecosystems. However, some savannas are being preserved, carefully monitored, and treated with fire on a regular basis.

Although savanna soils are extremely poor and trees are relatively stunted, in any area there is a comparatively rich diversity of plant species each represented by few individuals (see Wells 1932). Still, within several square meters, one may find pitcher plant, sundew, butterwort, and terrestrial bladderwort species along with native orchids and other flowering plants adapted to savannas.

Exploring the relatively few remaining healthy savannas on a fine spring day is enriching. If the day is clear, there is usually a pleasant, but admittedly warm, onshore breeze from the ocean several kilometers away, which moderates the sun and keeps mosquitoes at bay. A wet, pungent pine fragrance fills the air, and you can see vast distances. A compass is handy, unless you are within earshot of a road. Many times I have not been, and I had the pleasure of hearing only occasional insects and the soft breeze in pine boughs. Those days are increasingly rare, however, as more savanna is compromised or destroyed. The relatively flat topography causes the savannas to be susceptible to even widely spaced drainage ditches if they are deep. Once ditches are dug, perhaps after a sharp gasp at pitcher plant splendor for one more spring, the drained, mesic land is now ready for tree plantations (Schnell 1982a).

Sinkholes

Because much of the southeastern coastal plain lies over a limestone karst formation, depletion of the groundwater by wells and drainage leaves air under domes of limestone that sometimes collapse, resulting in a small lake or pond—usually a series of them. The shores and bottoms are rather sandy and most are now fed by springs, resulting in beautifully clear water. Two groups of lime sinkholes that I have explored include Boiling Springs Lakes in Brunswick County, North Carolina, and an unnamed series in Washington County, Florida. Because the shores of the large ones are desirable sites for vacation and retirement homes, needless to say, these natural ponds do not remain pristine.

The water of lime sinkholes is nearly neutral and rather high in calcium and magnesium. The shores are sandy but often drop off rather precipitously, as one might expect. Where the springs run down into the main water body and sometimes along shallower sand margins of these sinkholes, I get the impression of being in a modified marly fen, although very miniature in size. Many local carnivorous plants grow in these flats and spring areas, including some disjunct species such as the red threadleaf sundew (*Drosera filiformis* variety *filiformis*), which is far south of its usual range. Because you can see so far down into the clear water, the sinkholes of Washington County, Florida, are also an excellent place to view and photograph the rather magnificent bladderwort *Utricularia floridana*.

Another Wetland

Before ending this habitat section, I must mention another wetland that does not exactly fit any of the categories above. The magnificent Okefenokee Swamp is located in extreme southeastern Georgia, abutting and extending into Florida a bit. The Okefenokee, a bog mixed with swamp forest, covers nearly 2000 square kilometers and is located 120 km inland from the present Georgia shore, although prehistorically it was once part of the sea. The basin that is now the Okefenokee is walled of by a 64-km long sandbar and is largely watered by rain. The headwaters of the St. Marys and Suwanee Rivers emanate from it (Line 1999). The swamp, which is actually mainly a peat bog, has intervening solid islands and watery "prairies," as they are known to swampers. In this immense preserve, the peat beneath the water sometimes accumulates to masses that are 5 m thick. Anaerobic metabolism (as in sphagnous bogs farther north) creates methane (or swamp) gas, which may cause chunks of peat up to several hectares across to rise just beneath the surface, resulting in a prairie, or floating island. Green plants, including some carnivorous plants, may grow on these floating mats and create somewhat drier surfaces. Walking on these islands can cause the same sensation as the quaking bogs in the North, hence the name "land of the trembling earth."

The Okefenokee has been threatened several times, first by an unsuccessful attempt to channel it via the Suwanee Canal to make it more accessible for cutting timber and then by timber companies draining its perimeter. The latest threat, now thwarted by prompt action, was to mine the sandbar walling one edge of the swamp for aluminum ore (recall the high aluminum levels in coastal plain sands). Still, the preserve survives as a national treasure. There are narrated boat rides into the Okefenokee from several entrances, and you can rent canoes to follow your own isolated, quiet trip through well-marked waterways, from prairie to prairie —the best way to go.

Carnivorous plant enthusiasts are particularly intrigued by the consistently large forms of two pitcher plant species (*Sarracenia minor* and *S. psittacina*) that grow in a few Okefenokee locations, both around and within the swamp borders. There are also many bladderworts in the tannin-stained water and much other plant and animal life to see during a few days' leisurely trip through the land of the trembling earth.

Some General Notes on Cultivating Carnivorous Plants

In this section, I briefly outline my experience with cultivating North American carnivorous plants. (Information specific to particular genera and species will be mentioned in the main chapters.) Of course, many carnivorous species native to other places in the world may require different conditions, sometimes radically different. Every grower of plants knows that even under seemingly exacting greenhouse conditions, there are variations in different geographic areas. Some of these are obvious, such as variation in daylight hours; others are more subtle and are only detected indirectly by changing horticultural patterns slightly. In addition to my growing suggestions, some authors who may prove helpful for their areas are Slack (1979, 1986) for the British Isles, Pietropaolo and Pietropaolo (1986) for the northeastern United States, Carow and Furst (1990) for Germany and central Europe, and D'Amato (1998) for the Pacific Coast region of North America.

Another thing you must remember is that all cultivated plants are under stress to some degree. Plants are carefully attuned to their native environments. All things being equal, a plant will never do as well in cultivation as it does in a healthy native habitat. Although cultivated plants may often seem to do very well, they look fine, grow large, have excellent color, and propagate vegetatively and by seed, they are still in some distress. Stressful conditions will cause your plants to be more susceptible to deficiencies, some of which are not clearly defined, and to disease as well. For these reasons, you will have to be alert to any developing problems early in their course so that they do not progress to the point that you lose your plant. Certain diseases progress very rapidly in plants already battling the challenge of a cultivated environment that we believe closely matches their native habitat. The lesson is to watch your plants carefully and never take their health for granted.

Places to Grow Carnivorous Plants

Depending on local climate and available facilities, you may wish to grow your plants outdoors, indoors in terraria or on windowsills, or in a greenhouse. The ultimate dream of any serious grower is always a greenhouse, but these are expensive. Also, in our mobile society, owning a greenhouse is not always possible. However, you do not have to use a greenhouse to successfully grow many carnivorous plant species.

Outdoors

You may grow your outdoor plants in pots, being careful to follow the requirements for other factors in this section. In areas that freeze in winter, however, you will have to take them indoors for that season. In natural habitats, freezing air does not surround rhizomes and roots; therefore, potted plants do poorly outdoors in winter.

You may also build an artificial bog. I have reliable information of growers in Saginaw, Michigan, and Bedford, New Hampshire, growing plants in homemade outdoor bogs. Depending on how many plants you wish to grow and how many you can take care of, you must first dig a suitably sized hole. Children's wading pools that are at least 40–50 cm deep make ideal liners. You may also purchase a similar pool form from nurseries that deal in water gardening supplies or you can line the hole with flexible plastic pool liner. Next, punch a few holes in the liner. This step may seem contradictory to maintaining a wet bog, but stagnation is not desired, nor is buildup of salts from evaporating surface water. Four or five evenly spaced 0.5-cm holes in the bottom of a small or moderate size bog will allow sufficient slow drainage.

I recommend using Canadian peat for artificial bogs. Prewet the material by getting it out of the bale into a large tub of water. Mix it well and let the mixture sit for a day or two until a thick slurry remains in the tub. Pour this peat mixture to the top of the bog to allow for shrinkage after evaporation. Before you plant the bog, you may want to place a stone or other border around it. Carnivorous plant companion plants from sphagnous and savanna bogs look attractive, but beware of weedy, spreading plants, no matter how attractive—they will take over your bog and be difficult to weed out. Remember to keep the bog wet (with standing water immediately after watering, but not necessarily after that).

In certain areas, frost heave is a problem with outdoor bogs. If you have ever walked along a bare, wet roadcut on a crisp frosty morning, you may have noticed little columns of ice, known as hoarfrost. This can also form in your bog. Hoarfrost tends to lift smaller, recently planted material up and leave it to dry after the frost columns melt. You will have to inspect your bog daily in such weather and push the plants back down so they will not dry or freeze.

Terraria

Growing carnivorous plants under lights in glass terraria inside the home is very productive. Even though I have a greenhouse, I find growing some plants in terraria more useful. The easiest terrarium to construct is a large fish tank with a plate of glass over the top. Rather than planting everything in a layer of medium in the bottom of the terrarium, I prefer to place my plants in pots and set them in a few centimeters of water in the bottom because it is easier to move these around if I must clean out accumulating algae.

For lighting, I use fixtures with four 40-watt fluorescent tubes placed nearly on the glass, because light loss is exponentially related to the distance of the tubes from the tops of plants. Timers allow easy light management—try starting at six hours of dark at night and eighteen hours of light. If you can afford the various special growing lights available, they are fine, but most growers find the cool white bulbs just as good and they are relatively inexpensive.

There are a couple of concerns when growing plants in terraria. First, you must provide some cooling to account for winter dormancy of North American carnivorous plants. Placing terraria in an unheated (but not much below freezing) basement of the home in northern regions is excellent and takes care of temperatures automatically. Second, terraria limit the size and particularly the height of plants. Small, spreading pitcher plants, for instance, do fine, but tall pitchers will often outgrow the terrarium. If you try to make the terrarium taller to accommodate the tall pitchers, your lights are now farther away from your smaller plants and the tall pitcher plant growth points on the ground. This results in etiolation—weak, abnormal soft growth with poor development and color.

Determined growers set up banks of severely slanted lights to provide lighting at the sides of the terraria to overcome etiolation in tall plants.

Be careful of placing a closed, transparent container of plants on the windowsill. Direct sunlight on a closed glass or plastic container will literally cook the plants. Place the container on a sill that will not be in direct sun during the day, but that will at least receive adequate "bright shade" light.

Indoors

Both Slack (1979, 1986) and D'Amato (1998) reported how easy it is to grow some carnivorous plants on the windowsill. However, the key here is that it is in their specific areas (the British Isles and Pacific Coast, respectively) and probably without exposure to drying heat or air conditioning. You may wish to try some potted plants on the sill over the winter at least, and then place them outdoors in humid areas for the growing season. For potting, light, and media, follow the principles described below.

Greenhouses

Detailed descriptions of greenhouse management are beyond the scope of this book, except to mention a few basics pertaining to carnivorous plants. Be sure you have a system for heating in winter and cooling in summer. For the latter, an exhaust fan with louvers at one end of the greenhouse and an intake with motorized automatic louver at the other works well. The airflow should go down the center aisle and never pass directly over plants. I always screen the outside of the intake louver with 0.5- to 0.75-cm hardware cloth to prevent cutworm moths from coming in—these pests can decimate a butterwort (*Pinguicula*) planting.

West of the Mississippi, you will need humidification equipment (see a greenhouse equipment catalogue for your needs and size of greenhouse) to maintain minimum humidity during the growing season. You may decide to use a timed misting system instead, if your water source is of sufficient quality (see below). Shading, usually in the form of woven plastic shading cloth sold by greenhouse suppliers, may be necessary west of the Mississippi particularly. Carnivorous plant greenhouses always have a wet, mossy appearance, which helps maintain humidity levels in microhabitats.

Pots

Of the two choices of pot—clay and plastic—most carnivorous plant growers prefer plastic by far, unless the clay pot is glazed. Plastic pots are far easier to clean, do not break as readily, and are less expensive. Also, unglazed clay pots tend to absorb water; as it evaporates, salts build up on the outside surface. These incrustations at the top of the rim may then wash down into the soil and be toxic to the plants.

Square pots have more soil volume per footprint—there is a lot of wasted space among the circles of round pots and, in spite of the best plans, a terrarium or greenhouse turns out never to be large enough.

A short section of bench in a successful carnivorous plant greenhouse. Note that the pots are in trays of water and everything looks wet and mossy.

Place your pots in saucers or plastic trays with a few centimeters of pure water, which keeps the soil constantly moist. The water for initially mixing the dry soil and for the tray bottom must be as pure as possible. Evaporation of water at the soil surface causes upward wicking of water through the medium, but any salts present will concentrate near the surface as water evaporates and may become toxic or at least encourage unpleasant and possibly toxic algal growth. Repotting at least every couple of years is necessary in even the best situations.

Humidity

North American carnivorous plants inhabit bogs, which have very high air humidity. Thus, the question for cultivation is the lowest relative humidity levels needed to maintain proper growth and development of these plants. In general, carnivorous plants seem to do well if the minimum relative humidity is 45–55% at growing temperatures. Brief periods of lower humidity will do no harm, as long as there is not a consistent decrease. Warmer air has the capacity to hold more water vapor, so that the same amount of vapor in cold air will read as lower relative humidity at higher temperatures. The figures of 45–55% relative humidity will do for an air temperature range of about 4–30°C. Misting plants and surfaces daily (or several times a day in very hot, sunny weather) is helpful to keep humidity levels up and to provide evaporative cooling in very warm locations.

Growing Media

Canadian peat is the best all-around growing medium I have found. It is acidic and very low in salts. The brown, rather fibrous Canadian peat must be distinguished from Michigan peat. The latter is a black material from richer grass-sedge bogs in Lower Michigan that is often used as a soil amendment for growing plants other than carnivorous plants. Michigan peat has the wrong pH and too many salts and nutrients for growing carnivorous plants and is very messy to work with when wet. In other countries, suitable peats may also be found, including German peat, which many claim to be superior to all others. However, it is becoming rare as peat-mining restrictions are enforced in that nation. The important criterion is that the peat be of *Sphagnum* origin.

Some growers add materials to the peat, such as sand, perlite, or vermiculite, but I find no advantages to these. Sand makes a heavier soil, and perlite lighter. Plain, brown, sphagnous peat seems to work best. Other materials to consider include plain, igneous rock sand. Beware of river or lake sands because these may contain impurities from those bodies of water as well as granules of limestone or mollusc shell, which are not desirable. Sands sold as additives for concrete or use in sandboxes also may contain limestone (read the label). The best and purest bagged sand is sold for sandblasting.

So-called long-fiber *Sphagnum* moss is sold in bales or bags and is dead, dried sphagnous moss in whole strands. It is a good medium and retains some of the salt-binding and pH-lowering properties of the live material for at least one pass (see the *Sphagnum* section above). It is best used for larger plants, such as pitcher plants, because the medium is too coarse for finer roots. When using dry long-fiber *Sphagnum*, you must prewet it, as with peat. Pack the moss well into the pots so that smaller roots will have medium contact. For attractiveness, you can top the pot with a layer of green living *Sphagnum*, if this is available in your area. Live *Sphagnum* is a good indicator of the chemical health of your overall growing system. If the live moss dies, remove your plants immediately, wash them thoroughly, and repot. Also, live *Sphagnum* will tend to reward you with a continuous supply of itself. The moss grows so well for me that each year I harvest the excess off the tops of pots (so it does not bury the pitcher plant growing points too deeply) and save it in trays for additional potting later.

Repotting in fresh medium is required at least every two to three years, on average, or more often if salts and nutrients are accumulating. Peat and plain, dead *Sphagnum* (uncovered with live moss) also tend to grow nonsphagnous mosses on their surfaces after a few years. Although seemingly attractive at first, these must be removed. Nonsphagnous mosses tend to grow in thick mats and crowd our smaller plants, such as sundews or seedlings. There is also some evidence that they secrete toxins to depress the growth of seed plants. When these mosses come to occupy more than half of the soil surface, it is time to repot. When repotting, you will have to pick away the moss plants adhering to your carnivorous plants with forceps.

Water

Quantity and quality of water are extremely important factors in successful cultivation. North American carnivorous plants should be continually moist, although the medium may be allowed to become just damp at the surface during dormancy—and this may discourage rot if your dormancy temperatures are not low enough.

The three biggest problems with water supplies are possible organic toxins in natural water sources (streams and lakes), chlorine in municipal water supplies, and salts in any water source (even potable). The possible organic toxins in natural sources can be discovered through discussions with local authorities.

Chlorine in water supplies has been shown to be moderately toxic to plants, particularly those in small pots. It is of less concern in comparatively massive plantings, such as an artificial outdoor bog, where the chlorine is readily detoxified by the peat or dechlorinated by air exposure. You can dechlorinate your water source to safe levels by simply letting a container sit out in the open air for a day or two.

Hard water arises from sources that have a limestone geologic base, as opposed to an igneous rock base, where the waters are usually salt-free and of a slightly acidic pH—so-called soft water. The salts in hard water are mainly calcium and magnesium bicarbonates, similar to the water flowing over marl fens. The degree of hardness varies from location to location. Generally, hardness levels below 40 ppm are acceptable to carnivorous plants, but you will still have to beware of surface salt collection on your medium due to evaporation. Inexpensive kits for measuring hardness are available from most large variety stores or you can arrange a hardness and/or electrical conductivity water test through your agricultural extension agent.

Those who live near the southeastern coast of the United States will likely have hard water and quite possibly some salinity as well because of groundwater backflow from the nearby ocean. Do not treat your hard water with a water softener and believe it is safe to use. Most commercial water softeners simply replace the calcium and magnesium salts with sodium chloride, which is as bad for your plants. You may have to consider a reverse-osmosis unit or even a deionization unit. You can discuss these options with a sales representative of a local commercial water treatment company. If you have small plantings, dispensers of reverse-osmosis or deionized water can be found at many large variety stores, where you may fill your own containers.

Some growers have experimented with acidifying their carnivorous plant water with dilute vinegar (acetic acid), sulfuric acid (battery acid), or even by dissolving commercially available tannic or humic acid powder. The last two are derived from peat or acidic peat waters; they are expensive and available in some hobby fish stores as water blackener. Actually, you need not add anything to the water. In fact, it is far safer for your plants if you do not.

Rain provides a fine water source, and the roof of your home is a good, large collecting surface for rain. You may cut off your roof's drainpipe and collect water in a large plastic barrel. There are special barrels with outlet spigots at the bottom and connectors so you can link several barrels in a series. For the spigots to be useful, you will have to set your barrels up on cement blocks. If it has been a while since a good rain and a lot of pollen or plant debris has collected on the roof, allow for some washout at the beginning of the rain before collecting. Rainwater is of surprisingly good quality and is quite useful for watering carnivorous plants. You would be surprised with how much water you can collect from the average-sized home roof after even a moderate shower. I use rainwater to supplement my deionization system.

Light

Using the brightest light possible outdoors or in the well-ventilated greenhouse is advisable. This may require modification in very hot, sunny weather with either shade cloth or moving your plants to open shade, which is defined as the brightest light without being able to see your shadow. A dappled light effect under an open tree or overhead trellis is ideal in such situations.

For discussion of artificial fluorescent lighting and windowsills, see the Terraria and Indoor Open Pots sections. I have not tried the new focused incandescent lamp systems, however, I have spoken to a few carnivorous plant growers who have tried them. The growers were not pleased, mainly due to heat and difficulties with the proper light intensity for various plants. These incandescent systems seem to work better for other kinds of plants.

Dormancy

All North American carnivorous plants require a cool winter dormancy period. Watering should be decreased to just keeping the medium damp. Light intensity is not important as long as it does not lead to increased warmth; a maximum temperature of about 7–8°C is ideal. In my experience with growers, improper handling of dormancy is the most common cause for failure with North American carnivorous plants.

Some growers uproot their plants, wrap them in damp *Sphagnum* in plastic bags so they will not dry, and place them in the refrigerator for the winter. Beware of especially cold spots in your refrigerator where local freezing might occur. An uprooted plant is not as well protected against freezing as one in the ground. This method reportedly works well, but there is frequently some minor loss among smaller plants due to fungus attacks. Lightly dusting rhizomes and roots with sulfur (available from gardening supply stores) may help prevent fungus infestation. As I mentioned previously, if you grow in terraria in a cool, unheated basement, dormancy should be essentially automatic.

The timing of dormancy is of some importance. Studies (such as Winston and Gorham 1979a, 1979b) have shown that dormancy can be divided into two phases: (1) innate or obligatory; and (2) facultative. Innate dormancy is the inherent time a plant must remain dormant before dormancy can be safely broken. Efforts to force growing before innate dormancy is complete usually result in dead or at least diseased plants. The facultative phase is extra dormancy imposed by continued cold or decreased light. Dormancy is somewhat analogous to your own sleep cycle. As an individual, you require a minimum number of hours of sleep to function well—your innate sleep requirement. But on Saturdays you may like to sleep longer—facultative sleep—until your neighbor's lawnmower awakens you.

In essence, innate dormancy periods are usually shorter than actual dormancy set by external conditions. For most North American carnivorous plants, this innate period is six to ten weeks. This can be safely met even in a cool, temperate greenhouse. In my greenhouse, even though I have my ventilation system set to come on at 8°C in winter, around late February the photoperiod increases and sunlight pours in so that the plants resume growth—having satisfied their innate requirements—long before they would overcome facultative restraints in nature.

Temperatures

Generally, plants grown in the ground can survive surprisingly low winter air temperatures, and, of course, some carnivorous plants grow well up into Canada. Venus flytraps (*Dionaea muscipula*), which are native to the eastern North Carolina–South Carolina border, have survived regularly in a Pennsylvania *Sphagnum* bog, as have yellow pitcher plants (*Sarracenia flava*), whose native habitat extends from southernmost Virginia south. In fact, the latter did so well they even hybridized with native *S. purpurea*. There is a "carnivorous plant legend" about a field botanist who came across this situation and was unaware that the exotics had been planted. He dutifully prepared a paper on his exciting new find for a botanical journal. Fortunately, an alert reviewer recalled the plantings and was able to stop the paper from embarrassing the journal and the author.

The safest predictor of lowest winter temperature for cultivated plants is to be conservative and look to the natural habitat. Also, remember that plants kept above ground and in small containers are most liable for a damaging freeze, and, as mentioned, you must account for frost heave in outdoor bog plantings. The highest safe temperature for cultivated plants is about 30°C, at which point you may wish to consider cooling by temporary shade, more frequent surface misting, or more ventilation. Carnivorous plants native to more northern areas are surprisingly tolerant of warm air temperatures, as long as the roots are not warmed excessively. More frequent watering with cooled water may be helpful here. In arid regions west of the Mississippi, greenhouse cooling pads or evaporative coolers in the greenhouse are very useful.

Feeding

Although everyone is tempted to feed carnivorous plants, this should be done cautiously. They are genetically adapted to a particular diet and do not do well with bits of fatty hamburger or drops of milk, for instance. Never feed your carnivorous plants table food. Feeding insects caught against windows or from flowers in the yard (beware of handling stinging insects) is fine in moderation. In spite of some research wherein carnivorous plants have been kept alive for several years sealed in terraria with no external nourishment source, the plants do best when they can catch prey.

I hesitate to mention this for fear of it being overdone and having someone destroy a carnivorous plant collection, but plants deprived of insects, such as in a greenhouse or terrarium, may be lightly foliar fed. (One of my chemistry professors in college remarked that it seems to be an American tendency to feel that if a little does good, then more will do better. He supported his observation by pointing to the chemical stains on the laboratory ceiling.) Many gardeners know about foliar feeding. When applied to leaves, soluble fertilizer solutions can be absorbed through cuticle breaks—such as open stomata—and will be more quickly metabolized than if applied to the ground for root absorption. In carnivorous plants, nutrients are also absorbed through the leaf glands. Because ground application of fertilizers to carnivorous plants cannot be easily controlled and may be dangerous, light foliar feeding is an option when insects are lacking. The plants do seem to do better, but I must emphasize again—a *light* feeding.

Foliar feeding should only be done during the active growing season and no more often than monthly to be safe. I use a solution of a fertilizer labeled for acid-loving plants (such as azaleas) made up to no more than one-tenth of the recommended strength for noncarnivorous plants. Because most fertilizer labels are in English units, if the dilution on the label is 1 tablespoon per gallon of water, then use no more than $\frac{1}{10}$ tablespoon, or about $\frac{1}{4}$ to $\frac{1}{2}$ teaspoon, per gallon. Do not make the solution too strong. You may add to this solution about 5 ml of any liquid seaweed extract, which supplies many micronutrients. This solution is then sprayed on the leaves of the plants until their surfaces are just damp. Do not allow the solution to drip excessively on the soil surface.

Again, although foliar feeding seems very useful and, indeed, has been used in many carnivorous plant nutritional experiments as far back as Darwin, do not overdo the strength of your foliar feed solution or the frequency of application.

Pests

Both in nature and in cultivation, carnivorous plants are susceptible to pests, insect and otherwise. In this section, I discuss those pests most commonly encountered in cultivated plants. Specialized pitcher plant insect associates that may come into your collection through plants collected in the wild will be discussed in the pitcher plant chapters.

Scale insects most often infest pitcher plants. The name scale is applied to several genera of flat, brown, domed, 0.2–0.4 cm long insects that remain essentially stationary on the leaf once established. These pests are difficult to spot until a rather heavy infestation occurs. The mobile phase consists of similarly shaped organisms, but they are soft and pale green to yellow. These pests are extremely difficult to eradicate and their bodies remain attached even after death. If only a few plants are infested, disposal may be seriously considered before the organisms spread to the entire collection.

Aphids are 0.1–0.2 cm long, soft-bodied, yellow or green pests that attach most often to peduncles (flower stalks) of butterworts (*Pinguicula*). As do scale insects, aphids insert oral suction devices into vessels of the plant and suck juices from it. Aphids may also appear on other species' peduncles and occasionally on the backs of butterwort leaves. These insects tend to be seasonal (cooler spring or autumn) and can be treated rather easily.

Cutworms are larvae of several moths that feed on leaves of butterworts, in particular. Seemingly overnight, they can defoliate the plants, leaving only the central growing point. The larvae are relatively large but well camouflaged and difficult to spot. The best treatment is to find and remove them; there are usually relatively few in an infestation. This pest is the main reason I screen my air intake in the greenhouse.

Mealy bugs also belong to several genera. They usually come into your collection by two routes. One is with other plants you may grow with your carnivorous plants, particularly succulents. The other is through a natural rhizome infestation in eastern pitcher plants (*Sarracenia*) in the wild, particularly savanna plants. Mealy bugs are generally 0.2–0.4 cm long and have a powdery, white fluff covering their bodies and eggs. They often appear as a mass of fluffy white deposits. Although they most often infest aerial parts of plants, where they are visible, mealy bugs also infest underground parts, particularly the interstices of rhizomes. These are stubborn pests that are difficult to totally eradicate, but they can be controlled. You may have to make a choice between your infested carnivorous plants versus your succulents; the latter, once infested, always seem to remain so.

Treatment of pest infestations is a delicate problem where one wishes to use a minimum of potentially dangerous chemicals. However, chemical treatment will be required ultimately, except for cutworms, which can be removed manually. I cannot recommend insecticidal soaps because they wreak havoc with delicate small plants and *Sphagnum*. Pyrethrums, mixed and sprayed according to label precautions, work fairly well, but are not truly insecticidal, being better known for their knockdown capabilities. Also, the newly modified chemical derivatives are potentially toxic to humans.

The best treatment others and I have found is one of the commercial preparations of acephate liquid. Acephate is an insecticidal systemic; that is, it is absorbed into the plant's vascular system for several days. Along with suffering the immediate toxic effects of the applied spray, sucking pests ingest it and die. In my experience, this material has not damaged plants or live *Sphagnum*, but you should be cautious at first, with perhaps a limited trial spraying. Liquid preparations of acephate are foul smelling, and the bottle should be opened and dilutions made only outdoors in well-ventilated areas. Follow dilution, application, and personal safety directions on the label explicitly. A second application will be required in ten to fourteen days because the material does no affect eggs.

Heavy mealy bug infestations of pitcher plants will require repotting and disposal of the old medium—use fresh medium to repot. To physically remove as many mealy bugs and egg masses as possible, wash off the roots and rhizomes with a strong stream of water outdoors. Then, while wearing rubber gloves, spray the rhizomes and roots with diluted acephate when repotting. Respray your repotted plants again in ten days.

Cultivating *Utricularia*

In general, terrestrial and semiterrestrial bladderworts (*Utricularia*) can be treated like other carnivorous plants, although they prefer a wetter medium, so use a lower profile pot with water in the tray near the level of the medium surface. Some species, such as *Utricularia subulata*, will grow practically anywhere. This rampant growth may be alarming as it spreads through the collection, but the plant is harmless to others.

Aquatics, those plants that must grow in water in nature, may also grow in very wet slurries of Canadian peat, but usually less well than in their natural habitats. If you have an established pond that has not been treated with toxic algaecides, you might try aquatic bladderworts there. You can also make an artificial pond similar to the bog described above, only without the drainage holes. A deep tray may be suitable for growing these plants in the greenhouse. You can place good-quality, clean sand in the bottom of your pond or container; peat will tend to float to the surface. Algae may be managed by encouraging snails that are native to the ponds and ditches where you collect the bladderworts. Some snail species will consume the plants, but those growing with the bladderworts are probably safe to use.

Propagation Principles

There are many ways horticulturists increase numbers of (propagate) plants. Most applicable to carnivorous plants are use of seeds and rhizome and leaf cuttings, as outlined below.

Seed

The cultivation sections in the species chapters contain comments on producing seed. Those seeds that mature early in the season can usually be sown successfully on Canadian peat in a pot and kept under humid, well-lit conditions, the latter to discourage algal and fungal growth. Do not cover carnivorous plant seed with soil. Those seeds produced in autumn will likely require stratification. Autumn seeds usually have a protective chemical mechanism to prevent germination just before severe weather, with germination then taking place more safely in the spring. Horticulturists use a procedure called stratification wherein a pot of damp peat with seeds sown on the surface is sealed in plastic wrap and refrigerated for six to eight weeks, after which it is removed from the refrigerator, unwrapped, and placed in the greenhouse or terrarium. Seeds that self-sow in the bog will come up on their own in the spring.

Rhizome Division

Plants with rhizomes, particularly *Sarracenia* and *Darlingtonia*, will often branch to produce clumps of plants. This clonal growth habit is frequently noted in the wild. Such plants can be lifted from pots; if the rhizome branches have roots, they can be separated from the main rhizome and planted separately. Where applicable, propagation from rhizomes using other techniques is mentioned in the species chapters.

Leaf Cuttings

Leaves removed from some plants, particularly sundews, butterworts, and the Venus flytrap, can be induced to bud. Leaf propagation suggestions for butterworts and the Venus flytrap are mentioned in their respective chapters. For sundews, I recommend the technique first mentioned to me years ago by David Kutt. Pack a small, plastic pot with either live or moistened, dead *Sphagnum,* leaving a definite tight mound above the pot rim. Pull leaves from the sundew plants and lay them on the *Sphagnum* surface, with the top of the leaf up. A method to ensure that the leaf is snugly pressed against the moss surface so budding will occur is as follows. Unfold a plain (nonantiseptic) piece of wound-dressing gauze until it is a single layer. Stretch the cotton gauze snugly over the moss dome with the leaves, so that the dome is slightly depressed, and affix it by placing a rubber band around the pot rim. Place the pot in a warm, humid, well-lit place; in several weeks, plantlets will bud from the leaf glands. Because the gauze eventually rots, you do not have to worry about disentangling the plantlets from it.

VENUS FLYTRAP

M OST PEOPLE CONSIDER the Venus flytrap to be the epitome of a carnivorous plant. In addition to its odd beauty, its adaptations and carnivorous functions are truly remarkable. Darwin is often quoted as having called the plant "the most wonderful plant in the world," and indeed he did in a letter to American botanist Asa Gray in 1873 (reproduced in facsimile in Jones 1923). However, in his 1875 book, *Insectivorous Plants*, Darwin called the Venus flytrap "one of the most wonderful plants in the world." It seems the great naturalist hedged his bet along the way.

Dionaea muscipula Ellis

Dionaea is usually placed in the family Droseraceae. However, many botanists have proposed a separate family, the Dionaeceae, because there are several differences between the sundews (*Drosera*)—particularly of North America—and the Venus flytrap. The trapping mechanisms and leaf morphology are entirely different, *Dionaea* has a rhizome, and there are consistent and important flower differences. I would support a separate family (as in Radford et al. 1968).

There is also some disagreement concerning the common name for *Dionaea*, which, of course, is why we have scientific names. The following is a list of spellings of the common name, basically from Nelson and

McKinley (1990) with additions by me: Venus's flytrap, Venus's fly-trap, Venus's-fly-trap, Venus's fly trap, Venus' flytrap, Venus' fly-trap, Venus' fly trap, Venus flytrap, Venus fly-trap, The Venus Fly Trap, flytrap, and fly-trap. For this edition, I have chosen Venus flytrap as the most straightforward and most commonly used.

Alas, the plant's scientific name presents even more controversy. Prior to description by the botanist John Ellis in the eighteenth century (in a newspaper article, repeated in his pamphlet of instructions on transporting plants by sea), the plant was known informally by several names such as fly-trap sensitive and the seemingly odd name tipitiwitchet. The latter had been attributed to Native Americans, however, there is no such term in Native American languages now or of the time. It turns out that tipitiwitchet was a European vernacular term for female genitalia, and these somewhat bawdy eighteenth-century botanists were amused by the trap's supposed resemblance to the term's subject. Some scholars feel that botanists sought to legitimize and tidy up tipitiwitchet with a Latin reference to the goddess Dione, hence *Dionaea*. The epithet *muscipula* was supposed to indicate flytrap, but there was an error in the Latin used—the name actually translates as mousetrap. So, we have Aphrodite's mousetrap. However, further research into old letters disclosed several references to the trap being like a rat trap. Perhaps the epithet is not so far off after all. This information and much more is very delightfully and readably developed in Nelson and McKinley (1990), which every serious student of *Dionaea* must read, especially for the brilliant analysis leading to the unraveling of tipitiwitchet, which I have only hinted at here.

Description

Dionaea muscipula Ellis is a perennial, rhizomatous herb with black fibrous roots having white tips to 15 cm long. The short rhizome is covered with the fleshy petioles of the leaves, with the whole often erroneously referred to as a "bulb" commercially. Leaf blades to 12 cm long with variably winged, leaflike, green petioles terminating in a bivalved trap to 4 cm in length. Lobes of trap nearly reniform with strong marginal bristles to 6 mm, usually green externally (abaxially) and variably red inter-

A Venus flytrap in cultivation. Note the variable coloration of the trap interiors, which is probably related to light in this situation. The plants are in flower and there is some early seed capsule formation in spent flowers.

nally (adaxially). Scapes (naked flower peduncles) to 30 cm; inflorescence cymose and flowers actinomorphic, generally with five parts and non-fragrant; petals cuneate, white with faintly green veins; ten to fifteen stamens with yellow anthers; nearly spherical, superior ovary; stigma plumose when mature; seed capsule up to 0.6 cm across, flat, opening when seed mature; seed adherent to capsule, 0.1 cm, shiny black, roughly pear shaped. Seed is likely dispersed by water or in mud picked up by the feet of birds. Chromosome number $2n = 32$.

Flowering Season
From mid-May into the first two weeks of June

Distribution
Map 2 shows the distribution of the Venus flytrap. The historical area is extreme southeastern North Carolina into a narrow band of northeastern South Carolina. Roberts and Oosting (1958) thoroughly reviewed recorded locations of specimens in herbaria and mapped those still extant as well as those no longer found. At that time, they noticed a considerable shrinkage of the range. Since 1958, those of us active in the field have noted still more reduction.

Flowers of a Venus flytrap plant in Brunswick County, North Carolina. Petal and stamen details can be seen.

Mature *Dionaea muscipula* seeds in August.

Note the small location in northern Florida. Leonard (1978) discovered this area, which is in the Apalachicola National Forest west of Tallahassee. While inspecting savannas in the spring, he saw the flowers first and counted eighty-six plants. He noted seedlings as well, an indication of a healthy location with expansion. No regional botanists could recall anyone admitting planting *Dionaea* in the area, so the question of how they got there is outstanding. In my own investigations in the Apalachicola National Forest area, I have found small stands of *Dionaea* here and there in residual wet areas adjacent to roadside ditches. These, too, could have been planted, but the numbers and distribution seem to oppose that idea. Indeed, they may have been dispersed from Leonard's main site on the feet of birds.

The whole pattern, as I have observed it, suggests another possibility. One leg of migratory bird routes passes over the coastal Carolinas and then directly over the Apalachicola National Forest. The possibility of the original site being colonized by seeds on birds' feet must be considered. A sort of selection undoubtedly would have been in operation because we have not yet found evidence of additional range disjunctions between this location and the Carolinas range. But the Leonard location and the others nearby with seedlings in addition to adult plants suggest a particularly salubrious location.

Habitat

Dionaea muscipula is an inhabitant of southern pine savannas, where it grows in peaty, sandy soil and is subjected to continuous moisture in ideal weather. The plant may withstand being covered with water for brief periods in case of flood and is capable of tolerating temporary dry conditions as well. Frequent fire encourages exuberant growth.

Map 2. Distribution of *Dionaea muscipula*.

Variations

There is considerable variation in the coloration of *Dionaea* traps. Most trap interiors are varying degrees of bright red, with the pigment largely deposited in the glands. Newly emerged traps are usually lighter until exposed to light for a period. However, there are a few plants where red pigment is never present, with the trap interiors remaining yellowish green even in full light. At the opposite extreme, a few plants have been seen with extensive bright red coloration not only on the leaf interior but

A color variant of Venus flytrap in Brunswick County, North Carolina, that is red on both the trap exterior and interior.

also on the external portions as well, this coloration rarely becoming a deep wine red. One of the latter has been selected and propagated by tissue culture and has been named 'Akai Ryu' (red dragon in Japanese; Gagliardo 1996). Because it is propagated by tissue culture, this cultivar is commercially available, but it is difficult to find.

There are also variations in petiole shape and width and whether the leaf lies flat on the ground or extends up at an angle of about 45–60°. Japanese growers apparently recognized several cultivars on this basis, although I cannot find publication of these (J. A. Mazrimas, personal correspondence). These four are 'Typica', the most common, with a broad decumbent petiole; 'Erecta', with leaves at a 45° angle; 'Linearis', petioles narrow, leaves at a 45° angle; and 'Filiformis', with petioles extremely narrow or linear. Except for 'Filiformis', all of these can be seen as stages in leaf production of any plant depending on season (decumbent in summer versus semi-erect in spring), length of photoperiod (long petioles in spring versus short in summer), and intensity of light (wide petioles in

low light intensity versus narrow in brighter light; Roberts and Oosting 1958; personal observations). Thus, spring leaves are most often erect, later leaves decumbent; petioles in early spring are more likely to be broader as are those in varying degrees of shade, but the light intensity of later spring and summer produces less photosynthetic petiole tissue. I have not noted these forms to be consistent in any plants I have grown, but instead to be related to the factors listed above. The entire subject probably deserves further study.

Another interesting anomaly is the occasional production of vegetative plantlets within flowers. Botanically,

Vegetative apomixis, the aberrant production of plantlets in flowers, in *Dionaea*. These plantlets can be excised, rooted, and grown.

flower parts (sepals, petals, stamens, and carpels) are understood to be modified leaves. Occasionally in Venus flytrap and some sundews, an unknown stimulus causes these flower parts to revert back to a vegetative state as the flowers develop and vegetative plantlets are produced. These can be removed from the inflorescence, rooted, and grown as healthy plants that later flower. The process is best called vegetative apomixis and has been repeatedly observed and reported on over the years (such as Harshberger 1892; Hooft 1974 in most detail). I have noticed the phenomenon in many of my plants at times. Vegetative apomixis is intermittent and therefore not likely under genetic control. I have noticed it most in plants stressed by cold snaps and frost in spring, as flower scapes with their buds begin to grow.

Pollination

No detailed studies have been published on the subject of pollination in Venus flytrap flowers. We do not know the agent or the mechanisms. The flowers appear to be protandrous; that is, anthers mature and produce pollen before the stigma is receptive. This would encourage cross-pollination. The stigma is knoblike when the flower first opens and as initial pollen is being shed. In a few days, the stigma knob opens into a short, brushlike (plumose), pollen-receptive structure. Informally, several authorities feel that there is also an intrinsic block against self-pollination because plants of different strains (usually geographically separated) are required for pollination to be successful. However, there are recent oral accounts of apparently spontaneous successful pollination and seed production by plants isolated from insects (possible pollinators) in greenhouses and by single plants kept by growers (T. L. Mellichamp, personal correspondence). Self-pollination may indeed be possible, and this is another area requiring further study.

Trapping Mechanisms

Here, I briefly summarize trapping mechanisms and the extraordinary physiology of *Dionaea*. However, a very detailed and technical summary of the activities of Venus flytrap with complete bibliography can be found in Degreef (1998).

Juniper et al. (1989) divide the trap of *Dionaea* into three zones. The first contains the fourteen to twenty marginal teeth of each lobe periphery, which point more or less vertically. Once a trap has digested an insect and reopens, the teeth are at a 20–30° angle inward. When the trap closes, the teeth interlock and form a cage to prevent prey escape. The marginal teeth can vary from the usual number and thickness, and rarely they are absent. Sometimes the teeth are much stouter and fewer and are referred to as dentate (coarsely toothlike). The second zone is the peripheral band, a few-millimeter, narrow zone running just below the teeth. This zone has minute, colorless glands that secrete carbohydrates, presumably as a prey attractant. The third zone is the digestive surface, which is the remainder of the internal trap surface of both lobes. This zone has numerous pigmented digestive glands as well as the trigger hairs, usually three to a lobe. I have noticed no fragrance from the trap leaf.

In the Introduction, I quoted the results of Williams (1980) and Jones (1923) in their studies of prey composition. Briefly, Jones noted flying insects to be the majority of prey, whereas Williams found mostly crawl-

A trap of *Dionaea muscipula*. Note the marginal teeth and the pigmented glands of the interior, which can be seen as little dots. The three trigger hairs on each lobe are also visible.

ing insects consistently throughout the trapping season. Again, these divergent results might indicate varied insect populations and possible secondary effects of other plants in the area on insect populations.

Detection of Prey

Prey is detected by activation of one or two triggering mechanisms, both involving specialized, modified plant hairs. The main triggering hairs are located on the interior surfaces of the two trap lobes, normally three such hairs to a lobe. As a prey animal wanders into the trap, whether attracted by color or the carbohydrate secretions of the peripheral zone or just incidentally, it may brush against one of the trigger hairs. In normal spring and summer temperatures, nothing will happen. But if the prey brushes the hair again or a second hair within twenty to forty seconds of the first contact, activation is complete and the trap snaps closed very quickly (Burdon Sanderson and Page 1876). If the summer temperatures are quite hot, only one stimulus may be required.

In addition to the trigger hairs, another set of special stimulus points has been discovered. Scattered over the external surfaces of the traps are numerous tiny (80 μm), stellate trichomes (star-shaped plant hairs). These have a central point from which radiate usually eight hairlike structures, resembling the spokes of a wheel. Lightly brushing these hairs with a fine paintbrush over the external trap surface with eight to ten strokes changes electrical polarity in the trap, setting up something called an action potential. As a result, only one internal trigger hair stimulus is required to effect rapid trap closure. The process of stimulating the external hairs thus sensitizes, or alerts, the internal trigger hair mechanism. Furthermore, if one continues to stroke the trichomes so that five or six action potentials have occurred (forty to sixty strokes), the trap will close without stimulation of the internal trigger hairs (DiPalme et al. 1966).

Darwin (1875) noted that when the tip of the trigger hair was touched, movement or bending of the trigger hair occurs at the narrowing near the base. In fact, experiments in which the trigger hair is incrementally trimmed from its tip down show that its ability to respond to a stimulus is not lost until the narrow band is destroyed (Benolken and Jacobsen

1970). At Darwin's request, physiologist Burdon Sanderson (1873) was able to measure an electrical potential in stimulated traps similar to that of an animal nerve. For a review of this work, see Williams (1973b). Because *Dionaea* lacks animal-like nerves or nerve fibers, it is believed that this electrical action potential travels from the stimulus hair along cell plasma membranes by plasmodesmata (minute channels connecting cells) at a speed of about 10 cm per second (Sibaoka 1966).

The narrow time period (twenty to forty seconds) between the initial sensitizing trigger hair stimulus and the second actual closing stimulus has been termed "memory." The time lapse tends to prevent accidental closure of a trap by a drop of rain, a blowing plant fragment, or a prey that has escaped. This is of some import because nonfeeding closure of a trap can only be accomplished eight to ten times, on average, after which the trap will no longer respond but remains on the plant. If the interval between stimuli is increased, the number of stimuli must also be increased to effect closure. For instance, stimuli delivered at one-minute intervals will require six trigger hair deflections for closure to occur (Burdon Sanderson and Page 1876; Williams 1973a).

Rapid Closure

After the stimulation and electrical activation, the trap snaps partially closed, the speed depending mostly on temperature coupled with the condition of the plant. This phase of closure results in interdigitation of the marginal teeth so that prey cannot escape. Many years ago, trap closure was compared to a rat or bear trap with the two lobes supposedly swinging on the hinge where the two lobes attach. Now, it is known that this movement is caused by a partial fluid shift and almost immediate growth of the cells of the trap's outer surface, termed *acid growth* after the cellular pH changes that can effect similar growth (Stuhlman 1948a, 1948b; Williams and Bennett 1982, 1983).

If you examine an open trap of *Dionaea* closely, you will notice that the lobes have an inwardly directed convex curvature, whereas the outer surface is concave. After stimulation is complete and the trap closes, you will notice that the outer surface is now convex and the inner concave.

This inversion of the lobes' shape is sufficient to result in closure. Because this process involves rapid cell growth, the traps are a bit larger after each closure than they were before. The rapid-growth concept may also help to explain the finite number of closures possible in any trap because growth potential may be limited.

Slow Closure and Sealing

After rapid closure secures the prey, it must be digested and absorbed. To prevent the digestive secretions from drying or running off the trap, the whole trap is sealed into a tight pouch. Because it takes several hours to occur, this is known as the slow phase of closure. Several old beliefs were

Traps of Venus flytrap. The open one on the left (still containing the chitinous remains of a previous meal) has the typical shape of an open trap, with the internal surfaces convex and the outer concave. The trap is set. The trap on the right has just closed; note that the outer surface is now convex and the inner concave.

that the slow narrowing phase crushed the prey or impaled it on the trigger hairs, neither of which is true.

Darwin (1875) found that chemical stimuli were the main agents effecting narrowing. As the trap's margins get closer, the teeth turn outward, resulting in a tight seal. This is followed by secretion of mucilaginous material by the peripheral zone, which forms a gasket (Joel 1986) More recent studies indicate that chemicals—probably from the prey's excretions during its excitement—and mechanical stimulation of the struggling prey further the slow, sealing phase (Affolter and Olivo 1975; Robins 1976; Lichtner and Williams 1977).

Fagerberg and Allain (1991) mapped the growth regions in the trap during slow sealing. Unlike the initial closure phase, when rapid acid growth results in a sudden trap lobe shape inversion, tight sealing is effected by localized areas of growth. One zone is the external surface near

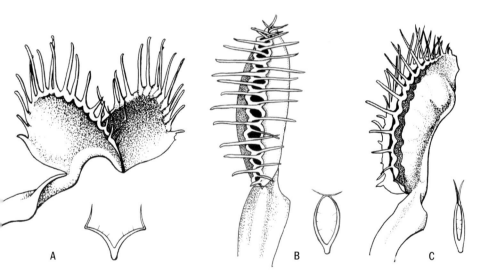

These drawings show the changes in surface contour as a result of trap closure. (A) The trap is set, with the internal surface convex and the outer concave; (B) the trap has rapidly closed with reversal of surface contours actually effecting the closure; and (C) the trap has narrowed into a tighter closure. Drawings by David Kutt.

the hinge; the growth of these cells tends to press the margins closer together. This closure is facilitated by growth on the internal surface in the peripheral zone near the teeth; the edges evert to get the teeth out of the way so sealing may occur at the narrow peripheral zone. Still to be worked out are the point stimuli that initiate these narrowing growth patterns and how growth is limited to these most useful zones.

Digestion and Absorption

Now that the prey is safely sealed in an essentially leak-proof chamber, its soft parts are broken down and the digestive products are absorbed. The glands that rather densely cover the inner surfaces of the trap lobes are sealed beneath cuticle prior to the trap's very first closure. Because the glands are to secrete the digestive enzymes as well as act as sites of absorption, they must be opened to the interior milieu. The digestive gland of *Dionaea* is the only plant digestive organ to develop discontinuities in the cuticle over the glands after stimulation (Joel et al. 1983), although exactly how this happens requires further study.

A trap in *Dionaea* after the slow sealing phase is complete. Note the narrowing and sealing at the peripheral zone and that the teeth are now standing almost erect. The prey can be seen inside through the lobe tissues.

As a result of mechanical (if the prey is still alive) and chemical (such as uric acid in prey excretions; Juniper et al. 1977) stimulation, digestive juices pour from the now uncovered glands. The excreted enzymes consist of proteases, phosphatases, nuclease, and amylase (Scala et al. 1969; Robins and Juniper 1980). Robins and Juniper (1980) proved that enzymes arise de novo from the glands rather than from microbial contaminants in *Dionaea*.

The duel-role glands now begin absorption of useful digestion products through complex cell membrane chemistry outlined in Juniper et al. (1989). Digestion reaches peak activity in about three to four days and is usually complete in seven to ten days. As mentioned previously, too large a prey will result in blackening of the still-closed trap in about two weeks, ultimately resulting in death of the trap leaf.

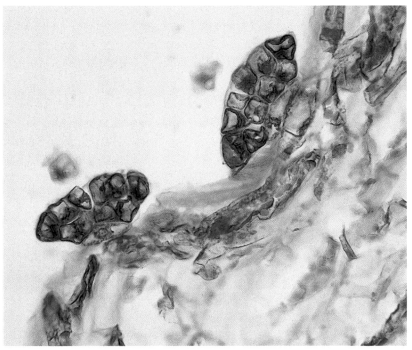

A photomicrograph of two decuticularized Venus flytrap digestive glands standing above the epithelium.

Trap Reopening

When digestion is completed, the trap opens. Juniper et al. (1989) describe this stage as very slow growth. However, reopening is faster than the ensuing bulging stage, which gives the trap a reset contour. The marginal teeth are not as erect in this reopened trap as they are in virgin traps, and, of course, the glands are now uncovered. Details of what kinds of growth occur in this reopening phase are still being researched. The chitinous exoskeletal remains of the prey may stay in the reopened trap, drop out after drying, or be washed out by rain. Each trap is capable of three or four digestive cycles of small prey during its lifetime (again, probably related to some growth limit), after which it is a quiescent photosynthetic organ—just an exquisitely shaped leaf.

Cultivation Notes

To grow Venus flytrap, follow the general cultivation requirements in the Introduction. The plants do best in a peat or peat-sand mix; live *Sphagnum* may grow too much and overwhelm the plants. The Venus flytrap must be allowed to go dormant in autumn, at which time the medium should be kept barely moist and cool. Resume heavier watering when the plant begins to grow again. Do not overfeed the Venus flytrap—no hamburger or table food and no more than three or four insects per plant in a season. If a leaf is fed too large an insect, it may die and turn black, but another will grow to take its place. After the flower scape has one or two flowers, you may cut it off to reduce energy loss from the rhizome. Cutting the scape before at least one flower appears, however, causes a new scape to initiate and begin growing, which uses even more energy reserves.

Without tissue culture facilities, propagation is by means of seed or leaf cuttings. You may achieve artificial pollination by gently rubbing the faces of two flowers of two different plants together in a circular motion. When seed matures in a few weeks, it may be immediately sown in peat or peat-sand mix. Do not cover the seed with soil. Germination should occur in two to four weeks. After a season or two, the little plants may be picked out and potted up separately. Germination rate decreases markedly when seed is stored at room temperature and approaches zero by one hundred days (Roberts and Oosting 1958). However, I have found that storing dry seed in a sealed glass vial in the refrigerator maintains high levels of viability for at least five years. Propagation by leaf cuttings, or pullings, is slower and less certain. Lift the rhizome from the soil, peel back three or four live leaves from the rhizome, and break them off at the

Anomalous double-trap formations occasionally appear in *Dionaea* traps. This formation arose apparently spontaneously in one of my plants several years ago, and I imagine
other growers have seen it. Although my plant's double trap closed, the slow sealing phase
was disturbed by the abnormal leaf configuration. In 1999, David Kutt had several of
these traps appear on plants he had treated with a fungicide earlier in the season. Kutt's
plants were also capable of the rapid closure phase.

base. Replant your large plant, and insert the bases of the peeled off leaves 1–2 cm into a pot of peat. Cover the pot in a plastic bag to maintain maximum humidity and place it in open shade (not direct sun) or under fluorescent lights in a warm place. Budding from the leaf base may occur in four to six weeks.

As dormancy approaches at the end of the season, most leaves will turn black and dry. Trim these away at the soil surface. Some rhizomes of *Dionaea* may maintain living, functioning trap leaves throughout the winter. David Kutt, a carnivorous plant botanical artist and grower, has made some interesting preliminary observations about overcoming dormancy in growing *Dionaea*. He is able to keep indoor plants at room temperature all winter and they continue to produce traps if a fluorescent-light, eighteen-hour photoperiod is used. The plants exhibited no evidence of rot or growth setback.

EASTERN NORTH AMERICAN PITCHER PLANTS

Sarracenia

THE GENUS *Sarracenia* was named after Michel Sarrazin (1659–1735), who has been called the founder of Canadian science. A French naturalist and surgeon, he became acquainted with the French botanist Tournefort and sent him examples of the New World northern pitcher plant, *Sarracenia purpurea*, after being appointed as surgeon-major in Quebec. Sarrazin contracted ship's fever while attending patients at Hotel Dieu and died in 1735 (Anonymous 1984).

The genus *Sarracenia* Linnaeus is in the family Sarraceniaceae, which also includes *Darlingtonia* Torrey and the South American genus *Heliamphora* Bentham. Several others and I have informally concluded that the differences between these three genera, which together comprise the entire family Sarraceniaceae, are of such a degree that *Darlingtonia* and *Heliamphora* probably should be placed in their own families. The main commonality is that all three are New World pitcher plants; however, there are significant floral and vegetative differences among the genera.

There seems to be nothing subtle about pitcher plants. Their general appearance begs attention, and when we encounter them we are almost startled. But once we look for awhile, then wander among them, we can begin to peel apart layers of subtlety and see many little secrets that collectively fit these plants so neatly into their bog habitat—and we still do not know all the secrets.

Description

Sarracenia is a rhizomatous, long-lived, perennial herb with reddish brown fibrous roots to 20 cm. The rhizome grows parallel just beneath the ground surface or, in very wet locations, at an angle or nearly vertical, often branching, each branch with a growth point. Just above ground is a ring of cladophyls (scale-like leaves), which are variously red to green and pointed, measuring to 2 cm. The leaves grow in a basal rosette, are adapted as hollow tubes or pitchers containing moisture and digesting prey, may be vertical or decumbent, have a flap at the end (lid or hood), and are variously shaped and colored according to species. Some species regularly and others occasionally produce seasonal flat, sword-shaped, nonpitcher leaves (phyllodia). The flowers are perfect, actinomorphic,

A dense stand of the white-topped pitcher plant, *Sarracenia leucophylla*, in Baldwin County, Alabama. Locations with this level of pitcher plant density are becoming increasingly uncommon.

protogynous, and appear singly on a scape nearly as tall as or taller than the pitcher leaves. The flower parts are hypogenous; there are three bracts, five sepals, five pendulous petals, and many stamens in fascicles (numbering from ten to seventeen with two to eight stamens each). The anthers are yellow; the pistil contains a nearly spherical 0.8–1.5-cm, five-compartmented ovary with a tubercular surface; the style is elongate, usually green, and expands into an umbraculate (umbrella-shaped) structure near the end; this umbrella has five cleft points; just proximal and internal to the clefts are located the five stigmas, which are 1–2 mm and papillose. The seed capsule is tan to brown and five valved. The abundant, slightly elongate seeds are shed in autumn, average 2 mm in length, and are tan to purplish brown. Chromosome number $2n = 26$.

Habitat
Members of the genus *Sarracenia* grow in sphagnous bogs, mountain seeps, and coastal plain savannas. Except for *Sarracenia purpurea* subspecies *purpurea*, which extends well into the Northeast and Great Lakes region and then far into Canada west to northeastern British Columbia, pitcher plants are largely confined to the arc of coastal plain from southeastern Virginia down to northern Florida and then west to eastern Texas, with a few noteworthy, more interior locations into the Appalachian Mountains. Harper (1918) mentioned eighteenth- and early-nineteenth-century travelers reporting that it was difficult to lose sight of vast pitcher plant savannas as one traveled from western Florida through southern Mississippi.

Comments
Although the eight species (with several subspecies, varieties, and forms) are distinct in appearance with respect to pitcher and certain flower characters, *Sarracenia* species are very closely related genetically to the extent that all are capable of hybridizing with one another. The hybrids are fertile and capable of crossing back with the parents and even with each other. Where two or more species grow together, hybrids are commonly seen and often occur as "hybrid swarms," sometimes to the extent that

with backcrossing and incrossing it becomes difficult to distinguish a pure example of a species. (Hybridization is discussed more at the end of the chapter.) This behavior as well as a matrix in a cluster analysis (Schnell and Krider 1976) strongly suggests a pattern of reticulate rather than strictly linear evolution of these species; that is, most characters are shared with one or more other species in the genus but in differing combinations, with the combination ultimately defining the species in many cases.

McDaniel (1966) and Gibson (1983) have pleaded a case for nonrandom placement of different *Sarracenia* species when two or more grow together. There is some indication that the tall species rarely intermingle because they would be competing with each other for the same spatial distribution of insect prey, whereas there would be little or no such competition between tall species and smaller, decumbent species growing closer to the ground. Where two or more tall species (or the two decumbent species in their more lowly realm) grow together, McDaniel and Gibson observed zonation; that is, the tall *Sarracenia flava* plants grow in the drier end of the bog, while the tall *S. leucophylla* plants grow in the wetter end of the same bog. Although this pattern is found in some locations, I fear these concepts have been idealized to some extent—I have found perfectly vigorous and densely populated stands of these two species growing intermingled (and often with extensive hybridization) in the same bog. *Sarracenia flava* is capable of growing in a relatively drier savanna habitat, but it is equally at home and even more vigorous in wetter places throughout its range. After seeing nearly a hundred locations of these two species, my experience suggests that the observed zonation is a random event. Certainly, more research is required on the problem of pitcher plant species competition and prey partitioning (see Introduction).

The Pitcher

Sarracenia pitchers are uniquely structured, both as a group and individually. Furthermore, each species can be identified by pitcher characteristics alone. Unfortunately, along with pitcher characters most botanical keys for the genus also use flower color characters and the presence or absence and character of any phyllodia. I have devised a key based on pitcher characters alone (Schnell 1998a), which is more useful because flower and phyllodia characters are seasonal.

At the very tip of most pitchers is a flattened to slightly curved, flaplike structure called the lid, or hood. The lid may be erect, as in *Sarracenia purpurea*, or it may be variably approximated to the pitcher opening. Some plant anatomists feel that the lid is derived from the blade portion of a leaf, whereas the hollow tube is derived from the leaf stalk (petiole). This concept is open to debate. The lid is often supported by a narrower band of tissue called the column, which attaches to the back (abaxial) edge of the pitcher tube. The pitcher tube margin is frequently rolled outward. On the front (adaxial) side of the pitcher, there is a variable seam with a narrow or widened wing (ala) that extends from the upper edge of the tube down to the base; a well-developed ala may be wavy (sinuate). The entire external surface of a pitcher is covered with small nectar glands; these are more numerous and dense in various areas to be mentioned later, as well as in the flower.

From the viewpoint of trapping, digestion, and absorption of prey, pitchers are divided into zones that are more or less visually discernable. These zones number from three to five, depending both on the author and to some extent on the pitcher plant species because some zones are indeed combined. *Sarracenia purpurea* best illustrates these zones, with all five present and clearly separated (Lloyd 1942).

Zone 1 is the lid, which is flaplike in most species, but in *Sarracenia psittacina* it is globose and in *S. minor* very closely approximated to the pitcher mouth. The lid, or hood, is densely lined with stout downward-pointing hairs to direct prey to the pitcher opening. Among the hairs are numerous attracting nectar glands; venation is often prominently red, which is probably also attractive.

Zone 2 is the attracting and conducting zone. It extends from the rolled edge of the tube directly to where the surface suddenly becomes shiny, usually a distance of 1–2 cm, but up to 10 cm in taller pitcher species. The rolled margin is often called the nectar roll because many glands secrete copious, visible nectar drops upon which insects feed. As the insect stretches down into the pitcher from the roll, often hanging only by its hind legs, it seeks more nectar being secreted in the conducting zone, but also happens upon a peculiar surface constructed much like the shingled roof of a house. The cells have downward-pointing protuberances, and the prey is unable to keep footing and slides down into the lower zones.

Zone 3, one of the longest, is the shiny-surfaced glandular zone. Here there are no hairs or epidermal cell protrusions, just many digestive glands and a smooth surface that provides no footing. Zone 4 is the retentive and absorptive zone. Downward-pointing hairs reappear to help hold the struggling prey or at least prevent it from climbing. There is usually a pool of digestive juices mixed with prey in this zone, and digestion and absorption occur here. Zone 5, which is located below the hairy zone 4, is apparently present only in *Sarracenia purpurea*. There are no glands or hairs and it is smooth and glassy. Originally thought to be absorptive, the function of zone 5 is not known. Variations in *Sarracenia* species include the usual absence of zone 5 and combination of zones 3 and 4.

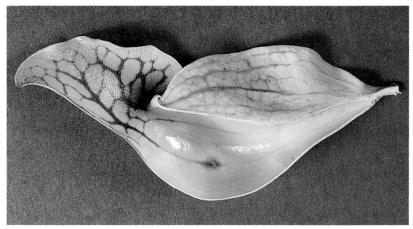

An open pitcher of *Sarracenia purpurea* revealing the internal zones. Note the prominent, wavy ala (pitcher wing) above. Zone 1 includes the hood to the left. Zone 2 (the conducting zone) extends from the rolled margin of the tube down to where the glass-smooth area begins. Zone 3, the glandular zone, is glassy and smooth in the photograph. Zone 4, the retentive and absorptive zone, has downward-pointing hairs. Zone 5 to the far right is smooth again.

Many species of *Sarracenia* also have interesting structures in their pitcher's upper portions; these are variously called areoles, fenestrations, or light windows. Light windows are groups of cells that lack chlorophyll, which allows more light to penetrate into the pitcher. Light windows lack vessels, glands, or hairs and, due to their lack of pigment, appear either white or translucent depending on how the cells are packed together and the degree of intercellular spacing. Insects tend to avoid entering dark places, and the windows lighten the interior of hoods and pitchers. In their extreme, such as in *Sarracenia leucophylla*, these windows may also have an external attractive function as well. In a pitcher such as *S. minor*, where the hood is closely oppressed to the pitcher opening, the prey may attempt flight and escape toward the light window area, only to strike a solid wall and fall back into the pitcher.

In addition to protease production by *Sarracenia* pitchers, the enzymes esterase, acid phosphatase, and amylase are also produced by various species (Parkes 1980). Mellichamp (1875), a country doctor in South Carolina near Charleston, observed *S. minor* (then known as *S. variolaris*) from his buggy while on rounds and then in experiments in his kitchen. He noted that the pitcher fluid had an intoxicating and anesthetic influence on various insects. After being removed from the liquid, however, the insects recovered. Mellichamp also observed evidence of digestion and increased growth caused by insect entrapment in the plants. There is more on Mellichamp's research in the section on *S. minor*.

Although somewhat limited, Hepburn et al. (1920b) produced the earliest general study of pitcher plant digestion using chemical methods. For the time, these experiments were carried out with remarkable attention to detail. Hepburn et al. used classical chemical analytic methods to note the reduction in quantity of certain simple and more complex nitrogenous and phosphate compounds added to pitchers. Allowance was made for dilution by increased water secretion, and pitchers were plugged to prevent insect entrapment or dilution by rainwater. Noting that developing, unopened pitchers produced sterile fluid, Hepburn et al. also experimented with these pitchers to overcome the confounding effects of bacterial contamination after pitcher opening, concluding that intrinsic enzymes digested prey and that simpler nutrient compounds were absorbed. They also realized that bacterial activity contributed to digestion in pitchers that had been opened for some time. They quoted an older, unavailable paper by Batalin in which dissolution of the cuticle overlying the digestive-absorptive glands took place soon after pitcher opening. Hepburn et al. also noted an increase in secretion of pitcher liquid into the tube after glandular stimulation.

Plummer and Kethley (1964) were able to use more sophisticated methods to track radioisotope-labeled nutrients as they were absorbed by the pitchers and distributed throughout the plant, including the rhizome for storage. Autoradiograms in the paper nicely illustrated this activity. This work was confirmed and taken one step further by use of actual insects fed radiocarbon-labeled glucose (Williams 1966). The tagged insects (fruit flies, *Drosophila melanogaster*) were then fed to pitcher plants (*Sarracenia purpurea*) and digestion and absorption were clearly demonstrated. Younger pitcher tissues incorporated the tagged compounds at a greater rate than older pitchers.

Experiments with *Sarracenia purpurea* also suggest that drugs may effect enzymatic secretions. Pilocarpine, morphine, and ethyl alcohol had a positive effect on digestive secretions in the pitcher; however, unlike in animals, atropine had no suppressive affect (Boldyreff 1929).

As discussed in the Introduction, bacterial enzyme activity undoubtedly plays some part in digestion and absorption once a bacterial flora is established in opened pitchers, but this flora is not the sole source of enzyme activity in pitcher plants. *Sarracenia* also digest prey by means of intrinsic enzymes, then absorb and transport these nutrients throughout the plant. The value of these nutrients is also discussed in the Introduction. The role of pitcher insect associates in processing certain prey will be discussed later.

Flowers

In their southernmost distribution along the Gulf Coast, pitcher plants begin flowering in mid-March. In the most northern distribution of *Sarracenia purpurea* in Canada, flowering may occur as late as early August

—a short summer to achieve flowering, pollination, and seed maturation. In between these extremes, flowering time predictably varies by latitude and altitude. Given the ease of hybridization among *Sarracenia* species, Bell (1952) felt that isolating mechanisms to prevent complete swamping of individual species where they grew together largely revolved around timing of flowering among species in any one bog and, of course, which species grew together. Still, the bell-shaped time curves of flower initiation, peaking, and waning usually overlap at their extremes so that isolation barriers potentially break down almost yearly.

Depending on the species, flowering occurs as either the first event of the season or concurrently with pitcher growth. The naked flower peduncle (scape) sprouts from the rhizome growth point with the spherical flower bud at the top. At this stage, the future three bracts of the flower can be discerned. As the scape grows, the bud begins to enlarge up to 1.5 cm,

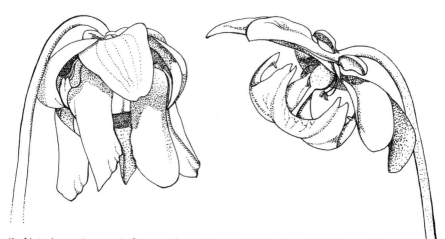

(Left) An intact *Sarracenia* flower with pendulous petals in place. (Right) A partially dissected *Sarracenia* flower in which the petals have been removed. The flower is an enclosed chamber bounded above and laterally by sepals and petals and below by the umbrella of the style. Stamens in fascicles ring the base of the spherical ovary. Pollen is shed into the cup of the umbrella along with drops of nectar secreted by the surface glands of the ovary and additional abundant nectar glands at the bases of the ovary and stamens. Note the stigma lobes at the umbrella tips. Drawing by David Kutt.

A newly opened flower of *Sarracenia purpurea* subspecies *venosa* in eastern North Carolina. Note the hook-shaped scape at the top so that the flower hangs pendantly. The three bracts can be discerned above the wedge-shaped sepals. The panduriform petals hang down over the dips in the umbrella-shaped distal style. To the right, beneath the scape and between a sepal and a petal, one can see a cleft tip of the umbrella with the nublike stigma protruding up.

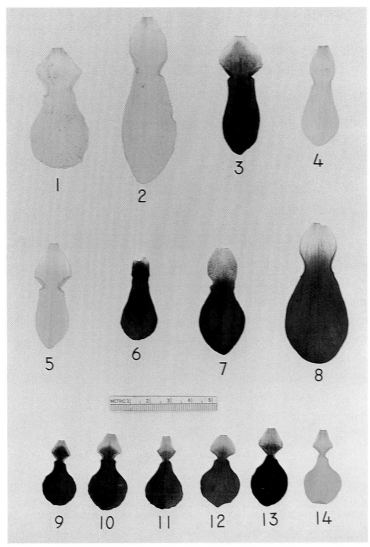

On the basis of measuring dimensions of numerous petals of each taxon (Schnell 1978b), an average petal shape and color can be presented for each: (1) *Sarracenia alata*; (2) *S. flava*; (3) *S. leucophylla*; (4) *S. minor*; (5) *S. oreophila*; (6) *S. psittacina*; (7) *S. purpurea* subspecies *purpurea*; (8) *S. purpurea* subspecies *venosa*; (9) *S. rubra* subspecies *rubra*; (10) *S. rubra* subspecies *gulfensis*; (11) *S. rubra* subspecies *alabamensis*; (12) *S. rubra* subspecies *wherryi*; (13) *S. rubra* subspecies *jonesii*; (14) *S. rubra* subspecies *jonesii* yellow-flowered.

depending on species. Before the flower emerges, the scape grows and shapes into a hook at the top so that the bud is now hanging down, or nodding, as is the flower when it opens. The flowers are protogynous (Schnell 1978d, 1983); that is, after flower opening the stigma is immediately receptive to pollen, but pollen production in a flower does not begin until two to five days later.

Flowers vary by color, size, fragrance, some sepal properties, and average shape of the pendulant panduriform (fiddle-shaped) petals. Although usually pushed behind pitcher characters as species discriminates, recent studies show that flowers are highly specific (Schnell 1978a, 1978b). Generally speaking, *Sarracenia* flowers are either shades of red or yellow, although the petals of *S. alata* are more yellowish white and some examples of *S. purpurea* are purple. Pigment chromatography (Schnell 1978a) produced a matrix that is of more theoretical than practical field value. However, the matrix shows the polymorphic character of pigmentation in *Sarracenia* flower petals in which species and some subspecies are discernable as well as some infraspecific relationships, such as the closeness of the *S. rubra* subspecies compared to other recognized species (see discussion under *S. rubra*).

In a companion paper (Schnell 1978b), I produced a matrix table of more easily discernable flower characters, which indicated that flowers could be used to help identify species in the field or in healthy horticultural situations. These various characters will be mentioned later with the individual species. Bell (1952) prepared a comparison drawing of various *Sarracenia* petal shapes and mentioned that these could be useful taxonomically. In my flower studies (Schnell 1978b), from each taxon I collected, pressed, and measured several hundred petals. Averaging these measurements allowed me to illustrate an "average" petal from each taxon.

Pollination

Experience indicates that although *Sarracenia* flowers are capable of producing seed when manually self-pollinated, on average, the largest seed sets and most viable seeds are obtained by cross-pollination (Sheridan and Karowe 2000). In nature cross-pollination requires a pollinating agent, usually an insect. Flowers that are experimentally bagged during anthesis to prevent insect activity only occasionally produce a few seeds (Mandossian 1965; Burr 1979; Schnell 1983).

The pollination process has been examined in depth for *Sarracenia purpurea* in Michigan (Mandossian 1965) and Vermont (Burr 1979) and for *S. flava* in North Carolina (Schnell 1983). In each case, the primary pollinators are queen bumble bees (*Bombus*), which are abundant in early spring when both pitcher plant species flower in their habitats. Honey bees (*Apis mellifera*) occasionally visit flowers, but not in large enough numbers to be efficient pollinators, and they do not work the flower in the same way as bumble bees. Most importantly from an evolutionary and historical viewpoint, honey bees have only been in North America since the arrival of European settlers. Certain flies (*Sarcophaga sarraceniae*) have been noted to be occupants of *Sarracenia* flowers and to travel

This flower of *Sarracenia flava* has had one petal removed to expose the dip, or swag, between two umbrella points, the latter having the stigma tips upon which pollen must be deposited. Note that the base of an adjacent petal covers the stamens (as the removed petal did) so pollen cannot reach a stigma tip, thus preventing self-pollination. The stigma tips protrude out under the sepals between two petals.

among them (such as Mandossian 1965), but the flies seem to be resting or taking shelter and consuming nectar. Again, these potential pollinators are the wrong size to work the peculiar configuration of the flower.

In early spring, queen bumble bees seek out unoccupied mouse holes to begin their nests. Bumble bees have voracious appetites and must feed a great deal. Because they have little energy reserves, their energy balance depends on regular food intake (Heinrich 1979), and the large pitcher plant flowers, which contain prodigious quantities of nectar and pollen, are excellent food sources. Some early spring days and nights are very cool, but poikilothermioc (cold-blooded) insects are quite capable of achieving an early morning warmup—they shiver. Do not look for them to be shivering on a branch the way we shiver. They shiver inwardly because their flight muscles are attached under the exoskeleton, so you will not see a thing through the armor. Then they are ready for a full day.

A bumble bee initially approaches the flower in a straight line, suggesting visual attraction. As the bee nears the pitcher plant stand, she circles and then approaches in a serpentine pattern as though catching fragrance on the air. The bee lands on the sepals and immediately goes beneath to the petal bases (from which most flower fragrance emanates). She then circles the petals one or more times. The bee then faces a stigma lobe on an umbrella point and forces her way between two petals into the interior of the flower. A strong insect is required to enter the flower, and as the bee does so, she brushes any pollen on her back from a visit to another flower over the stigma lobe, thus achieving cross-pollination.

An important point concerns how the bee exits the flower. If she left the same way she came in, self-pollination might occur. But the bee lifts a petal with her body and exits the flower over the dip in the umbrella between two stigma tips, avoiding these. This is the only way it could work. The large queen could not enter by raising a petal and uselessly going over the swag because this is not anatomically possible. Forcing entry directly between two petals is the pathway, and this brings the bee in over the stigma lobe. Exit over the stigma lobe is not the path of least resistance, so the bee instead simply lifts a petal and takes off.

You can hear much buzzing from inside a bumble bee–occupied flower and actually see the flower moving. As far as stinging insects go, bumble bees are rather even-tempered. With care, you can lift the petal a bit and see the bee walking about the umbrella as she gathers nectar and pollen, with the buzzing of her wings causing more pollen to shower down on her from the anthers above.

A bee will work an average of eight flowers (as few as two and as many as forty-nine in my count) before returning to her nest. After exiting, a bumble bee will often go to the top of the flower and clean her pile, leaving a dusting or clusters of pollen on the sepals and upper petals. I call these deposits "bee tracks" and they are a definite sign that a bee has worked that flower.

After an average of ten to fourteen days, the flower's petals dry and fall off. The bend in the upper scape then begins to change and the flower

In this photograph of a bumble bee queen on an intact flower of *Sarracenia flava*, the bee has positioned herself so that her head is pressed nearly against the stigma lobe. She will then swing forward, brushing her pollen-dusted back over the stigma as she enters the flower upside down between two petals.

slowly assumes a more lateral or even completely upright position. Some have supposed that this change may then result in the pollen still contained in the umbrella falling onto a stigma. In case insect cross-pollination had not occurred, this would assure some seed production by selfing. However, after examining many of these spent flowers, I am convinced that the geometric configurations related to curvature of the stigma points would not allow this to occur. In addition, most of the umbrellas are emptied of pollen at this stage due to earlier bee activity and any remaining pollen-nectar mixture has become a solid mass mixed with mold.

As summer progresses, the flowers, still with their umbrellas and sepals, stand in the bog as the ovary increases in size. The sepals tend to recurve outwardly to a varying degree depending on species. In late sum-

Bee tracks on a *Sarracenia flava* flower. The clumps of pollen on the sepals and petals indicate that a bumble bee has cleaned herself after visiting the flower and strongly indicate that the flower has been pollinated.

mer or autumn, depending on species and latitude, the ovary has dried and turned tan or brown and is now a seed capsule. When fully ripe, the capsule splits open and the five parts of its wall lift out, usually at the tip of the capsule, exposing the mature seed.

Although we presume that bumble bees are also important pollinators of the other six species of *Sarracenia*, this may not be the case. Rymal and Folkerts (1982) and Folkerts (1982) point out that the flowers of *Sarracenia psittacina*, *S. minor*, and *S. rubra* are smaller than those of *S. flava* and not suitable for pollination by large bumble bee queens, even though there is much variation in size among *Bombus* species. Further observations are required, but I would point out that these three species flower somewhat later than the larger-flowered ones in their latitudes, at which time smaller *Bombus* workers are available. I have seen bumble bee workers smaller than honey bees, and, of course, in the Deep South workers would appear sooner than they would farther north.

Animal Associates

In the Introduction, I discussed some complex relationships between carnivorous plants and other plants and animals in their habitats. Pitcher plants do not consume every insect or other small animal. Indeed, some insects have adapted to living in or on the plants. In some cases, the insect does no harm (commensalism) or may even provide some benefit (mutualism). In other cases, the insect does a great deal of harm to the plant (parasitism). Insects that live in close relationship in or on a plant are often called inquilines, although there is some criticism of the use of the term (Juniper at al. 1989).

Two relatively common commensals of pitcher plants, especially the tall species, are the green tree frog (*Hyla cinerea*) and several species of small, yellowish green crab spiders. These animals hang just at or inside the pitcher rim to partake of some of the inflow of prey. Pitchers containing these animals seem to have no less prey in their depths, so these small robbers apparently do little harm. Of course, if a frog slips and goes in, it does some good—as indicated by the occasional presence of green tree frog bones in a pitcher. Because the color of crab spiders very closely matches the pitcher linings, the spiders are difficult to detect as they sit quietly in wait with front legs outspread. Indeed, the relationship between these two animals and pitcher plants may be mutualistic, as the animals may contribute to plant nutrition through excretions.

There is a mosquito whose larvae inhabit pitcher plant traps. Somehow, the larvae of *Wyeomyia* are able to overcome enzyme action. Smith (1902) noticed that larvae of *W. smithii* (which was later named for him) were able to exist in dormancy through the northern winter in the frozen watery contents of *Sarracenia purpurea* pitchers, with the dormancy being broken by the increasing photoperiod (not temperatures) of rising spring (Bradshaw 1976). *Wyeomyia* deposits eggs only in pitcher plants (Istock et al. 1983). The larvae feed on small protozoa, bacteria, particulate matter, and assorted detritus (Addicott 1974; Bradshaw 1983). Because mosquito larvae are mainly filter feeders, they require others organisms to break down larger fragments of trapped insects for them. In the North *Wyeomyia* does not require blood meals prior to egg-laying, but in the South may bite occasionally (Smith 1902; Bradshaw 1980; Lounibos et al. 1982).

Although largely confined to *Sarracenia purpurea*, in the South *Wyeomyia* may also occasionally be found in *S. leucophylla*, *S. alata*, and the hybrid of *S. flava* and *S. purpurea* (Bradshaw 1983). Dodge (1947) recognized the southern *Wyeomyia* as a separate species, *W. haynei*, leaving the northern population as *W. smithii*. Goins (1977) concurred with this, but some workers feel that the two populations are subspecies of the one species, *W. smithii* (Lounibos and Bradshaw 1975; Bradshaw and Lounibos 1977). *Sarracenia purpurea* is also divided into two subspecies by reason of morphologic differences as well as range, the northern being subspecies *purpurea* and the southern subspecies *venosa*. Whether species or subspecies, the two *Wyeomyia* mosquitoes tend to stay with their northern or southern subspecies of *S. purpurea*. Wherry (1972) recounts a discussion he had with H. R. Dodge concerning the ranges of the two *S. purpurea* subspecies. Wherry then went to visit entomologist Frank Morton Jones in Wilmington, Delaware, because the southernmost extent of *S. purpurea* subspecies *purpurea* is southern Delaware. Jones had a preserved mosquito larva from Delaware plants that indeed proved to be the northern *Wyeomyia.*

Most eggs of *Wyeomyia* are laid in new pitchers, with the insect usually dividing the season's eggs among several different pitchers. There is a chemical stimulus, a water-soluble compound found only in new pitcher tissue, that acts as an attractant (Mogi and Mokry 1980; Istock et al. 1983). Because the larvae must undergo several growth stages (instars), they frequently overwinter in the frozen pitcher contents. *Sarracenia purpurea* maintains its pitchers over the winter and gradually replaces these during the next season, whereas most other pitcher plant species have complete pitcher dieback each autumn.

The presence of the mosquito larvae may be of value to the pitcher plant in that it is able to more efficiently digest and absorb larval excretions. The absence of other mosquitoes in pitchers of *Sarracenia purpurea* is an interesting problem. Apparently, the midge *Metriocnemus knabi* directly suppresses species other than *Wyeomyia smithii*; water from pitchers in which *M. knabi* is growing does not suppress other mosquitoes, and *Wyeomyia* is apparently able to resist the midge's negative effects (Peterson et al. 2000). Pitchers of *S. purpurea* without *Wyeomyia* or *M. knabi* larvae often have heavy growths of algae in the pitcher cavities (Stewart et al. 2000).

There are also several larvae of fly and midge species that inhabit pitcher plants. *Blaesoxipha fletcheri*, a sarcophagal fly, floats from the water surface using two posterior spiracles at the surface for air exchange; this fly feeds on floating prey corpses (Forsyth and Robertson 1975). *Blaesoxipha fletcheri* is found only in prime pitchers at the best of their insect-catching ability (Fish and Hall 1978). The larvae of the midge *Metriocnemus knabi* live at the bottom of pitchers and bore holes into sunken insects; when such insects are extracted from the pitchers and examined, they are writhing with surface midge larvae (Fish and Hall 1978). The midge is also able to control its dormancy by photoperiod (Paris and Jenner 1959), as does *Wyeomyia.* Among these organisms, we see a system: *B. fletcheri* feeding on surface insects, *M. knabi* on insects in the depths, and *Wyeomyia* on smaller debris from these two (Buffington 1970).

Sarracenia species interact with additional dipteran larvae, particularly the pitcher plant fly, *Sarcophaga sarraceniae*, which was mentioned earlier as a possible pollinator. These large larvae, measuring up to 1.7 cm, are usually found one to a pitcher and infest a broad range of *Sarracenia* species (Jones 1935; Plummer and Kethley 1964). The fly is ovoviviparous; that is, eggs develop within the mother's body. The adult lands on the rim of a pitcher, deposits one small larva into the depths, and flies on to the next. The larva of *S. sarraceniae* is the only one shown to actually produce an antiprotease to counter the plant's digestive enzymes (Jones in Hepburn and Jones n.d.). In the autumn, the *Sarcophaga* larva exits the pitcher and becomes a pupa partially hidden in ground debris. These pupae are sometimes found and consumed by birds.

Several other dipterans that use the pitcher plant trap include *Dohrniphora cornuta* (Jones 1918) and *Bradysis macfarlanei* (Jones 1920). An aphid, *Macrosiphum jeanae* has been found living, possibly exclusively, on the inner pitcher walls of *Sarracenia purpurea* in Manitoba (Robinson 1972). The wasp *Isodontia philadelphicus* builds nests in pitchers of *S. flava*. These consist of alternating plugs of grass and nest chambers containing a single egg and several paralyzed crickets and grasshoppers for larval food (Jones 1904). Several leafcutting bees of the family Megachilidae do something similar, often cutting out neat sections of pitcher plant petals as the nesting material.

I have had a couple of amusing experiences with leafcutting bees. When I lived in North Carolina, I grew several sunken tubs of pitcher plants outdoors next to the greenhouse. To facilitate watering in dry weather, I tied a length of standard hose to a short pole and ran fine water lines out to the tubs. To water the entire set of tubs, I simply plugged my main hose into the piece on the post. One day I noticed no water coming from the ends of the fine tubes. Tracing back, I found bits of green leaf stuffed deeply into my hose end on the post. The children denied everything and I finally decided it was the work of a leafcutting bee, which repeated this maneuver several times until I corked the hose end when not in use. When we moved to the mountains of southwestern Virginia, we would leave several detachable watering wands lying about on the back porch.

The wands became plugged, and I once again took them apart to find packed bits of green leaf. Apparently, both the wasp and the leafcutting bees are found away from pitcher plant locales and clearly use other cavities when necessary.

There are several moths that infest pitcher plants. Because these parasites consume plant tissue, they do a great deal of damage in the process (Jones 1904, 1907, 1908, 1921, 1935; Hilton 1982). Frank Morton Jones wrote thoroughly and delightfully of these moths. In fact, his work is the standard reference to this day. His papers in *Entomological News* always contained nicely executed drawings as well.

The first moth to consider is *Papaipema appasionata*, an exotic name for the *Sarracenia* root borer. Until the late nineteenth century, it was considered to be one of the rarest moths in the world, with only one specimen from America in a European collection. Finally, someone learned to look for the moth in pitcher plant savannas, and then it was considered common. The adult moth lays an egg on the growth point of a *Sarracenia* rhizome. The small larva quickly bores into the rhizome, consuming a great deal of tissue and attaining a relatively huge size, 5–6 cm. It always gives itself away, however, by its accumulating bright orange droppings, or frass, at the pitcher plant growth point. The larva consumes enough

A nest of the *Sarracenia* wasp, *Isodontia philadelphicus*, in a *Sarracenia flava* pitcher. Note the grass plugs and a chamber of chitinous exoskeletons of crickets and grasshoppers. The wasp has already pupated and left the nest, having fed well as a larva.

tissue to considerably weaken, if not kill, the plant by the time it pupates. If the telltale frass appears in your cultivated collection, you can sometimes save the plant by reaching into the rhizome cavity with a fine forceps and pulling the wriggling larva out.

Endothenia daeckeana is a small moth whose larvae attack *Sarracenia* flowers, especially early seedpods. These moths were a particular nuisance to Mandossian (1965), who was trying to count seed production and came back to her study bogs in late summer to find severely damaged flowers. They particularly infest *S. purpurea* in the North, and a severe infestation can decimate a season's seed production. Fortunately, seed production in any one flower is prodigious (400–600). In autumn, the larva burrows down inside the scape to pupate (Hilton 1982).

Probably the most interesting of the pitcher plant moths are the three species of *Exyra*. Often, nearly every plant in a stand of *Sarracenia* is infested. A botanist friend (who shall remain nameless) was curious about the moth and its life cycle and thought he would study it in "one or two"

Note the brown-orange castings, or frass, around the growth point of this plant of *Sarracenia rubra* subspecies *rubra*, a sure sign that the root borer *Papaipema* dwells within.

of the plants in his extensive greenhouse collection. Before long, nearly the entire collection was captured in the "study," and he put a great deal of time and work into clearing the infestation.

The small *Exyra* moth, with a resting width of no more than 1.0 cm, has yellow, black, and white crossbands. The three species are largely confined to certain pitcher plant species. *Exyra rolandiana* is found in *Sarracenia purpurea* only, both in the northern and southern parts of the plant's range. *Exyra ridingsii* is found in *S. flava*, and *E. semicrocea* in the remaining species of the southern coastal plain. Occasionally in the South the moths do cross over to other pitcher plants.

Exyra moths are rarely seen flying about because their only movement seems to be from one pitcher to another, usually at night. You can lift back a pitcher lid in daytime and often see from one to several moths resting on the inside of the upper part of the wall. *Exyra* moths apparently have no special foot adaptation to overcome pitcher plants' conduction and glandular zones, but they are able to rest quietly as well as move around

A rhizome of *Sarracenia rubra* has been opened longitudinally to show *Papaipema appasionata* inside.

at will. Movement seems to be by means of a combined hopping and minimal wing flutter, perhaps timed to overcome the conduction zones of pitchers, although this does not explain their capability to rest in place.

The damage to pitchers is done by the larvae, of course. At dusk, the *Exyra* female flies from pitcher to pitcher and usually deposits one egg on the inside wall of the pitcher on the conducting zone. If more than one egg is deposited, perhaps by separate females, the resulting larvae will kill each other off until only one remains in that pitcher. The newly hatched larva of *E. ridingsii* at first lies in the shallow groove of the inside of the hood column of *Sarracenia flava*. The larva weaves a small web over itself and begins to feed on the column. It then begins to feed on the plant tissues of the inside wall of the pitcher, at first girdling the wall so that the remaining outside wall becomes paper thin and often collapses, sealing the larva safely in its feeding chamber. In uncollapsed pitchers or prior to pupating, the larva spins a thin, waterproof web across a pitcher opening to keep out water, prey, and possibly enemies. *Sarracenia psittacina*'s uniquely small lateral pitcher mouth is plugged with web and debris instead of just a woven web.

The lid of this *Sarracenia leucophylla* pitcher has been clipped off to disclose an *Exyra semicrocea* moth resting on the inside of the upper part of the pitcher.

The larvae grow rapidly and pass through molts (instars). As they develop, the larvae assume easily visible species characteristics. The larvae of *Exyra semicrocea* and *E. ridingsii* grow four lateral bristled tubercles, or lappets, on each side of their bodies, those of *E. semicrocea* being most prominent. The lappets are supposed to prevent the larvae from being wedged in the depths of tall, narrow pitchers. The larvae of *E. rolandiana*, which inhabit the wider pitcher body of *Sarracenia purpurea*, would be less likely to become wedged and do not have lappets.

Larval maturity with resulting pupation and emergence of an adult rarely occurs in one season. The larvae overwinter in their sealed, dried pitchers, buried in their own frass and silk for protection. In spring, they may emerge from torpor before a green pitcher is available, in which case they may feed on early flowers and buds. As new pitchers emerge, the larvae enter them even before the pitcher opens, the pitcher top then ringed and sealed.

Prior to pupation, *Exyra rolandiana* spins a dense, waterproof cocoon of silk around itself in a fresh pitcher of *Sarracenia purpurea*. In the South, the other two *Exyra* species seek fresh pitchers for pupation. If the

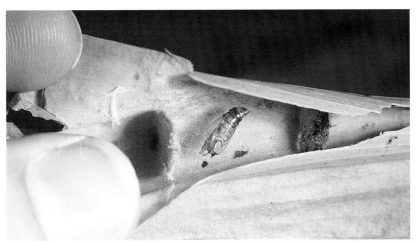

An opened pitcher of *Sarracenia minor* containing an empty pupal shell of *Exyra semicrocea*. The adult moth has already matured and exited, but note the upper and lower woven ceilings of the pupal chamber and the light webbing in which the pupa was suspended.

top of the pitcher is not then collapsed because of larval feeding, the larva seals off its chamber with a silken web. Then it cuts an emergence hole in the pitcher wall just below the ceiling for the adult's egress. (In *Sarracenia psittacina*, this emergence hole is at the top of the spherical hood.) Down below, a smaller drainage hole is cut for runoff, should water enter the tube, and the chamber just above this may be sealed as well. The larva then pupates. The adult emerges to begin the whole remarkably adapted process anew.

This thumbnail sketch of the complex life of pitcher plants and their denizens is in fact much more complicated. Sometimes the *Exyra* egg on the inside of a pitcher wall does not yield a minute moth larva, but an equally minute and quite mature *Chalcis* wasp, whose parent had been directed to lay its egg on the moth egg by chemical signals. Also, a dozen or so tiny wasps may emerge from the ovoid *Sarcophaga* pupa seemingly safe in the debris. Similarly, *Exyra* larvae hurriedly making their way from one pitcher to another may be parasitized by wasps. The connection between wasps and lepidopteran larvae is an old and widespread one. *Papaipema*, housed deep in the cellar of a pitcher plant rhizome, also has its wasp enemies. And even the *Isodontia* wasp's larvae sealed in with crickets and grasshoppers between dense plugs of dry grass fall victim to ants exploring the dried, dead pitcher. *Exyra* larvae sealing off the tops of pitchers for their own use may cause dipteran larvae at the bottom of the pitcher to starve for lack of an inflow of food. Finally, in early spring as we pad through a fine stand of pitcher plants, we may notice some with obvious *Exyra* damage that have mysterious longitudinal slashes near their bases. Birds have learned to recognize the drainage and escape holes and have pecked into the pitcher for a rich bit of food.

Cultivation Notes

Pitcher plants are easily grown following the general instructions in the Introduction. They do equally well in dead or live *Sphagnum* or in Canadian peat. The plants must be allowed a period of dormancy. During the winter, pitchers of the erect species will gradually brown and all dead portions should be cut away. If any phyllodia are present, leave them in place until they die in the spring. The pitchers of some species overwinter (see the following species accounts) and should not be trimmed off until they die back naturally, after new pitchers appear in the spring.

Feeding solid bits of material to pitcher plants is to be discouraged. These bits are usually rich and may wedge in the tall pitchers above the bottom, thus causing necrosis of the wall at this point. You may wish to conservatively and cautiously try foliar mist feeding, as described in the Introduction.

Propagation is by seed or rhizome division. No one has had repeated success with leaf cuttings, although you may wish to experiment. Seeds require six to eight weeks of stratification for a good flush of germination. Rhizome division may be accomplished in two ways. If the rhizome branches and has two growth points, these may be separated as long as each portion has adequate roots. Steve Clemesha (personal correspondence) of Australia, who grows *Sarracenia* well, has devised a method of encouraging budding of horizontal rhizomes. Raise the horizontal rhizome to a level so that its top surface is above ground. With a sharp knife or single-edge razor blade, make sharp cuts halfway through the living part of the rhizome every 2–3 cm along its course. In time, fresh growth points will bud from each cut. Eventually when good root systems are established, you may finish breaking the old main rhizome into smaller ones with the new growth points.

Sarracenia purpurea Linnaeus

Synonyms
One may encounter the following synonyms, most often in older literature: *Sarracenia gobbosa, S. venosa, S. terrae-novae.*

Common Names
Sarracenia purpurea is commonly known as the northern pitcher plant, southern pitcher plant, sidesaddle plant, pitcher plant, huntsman's cap, frog's britches, and dumbwatches. The last is an interesting local term used in the New Jersey Pine Barrens—the expanded style and sepals that

remain after flowering were thought to look like the old-style watches whose cover opened in a star-shaped pattern, but in this case without hands and therefore mute.

Description

Rhizome short and usually angled or nearly vertical. Leaves decumbent, gibbous, becoming more vertical at ends, to 30 cm; hood erect, margins often wavy, expanded, and not covering pitcher mouth; external surface of pitcher variably hirsute; prominent wavy pitcher wing, or ala. Flower scape 20–40 cm, often with pale red coloration near top; bracts, sepals, and petals usually red to reddish purple; fragrance varies from sweet in the North to mixed sweet and "feline" in the South.

Flowering Season

Mid-March in the South to as late as August in the far north

Distribution

This species is the most widely distributed of our North American pitcher plants. Map 3 indicates the historical limits of distribution. While the range is shrinking in some areas, due mainly to habitat destruction and water-table changes, it occasionally expands, such as the discovery of a colony near Fort Nelson, British Columbia (Krajina 1968), although this location is still east of the Continental Divide.

Habitat

In the North and the Appalachians, *Sarracenia purpurea* is associated with sphagnous bogs and marly fens, but the species does not have any consistent plant associates (Mandossian 1965). In the southern coastal plain, the species grows in savannas and pocosin margins, often associated with other *Sarracenia* species.

Comments

This is the only *Sarracenia* with an erect hood that does not cover the pitcher orifice. In spite of early studies indicating that *Sarracenia purpurea* does produce digestive enzymes (Hepburn et al. 1920a), the notion that the plant does not has grown over the years. The hood placement of other pitcher plants protects the pitcher contents from dilution by rain. However, the erect hood of *S. purpurea* allows rain to enter the pitcher cavity freely; if intrinsic fluid and enzyme production does not occur, this rain would produce a pitcher pool for the activities of inquilines and bacteria in digestion. But a more recent study (Gallie and Chang 1997) confirms intrinsic pitcher fluid and enzyme production. Interestingly, the pitcher also harbors nitrogen-fixing bacteria (Prankevicius and Cameron 1989). The pitchers are decumbent and, in general, the plant is a low-ground rosette, often with the tubular portion of the pitcher nearly buried to the rim in northern sphagnous bogs. Thus, the erect hood's bright red venation and nectar glands may serve as an attractant flag as well.

Unlike many *Sarracenia* species, the pitcher leaves of *S. purpurea* do not die back at the end of the growing season. In the North, many leaves

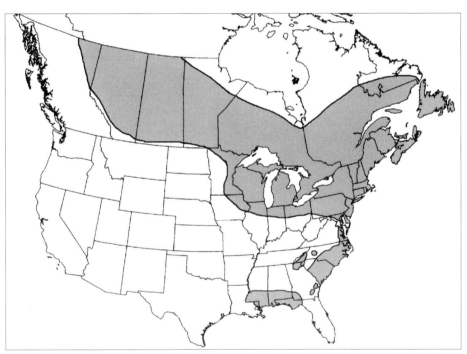

Map 3. Distribution of *Sarracenia purpurea*.

turn dark red and then become green again in the spring. As new leaves sprout, with spring growth at the rate of one every ten to fourteen days, the leaves of the previous season die back slowly throughout the summer. During northern winters, both the surrounding bogs and the liquid within the leaves often freeze solid with no harm done to the dormant leaves. However, a snap freeze during spring can damage the softer pitchers severely.

Infraspecies

As one might expect in a species with such a large range, there is considerable variation in form and color among *Sarracenia purpurea* plants. These variants were noted in the eighteenth and nineteenth centuries. With little knowledge of ecology, absolutely no concepts of genetics, and no guidance from the contemporary International Association for Plant Taxonomy (IAPT) and its International Code of Botanical Nomenclature (ICBN), botanists tended to designate a lot of these variants with quasi-formal names. The slow lines of communication in those days furthered confusion.

Wherry (1933b) critically reviewed some of these named variants (see also Schnell 1979a). The following should be eliminated from formal designation within the species *Sarracenia purpurea* because they most certainly are either ecophenes (ecological or site variants that are not genetically consistent) or are aberrant, unpredictable, and/or inconsistent variations in single plants: forma *incisa* Rousseau, forma *plena* Klawe, variety *stolonifera* Macfarlane and Steckbeck, variety *ripicola* Boivin, and variety *terrae-novae* La Pylaie. For the details of my reasoning, see Schnell (1979a). Within *Sarracenia purpurea*, I recognize the following taxonomic infraspecies, which will be discussed in more detail and illustrated below: subspecies *purpurea*; forma *heterophylla* (Eaton) Fernald; subspecies *venosa* (Rafinesque) Wherry; variety *burkii* Schnell forma *luteola* Hanrahan and Miller; variety *montana* Schnell and Determann; and variety *venosa*.

The division of the species *Sarracenia purpurea* into two subspecies, *purpurea* and *venosa*, is generally accepted and is based on reasonably consistent criteria (Wherry 1933b, 1972; Schnell 1979a), although not all botanists accept it (such as Bell 1949; McDaniel 1966), feeling that there is gradation between the two subspecies as well as intermingling of plants out of range. *Sarracenia purpurea* subspecies *purpurea* occupies the portion of range from the narrow waist (see Map 3) in Delaware and Maryland north, whereas subspecies *venosa* grows in the southern portion of the range. Given the ease with which all *Sarracenia* species hybridize and backcross, it is not surprising to find intermediate plants where the two ranges meet; but at the further extremes of the ranges, the plants are consistently quite different. Also, considering the nature of biological variation, it is not surprising to find single or small groups of plants in the upper southern half of the range that have an appearance close to subspecies, as in the southern portion of the range. Combining the evidence from examining many field locations over the years, I feel that subspeciation is genuine.

There are four chief differences between the two subspecies. In subspecies *purpurea*: (1) the ratio of the length of the pitcher tube to the width of the mouth is 3:1 or greater; (2) the external pitcher surface is smooth to the touch (even though a few hairs are present under magnification); (3) flowers are dark red to reddish purple; and (4) when viewed sideways as the lobes of the pitcher hood are pinched together in front, the lobes do not or just barely exceed the front edge of the mouth. In subspecies *venosa*: (1) the ratio of the length of the pitcher tube to the width of the mouth is 3:1 or less; (2) the external pitcher surface is densely hirsute to touch; (3) flowers are most often brighter red; and (4) the pinched hood lobes easily exceed the front edge of the pitcher mouth. The most variable characters are items 3 and 4; but all four taken together are diagnostic.

Mandossian (1965) studied *Sarracenia purpurea* subspecies *purpurea* in Michigan bogs and found variations induced by where the plants grew. Plants in the shade always had less color. Plants growing in *Sphagnum* bogs were largest and had the best red venation of the pitcher. However, plants growing in marly fens were smaller when mature; had a brittle, hard character to the pitcher tissue; and were usually dark red. Mandossian's reciprocal-transplant experiments indicated that these were not permanent

A clump of *Sarracenia purpurea* subspecies *purpurea* in a Michigan bog. Note the dark red to maroon flowers.

genetic effects—the transplanted individuals assumed the characteristics of their new neighbors after a few seasons.

An interesting variant of the northern subspecies is forma *heterophylla*, a plant that is without a trace of the red pigment (anthocyanin) so pervasive in most carnivorous plants. The bright yellowish green foliage (in full sun) and the yellow flowers stand out. Sites for forma *heterophylla* are uncommon, and the form usually grows in bogs with its heavily red-pigmented brethren and their hybrids. The original location found by Eaton, who described the form, is in Massachusetts. In recent publications the plant has been noted in Montmorency County in northern Lower Michigan (Case 1956); in Connecticut, behind a college in a bog that had been visited by students for years but not noticed earlier (Robinson 1981b); and in Gros Marne National Park in Newfoundland (Robertson and

Sarracenia purpurea subspecies *purpurea* on the Bruce Peninsula of Ontario. Note the smaller hood and the glistening, smooth appearance of the external pitcher surface.

Roberts 1982). Steve Smith (personal correspondence) found a location in New York, and Phil Sheridan wrote me of a location at Bear Lake, Pennsylvania, found in 1958, but not seen since 1978. Others have written to me of *heterophylla* plants in locations in Ontario and Minnesota, and I have found plants in Michigan's Upper Peninsula.

There are strict criteria for identifying forma *heterophylla*. This is because many shaded, ordinarily red-pigmented plants may have little red coloration and appear almost totally green. Proper identification of these shaded plants can be difficult for the beginner if flowers are not present (they retain some red, even in the heaviest shade). One should examine the leaves closely for even the faintest red venation. Then, pull back *Sphag-*

Sarracenia purpurea subspecies *purpurea* forma *heterophylla* in a sphagnous bog in Michigan's Upper Peninsula. Note the almost translucent yellowish green color of the mature and budding pitchers as well as the green scape.

num and examine the cladophyls at the growth point. In red-pigmented forms, even in heavy shade, there is always some red pigment in these structures; in forma *heterophylla*, the cladophyls are a clear yellowish green.

Moving to the southern populations of *Sarracenia purpurea*, subspecies *venosa* grows south of Delaware. The subspecies grows sporadically in mountain and piedmont seep bogs, but more commonly in the coastal plain savannas. Because several varieties have recently been named for the subspecies, by ICBN rules any remaining plants are variety *venosa*, until and unless additional varieties are pulled from this pool.

On Map 3, the range for variety *venosa* is indicated for eastern North and South Carolina, with a few isolated colonies recorded for coastal Georgia that are perhaps no longer extant. A field study with observations, counts, and reciprocal and garden transplants disclosed two main color variants of variety *venosa* (Schnell 1981). When grown in full sunlight and intermingled, one variant has a nearly completely dark red

Flower of *Sarracenia purpurea* subspecies *purpurea* forma *heterophylla*. All parts are yellow or yellowish green. Because the plants readily set seed, this anthocyanin-free variant seems to make no difference to bumble bee pollinators. The sweet flower fragrance of the northern subspecies is still apparent in this form.

pitcher, which obliterates venation. The other variant is green with red veins. There are numerous intermediate hybrids between the two. Because these variants grow intermingled, without any evidence of ecological zonation, and there is seemingly no prey-trapping advantage of one variant over another, there seems to be no selective adaptation for either variant.

Phenolics in plants (such as anthocyanin) appear to discourage predator attacks and have antimicrobial properties (Cooper-Driver 1980). Anthocyanins in the epidermal layers also absorb potentially harmful

Sarracenia purpurea subspecies *venosa* variety *venosa* in a savanna in eastern North Carolina. The range of the variety extends into the coastal plain of South Carolina as well. Compared to subspecies *purpurea* in the North, note the more expanded hoods, the stockier pitchers, and the dull external surface due to hirsutism, which can be best appreciated by feel.

ultraviolet rays and perhaps protect deeper photosynthetic tissues (Lowry et al. 1980). However, anthocyanin-free variant plants grow side by side with normal forms and do not appear challenged. One must consider founder and quantum effects during colonization of the coastal plain from higher and more inland bogs as well as balanced polymorphism.

The genotype of the plants may have originated in separate bogs (polytopic) prior to coastal plain migration and simply retained a random variation or one that was advantageous in a previous situation and neutral in the coastal plain. Finally, one must consider the possibility of transposons effecting neighboring genes, a linkage and epistatic effect. Presently, then, these two variants seem random and may in effect be waiting for a challenge.

On Map 3, note the localized populations of plants in the North Carolina piedmont and in an area extending from extreme southwestern North Carolina in an arc into northeastern Georgia. These plants of *Sarracenia purpurea* subspecies *venosa* are distinct from the coastal populations with

Compare the pitchers of *Sarracenia purpurea* subspecies *venosa* variety *venosa* (top) and *Sarracenia purpurea* subspecies *purpurea* (bottom). The four differential criteria mentioned in the text are apparent.

uniform characters among them. Distally on the pitcher leaf, the hoods curve inward and nearly touch at this point; the hairs lining the hood in the upland plants average 0.8–1.0 mm long, whereas the coastal plain plant hood hairs are greater than 1 mm. Also, the upland plants have a particularly striking bright red venation with wider, coarser veins. These upland plants have been designated variety *montana* (Schnell and Determann 1997). Transplant and horticultural studies done separately by myself and Determann indicate that these characters are consistent and genetic in origin.

Lastly, Map 3 indicates a range of *Sarracenia purpurea* subspecies *venosa* nearly disjunct from the Carolinas and upland plants except for a few small, historical populations in coastal Georgia, these being on the Gulf coastal plain extending from the eastern end of the Florida Panhandle through southern Mississippi. The small extension into northeastern

Pitchers of *Sarracenia purpurea* subspecies *venosa* variety *venosa* in the Carolina coastal plain. The pitcher on the left is the nearly all-dark-red variant, whereas the one on the right is the veined variant. The pitcher in the middle is a hybrid of the two.

Louisiana represents plants collected in 1871 but not seen since (Murry and Urbatsch 1979).

Wherry (1933b) reported that Frank Morton Jones found near Theodore, Alabama, "rare mutant" plants of *Sarracenia purpurea* with a pale style umbrella and rosy pink petals. Although he arrived in the Theodore area past flowering season, in 1932 Wherry randomly collected plants that flowered the following year in the Philadelphia greenhouse of a horticulturist named Louis Burk. These all had the characteristics that Jones had described, and Wherry unofficially dubbed them "horticultural variety Louis Burk."

I have made some thirty-five botanical explorations along the Gulf Coast over the years, both in and out of flowering season. Far from being a "rare mutant," the plants with flowers that Jones described were actually the overwhelming, if not only, expression of *Sarracenia purpurea* variety

Flowers of *Sarracenia purpurea* subspecies *venosa* variety *burkii*. Note the white umbrella and the pink petals. The sepals retain their usual red color.

venosa on the Gulf coastal plain. I have described them as variety *burkii* (Schnell 1993). The umbraculate portion of the style is indeed nearly white, as is the ovary, and the petals are pink. C. R. Bell (personal correspondence) has suggested that the pallor of the pistil parts may be due to growing in the shade; however, the umbrella and ovary express the greatest whiteness in full sunlight, whereas shade-grown plants have a green, albeit pale, pistil. The pink petals are consistent in sun or shade. The pitchers of the plants are also rather distinctive compared to the Appalachian and Carolinian varieties in that they are much larger, with gaping mouths and a wider, more undulating hood.

Naczi et al. (1999) have suggested that the differences between variety *burkii* and other infraspecies of *Sarracenia purpurea* are sufficient to warrant designation as a separate species, *S. rosea*. They cite the differences already mentioned and place a great deal of emphasis on a thickening of

A comparison of the pitchers of the three varieties of *Sarracenia purpurea* subspecies *venosa*. On the left is a pitcher of variety *burkii*, with its large, undulating hood. Second from the left is variety *venosa* from the Carolinas coastal plain. The remaining two pitchers on the right are variety *montana* from the Carolinas and northeastern Georgia mountain bogs; note the characteristic hood configuration.

the pitcher lip in variety *burkii* (their *S. rosea*). There are a number of deficiencies in their paper, among them not considering the measurement length of pitcher versus mouth width as well as reordering their basic measurement data according to accepted *S. purpurea* infraspecies; grouping the data together has resulted in bias of measurement averages. For instance, the fact that plants of *S. purpurea* subspecies *purpurea* forma *heterophylla* most often also have a thickened pitcher lip is buried and therefore lost in the combined data. Lip thickness is, after all, most likely related to overall pitcher size, expansion, and volume. Allozyme studies (Godt and Hamrick 1999) show variety *burkii* somewhat more segregated from the other infraspecies, but not of sufficient extent to designate a new species as clades are understood. Overall, the infraspecies of *S. purpurea* are so closely related and so different from other *Sarracenia* species as a group that I do not feel that Naczi et al. (1999) have made a clear and definitive

An example of *Sarracenia purpurea* subspecies *venosa* variety *burkii* forma *luteola* growing in the author's greenhouse. Note the lack of red pigment but usual expanded hood of variety *burkii*.

case for separate species designation of the Gulf Coast plants. Therefore, I strongly recommend continued consideration as variety *burkii*.

Professional and amateur botanists often look for rare color variations of *Sarracenia* species in the field, particularly anthocyanin-free forms of usually red-flowered and red-pitchered plants in the South (similar to *Sarracenia purpurea* subspecies *purpurea* forma *heterophylla* in the North). A yellow-flowered plant of *S. purpurea* subspecies *venosa* variety *burkii* has indeed been found, thus far in small numbers. It has been described as *S. purpurea* subspecies *venosa* variety *burkii* forma *luteola* (Hanrahan and Miller 1998). The pitchers also lack red pigment and are a pale yellowish green color in full sun.

Cultivation Notes

Sarracenia purpurea is generally easy to grow if one follows the suggestions at the beginning of this chapter. This species is an ideal terrarium plant because it is decumbent, although one would have to deal with the tall annual flower. The yellowish green forms present some problems, particularly subspecies *purpurea* forma *heterophylla* if grown in the South, where summers are relatively hot. The plants seem more susceptible to fatal fungal and bacterial diseases under these circumstances. Growing plants in indoor terraria in moderate temperatures helps, as does placing the plants under the greenhouse bench in bright shade during summer. The possible protective effects of anthocyanins in regard to plant infections are somewhat borne out by the greater resistance of ordinary red subspecies *purpurea* to warmer temperatures when grown in the South.

Sarracenia flava Linnaeus

Even though *Sarracenia flava* has a far smaller historical range than *S. purpurea*, individual *S. flava* plants far outnumber those of *S. purpurea*, which is due to the density of *S. flava* plants in a good site. Alas, the large old stands of this magnificent pitcher plant have dwindled remarkably, particularly since the mid-1950s. The huge colonies depicted in the centerfold photograph of Macfarlane (1908) are now extremely rare and largely maintained by careful artificial management, but still susceptible ultimately to a falling water table. I remember locations several hectares in extent.

Synonyms
A few of the more recent but still relatively old synonyms include *Sarracenia gronovii* variety *flava*, *S. rugelii*, and *S. fildesii*.

Common Names
These include yellow trumpet, trumpet, huntsman's horn, yellow pitcher plant, and lily. The last is attributed to local folk who thought the large, colorful pitchers were flowers, specifically lilies.

A fine colony of *Sarracenia flava* variety *rugelii* in Toombs County, Georgia. This site was adjacent to a pasture. After several years of trying, the owner was finally able to ditch and drain the site to extend his pasture.

Description

Rhizome robust, elongate, and parallel to the surface of the ground. Summer leaves erect, smoothly expanding to pitcher mouth, to 120 cm tall with mouths to 12 cm wide; narrow, linear ala; lid mounted on an erect column with markedly recurved margins to more than halfway to midline; lid nearly circular when viewed from top; tip filamentous apiculate with no keel; lids up to 20 cm across; winter leaves (phyllodia) ensiform (sword shaped and straight), 20–40 cm long. Flower scapes appearing before pitchers in spring, slightly shorter than mature pitchers; parts yellow to yellowish green with yellow petals; flowers have strong feline fragrance; mature seed capsule to 2 cm.

Flowering Season

Mid-March in the South to mid-April and early May in the Carolinas

Distribution

Map 4 depicts the historical distribution of the species. *Sarracenia flava* was thought to be extinct in southeastern Virginia, but Phil Sheridan (personal correspondence) has found remnant sites and is making recovery attempts. The small location in the North Carolina piedmont is disjunct and will be mentioned again in the conservation chapter, unfortunately. The southernmost extension is just over the western Florida line.

Habitat

Sarracenia flava is a classic example of a savanna carnivorous plant, but can also be found rather commonly in wetter seeps, shallow standing water, and even sphagnous seep bogs. I certainly have not found the claim of its "preference" for more "dryish" areas to be true (cf. Folkerts 1982; Rymal and Folkerts 1982). The plant can tol-

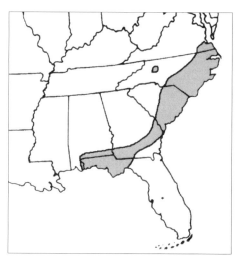

Map 4. Distribution of *Sarracenia flava*.

erate drier areas, more so than some other species (such as *Sarracenia leucophylla*), but it is nicely adapted to wet locations, which is where I have seen the most robust plants.

Comments

The flowers of this species are characteristic (Schnell 1978d) and large, up to 12 cm across. Pollination has been well worked out (see earlier in this chapter). The fragrance is strong and unusual, often described as "musty." My wife, Brenda, pointed out that the flower smells like the urine of an intact, male domestic cat. I concur and refer to the fragrance as "feline" for that reason, although I found out much later that Wherry (1933a) actually used "feline" to describe the fragrance of *Sarracenia flava* flowers first, but the term was never commonly used. The family cats also agree— one hot and sunny early March day, plants in the greenhouse were in full flower and the exhaust fan at the back of the greenhouse came on. The

A flower of *Sarracenia flava*. The flowers of all the varieties are essentially identical. Some individuals may have a reddish blush (not related to varietal status) to the proximal sepals and bracts.

cats gathered in a semicircle just beneath the outflow with intensely interested noses twitching in the air.

Phyllodia (winter leaves) are long, linear leaves usually about half the length of a pitcher. They have a prominent midrib on one margin and the flat portion of the leaf looks like a widened ala. At the upper end of the phyllodium is an apiculate tip similar to that on the tip of the lid. Two species of *Sarracenia*, *S. flava* and *S. oreophila* (discussed in the next section), regularly produce phyllodia in late summer. Some other species produce phyllodia occasionally, as will be discussed. The phyllodia of *S. flava* are long and straight, and those of *S. oreophila* are shorter and sharply curved. A comparison photograph of these is in the *S. oreophila* section. The function of phyllodia is not clear; however, pitchers of *S. flava* die back in the autumn, whereas phyllodia remain green all winter, suggesting that they may photosynthesize during warmer, sunny spells in autumn and winter. In early summer, when new pitchers have grown, the previous autumn's phyllodia die back.

True phyllodia must be differentiated from etiolated pitchers. The latter have a somewhat phyllodia-like (phyllodiform) appearance, but the midrib portion on the margin is usually slightly expanded into an incompletely formed pitcher, with the small opening and lid at the top. Etiolation is usually caused by growth in deep shade or other stressed conditions. The atypical pitcher formation coupled with a markedly widened ala makes the etiolated pitcher look like a phyllodium.

Infraspecies

As I look out over a large, Carolina savanna of *Sarracenia flava* and then walk through them, I am impressed by the variation in color forms in the species. The variation is usually described as polymorphism, and initially it seems hopeless to try to make any sense of it all. Bell (1949) and McDaniel (1966) felt it was useless to try to discern and name any varieties. During the nineteenth century, British horticulturists had an avid interest in *Sarracenia* species, but few were fortunate enough to spend any time in the field in the southeastern United States. Consequently, plants were first artificially selected by the collector and then the grower, who had little knowledge of the plants' origins or the native habitat. As a result, names flourished. Because this was before ICBN, any interesting plant (often represented by only one individual) was given a species, variety, or horticultural variety name, with little clarification. Often, the same plant was given different names, and no one knew for certain if they were dealing with a species, multiple species, and/or hybrids.

I reviewed this process in several articles (Schnell 1978b, 1995b, 1998b), including the efforts by Masters in *Gardeners' Chronicle* articles (for bibliography, see Schnell 1998b). (*Gardeners' Chronicle* was a highly regarded late-nineteenth-century British horticultural journal.) Although Masters did a fine job in straightening out most of the mess, he unfortunately was also victim of insufficient plant material and information, so that some of his varieties of *Sarracenia flava*, for example, were actually other species or clearly hybrids.

I published a review article of *Sarracenia flava* variants in the Carolinas coastal plain (Schnell 1978b). After countless field trips over several years, I felt that there was some sense to the seeming spectrum of variation. I was able to reduce the plants to five clear varieties that were genetically consistent, and I decided that the remaining plants of the spectrum were hybrids of the five varieties to varying degree: simple hybrids, backcrosses with varietal parent types, hybrid crosses with one another, and even hybridization with other species of *Sarracenia* with resulting introgression. I concluded that, as is the case with *Sarracenia purpurea* subspecies *venosa* variety *venosa* in the same area and indeed the same savannas, there was no discernible advantage for one variety over another. In fact, *S. flava* variants grow intermingled in the same savannas.

I confronted the Gulf coastal plain in an article with similar results (Schnell 1995b) and finally settled on seven named varieties for the entire range of the species (Schnell 1998b), with two newly named varieties among the seven, the other five being derived from Masters. Some of the varieties grow throughout the range, although more prominently in the Carolinas; two varieties are confined largely to the Gulf Coast. I will begin the descriptions with the five varieties of *Sarracenia flava* most prominent in the Carolinas; the last two of the seven are confined to the Gulf Coast.

Variety *flava*

Prominent deep red to purple pigment deposition in pitcher throat (interior lower lid, column, and just below mouth of pitcher) with variably prominent red venation radiating from this over the interior lid and upper pitcher tube. Because this is the predominant variety in the type area for the species, it automatically bears the specific epithet without authority. This variety is very common in the Atlantic coastal plain.

Variety *atropurpurea* (Bull) Bell (1949)

Lid and external pitcher tube deep red in ideal growing conditions; pitcher interior pale tan or also red. When cultivated, the deep red color is often difficult to maintain and even plants brought in will fade perceptibly in a few weeks. Full sunlight as many hours a day as possible and an acidic soil help to maintain color. This variety flowers reluctantly. It is uncommon on the Atlantic coastal plain of the Carolinas, and even more rare in the Florida Panhandle.

A single pitcher of *Sarracenia flava* variety *flava*. Note the prominent veins radiating from the central purple area and the prominent purple blotch in the pitcher throats.

Variety *maxima* Bull ex Masters (1881a)

The epithet *maxima* is unfortunate for this variety because one would assume that it refers to pitcher size, and the name has been mistakenly regarded in this respect. The pitchers may be large, but no more so than any of the varieties. In fact, the key early descriptive feature of this variety is that the pitchers are green with no red venation or purple throat markings. These plants are not the equivalent of other anthocyanin-free taxa in the genus (such as *Sarracenia purpurea* subspecies *purpurea* forma *heterophylla*) because the very bases of the pitchers and cladophyls of variety *maxima* do indeed have some red

Sarracenia flava variety *atropurpurea* in eastern North Carolina. This plant is in relatively high vegetation, and the red color in the lower portions of the pitcher is fading due to relative shading.

Sarracenia flava variety *maxima* in eastern North Carolina. There is no evidence of red pigment in the upper portions of the pitchers.

pigmentation. This variety is uncommon throughout the range, being more easily found in the Carolinas coastal plain and far less common in northwestern Florida.

Variety *ornata* Bull ex Masters (1881b)
There is deep red to purple throat pigmentation nearly obliterated by heavy venation throughout the pitcher tube and lid—a truly ornate pitcher. This variety is frequent in the Carolinas coastal plain, far less easily found in northwestern Florida. One should be careful when identifying this variety because hybridization with variety *maxima*, for instance, will result in a pronouncedly veined pitcher but not to the extent of pure variety *ornata*.

Variety *cuprea* Schnell (1998b)
This variety is characterized by a distinctive deep copper color of the external lid surface, which often extends down into the upper one-fifth of the pitcher. Variety *cuprea* is relatively common in the Carolina coastal plain and rare in northwestern Florida.

Variety *rugelii* (Shuttleworth ex Alphonse de Candolle) Masters (1881c)
The top of the pitcher is more widely expanded and has a proportionately larger lid than other varieties. The key is a large, deep red to purple area in the pitcher throat that is often fractured with smaller close satellite areas but no true venation emanating from it. Due to the pitcher's proportions, *rugelii* has erroneously been called variety *maxima* by some. This is the common and predominant variety in

Sarracenia flava variety *ornata*. This close-up view of the upper and throat portion of the pitcher shows the dense red veining that extends top to bottom and the nearly obliterated purple throat blotch.

southern Georgia and northwestern Florida, although I have seen an isolated colony as far north as Summerville, South Carolina. Good savannas of this plant are particularly impressive due to the pitcher density caused by many short rhizome branches, each with a growth point. Thus, a large, close cluster of pitchers may be 1 m or more in extent, although they are genetically the same plant (genet) with many extensions (ramets).

Variety *rubricorpora* Schnell (1998b)

The external tube is entirely deep red to reddish purple in full sun, the tube lining is yellowish buff, but the lid is green with prominent red veins. This strikingly beautiful variety is restricted to the Florida Panhandle. It

This overhead photograph shows the copper color of the lid of *Sarracenia flava* variety *cuprea* very clearly. The copper color varies in intensity somewhat, being most prominent in unshaded pitchers.

Sarracenia flava variety *rugelii*. The backlighting emphasizes the purple throat patches. Note the fracturing of some of the patches and separation, but no true venation.

is not common in the global sense, but locally may grow in relatively large stands, where it affords a spectacular view. The plant does not grow in bunches, as does variety *rugelii* of the same region.

Cultivation Notes

Sarracenia flava is easily grown and somewhat readily available from commercial sources. Because this species is tall, it is not a plant for the lighted terrarium. If your house is not too dry, the plant may be cultivated open on a sunny windowsill. It does well outdoors in the mid-

Sarracenia flava variety *rugelii* in southern Georgia. This medium-range photograph emphasizes the bunching growth pattern due to much short rhizome branching. One can almost pick out the genets.

A close-up view of *Sarracenia flava* variety *rubricorpora* pitchers. There is a purple throat blotch from which fine veins radiate.

Atlantic to Southeast, and successful outdoor bog growth has been reported in New Hampshire, Massachusetts, and Michigan. As with all *Sarracenia* species, *S. flava* must be allowed to go dormant. For best color and pitcher development, grow plants in as full sunlight as possible and in an acidic medium, such as Canadian peat.

A stand of the striking *Sarracenia flava* variety *rubricorpora* in the Apalachicola National Forest of northwestern Florida. Note that the variety does not grow in bunches. Among the mature pitchers are newly emerging pitchers that have not yet achieved full color.

Sarracenia oreophila (Kearney) Wherry

Synonyms
Sarracenia flava catesbaei, S. flava variety *oreophila, S. catesbaei*

Common Names
Sarracenia oreophila is commonly known as green pitcher plant and fly-catcher.

Description
Rhizome horizontal; scales and cladophyls to 1.5 cm and green to pale red. Pitcher leaves erect to 70 cm; ala narrow and linear; leaves finely veined, slightly reddish yellow at top; hood column erect with marginal reflection ranging no more than one-third to midline; hood at about 80° angle upward, nearly circular when viewed from top; tip of hood with small, coarse keel on a slight platform (mucronate); winter leaves recurved or falcate phyllodia. Flower scape about two-thirds as tall as pitchers; bracts, sepals, and pistils green; petals bright yellow; flower fragrance weakly feline.

Flowering Season
Mid-April to early June

Distribution
Map 5 shows the very limited distribution of *Sarracenia oreophila,* which is on the federally endangered list. The well-known location is extreme northeastern Alabama, particularly on and around the Sand Mountain plateau, where the species is now infrequent.

Map 5. Distribution of *Sarracenia oreophila.*

The map shows an area along the northern border of Tennessee, in Fentress County. One would expect that

Sarracenia oreophila in full pitcher in early summer in Towns County, Georgia. Note the relatively fine venation, which weakens in the hood. The column leans slightly forward, and many lids are not squarely over the pitcher mouth but at about an 80° angle.

any extension of the species into neighboring Tennessee would be along the plateau extending from Alabama into southeastern Tennessee (as suggested by McDaniel 1966), but the plants have not been found there. An exploratory party led by Jennison (1935) found a single *Sarracenia* with no flower or seed capsule growing in a bog near Clark Range. The pitchers were not described, and an enthusiastic member of the party dug the single plant, potted it up, and placed it in the University of Tennessee greenhouse for further study. Unfortunately, a student worker in the greenhouse knocked the pot off the bench, breaking it and sending plant and potting mix across the floor. Not realizing the value of the plant and thinking it would not be missed, he swept up the entire mishap and disposed of it (Sharp and Baker 1964). In 1948, while working on his *Sarracenia* study Bell had a considerable living collection of pitcher plants growing in the University of North Carolina greenhouse in Chapel Hill (Bell 1949). A. J. Sharp, who had been in the original Jennison exploratory party in Fentress County, visited and was struck by the *Sarracenia oreophila* plants, which he identified from memory as exactly what he saw on the expedition. Sharp listed it in a later inventory (Sharp and Baker 1964). Unfortunately, the Fentress County bog no longer exists.

There are vague, anecdotal suggestions that the species was once in northwestern Georgia, specifically the Cloudland Canyon area, but there is no official record. *Sarracenia oreophila* has not been seen there in more recent searches. However, an excellent, disjunct location was found recently in Towns County in northeast Georgia (Dennis 1980). The population is

A flower of *Sarracenia oreophila*. Note the absence of any red color in the flower parts as well as the yellow petals. The yellow is not as deep as in *S. flava*, and the petal shapes and sizes are different.

very healthy, with plants producing more than one hundred genets in full light. The location almost never was—it is on the immediate shore of a Tennessee Valley Authority impoundment, the Chatuge Reservoir. The location is a gentle seep slope adjacent to a small run going into the reservoir.

Note on Map 5 that the Towns County area extends over into southwestern North Carolina. Spurred on by the northwestern Georgia location, exploration was undertaken in the broad area around the Chatuge Reservoir, lands that extended into North Carolina. Local residents seemed to remember similar plants along a creek, now deep under the surface of the reservoir. But Govus (1987) did find two locations just over the North Carolina state line. One population contained less than a dozen plants and seemed doomed to eventual extinction. The second location occupies an area about 0.2 hectare in extent and seems more viable. Again, these locations are in seepage areas.

Two other areas are marked with tiny, incomplete circles on Map 5 because they probably represent mistaken identity. In middle Alabama north of Montgomery, an area near Draper Prison in Elmore County down the tracks from the old railroad depot has been anecdotally described. As one witness put it to me, "There they were, *Sarracenia oreophila* growing among *S. rubra.*" Unfortunately, when I finally got to the area in 1968, a sheriff's deputy led me to where the plants had been but said they had long since disappeared, probably not dug out and collected, as rumored, because the area was now quite dry. What does grow in Elmore and adjacent Autauga and Chilton Counties is the rare *Sarracenia rubra* subspecies *alabamensis*, which I will discuss in the next section. Subspecies *alabamensis* has an interesting habit of growing spring pitchers looking very much like typical *S. rubra* subspecies *rubra* and summer pitchers with larger, more expanded tubes with yellowish tops. To this day, the latter phase is often confused with *S. oreophila* by people looking at and photographing plants in cultivation, and I believe the two kinds of pitcher of *S. rubra* subspecies *alabamensis*, not defined until 1974, were confused with *S. oreophila* and *S. rubra* subspecies *rubra* supposedly growing together.

The second dubious *Sarracenia oreophila* area is the south-central Georgia location in Taylor County. Wherry (1933a) reported a collection by Neisler in the New York Botanical Garden Herbarium with the notation "flowers not odorous," so apparently there were flowers of no description. McDaniel (1966) was unable to locate this specimen for his monograph, however, he did find a specimen from Neisler that was barren of locality data in the Gray Herbarium of Harvard University that he felt was *Sarracenia oreophila*. Exactly where this came from is, of course, unknown. Since then, searches for the species in Taylor County, Georgia, have been fruitless. What does grow in the county to this day is a variety of *Sarracenia rubra* that is rather tall, has an expanded top, and has closest affinity to subspecies *gulfensis* of that species (see the following species section). There are two likely possibilities of what happened: Either McDaniel should not have assumed the orphan specimen is from Taylor County or the specimen is not *S. oreophila* but the variant of *S. rubra*.

Habitat

Sarracenia oreophila grows predominantly in seepage bogs usually in a heavy, clayey sand soil. As Bell (1949) noticed, the plant is also occasionally found along the sandy shores and spits of shallow streams, probably as a washdown from seepage slopes upstream. The plant does best in open, sunny locations with a minimum of competition from other species. McDaniel (1966) also felt that *S. oreophila* frequented moist oak woods, but its presence there was probably residual as its preferred habitat transformed to forest. As we would therefore expect, the oak woods location is no longer extant.

During the period of summer known as "dog days" (so-called because the dog star Sirius is so prominent in the night sky), usually from middle July into late August, the weather in the Alabama range is quite warm, very humid, but with little rainfall. As a result, the seepage bogs begin to dry to varying degrees. *Sarracenia oreophila* has adapted to this by easing into dormancy far earlier in the season than other *Sarracenia* species. The pitchers begin to assume a mottled red appearance and the typical falcate or curved phyllodia of the species emerge around the base of the plant; then the pitchers die back over a period of a few weeks. Although this apparently responsive behavior in habitat is unique in the genus, even more interesting is the fact that in cultivation, where we can continuously supply abundant water, the same series of genetically programmed events ensues in mid-July (Schnell 1980b). The response may be triggered by the shortening photoperiod.

Comments

Sarracenia oreophila has close affinity to *S. flava* (Schnell and Krider 1976; Schnell 1978a, 1978d), as evidenced by the confusion in naming the plant early in its botanical history. In 1897, Mohr identified the plants on the Little River in northeastern Alabama as *Sarracenia catesbaei* Elliot, but

In late July, the pitchers of *Sarracenia oreophila* assume a mottled red appearance as the dog days of summer advance. On the lower middle edge of the photograph, flattened and curved phyllodia can be seen down in the grass.

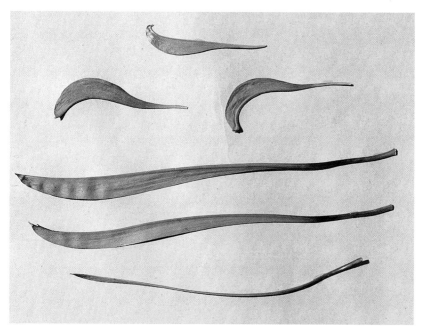

Compare the three typical curved (falcate) phyllodia of *Sarracenia oreophila* (top) with the sword-shaped (ensiform) phyllodia of *S. flava* (bottom). You would never have to use these characters for differentiation in the field, however, because the species are widely disjunct.

Hood tips of *Sarracenia oreophila* (left) and *S. flava* (right). Note that the apiculate tip of *S. flava* is more delicate and filamentous, whereas that of *S. oreophila* is shorter and coarser.

An abaxial view of pitchers of *Sarracenia oreophila* (left) and *S. flava* (right). The pitcher of *S. flava* has a more graceful concave ascension of the pitcher curve toward the mouth; *S. oreophila* has lateral bulging before reaching the mouth. One can also appreciate the increased hood column reflection of *S. flava* compared to *S. oreophila*.

changed his mind and renamed them *S. flava catesbaei.* In 1900, Kearney noted sufficient similarity to *S. flava* to rename the plant *S. flava* variety *oreophila* (Wherry 1933a). Wherry (1933a) felt that discontinuities were sufficient to designate the plants as a separate species, *S. oreophila.*

Most *Sarracenia* species flower just prior to pitcher growth in the spring, but *Sarracenia oreophila* flowers commensurate with or even after pitcher growth. There seems to be no ready explanation of advantage or disadvantage for this.

Finally, there is some confusion regarding flower fragrance. Wherry (1933a) noted a faintly "musty" odor, whereas Bell (1949) could not detect any fragrance. I find that the flowers of *Sarracenia oreophila* clearly have the feline fragrance characteristic of *S. flava*, but about half as intense, to the extent that it is not unpleasant (Schnell 1978d, 1980b).

Cultivation Notes

The comments in the genus and *Sarracenia flava* sections apply here. Although *S. oreophila* does not grow in *Sphagnum* in its native habitat, the moss is an excellent growth medium, but Canadian peat or peat-sand mixtures work as well. After the pitcher leaves turn completely brown, they may be pulled or cut from the plant, but leave the phyllodia on over the winter. This species has a bit more tendency to rot if kept too wet after leaf dieback and through the winter, so the medium should be kept just damp until spring. Because of strict federal regulations concerning this endangered species, you are not likely to find it on the market. Specimens with stringent proof of having been produced by propagation or tissue culture require permits for interstate shipment or even the buyer carrying the plants across state lines.

Sarracenia rubra Walter

The taxonomic classification of *Sarracenia rubra* is problematic. The controversy centers around the species' variability, with the variants geographically separate, unlike the case with *Sarracenia flava*, whose variants are often intermingled. As a result, taxonomists have viewed *S. rubra* variously as one species, two species, three species with one subspecies, and most recently one species with five subspecies. The discussion is far from concluded, even with the use of sophisticated molecular analyses, which tend to fray at the margins and show their limitations with this problem. Unfortunately, as with much science, politics and pride may be playing a part in this controversy.

At the outset, I will say that I have a conservative viewpoint regarding the taxonomy of *Sarracenia rubra*. I classify it as one species with five subspecies. I do not consider the variations among the disjunct populations to be sufficiently discontinuous to be called separate species, and from a differentiation point the variants fall nicely into five subspecies. Furthermore, close observation indicates that some of the differences that are allegedly specific to certain populations are actually common to several or all of the others.

Synonyms

During various times, applicable synonyms (in part) include: *Sarracenia gronovii* variety *rubra*, *S. minor*, *S. sweetii*, *S. rubra* variety *acuminata*, *S. jonesii*, *S. rubra* forma *jonesii*, *S. alabamensis*, *S. alabamensis* subspecies *alabamensis*, *S. alabamensis* subspecies *wherryi*.

Common Names

Overall, *Sarracenia rubra* is referred to as the sweet pitcher plant either because of the roselike fragrance of its flower or possibly after a botanist named Robert Sweet (1783–1835). Common names applied to some of the subspecies will be mentioned below.

Description

The reader will note that some dimensions are rather far ranging in this species description, but these will be sorted out in the subspecies discussion below. Rhizome elongate, usually parallel to the ground surface but frequently angled or even vertical in very wet situations. Summer pitcher leaves erect, 15–65 cm with prominent ala wider about midway up the pitcher; most subspecies with prominent, fine, red, reticulate venation of at least the upper two-thirds of the pitcher on a tannish green background; pitchers expand upward to mouth 1.5–5.5 cm across; hood on short, minimally recurved column; hood ovate (longer than wide) often with apiculate tip; spring leaves often phyllodiform and curved into C or S shapes; bears many flowers, often all subspecies may have two scapes per growth point of branched rhizome, each point flowering yearly; scape 15–75 cm, often with red flush to lower portion; bracts and sepals dark red to nearly maroon; sepals usually sharply recurved by the time of petal fall; petals also red to maroon; undersurface of petals usually green to tannish green with prominent red vertical streak down middle; minority of petals with red undersurface; pistil green with spherical ovary; flower fragrance strong, pleasant, and roselike.

Flowering Season
April to May on the coastal plain, June in the mountains

Distribution
The half dozen location zones marked on Map 6 represent the ranges of the five subspecies. The zone for each subspecies will be mentioned below.

Habitat
In the coastal plain, *Sarracenia rubra* grows in savannas and on the margins of bays and streams. Inland, subspecies grow in seepage bogs on sandhills or the mountains. The species reaches best development in full light, but is often shaded by advancing shrub growth.

Comments
Overall, *Sarracenia rubra* is decreasing in numbers throughout its range. Two of its subspecies have been placed on the endangered species list (subspecies *jonesii* and *alabamensis*), but

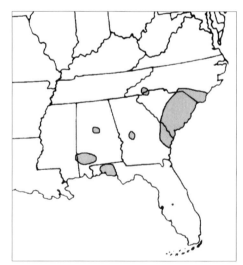

Map 6. Distribution of *Sarracenia rubra*.

there is also concern about the remaining subspecies. In drying habitats, where the water table has fallen mostly due to human activity, and particularly in drought years, the plants are small, to 10–15 cm. Their flowers are no more than 1.5 cm across and are frequently seedless at the end of the growing season. This is so common that many think the plants never reach greater size. I have even seen *S. rubra* advertised in native plant catalogues as "a small pitcher plant, to six inches [15 cm]."

There are several characteristics of *Sarracenia rubra* mentioned in the description that require emphasis because they have previously been attributed to only one or two subspecies. All subspecies are capable of bear-

Pressed petals of several *Sarracenia rubra* subspecies *rubra* plants growing in various locations in southeastern North Carolina. The top two rows are external surfaces. In spite of some size variation reflecting plant size, the general shape of the petal is uniform. Color is generally dark red to maroon, but there are lighter petal variations. The bottom row shows the undersurfaces. Most have a uniform tannish green color with a prominent red streak down the center—a characteristic of the species as a whole—although some of the petals are red on the undersurface.

ing two flower scapes per growth point, which is uncommon in other *Sarracenia* species. With multiple growth points in a genet (clump), the spring flowering display, with the deep red to maroon flowers, is often spectacular.

A second characteristic of *Sarracenia rubra* is the similarity of the subspecies flowers. Except for a general modal variation in overall size that reflects pitcher size in various subspecies, the petal structure, color, and flower fragrance are identical (contrasting with Wherry [1933a], who could not detect a fragrance in subspecies *jonesii*). The color pattern of the underside of the petals is a feature unique to the species as a whole and is found in all five subspecies. In about 55–80% of cases, the background color of the petal underside is tannish green with a prominent red streak running down the center. Other petals, sometimes in the same flower, have red undersides.

A third characteristic of *Sarracenia rubra* is that all subspecies often bear specialized spring leaves that are phyllodiform, that is, they superficially appear similar to the true late-summer phyllodia of *S. flava* or *S. oreophila*, but closer examination discloses minute pitcher tubes along one margin, complete with small mouths and lids. These spring leaves resemble etiolated leaves, which are flattened, malformed, and weak often due to a sun-loving plant growing in shade. However, in the case of *S. rubra*, these leaves appear even in plants growing in the open, although they do not appear in all plants every year. There may be a genetic propensity to produce such leaves, or perhaps an environmental factor other than light intensity triggers the activity, for example, a combination of temperatures and photoperiod.

Finally, my studies indicate that all pitcher textures of *Sarracenia rubra* are relatively soft and pliable, not waxy as in most other species. The external surfaces all have fine pubescence (Schnell 1977).

Subspecies

The problem of subclassifying the *Sarracenia rubra* "complex," as it is often called, boils down chiefly to the studies of two sets of authors: Case and Case (1974, 1976) and Schnell (1977, 1978a, 1978c, 1978d, 1979b, 1982c). Those who wish to pursue the problem in depth should read these

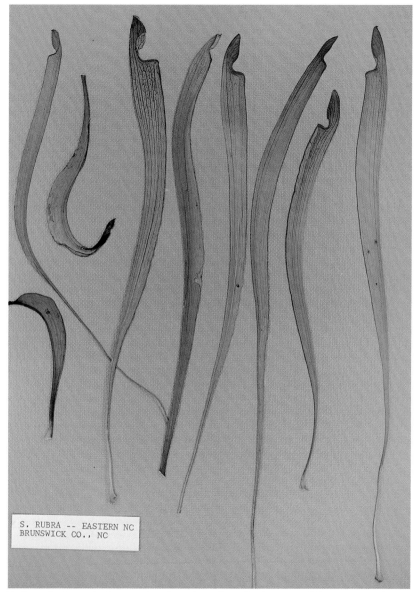

S. RUBRA -- EASTERN NC
BRUNSWICK CO., NC

Early spring leaves in *Sarracenia rubra* subspecies *rubra* in Brunswick County, North Carolina. Note the flattened, C- and S-shaped phyllodiform character, but with some leaves developing weak pitcher characteristics. True phyllodia do not have tubes, mouths, and lids. These plants were growing in open sunlight.

sources in addition to others cited in the subspecies accounts. At the end of the subspecies descriptions, I will briefly summarize my arguments.

Subspecies *rubra*

By virtue of its occurrence in the original species type distribution, this subspecies bears the species epithet without authority. Commonly called the sweet pitcher plant, it inhabits the southeastern North Carolina, South Carolina, and northeastern Georgia coastal plain, as indicated in

An early summer *Sarracenia rubra* subspecies *rubra* in Brunswick County, North Carolina. Flower petals are past. Note the hood and column contour and the relatively wide ala midway up its course. The finely reticulate red venation of the pitcher is obvious.

Sarracenia rubra subspecies *rubra* in eastern North Carolina. The plant is at the edge of a shrubby thicket, but is easily spotted by the number of spring flowers.

A late spring plant of *Sarracenia rubra* subspecies *rubra* in South Carolina that is not flowering. The plant is relatively small. Note the small mouth and lid in relation to tube length. There is minimal lid column reflection. Phyllodiform spring pitchers are lying on the ground.

the largest zone on Map 6. The summer pitchers are narrow and elongate (tube length:mouth diameter = 20:1 average), the mouth is ovate, there is only a slight dip in the lip just above the ala, and the hood is not prominently yellow. In good growing conditions, pitcher heights range from 26 to 45 cm with a mouth width of 1.5–2.3 cm.

Subspecies *jonesii* (Wherry) Wherry

Sarracenia rubra subspecies *jonesii* is historically native to a very small area in Buncombe, Transylvania, and Henderson Counties in North Carolina and adjacent Pickens County in South Carolina. On Map 6, its range

Spring in a *Sarracenia rubra* subspecies *jonesii* bog near Etowah, North Carolina. Note the masses of flowers, which reflect the multiple scapes per growth point. Pitchers are just emerging. In the extreme upper right, you can see a few yellow flowers of the anthocyanin-free plants.

Later spring into early summer in a *Sarracenia rubra* subspecies *jonesii* bog in Henderson County, North Carolina. Petals have fallen and sepals are recurving. Even at this distance, the upper pitcher bulge can be seen in profile, the reticulate red vein pattern is evident, and there is slight reflection of the column margins.

is the small zone straddling the western North Carolina and South Carolina border. The plants grow in mountain seepage bogs, sometimes associated with but not in *Sphagnum*, and in a few cases, especially in Pickens County, on the shores of fast, steep mountain streams, probably as a result of washing downstream from higher seepage bogs, which may or may not still be extant.

Commonly called the mountain pitcher plant, the subspecies has a checkered taxonomic history. Wherry (1929) first noted the plant near East Flat Rock, North Carolina, and named it *Sarracenia jonesii* in honor of entomologist Frank Morton Jones, who worked with many of the *Sarracenia* moths. Wherry recognized the *S. rubra* affinity, but felt the pitcher size, disjunct location, and lack of flower fragrance (to him) called for a separate species designation. Bell (1949) thought the mountain pitcher plant was clearly an infraspecies of *S. rubra* and changed the name to *S. rubra* forma *jonesii*; he also felt that all *S. rubra* plants west and south of the Carolina mountain zone were the same form with variable pitcher size. In 1972, Wherry concurred that the mountain plants were indeed an infraspecies of *S. rubra*, but felt that the subspecies level was more appropriate, so they became subspecies *jonesii*. However, Case and Case (1976) preferred the original species designation, *S. jonesii*, whereas I preferred subspecies *jonesii* (Schnell 1977, 1978c), which I still believe is the correct level. The subspecies *jonesii* is on the federal endangered list.

A single pitcher of *Sarracenia rubra* subspecies *jonesii* in Pickens County, South Carolina.

The summer pitcher reaches a height of 43–61 cm, with a pitcher mouth of

Green pitchers of the anthocyanin-free variant of *Sarracenia rubra* subspecies *jonesii*. Note the subtle mottling of the green of the pitcher near the top of the tube.

2.8–4.2 cm. There is slightly more hood reflection than in the smaller coastal plain subspecies (*rubra*). An interesting feature of subspecies *jonesii* is that when a mature pitcher is viewed from the side, the generally smooth widening of the pitcher toward the top is interrupted by a bulge on the alar (inner) side about one-fourth to one-fifth of the way to the lip. At the lip, the pitcher contour pulls in somewhat.

In at least two bogs that I know of, there is a small intermingled population of anthocyanin-free plants with yellowish green flowers and all-green pitchers, which is equivalent to the northern *Sarracenia purpurea* subspecies *purpurea* forma *heterophylla*. Occasionally, one can see intermediates that indicate hybridization. Many of the bogs with subspecies *jonesii* also contain populations of *S. purpurea* subspecies *venosa* variety *montana*, with rare hybrids between these and subspecies *jonesii*.

Sarracenia rubra subspecies *jonesii* with a yellowish green (anthocyanin-free) variant flower (left) and the usual dark red flower (right).

Subspecies *alabamensis* (Case & Case) Schnell

Summer pitchers are 18–49 cm tall, mouth width is 6–5.8 cm, and the hood column is moderately reflexed. There are faint areoles near the top of the pitcher. The typical reticulate, fine red venation of *Sarracenia rubra* pitchers is limited to about the middle third of the pitcher, and externally it only extends rather faintly into the column and hood with occasional streaks. However, venation is stronger on the internal pitcher surface. In full sunlight, the upper quarter or so of the tube and column and the hood are yellow. Occasionally, the entire external surface of the tube is bright red.

Sarracenia rubra subspecies *alabamensis* in Autauga County, Alabama, growing in a sandy seep. Note that in many pitchers, the fine, external, red reticulate venation is not strong and that the hoods are yellow. There are not many spring pitchers in this group, although some authors claim they are more prominent in this subspecies.

Subspecies *alabamensis* is the most problematic in *Sarracenia rubra*. Morphologically, the pitcher diverges from the mean the most of any of the subspecies. Even so, flowers are clearly *S. rubra* in all characteristics and species characters are evident in the pitchers as well as the biological behavior of the plants. Commonly known as the cane-break pitcher plant, subspecies *alabamensis* is limited to a few bogs in the central Alabama counties of Elmore, Autauga, and Chilton (see the small, central Alabama zone on Map 6). The area is an inland coastal plain sandhills province with a conglomerate rock base. The plants grow in sandy or gravelly to mucky seepage bogs, some of these located rather high on ridges, and along the borders of small streams.

This shaded group of *Sarracenia rubra* subspecies *alabamensis* in another seepage bog in Autauga County, Alabama, has more apparent spring leaves with even less red venation, but also less pronounced yellow in the upper pitchers.

Sarracenia rubra subspecies *alabamensis* in early spring in Elmore County, Alabama. The large number of flowers for the size of the clump is noteworthy, the typical *rubra* petals are apparent, and some of the spring leaves are assuming a phyllodiform character.

In this example of *Sarracenia rubra* subspecies *alabamensis* in Chilton County, Alabama, growing in the open on a sandy seep, the internal pitcher tube venation can be seen, and there is more external venation with the typically reticulate *rubra* pattern.

Sarracenia rubra subspecies *alabamensis* in Autauga County, Alabama. Variation exists in all plants, and this easily found variant has diffuse red coloration of the external tube in addition to venation.

Case and Case (1974, 1976) refer to this plant as *Sarracenia alabamensis* subspecies *alabamensis*. Bell (1949) included it in his sweeping map of *S. rubra* forma *jonesii*. Harper (1922) visited the region in 1918 and thought the plants were *S. sledgei* (as *S. alata* was then known) when he saw them from a train window. Later, when he saw the plants in flower, he recognized them as *S. rubra*.

Subspecies *alabamensis* is on the federal endangered list. At one time, the area in which it grows was quite primitive, consisting mainly of uninhabited woodlands. Since then, farming and logging have increased, with resulting fire suppression and lowering of the water table. In the early 1960s there were nearly thirty locations for the subspecies, although some were small. Murphy and Boyd (1999) published a very thorough survey of the remaining sites and plants; there were only eleven sites (one of these discovered during the course of their investigation), which ranged from 2 to 2200 square meters. Numbers of plants per site ranged from 8 to 2241, with a mode of about 129–140, and half of all the remaining plants were at one site. Seedpods and seedlings were only seen in the larger sites. Genets were mostly small. Based on this information, Murphy and Boyd estimated that only three of these sites would be viable ultimately, providing they were aggressively managed.

A backlit summer pitcher of *Sarracenia rubra* subspecies *alabamensis*. Between the reticulate veins in small patches of green leaf tissue, one can just discern faint areoles (light windows), tiny patches of almost white tissue.

To investigate genetic diversity and taxon differentiation, Godt and Hamrick (1998) did allozyme (isoenzyme) electrophoresis studies of leaf extracts of *Sarracenia rubra* subspecies *rubra* and subspecies *alabamensis*. They found the two subspecies to be very closely related, with little genetic differentiation. A calculated index was well within the range commonly found for conspecific populations, and there were no alleles that consistently differentiated the two subspecies. Fortunately, within each population studied, there was sufficient genetic diversity to indicate strong evolutionary potential with proper management of the sites.

Subspecies *wherryi* (Case & Case) Schnell

This subspecies is limited to the southwestern Alabama zone on Map 6 that just crosses over the Mississippi line. It has no common name. Its botanical history is largely limited to inclusion in Bell's (1949) large *Sarracenia rubra* subspecies *jonesii* range and Case and Case's (1974, 1976) preference to list this as *Sarracenia alabamensis* subspecies *wherryi*.

Briefly, the plant is a shorter version of subspecies *alabamensis* that grows disjunctly farther north. It retains the reticulate red venation of the species, does not have yellow in the upper pitcher, and does have faint areoles, which are even less prominent than in subspecies *alabamensis*. Pitchers are 28–43 cm, with a mouth width of 3.4–5.3 cm.

The plants grow in pine savannas as well as sandy seeps. Whereas *Sarracenia rubra* subspecies *alabamensis* farther north has no other pitcher plant species in its bogs, subspecies *wherryi* grows with several other Gulf Coast species. Thus, the field naturalist must be cautious of subtle hybrids and introgressions. Currently, the plants are not endangered but are of concern because their habitat is being altered so rapidly. From an automobile, you are much more likely to see these plants on the roadside than subspecies *alabamensis* or subspecies *jonesii*, whose sites tend to be far off the road.

Subspecies *gulfensis* Schnell

I described this subspecies after noting significant differences from subspecies *rubra* (Schnell 1979b). Mature summer leaves are 43–61 cm tall, and the mouth is 2.4–3.5 cm wide. The usual slight reflection of the hood column is apparent. The hood is somewhat more closely situated over the mouth compared to subspecies *alabamensis* and subspecies *wherryi*,

Sarracenia rubra subspecies *wherryi* in northern Baldwin County, Alabama. Note that the pitchers are less robust than in subspecies *alabamensis*, as seems to be the case with flowering in this particular genet. Reticulate venation is prominent. A casual glance might cause one to confuse this plant with a larger plant of subspecies *rubra*, but the hood and mouth are larger, the taller column has more reflexed margins, and the plant is disjunct from the range of subspecies *rubra*.

similar to subspecies *rubra*, but with a taller, narrow pitcher. The free margin of the hood is either straight or slightly undulate, red venation is prominent, and sometimes there is a high adaxial bulge to the pitcher, similar to subspecies *jonesii*. It is easy to see how initially the two might be confused (such as Bell 1949). Case and Case (1976) felt the plants were ecads (environmental variants) equivalent to subspecies *rubra*. Several examples of an unnamed green-pitchered, yellow-flowered variety of the subspecies have been found.

Summer pitchers of *Sarracenia rubra* subspecies *gulfensis* in Okaloosa County, Florida. Note the tall pitchers with relatively small hoods and mouths (compare to subspecies *jonesii*, *alabamensis*, and *wherryi*), the reticulate red vein pattern on pitchers, early reflection of sepals, and the relatively close approximation of the hoods over pitcher mouths.

Sarracenia rubra subspecies *gulfensis* in Santa Rosa County, Florida. This example shows a diffuse red background color. Although many *Sarracenia* hybrids of the Gulf Coast do indeed have a red background color, this is not exclusively confined to hybrids. There is clearly no evidence of hybridization in these plants.

Sarracenia rubra subspecies *gulfensis* with a relatively common, prominent bulge in the pitcher line just below the mouth, which is very similar to subspecies *jonesii*. The Gulf subspecies is quite disjunct from subspecies *jonesii*, the pitcher does not widen or flare as much as the Carolinas mountains subspecies, and the hood is smaller and more closely approximated to the mouth.

The subspecies is confined to the site in the western Florida Panhandle on Map 6. However, note the site located in southern Georgia, specifically Taylor County and environs. There are clearly *Sarracenia rubra* plants growing there in small, scattered locations. In my opinion, these plants have closest affinity to subspecies *gulfensis*, which is where I place them unless or until further studies indicate otherwise. There are private efforts underway to preserve and recover some of the Taylor County sites.

Sarracenia rubra subspecies *gulfensis* grows in seepage bogs and along small streams, the latter being particularly good locations within the huge Eglin Air Force Base in the region. Because there are several other *Sarracenia* species in the general area, one must be cautious with identifications and possible hybrids, which are very common. There are isolated colonies of the subspecies, especially along the streams in the region. Many of these are on Eglin, where they persevere because of relative lack of development. In the late 1960s, when my military status allowed me ready access to the base (except bombing and firing ranges), I was able to locate and study the subspecies. Even today, several public-access state highways cross the base and you can observe plants along the many streams that cross under the roads.

Concluding Remarks on *Sarracenia rubra* Subspecies

One of the major problems some people may have in seeing relationships within the so-called *Sarracenia rubra* complex is perspective. The genus *Sarracenia* is small, whether one chooses to see eight or ten species in it. All other species are well established and accepted, and I think it is important to look at *S. rubra* in light of what differentiates the other species.

Some authors have established morphology and size of pitchers as the major species determinants (such as Bell 1949; McDaniel 1966; Case and Case 1976). Although pitchers are important, the flowers should not be ignored. These same authors have lightly passed over flower color and morphology, but there are important and consistent flower characters across the genus (Schnell 1978a, 1978d, 1982c). In the case of *S. rubra*, the flowers of the subspecies are identical except for slight overall size differences (Schnell 1977, 1978d). Unlike other groupings of *Sarracenia* species, petal extract chromatography indicates a close clustering of the *S. rubra* subspecies (Schnell 1978a), thus supporting a single species. Also, comparison of flower petal morphology alone indicates a single *S. rubra* species. Based on these studies, I conclude that comparison of relative differences between pitcher and flower characters of *Sarracenia rubra* with other well-established species of the genus points to a single species with infraspecific variants, rather than three different species. Again, it is important to look at the whole genus and all parts of the plant, not just *S. rubra* or its pitcher in isolation.

In addition to petal extract chromatographic evidence (Schnell 1978a), pitcher leaf extract chromatography (Romeo et al. 1977) points to a separation of the *Sarracenia rubra* complex from other members of the genus by lack of certain compounds (uniformly absent in all infraspecific variant extracts) that are found in all other species of the genus. Romeo et al. suggest that this is evidence of a more recent evolutionary status of *S. rubra*, a concept that was previously noted on the basis of morphologic comparisons (Schnell 1977). In allozyme studies on only two subspecies of *S. rubra* (separated into *S. rubra* and *S. alabamensis* species by Case and Case 1976), Godt and Hamrick (1998) found that the genetic identity index was more consistent with a single species.

Finally, the disjunct distribution of *Sarracenia rubra* subspecies is insufficient evidence for separating *S. rubra* into several species, especially in light of the many other characters to consider as I have pointed out in this entire *S. rubra* section. I need not go into the countless other subspecies in botany that have disjunct ranges.

Cultivation Notes
Sarracenia rubra is generally easy to grow and propagate in either peat or *Sphagnum* using previously mentioned techniques for other *Sarracenia* species, but many growers have difficulty achieving plant sizes found in the natural habitat. All too often, the pitchers seem to fall back to the small size of many subspecies *rubra* plants growing in stressed field conditions. Full sunlight throughout the daily photoperiod is very important. Repot plants only when necessary because disturbance can set back

growth as much as two to three years. Keeping the plants wetter than average during the growing season is also helpful (this can be achieved with a deeper saucer or tray of water for the pots). Finally, I have found the species to be a relatively heavy feeder in horticultural terms, and regular foliar feeding as detailed in the Introduction seems necessary if your plants cannot trap insects.

Sarracenia alata (Wood) Wood

Sarracenia alata is an interesting pitcher plant for many reasons. Its disjunct distribution is divided into two zones. In the eastern zone, the species is fairly common, but its habitat is being vigorously assaulted by humans. *Sarracenia alata* also bears a close relationship to *S. rubra*, as I will discuss below.

Synonyms

These include *Sarracenia gronovii* variety *alata*, *S. purpurea* variety *alata*, *S. flava* variety *crispata*, and *S. sledgei*. Of these, *S. sledgei* is the most likely to be encountered in the literature well into the 1950s. Macfarlane (1908) described the species as *S. sledgei*, either ignoring or being unaware of Wood's work published in 1863, which has many years priority, as noted by Merrill (1948) and Bell (1954).

Common Names

Sarracenia alata is commonly known as the pale pitcher plant and flycatcher. If a common name must be used, the former is preferred because "flycatcher" is used for several other carnivorous plants.

Description

Rhizome to 3.0 cm thick and parallel to the ground surface. Summer leaves erect to 75 cm (but examples to 120 cm are recorded); yellowish green, sometimes narrow wing but most often to 1.0 cm wide midway, usually glabrous (without hairs externally; see exception in Comments); coarsely reticulate red veins near top of tube, but upper tube, hood, and lid may be deep purple; hood ovate and erect on short column with slight reflection, apiculate at tip; rare winter phyllodia are ensiform and half to

Sarracenia alata in Jackson County, Mississippi, in early summer. Note the veining and short hood column with minimal reflection of column margins. There is also red veining of the upper tube and lid. Several pitchers show signs of attack by the moth *Exyra semicrocea*.

two-thirds the length of pitcher leaves. Flower scape yellowish green and about half as tall as pitchers; bracts and sepals yellowish green but often suffused with some red; pistil green; petals creamy white or pale yellowish white; flower fragrance moderately feline.

Flowering Season
Early March into April

Distribution
Map 7 indicates the two-zoned distribution of *Sarracenia alata* (Murry and Urbatsch 1979; MacRoberts and MacRoberts 1991; Sheridan 1991). The plants extend east just over the Alabama River; on the western edge of the eastern zone, the species extends historically just into Louisiana, but it has not been seen in the field lately. There is a gap throughout most of Louisiana to just east of the state line, and the plants extend into the Big Thicket country of eastern Texas, where sites are uncommon. There are some interesting variations in eastern Texas. In a pasture, one site was found where the genets branched and bunched, much as *Sarracenia flava* variety *rugelii* does. This is also the region where pitchers of exceptional length (to 120 cm) have been reported. Some of these have faint, clear (not white) areoles (light windows; Sheridan 1991).

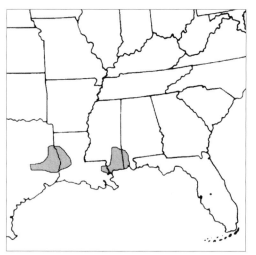

Map 7. Distribution of *Sarracenia alata*.

Habitat
In the eastern zone of the range, the species grows in pine savannas and seepage bogs. Frequently, the soil is a heavy sandy clay, rather than sand and peat silt. In the Louisiana portion of the western zone, *Sarracenia alata* grows in oak savannas, but in the Texas Big Thicket, it reverts to pine savannas. The species is not common in the western zone and is decreasing in the eastern zone, but still easy to find.

Flowers of *Sarracenia alata* in Washington County, Alabama. Note the creamy to yellow-ish white petals; no other *Sarracenia* species has petals this color. In this example, the bracts are slightly suffused with red.

Comments

Sarracenia alata was long thought to be closely related to *S. flava*, but indications are that the species is actually closely related to *S. rubra* instead, particularly *S. rubra* subspecies *jonesii* (Case and Case 1976; Schnell and Krider 1976; Schnell 1978a, 1978d, 1989). Some have informally suggested that *S. alata* is just a white-petaled variety of *S. rubra* subspecies *jonesii*. This is unlikely, however, because the white petals would then suggest an anthocyanin-free variant, which should also have pitchers without red veins.

There is an unusual variant of *Sarracenia alata* in the eastern zone, particularly in the broad environs of Mobile, Alabama. This is informally

Sarracenia alata with a deep red color to the upper pitchers, including inner hood and the throat of the tube.

referred to as the "stocky, hairy" variant and is characterized by a shorter pitcher to about 40 cm but with as wide a mouth (hence the "stocky" feature). The "hairy" reference is due to the fact that the external surface of the pitcher tube is clearly pubescent to touch. These plants, with the usual flower of the species, grow widely scattered in relatively small stands among the regular forms.

Many of the plants of *Sarracenia alata*, particularly in the eastern zone, have a deep red, almost purple, coloration to the upper quarter of the pitcher, including the inner part of the lid and throat of the pitcher. Again, the flowers are of usual appearance. The red coloration is maintained in cultivation if the plants are grown in bright sun.

As noted in the description, the plants of this species produce autumn phyllodia rarely, usually when the plants are stressed. I have never seen phyllodia in cultivation and only occasionally in the field, most often in sites with drying, shrub invasion, or even a heavy attack of *Exyra* moths. Certainly, phyllodia are not regularly produced as they are in *Sarracenia flava* and *S. oreophila*, where they are characteristic.

Sheridan (1991) noted some *Sarracenia alata* plants with areoles in the western zone. These were particularly tall plants with expanded pitcher tops and lids. In plants from Angelica County, Texas, that I am growing, I confirm the presence of these clear (not white), faint areoles, certainly far fainter than even those in *S. rubra* subspecies *alabamensis* or the green variant of *S. rubra* subspecies *jonesii*. Juniper et al. (1989) distinguish two sorts of areoles: (1) the white areoles of *S. leucophylla, S. minor,* and *S. psittacina*; and (2) translucent areoles caused by focal clearing of the tissue between veins, most likely due to stretching of tissues on an expanded pitcher top.

Cultivation Notes

Cultivation of *Sarracenia alata* is relatively easy. The plants are robust and grow well in either *Sphagnum* or peat. Because the plants are tall, growing them in terraria is not feasible. To achieve the deep red upper pitcher color in the red variants, full light is advisable, and the flower petals will also be whiter.

Sarracenia leucophylla Rafinesque

Sarracenia leucophylla is the favorite pitcher plant of many people. Especially spectacular when massed in the field, a colony of the species is easy to spot from some distance, even from an automobile at road speed. Unfortunately, easily accessible mass colonies are disappearing rapidly.

Synonyms

The most recent synonym, used until the late 1950s and the one that you are most likely to come across, is *Sarracenia drummondii*. Bell (1954) pointed out the erroneous use of the epithet. He also noted several comments by older, staid botanists who disapproved of the colorful, flamboyant Rafinesque in general terms and wished to suppress and generally discount what they felt was poor botanical practice across the board. In any event, Rafinesque's *Sarracenia leucophylla* takes precedence. Other, older epithets include *S. undulata*, *S. gronovii* variety *drummondii*, *S. laciniata*, and possibly *S. lacunosa*.

Common Name

Sarracenia leucophylla is commonly known as the white-topped pitcher plant.

Description

Rhizome to 3 cm thick and mostly parallel to the ground surface. Summer leaves erect to 120 cm; pitcher gradually expanding with upper one-fourth or so white (areolate) with coarsely reticulate green or red veins; hood on erect column with slightly reflexed margins and colored similarly to upper pitcher tube; hood itself usually with sinuate (wavy) margins; external surface of pitcher finely hirsute; occasional winter leaves true phyllodia, but more often phyllodiform with small abortive pitcher tubes and lids. Flower scapes about as tall as pitchers, usually red flush at top; bracts and sepals dark red to maroon; petals red to maroon; stamen filaments often red; umbrella of pistil hirsute externally and often flushed with red; style and ovary usually red to some degree; flower fragrance moderately sweet (as in *Sarracenia rubra*).

Close-up of pitchers of *Sarracenia leucophylla* in Mobile County, Alabama. The prominent white tops are quite evident. These are due to aggregated white areoles. The veins vary from green to red.

Flowering Season
Early March to late April

Distribution
Historically, *Sarracenia leucophylla* grew on the lower Gulf Coast from approximately the middle of the Florida Panhandle west through Alabama just into Mississippi, with slight northward extension into southwestern Georgia (see Map 8).

Habitat
The species is found in pine savannas and seepage bogs, in mostly sandy peat soil, often in masses. *Sarracenia leucophylla* prefers a more constantly wet situation than many other pitcher plants, and this may account for its seeming partition from other *Sarracenia* species in sloping sites. However, in a wet more or less level savanna, this species is frequently mixed with other pitcher plants. In very dry spring seasons, the appearance of flowers and pitchers may be markedly retarded, more so than most other *Sarracenia* species. In such situations, many rhizomes of *S. leucophylla* remain dormant for the entire season.

Comments
A unique feature of *Sarracenia leucophylla* is its rather consistent habit of forming two sets of pitchers during the growing season. There is the expected set in the early spring. Then, in late summer or early autumn, a second set of pitchers comes up as though the growing season were starting again, but, of course, the time for frost is nearly at hand. This feature follows through in cultivation, whether the plants are grown outdoors or in the greenhouse. Whereas other *Sarracenia* species may replace a few lost pitchers throughout the growing season, this flush of late summer pitchers is peculiar to *S. leucophylla*.

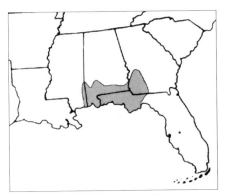

Map 8. Distribution of *Sarracenia leucophylla*.

Sarracenia leucophylla occasionally forms ensiform winter phyllodia, apparently more often in stressed conditions. Many of what seem to be phyllodia are actually phyllodiform leaves with narrow abortive pitcher tubes and even lids on one margin. I see these only rarely in the field. When I lived in the piedmont region of North Carolina, I never saw phyllodia or phyllodiform leaves in plants grown outdoors or in the greenhouse. Here in southwestern Virginia, I rather regularly see phyllodia and phyllodiform leaves in outdoor plants, but never in the greenhouse. I would expect more stress in plants grown outdoors at this latitude and greater altitude.

As is the case with other red-flowered *Sarracenia* species, several examples of a yellow-flowered *S. leucophylla* variant can be found. I have noted these on occasion and mentioned that there is no red in the pitcher either, the pale green veins making the white so prominent that the pitchers have a "ghostly" appearance (Schnell 1976). British growers seem taken by this

Red to maroon flowers of *Sarracenia leucophylla* in Mobile County, Alabama. The red blush of the external umbrella can be seen in the two end flowers. The sepals also tend to reflex moderately.

An anthocyanin-free *Sarracenia leucophylla* in northern Baldwin County, Alabama. Note the lack of red veins in the pitchers and the seeming increased whiteness of the pitcher tops. The flowers of this plant were yellow.

and refer to the plant informally as "Schnell's ghost," which I take in good humor.

There are many examples of *Sarracenia leucophylla* where red venation seems more prominent than usual. Close examination may disclose the usual broad lid with sinuate margins set on a tall column, whereas other examples have smaller pitcher mouths, shorter columns, and less wavy margins. The latter likely represent varying degrees of hybridization and introgression (Schnell 1989). Even a cursory examination of *Sarracenia* distribution maps indicates clearly the overlap of *Sarracenia leucophylla*'s range with several other *Sarracenia* species. Not only do hybrids form readily, the hybrids may breed back into species, possibly carrying characters from one parent species into the genome of the other parent species. As seeds from this backcrossing germinate and resulting plants grow to maturity, many of these plants may be readily identifiable as one species in general, but seem to have characters of another species as well. This process is known as introgression. I discuss more about hybridization in the last section of this chapter. Such variation in red color and form are very confusing to the beginner, who must then rely on strict criteria to identify examples of *Sarracenia leucophylla* species not involved in hybridization.

Folkerts and Folkerts (1989) noted that the seed capsules of *Sarracenia leucophylla* dehisce at their bases to release seed, whereas capsules of most other *Sarracenia* species open at the apices (the end near the base of the style). I concur with this observation. Folkerts and Folkerts (1989) offered a possible explanation for the tilting of *Sarracenia* flowers to a lateral or even vertical position from their pendant one after petals fall. Older explanations were that this ensured that some pollen from the cup of the umbrella would fall over the lowest stigmas during tilting, in case pollination had not been achieved. I have mentioned earlier that this is not likely because there is very little pollen left in the cup that late in anthesis and what pollen is there is stuck to the cup by a mixture of sticky nectar and mold. Also, the geometric configuration of the tilting cup with the stigmas placed at the umbrella points would not allow pollen to fall on them. Folkerts and Folkerts (1989) proposed that the tilting allows for

A possible *Sarracenia leucophylla* in northern Baldwin County, Alabama. Several features cause one to be suspicious of this plant. Note the very heavy red venation of the pitcher top, the shorter hood column, the smaller hood with less waviness of the margins, and the smaller mouth than a normal *S. leucophylla*. This plant's features likely represent a complex hybridization, perhaps with *S. rubra* subspecies *wherryi*, which grows in the same bog. In fact, the strong residual features of *S. leucophylla* may be due to a simple hybrid between the two backcrossing into *S. leucophylla*. Many plants of this sort in a bog can be either very interesting or frustrating, depending on one's viewpoint.

seeds to fall clear of the umbrella cup, where they might be trapped and prevented from reaching the ground. This concept should be further investigated.

Determann and Groves (1993) described a few plants of *Sarracenia leucophylla* in northern Baldwin County, Alabama, that have multiple sepals and petals ("double" in horticulture). These must be derived from flower-part primordia because there are few or no stamens and pistils in the flowers, which on my examination almost have a crestate appearance. Determann and Groves named this horticultural variety 'Tarnok' after the person who discovered the plant. This variety is sterile and can only be reproduced vegetatively.

Cultivation Notes

As is the case with most of the *Sarracenia* species described so far, *Sarracenia leucophylla* is very easy to grow. Due to the tall, erect pitchers, it should not be grown in a terrarium. The species grows best in a wetter habitat, and it should be kept amply moist in cultivation. If phyllodia or phyllodiform leaves do form in late autumn, they should be left on over the winter for additional photosynthetic activity during warmer periods.

Sarracenia minor Walter

Sarracenia minor is a very distinctive and easily identified pitcher plant that also has a rather distinguished botanical history. Efforts and keen insight by a family doctor practicing near Charleston, South Carolina, in the mid-nineteenth century set the stage for understanding many aspects of all pitcher and carnivorous plants, in general. I will review his work below.

Synonyms

These include *Sarracenia lacunosa*, *S. variolaris*, and *S. adunca*. Of these synonyms, the last two are most likely to be encountered in the literature.

Common Name

Sarracenia minor is commonly known as the hooded pitcher plant.

Description

Rhizomes horizontal and up to 1.5 cm thick. Pitcher leaves erect, to 30 cm average but up to 60–70 cm in areas; free margin of ala straight and widest to 1.0–1.5 cm at its midpoint; tube curved on inside edge of ala; pitcher expanding evenly to mouth to 3.0 cm across; hood column short, wide, and curved part away around lateral margin of mouth; hood closely approximating mouth and tip extending over edge and sloped downward; prominent white areoles of back of lower hood, column, and upper few centimeters of pitcher tube; occasional ensiform spring phyllodia half as tall as pitchers. Green flower scape half as tall as pitchers; bracts and sepals green although sometimes flushed with red; petals yellow; stamens and pistils green to yellowish green; faint watermelon flower fragrance.

Flowering Season

Sarracenia minor flowers from late March to mid-May, most often simultaneously with or just slightly after pitcher appearance.

Distribution

As indicated on Map 9, the range of *Sarracenia minor* extends from extreme southeastern North Carolina in a coastal plain arc approximately midway across the Florida Panhandle. This species is the only *Sarracenia* to extend nearly halfway into peninsular Florida near Lake Okeechobee.

Map 9. Distribution of *Sarracenia minor.*

Habitat

Sarracenia minor favors pine savannas, where it is capable of growing in drier areas (which present less competition), although it does best in moister areas. In southeastern Georgia, particularly Ware County and immediate environs, the plant often grows in very wet locations including standing water and on floating sphagnous prairies in the Okefenokee Swamp.

Sarracenia minor in Columbus County, North Carolina. Note the lemon yellow flowers on scapes that are about half as tall as pitchers. The light windows on the posterior upper pitchers are prominent. The hood column wraps around the side of the mouth about halfway, and the cupped hoods very closely approximate the mouths of the pitchers.

Comments

There are prominent nectar glands on the free border of *Sarracenia minor* pitcher wings; in humid situations, droplets of nectar are clearly visible along this margin. This arrangement creates an attractant trail for ants, in particular. Especially in drier locations (but see Ware County comments below), ants approach the pitcher petiole and march up the ala margin to the rim of the pitcher mouth, where there is abundant additional nectar. Eventually, many ants tumble into the abyss.

Generally, ants seem to be the primary prey of *S. minor*, representing one of the strongest partitions of prey known among pitcher plants. The plant traps other insects, including some flying beetles, but ants predominate. Even in Ware County, Georgia, where *S. minor* frequently grows in standing water, I have opened many pitchers and noted a pronounced predominance of ants as prey. The ants possibly negotiate their way to the pitchers during drier periods.

Many early botanists suggested that *Sarracenia minor* may be the most primitive member of the genus because the mature pitchers of this species look very much like seedling pitchers of other species. When a *Sarracenia* seed germinates, the first pair of seedling leaves (cotyledons) is small and straplike—not at all like pitcher plants. The next leaves are minute pitchers. These second leaves tend to look very similar among the *Sarracenia* species, until later, small pitchers begin to diverge in character. I think the first true pitcher leaves of various *Sarracenia* species look more like *S. minor* hybrids with erect pitcher plants rather than adult *S. minor*. If "ontogeny recapitulates phylogeny"—and there is likely some partial truth to this old adage—these observations may support the concept of many predecessor *Sarracenia* species having existed and then gone extinct.

There is some color variation in *Sarracenia minor*, although not to the extent of other species of the genus. Plants with a slight red blush of the hood are typical for the species, however, plants with much more red in the upper pitchers and even the bracts and sepals are fairly common.

Flower fragrance is very faint in *Sarracenia minor* and does not resemble sweet violets or felines, as in other *Sarracenia* species. To accent the fragrance, several flowers can be picked and sealed inside an unused plastic

Sarracenia minor near Charleston, South Carolina, with prominent red in the upper pitchers and even in the bracts and sepals. The petals remain clear yellow.

bag and set in the sun for an hour or so. The bag is then opened and the contents sniffed quickly before the fragrance dissipates. I liken the smell to watermelon.

There is an interesting size variant of *Sarracenia minor* that grows most prominently in Ware County, Georgia, in the environs of the Okefenokee Swamp as well as on a few sphagnous prairies in the preserve. These regularly have pitchers to 70 cm, sometimes up to 80 cm. Often, when transplanted to cultivation, the pitchers do not grow so large, perhaps no more than the average plant in a wet situation elsewhere. Bell (1949) and Case and Case (1976) felt that these plants were simply ecads, that is, they grow

The large variant of *Sarracenia minor* in Ware County, Georgia.

Brenda Schnell holding a large Ware County, Georgia, *Sarracenia minor* variant as seen near Manor, Georgia. The pitchers are obviously very elongate, although the tops have about the same dimensions as the smaller typical plants growing elsewhere.

large because of the environment and not for genetic reasons. These authors had the plants revert to average size in cultivation. However, my experience in cultivating these variants, as well as the efforts of David Kutt and George Newman, have resulted in very tall plants that approach the wild plants in size.

Even as seedlings and young plants, the Ware County variants are, to quote George Newman, "just different." The young pitchers have a very slender profile compared to *S. minor* of the same size and growth stage from elsewhere, although the mouths and hoods are about the same size. Growing side by side in cultivation, the typical plants and Ware County variants are indeed quite different, indicating a genetic variation that responds best to optimal conditions. These unique variants are sometimes referred to as the "Okefenokee giants."

Another interesting feature of the Ware County, Georgia, plants is that they rather commonly grow spring phyllodia, an unusual season for those structures. These are true ensiform phyllodia found among the fresh pitchers of the season. These structures do not regularly appear in most plants, as is the case of autumn phyllodia in *Sarracenia flava* and *S. oreophila*. Phyllodia are far less common among the typically sized *S. minor*.

In closing, recognition must be given to J. H. Mellichamp, a country doctor who in the mid-nineteenth century did pioneering work on *Sarracenia minor*, which grew in the area where he practiced around Charleston, South Carolina. His observations also led the way to understanding the nature of other *Sarracenia* species as well. In those days, many physicians were outstanding botanists. Because a doctor's pharmacy largely resided in nearby woods and fields, where plants supplied many of the drugs used for treatment, physicians were expected to be familiar with medicinal botany. Often, they carried the interest further into general botany.

Dr. J. H. Mellichamp of Bluffton, South Carolina, became curious of the hooded pitcher plants he noted in fields and savannas while on his daily rounds. The root of *Sarracenia minor* had been extracted by others as early as 1849 (Mellichamp 1875) to treat various gastrointestinal ailments, but other aspects of its botany were not understood. There was a general idea that the plants served as shelters for insects against weather and enemies. However, Mellichamp had a hunch that the plants were trapping insects, possibly for nourishment. He made detailed observations that culminated in a paper he read before the prestigious American Association for the Advancement of Science in Hartford, Connecticut, in 1874.

To briefly summarize his findings, Mellichamp noted the nectar secretions on the ala and lip of the pitcher mouth acting as a lure for ants, in particular, which he found dead in the depths of pitchers (he noted a few other kinds of insects as prey also). He did experiments that proved that the nectar lure itself did not contain an anesthetic compound, but that physical characteristics of the pitcher lining caused the insect to tumble into the trap. Mellichamp proved that sterile secretions taken from the interior of unopened pitchers possessed an anesthetic substance that incapacitated test flies. If the quiet and numbed insects were removed from the fluid puddles in time, they would slowly recover. He also tested sterile fluid collections for their capacity to digest small bits of meat and found that this did occur.

Mellichamp also noted the small larvae of *Sarcophaga sarraceniae*, which he sent off to an entomologist friend who named the fly; both puzzled over the larvae's capacity to thrive in the mixture of digesting prey. He also studied *Exyra* (then identified as *Xanthoptera semicrocea*), noting both the ability of the adult moth to negotiate the pitcher at will and its larval habits. Finally, Mellichamp watched flying prey taking off from the pitcher lip toward the light windows, apparently mistaking them as an escape route, crashing into them, and tumbling down into the pitcher.

Cultivation Notes

There are no problems in cultivating *Sarracenia minor*. Smaller examples of this generally shorter plant might be feasible in terrarium culture as well. Although the plant does tolerate drier habitats if required to do so, it does better with more moisture. If you have color variants with more red in the leaves, this feature will be expressed best if the plant is grown in full light.

Sarracenia psittacina Michaux

Sarracenia psittacina is the most unusual looking species of the genus. It is highly adapted for a wetter than usual, sometimes flooded, habitat. Regarding pitcher characteristics, the species has been compared to *Darlingtonia californica*, but they are not closely related at all.

Synonyms
These include *Sarracenia calceolata* and *S. pulchella*, although you are unlikely to encounter these synonyms in the literature.

Common Name
A sideways view of the upper pitcher indicates where the common name, parrot pitcher plant, originated. In fact, the epithet *psittacina* refers to parrots, the psittacine birds.

Description
Rhizome to 1 cm thick, usually angled or vertical. Leaves more or less evergreen, 5–15 cm long (up to 40 cm in special circumstances; see below); spring leaves angled; summer leaves decumbent; ascending and widening pitcher to 1.3 cm terminates in a semiclosed, globose hood with a prominent crest and a lateral adaxial (toward center of plant) mouth; wing sinuate (wavy) and up to 3.5 cm wide at midpoint; lower leaf green with more red toward the top and with prominent areoles. Flower scape to 40 cm, mainly green with reddish blush near top; bracts and sepals red to reddish green; petals deep red; pistil green but umbrella often with narrow red margin; flower fragrance is slightly sweet (as in *Sarracenia rubra*).

Map 10. Distribution of *Sarracenia psittacina*.

Flowering Season
Late March into May

Distribution

Map 10 indicates the historic distribution of *Sarracenia psittacina*, chiefly along the Gulf Coast but also into the Georgia Atlantic coastal plain. There is a slight extension into two parishes in extreme eastern Louisiana (Murry and Urbatsch 1979).

Habitat

Sarracenia psittacina grows in pine savannas and seepage bogs and achieves its best form in open, very wet, often partially submerged areas. Today, some of the best plants are in roadside ditches near the waterline. Drier savanna plants tend to be smaller in all respects.

Comments

The distinguishing feature of *Sarracenia psittacina* pitchers is the globose hood with a lateral pitcher mouth. Hemisection of the pitcher discloses

Leaves of *Sarracenia psittacina* in cultivation. The lateral opening of the mouths just above the pitcher wing is apparent in two pitchers near the center. Note the prominently crested hood and abundant light windows.

Sarracenia psittacina in flower in Florida. This plant clump is in open light and has excellent red coloration. The lateral view of the globose hoods shows the parrotlike appearance. There is a mix of semidecumbent spring leaves as well as decumbent leaves from the previous summer.

that just inside the mouth is a collar of tissue about 0.7–1.0 cm long around the mouth. One also notices that the pitcher hairs are prominent and interlock. This is a perfect design for capturing crawling or aquatic prey. The collar results in a lobster-pot effect in which the prey can enter the pitcher but cannot seem to make its way back out around the collar. Light windows direct the prey's attention away from the opening, as is the case with *S. minor*. Because there is no help from gravity in this decumbent trap, as the prey does work its way into the depths of the pitcher, the much longer than usual interlocking hairs secure the animal. The plants are often partially or entirely submerged for periods of time, and many water bugs are trapped.

This pitcher demonstrates well the difficulty with designating pitcher zones. Compared to *Sarracenia purpurea*, for example, zones 2 and 5 are absent and zones 3 and 4 are combined (glandular and hairy). Because this is a red-flowered *Sarracenia*, many people have searched for a yellow-flowered, green-pitchered variety. The search has been fruitful, with plants found in Baldwin County, Alabama, but probably existing elsewhere as well.

A longitudinally hemisected pitcher of *Sarracenia psittacina*. The tab of red tissue just inside the lateral mouth is a portion of the collar, which would be in a ring in the intact pitcher. Note the margins rolled slightly inward. The very long pitcher hairs are also apparent. The design serves very well for trapping crawling or aquatic prey in this decumbent pitcher.

When plants of the decumbent *Sarracenia psittacina* grow in deeper *Sphagnum* or duff, the rhizome sends up a green branch (stolonoid) from which the leaves and flowers bud and grow. This branch keeps the aerial portions of the plant above the growth medium. This structure is sometimes found in the other decumbent species, *S. purpurea*, as well (Folkerts 1989).

As with *Sarracenia minor*, there is a large variant of *S. psittacina* in and around the Okefenokee Swamp in southeastern Georgia, with pitchers measuring to 40 cm. The Okefenokee has many marked water trails, and you can rent or launch your own canoe or small-engine boat at one of several landings along the eastern edge of the swamp. Get directions to Chesser Prairie, where you can see abundant large forms of both *S. minor* and *S. psittacina*. The plants must not be disturbed, but you can take wonderful photographs.

Cultivation Notes

Sarracenia psittacina grows equally well in either *Sphagnum* or Canadian peat. The species does better in a wet medium and will develop firm pitchers with good color in full light. British growers remark about losing plants to fungus attack over the winter, although I have not experienced that problem in the United States. Some have found that the plant survives dormancy best in their area if it is entirely submerged in water over the winter. In my experience, *S. psittacina* is an excellent plant to grow in a terrarium because moisture, temperature, and good lighting can be easily maintained under fluorescent lights. Do not trim back the living pitchers at the end of the season; this will set back plant growth. In spring and early summer after new pitchers begin growing, older pitchers will gradually turn brown and may then be removed.

Sarracenia Hybrids

The maps showing the distributions of *Sarracenia* indicate that many species grow in the same or overlapping ranges. In the field, two or more species often grow in the same bog or savanna. As a result, crosses or hybrids between the various overlapping species may be frequent.

Not all species of plants, even those in the same genus, are capable of hybridizing. For example, there may be internal blocks such as pollen or stigma incompatibility. Also, the pollen tube may not grow and, if it does, pollen tube nuclei may be incompatible with ova. If those problems do not arise, sterile seeds may be produced. Even if seeds are viable, the resulting hybrid plant may be sterile and incapable of reproducing with other hybrids or parent species.

Such is not the case with *Sarracenia,* however. Not only can nearly all conceivable crosses be found in the field or made in the greenhouse, the hybrids are fertile. *Sarracenia* hybrids are capable of making additional crosses with a third species or with each other, and they can effect complex backcrosses with one or both parent species. Such backcrossing (introgressive hybridization) may result in an effective exchange of genetic material between two parent species through their hybrid as an intermediate. This process is an important mechanism for variation in evolution, and indeed many plant species are likely of hybrid origin. The ease of interspecific hybridization among *Sarracenia* species and other evidence of incomplete differentiation of species in the genus support the concept of many *Sarracenia* species being of complex hybrid origin (see discussions of reticulate relationships of *Sarracenia* species elsewhere in the this chapter, particularly in *S. rubra*).

There is a general rule in botany that plant hybrids become established only with difficulty. In theoretical ecological terms (and usually in actuality) hybrids should require a rather narrow habitat, intermediate in terms of space and character between the two parents, which themselves have become established as a result of environmental selection. But the various species of *Sarracenia* can generally grow well in very similar environments. Over the years, I have become impressed how more alike American pitcher plant habitats are than they are different, except for a possible moderating effect of temperature. As a result, if there is space, hybrids can generally establish themselves intermingled among the parents, which may be mixed in the bog anyway.

Several authors (such as Folkerts 1982) feel that *Sarracenia* hybrids establish mainly in sites disturbed by humans. In fact, over several seasons with students in the field, Folkerts observed hybrid seedlings in footpath disturbances. This would seem to suggest that hybridizations, including the extensive hybrid swarms in Gulf Coast bogs, have originated fairly recently as a result of human activity. However, in the Gulf area particularly, hurricanes, floods, lightning fires, and other natural disturbances may well have played important roles even before humans began to disturb and physically open habitat. In fact, natural systems are largely structured by natural disturbances (Pickett and White 1985; Huggett 1995), and in evolutionary terms, we must look to natural factors for the establishment of hybrids, backcrosses, complex intercrosses, and possible introgression in the reticulate genus *Sarracenia*.

If these species are so capable of hybridizing with each other and the hybrids are interfertile, then how have distinct species been preserved at all, especially in sympatric populations? The answer lies in isolation factors other than those already mentioned at the beginning of this section. For the species as a whole, geographic factors may be considered. Obviously, species such as *Sarracenia oreophila* and *S. alata* will never hybridize in nature because their ranges are widely separated. But what about such species as *S. alata* and *S. leucophylla*, which not only overlap in their ranges but freely hybridize and yet are still distinguishable species? Other isolation factors must come into play.

Wherry (1933a, 1935) proposed that *Sarracenia* species originated in isolated bogs of the ancient peneplain, which occupied the present-day Tennessee plateau, the Appalachians, and the piedmont. Thus, early physical separation may have helped fix and maintain early pitcher plant species. After the montane uprising and the new availability of the present coastal plain, propagules from residual populations washed down ancient river systems to establish in the newly opened habitat, again mostly in islands of suitable bogs. It is unlikely that all of these ancient river systems were the same as present-day ones, so we have difficulty tracking pathways exactly (see Schuchert 1955). A fanning out of species propagules to the new habitats may have helped keep some species physically separate. Clearly, though, there was some geographic overlap. In southern Baldwin County, Alabama, at least six species of *Sarracenia* have portions of their ranges overlapping in one area.

The main isolating factor for sympatric *Sarracenia* species appears to be differing peak flowering times (allochrony; Bell 1949). Thus, when pollen of one species is ripe and being carried abroad by bumble bees, the stigma of a different species nearby may not be receptive or the other species may not have even flowered. A quick scan of flowering periods across *Sarracenia* reveals overlap, but there are bell-shaped peaks in flowering periods. The majority may flower and be at peak over a week or two, but only a few functional outliers overlap. These outliers would be capable of producing relatively few hybrids, although there would be hybrids. Such a barrier is termed *leaky*.

Other barriers to hybrid viability exist. There must be a suitable site for seed to germinate and grow into young plants. If there is no disturbance, such space might not be available. Also, there might not be sufficient light penetrating to bare areas between larger plants, and hybrids therefore could not establish themselves. Another factor might be pollinator size. A large queen bumble bee may not be capable of negotiating a smaller flower early in the season, whereas later spring workers might be. There is the consideration of pollinator fidelity—bumble bees do have fidelity to proven pollen and nectar sources based on flower color, nectar quantities, and possibly fragrance, although this fidelity can be limited. But bees have a tendency to stay with one species in flower rather than use other species coming into flower in the same area indiscriminately (Heinrich 1979).

Within the flower, pollen competition must be considered. Pollen grains, somewhat analogous to seeds, require adequate space in a suitable seedbed. If the stigma is overloaded with pollen grains, only a limited number may germinate and/or be capable of sending their pollen tubes toward the ovary. Still, there seems to be a chance factor involved in what pollen grains will germinate and successfully fertilize an ovum.

Finally, one must consider seed dispersal. If hybrid seed is produced but the site is unsuitable for seedling growth, any seed produced is wasted. *Sarracenia* seed falls in the immediate area of the parent species, and if hybrid seed is to be transported to another suitable site, something must move it. Although wind and animal fur are clearly not factors, the seed does float in water. Thus, flooding may wash seed to a more suitable area for germination, or the seeds may just wash away. The feet of animals, particularly birds, could carry seed mixed with mud to another area.

All of these isolation factors are by themselves "leaky." However, taken in combination, they could be sufficient in preventing a mass genetic mixing and obliteration of individual species in certain areas of overlap.

The frequency of hybridization between species of *Sarracenia* caused a great deal of difficulty among early botanists. That, combined with a lack of ready communication or rules of nomenclature, such as our modern ICBN, resulted in near chaos. Looking at older synonyms listed in the preceding sections indicates how often certain ones cropped up within various species in varying capacities. Yet, the confusion among those early botanists is understandable because they were trying to understand a New World genus with many variations and hybrids. I can sympathize because I had a small taste of those difficulties while working on the true genetic varieties of *Sarracenia flava*.

As a brief introduction to nomenclature of hybrids, I will mention a few helpful rules that will apply to other species as well. In the early days of American botany, many hybrids were thought to be species and were given species binomials. One example is *Sarracenia catesbaei*, which after much study and backtracking was ultimately found to be a hybrid between *S. flava* and *S. purpurea*. To indicate that the binomial *S. catesbaei* is a hybrid, a multiplication symbol is placed before the specific epithet, *S. ×catesbaei*. The × is pronounced "hybrida" (hi-BREE-duh), by the way, which becomes somewhat amusingly awkward in the case of a *Drosera* hybrid, *D. ×hybrida*, which would be pronounced "*Drosera* hybrida *hybrida*." Sometimes in colloquial conversation the × is pronounced "ex." In either event, there are many of these old hybrid binomials around to deal with. Each has an authority and the publication of new binomials must follow certain rules. Also, one must have a ready reference to a list of hybrid binomials or a total memory for all of them to know their composition.

A second system in use is much better, namely to call the hybrids by their composition. This system is being used with increased frequency and does not require special publication because the naming is descriptive. I prefer this system because everyone knows what is being discussed, even the beginner who knows some species but not the gallery of hybrid binomials. The use for hybrid binomials now seems to be for historical study or to name a new hybrid after someone. Experts in *Sarracenia* hybrids might also find hybrid binomials useful for very complex, multi-parent hybrids, where one term suffices for a list of parent species, or for other hybrids. This case is unusual, however.

In the example above, *Sarracenia* ×*catesbaei* would be known as *S. flava* × *S. purpurea* in the new system. The multiplication symbol in this case is spoken as "by," although sometimes the mathematical meaning "times" is used colloquially. For those producing their own hybrids, this system can also help delineate which parent is the seed (female, or pistillate) parent versus the pollen parent. If known, the seed parent is listed first. Therefore, if I pollinated a flower of *S. purpurea* with pollen of *S. flava*, the hybrid is called *S. purpurea* × *S. flava*. If the hybrid is found in the wild (and therefore the direction of pollination unknown) or if I lost my records or labels, the two epithets are listed alphabetically, *S. flava* × *S. purpurea*.

As determined originally by Russell (1918), *Sarracenia* hybrids are intermediate in nearly all ways in both microscopic and macroscopic characteristics between the parents. No one color or physical attribute seems dominant over another. Thus, a red-flowered species crossing with a yellow-flowered species does not produce red- or yellow-flowered hybrids, but a plant with pink or orange flowers. The same would apply to pitcher colors and forms. A study to try and determine red dominance in which, for example, a very red *Sarracenia psittacina* is crossed with the all-green variety of the same species is doomed to failure if only the presence or absence of red in seedlings is counted. Older plants must be assessed for the degree and distribution of red color, in which case intermediacy would be noted.

There are a large number of *Sarracenia* hybrids that have been found and recorded in nature, and those not found have been produced in the laboratory or greenhouse with ease. I include photographs of a few representative examples of hybrids. When viewing these, leaf back to photographs of the parent species in their respective sections and note the intermediacy of the hybrids. Many of the hybrids are quite attractive, and growers like to collect them. Some of the hybrids exhibit a phenomenon known as hybrid vigor (heterosis), wherein the hybrids exceed either parent in some or multiple qualities such as size, color, or ease of growing in cultivation. Recently, certain hybrids that seem to have good horticultural qualities, including easy cultivation, long-lasting pitchers, and suitable size, have been selected for horticultural naming and reproduced by tissue culture so that clones are available for sale. These offer growers

Flowers of a natural hybrid between *Sarracenia flava* and *S. purpurea* in the field in Brunswick County, North Carolina. The bright yellow flowers of *S. flava* and the deep red to maroon flowers of *S. purpurea* have resulted in pink flowers in this hybrid.

Sarracenia flava × *S. purpurea* subspecies *venosa* in Brunswick County, North Carolina. A comparison of photographs of the species in previous sections emphasizes the intermediate character of the pitchers. The red color is likely from a red variation of *S. purpurea*.

Sarracenia leucophylla × *S. purpurea* subspecies *venosa* variety *burkii* in Baldwin County, Alabama. A second look reveals some peculiarities. Note the short column and slight overhang of the pitcher hood on the right, along with the red color of the upper pitcher. The *S. leucophylla* parent of this hybrid may have been introgressed with *S. rubra*.

Sarracenia minor × *S. purpurea* subspecies *venosa* in Brunswick County, North Carolina. The red color again is derived from the red variant of this coastal *S. purpurea*.

Sarracenia alata × *S. psittacina* in Jackson County, Mississippi. This uncommon hybrid derives its erect character from *S. alata* (the only erect pitcher species in this particular area), and the wide pitcher wing, light windows, and well-formed hood from *S. psittacina*. Due to the *S. alata* influence, the pitcher mouth to the right of the hood is more open than it would be in *S. psittacina*. When grown in cultivation without very high humidity, bright light, and warmth, the pitcher mouth frequently remains closed, but squeezing the hood easily breaks the seam.

Sarracenia rubra subspecies *wherryi* × *S. psittacina* near Perdido in Baldwin County, Alabama. Compare this hybrid with the *Sarracenia alata* × *S. psittacina* hybrid. Although very similar, the fine reticulate venation in this pitcher with a clear *S. psittacina* influence is due to *S. rubra*, which also results in smaller light windows.

proven plant material in culture and take collector pressure off dwindling natural populations of *Sarracenia*.

For convenience and reference, I list below some of the simple, two-parent *Sarracenia* hybrids under both systems of nomenclature:

HYBRID COMPOSITION NAME	HYBRID BINOMIAL NAME
S. flava × *S. purpurea*	*S.* ×*catesbaei*
S. leucophylla × *S. purpurea*	*S.* ×*mitchelliana*
S. minor × *S. purpurea*	*S.* ×*swaniana*
S. psittacina × *S. purpurea*	*S.* ×*courtii*
S. purpurea × *S. rubra*	*S.* ×*chelsoni*
S. alata × *S. purpurea*	*S.* ×*exornata*
S. flava × *S. leucophylla*	*S.* ×*moorei*
S. leucophylla × *S. minor*	*S.* ×*excellens*
S. leucophylla × *S. psittacina*	*S.* ×*wrigleyana*
S. leucophylla × *S. rubra*	*S.* ×*readii*
S. alata × *S. leucophylla*	*S.* ×*areolata*
S. flava × *S. minor*	*S.* ×*harperi*
S. minor × *S. psittacina*	*S.* ×*formosa*
S. minor × *S. rubra*	*S.* ×*rehderi*
S. flava × *S. rubra*	*S.* ×*popei*
S. psittacina × *S. rubra*	*S.* ×*gilpini*
S. alata × *S. rubra*	*S.* ×*ahlesii*

Macfarlane (1907), Bell (1949, 1952), Bell and Case (1956), McDaniel (1966), and Nelson (1986, 1992) provide additional information on pitcher plant hybrids including their tangled history, descriptions, and locations; the authors also describe some of the adventures in finding these hybrids.

CALIFORNIA PITCHER PLANT

Darlingtonia californica

DARLINGTONIA CALIFORNICA Torrey is a member of the family Sarraceniaceae, which also includes the genera *Sarracenia* and *Heliamphora*, the other New World pitcher plants. Because there are significant floral and vegetative differences between these genera, however, some reclassification may be in order (but see the comments on this at the beginning of the *Sarracenia* chapter). *Darlingtonia californica* has been compared to *Sarracenia psittacina*, but the California pitcher plant is unique in appearance; differences are clear on closer examination and, of course, the flowers are entirely different. Although this species was discovered in the mid-nineteenth century and is the only pitcher plant in western North America, more questions remain about the basic biology of *Darlingtonia* than its cousins in the East.

Synonyms

The only synonym is *Chrysamphora californica* (Torrey) Greene. When he described *Darlingtonia* in 1854, John Torrey had been anxious to name a plant genus in honor of his friend William Darlington of West Chester, Pennsylvania. Torrey had made two previous tries and hoped that the third would be successful. However, he overlooked the previous use of *Darlingtonia* for an obscure legume genus. Thus, his naming of the pitcher plant was ultimately invalid according to ICBN rules, even though, paradoxically, the legume *Darlingtonia* was eventually placed into another genus, leaving no plants for the generic epithet. In 1891 Greene found the problem and renamed the pitcher plant *Chrysamphora californica*. The latter then became the legitimate name for the plant, but was often ignored in favor of the more popularized *Darlingtonia*. In 1954, because the generic epithet *Darlingtonia* was then not in use, the International Botanical Congress narrowly voted to retain it for the pitcher plant; thus, we have come full circle back to *Darlingtonia californica* (Mellichamp 1978; Rondeau 1995).

Common Names

The plant's common names include California pitcher plant, cobra lily, cobra plant, and calf's head. It is interesting that many people on the West Coast thought their pitcher plants were lilies, as did those on the East Coast. The cobra designation reflects the fancied resemblance to a cobra with its hood expanded and ready to strike, complete with forked tongue in the form of the pitcher orifice appendage.

Description

A more or less evergreen, perennial, long-lived herb with a narrow horizontal rhizome and fibrous roots; vegetative stolons common; cladophyls to 1 cm, pointed, yellowish green to pink; leaves hollow, semidecumbent, and later ascending to 100 cm (average 40–60 cm), twisting average 180° (90–270°) as they grow; upper pitcher with translucent areoles, prominent keeled nearly globose hood with pitcher opening 2–3 cm and facing vertically; ala prominent to 1 cm; fishtail-shaped 3- to 5-cm appendage hanging from external lip of mouth, yellowish green to lightly suffused with red; peduncle nearly as tall as pitcher and with nine pointed 1.0- to 1.5-cm pink to yellowish green bracts, bent at the top with solitary actinomorphic opened flower pendant; five oblong, pointed 3- to 5-cm yellowish green to rusty sepals; five red to brownish red, heavily veined petals 2.5–3.5 cm long, ovate-lanceolate with pointed tips and margins closely appressed, 3- to 4-mm notches in lateral margins above pointed petal tips; fifteen stamens 5–7 cm long, arranged in ring around base of

Clumps of *Darlingtonia californica* with maturing seedpods. Note that the flower assumes an erect position from its usual pendant aspect after pollination. Photograph by J. A. Mazrimas.

ovary; pistil green; bell-shaped ovary 1.0–1.5 cm long; style 2–3 mm; stigma radiately, deeply five-lobed; five-valved fruit capsule to 3 cm, erect at maturation; seed 2–3 mm, club-shaped with spicules at wide end; daytime flower fragrance melonlike. Chromosome number $2n = 30$.

Flowering Season

Depending on altitude, *Darlingtonia californica* flowers from April to July.

Distribution

Darlingtonia californica grows locally in areas of northern California extending to the extreme northwestern coast, then more or less coastal in Oregon, with slight inland extension in the north (see Map 11).

Habitat

Darlingtonia californica is strongly associated with ultramafic rocks and their serpentine soils, the latter characterized by low levels of plant nutrients such as nitrogen, phosphorous, potassium, and calcium and high to nearly phytotoxic levels of magnesium, nickel, and chromium (Kruckeberg 1954). Because the plants of serpentine areas generally grow better on nonserpentine soils, plants native to these soils apparently are able to *tolerate* the toxic mineral levels rather than require them. Also, the plants' carnivorous nature allows them to compensate for lack of nutrients. Because *D. californica* is able to withstand toxic mineral levels, whereas most plants cannot, serpentine plants are able to grow with less competition. Such habitat use is somewhat analogous to eastern pitcher plants growing in nutrient-poor bogs and savannas.

True bogs of any sort are rare in the Pacific Coast states (Rondeau 1995). In fact, *Darlingtonia* is most often associated with cold, rapid seeps and streams, where the plants grow along or in running water that rarely exceeds 20°C but sometimes is

Map 11. Distribution of *Darlingtonia californica*.

as low as 9°C (Sheridan and Scholl 1993; Rondeau 1995). Cool water running over the rhizomes, roots, and stolons of *Darlingtonia* is a key factor in the plant's survival strategy, as shown by failed attempts to grow it in cultivation when the medium warms up. Besides temperature, the water's constant movement provides oxygenation of roots. Perhaps roots of *Darlingtonia* are less tolerant of the nearly anaerobic soil conditions in which *Sarracenia* species are able to grow well. In fact, the California pitcher plant only rarely grows in conditions where water movement is slowed (DeBuhr 1973; Rondeau 1995).

In many of the Oregon coastal sites near sea level, the rock is not ultramafic; however, cool, running surface water is still present. Some feel that the water may emanate from serpentine areas higher up and may still be charged with serpentine minerals (Juniper et al. 1989).

On a July day in Oregon, J. A. Mazrimas (personal correspondence) found an interesting and exceptional growing situation at about 500 m, with the air temperature at 38°C and the root water temperatures ranging from 23°C to 27°C. Because the water was running, aeration may be more important than temperature after all. The *Darlingtonia* discovered by Mazrimas bore fewer pitchers, with no new emergents in July, so the plants may have produced pitchers in the cooler early spring and gone into semi-aestivation by summer.

Pollination

Surprisingly, little is known of the pollination of *Darlingtonia* in the field, in spite of more than 150 years of observation. However, seeds are produced in nearly all flowers yearly and the flower design discourages self-pollination, although selfing may be effected manually, resulting in the production of large quantities of viable seeds.

Like *Sarracenia*, *Darlingtonia* flowers have stamens and pistils enclosed in a floral chamber of sorts, but the California pitcher plant does not have an umbraculate, expanded style. The floral chamber is entirely enclosed by the five pendant petals, which touch on the sides and at the tips. Fifteen stamens encircle the ovary's base. The ovary has a unique bell shape, and the distal spread of the bell exceeds the width of the five-lobed stigma hanging from the short style.

Two features of the flower seem to be especially important in pollination. First, any pollen that falls by gravity from the anthers would tend to be swept out and away by the bell-shaped ovary, so that pollen would not easily contact the five-lobed stigma, which is well shielded by the bottom of the bell. Second, apertures are formed where notches in adjacent petals touch. These are at the exact level of the stigma and seem to be good entry points for a pollen-laden insect to enter and brush against the stigma. Our hypothetical pollinator then might ascend the bell-shaped ovary to its base to collect nectar from the basal glands, as well as pollen. The unknown pollinator next might descend the sweep of the ovary, being prevented from retouching the stigma by the bell expansion, and then would exit the flower, either again through the petal apertures or by separating the tips of the petals. This mechanism seems to be a good hypothesis from which to work, considering parallels in *Sarracenia* flowers, where arrangement of flower parts discourages self-pollination and encourages crossing. The only thing we are lacking is a pollinator.

A flower of *Darlingtonia californica* with two adjacent petals removed to reveal the interior of the flower.

The first student of *Darlingtonia* to search for a pollinator was Rebecca Austin. She was born in Kentucky and botanically educated in Illinois; she then moved with her husband and children to California. From 1875 to 1877, she lived near two great sites for *Darlingtonia*, including the famous Butterfly Valley in Plumas County. In those days, of course, married women with children were largely expected to put aside personal interests for the sake of family duties, which in her case included running a boarding house. Nonetheless, Austin became interested in the mysterious pitcher plants. She spent much time studying them, often all day, sometimes with sewing and knitting in hand as she made her observations—even through several thunderstorms, where she satisfied herself that the structure of the pitcher prevented rainwater entry. She pitched a tent for multiple-day stays and some night observations. Austin corresponded with eminent botanists William Canby and Asa Gray in the distant East. These two botanists found her observations and insights clear and fascinating and encouraged further correspondence. They even sent her paper, pens, botanical supplies, and books to use in her studies. Her husband became somewhat impatient at times, but seemed to bear through it all. Unfortunately, her studies were terminated by the family's move further from the fine stands of *Darlingtonia*.

Rebecca Austin noted very few potential pollinator visits to flowers despite weeks of close monitoring, yet seeds were produced. An occasional fly and rarely a beetle entered a flower, but they seemed to rest inside and never visited in great numbers or consecutively among the thousands of spring flowers. Austin did note large numbers of spiders— a majority of flowers seemed to be home to their tight webs, which were spun among the sepals and sometimes into the interior of flowers. She felt that the spiders might be the elusive pollinators, but in modern understanding, this seems unlikely. In fact, spider webbing might interfere with efficient pollination by a suitable agent, depending on when in flowering the webs were in place.

Since Austin, many students have been watching. As of this writing, there is still no solid lead on pollinators (DeBuhr 1973; Elder 1994; Rondeau 1995). Elder noted a few bee and wasp visits to flowers, but again not in large numbers or with consistency. At this point, I would bet on a bee that has somehow slipped by all those bloodshot eyes over some 150 years since the plant's discovery. This question is truly a fascinating mystery begging resolution by solid pollination biology techniques (such as Kearns and Inouye 1993).

Comments

The recorded history of *Darlingtonia californica* began on 3 October 1841. An exploration party under the command of Lieutenant Emmons of the

U.S. Navy was winding down narrow mountain paths near Mount Shasta in northern California. They made their way through a general haze from forest fires meant to slow them, and hostile smoke fires signaled their route to unseen enemies ahead. The expedition was supposed to map a route from the Willamette River to Sacramento and San Francisco, but the Shasta tribe wished to disrupt their explorations.

With the group was the larger expedition's assistant botanist, J. D. Brackenridge. While lingering over plant collections, he became temporarily separated from the group and he hastily ran to rejoin them. While hurrying along, he spotted a strange plant and quickly grabbed a handful of leaves with no flowers or rhizome but with a broken seed capsule. Later that evening Brackenridge listed the new find among others in his daily journal as "Sarracenia species.—leaves 3 ft. long—flower stem exceeding the leaves in length, hab. wet places" (Maloney 1945).

The new pitcher plant specimen eventually made its way to John Torrey, often called the father of American botany. He thought it was allied to *Sarracenia*, but likely a different genus; however, he had insufficient material for a formal description. It was not until 1853 that G. W. Hulse brought Torrey plant material in flower, very likely from close to the spot where Brackenridge had first found it. Torrey described the new genus, naming it after his friend William Darlington, who felt the dedication was his greatest botanical honor (but see Synonyms; Jones 1950).

In 1914 Frank Morton Jones went to California to study insect associates of *Darlingtonia* as he had done for *Sarracenia* (Jones 1950). He set up housekeeping in the nearly abandoned mining town of Keddie in Plumas County, and eventually he found a nice pitcher plant site about a mile from his cabin. To reach it, Jones had to cross a small river, hike through a dense forest, then clamber up a rushing mountain stream, but he was not disappointed. For two months Jones made the daily hike to study the plants. He often brought home an armful of pitchers at night to study in his cabin, although he sometimes did fieldwork at night, leaving a trail of bits of paper, which were easily seen in lantern light. One afternoon, a butterfly settled on one of the pitchers in his bundle, unfurled its coiled tongue, and began feeding on pitcher nectar.

By a miraculous circumstance, while Jones was at Keddie he happened to meet the local visiting schoolteacher, Mrs. M. A. Hail, who turned out to be the daughter of Rebecca Austin. It was there that Jones found out about the Austin letters to Canby in Delaware. Later that year Jones returned to his home in Wilmington, Delaware, and contacted the son of the now-deceased William Canby. Together they searched the dusty attic that contained the elder Canby's correspondence and found the Austin letters in a forgotten trunk. Jones spent the winter sorting and organizing them, finally having a typewritten copy made for posterity. Jones remarked on the thoroughness of Austin's observations and that she had recorded things he had missed in his observations (Jones 1950). The letters are stored at the Society of Natural History of Delaware, and excerpts appear in several pages of Juniper et al. (1989).

California pitcher plants tend to grow on east-facing slopes in California seeps (Rondeau 1995), not exclusively on south-facing slopes as reported in Juniper et al. (1989). Rondeau attributes this to the fact that most mountain ranges run north to south. Growth on the eastern slopes is probably related more to hydrology than to any other factor. Of course, the coastal locations in Oregon face west, which is consistent with water drainage down to the sea. *Darlingtonia* is apparently one of several compass plants. Rebecca Austin discovered that the first two new pitchers of the year are the largest of the season and always orient north–south, whereas the third and fourth smaller pitchers orient east–west. Many observers have confirmed Austin's discovery (such as Jones 1950; DeBuhr 1973; Rondeau 1995). I have noticed this same orientation in cultivated plants here in the East, providing the pots are not moved too frequently. After making the observation one year, I turned the basket 90°. The next year, pitchers were produced in the old orientation, but the following year they were produced according to the new orientation. Apparently, when moved, the plants seem to require a season to reorient.

In addition to the first four new leaves each year emerging in compass quadrants, the pitchers twist approximately 180° as they grow so that all pitchers face outward (abaxially), compared to the pitchers of *Sarracenia*, which face toward the central axis (adaxial) of the plant. Observers think that this twisting allows for a form of advertising because the fish-tail appendage, with its high density of nectar glands, is then facing away from the plant to attract prey. Sheridan and Scholl (1993) attributed the general sweet aroma in springtime *Darlingtonia* bogs to the pitcher mouth appendages. In dense stands, the repositioning also minimizes new pitchers growing into the mouths of nearby mature pitchers.

Particularly in the Southeast, eastern *Sarracenia* species can be found growing in the same bog with several other carnivorous plant species. *Darlingtonia*, in contrast, is accompanied by *Drosera rotundifolia* or *Pinguicula macroceras* only rarely in northern Californian mountain locations, although *D. rotundifolia* is somewhat more common in southern locations and in Oregon (Rondeau 1995).

Prey is undoubtedly attracted by the sweet fragrance emanating from the nectar glands of the fishtail appendage and probably by pitcher and appendage coloration as well. The mouth of the pitcher has an inwardly rolled edge, not the deep collar of *Sarracenia psittacina*. Whereas large pitchers in older plants are erect or nearly so, smaller, semidecumbent

pitchers also emerge from younger plants and even older plants on occasion. Because of the twisting that occurs as pitchers grow, the mouths and fishtail appendages still face outward from the rosette, but the appendages often touch the ground or adjoining low vegetation and thus serve as crawling-insect conductors up to the pitcher mouth.

The rolled inside margin of the mouth

A backlit pitcher of *Darlingtonia californica*. Note the fishtail appendage, which is colored partly red as an additional attractant, hanging from the outside edge of the mouth. Looking into the mouth, one can see the collarless, low lip roll. The interior is well lit by the translucent areoles.

encourages prey to topple over into the pitcher depths. Well-developed, translucent areoles light the interior of the pitcher very well, so that prey that might be repelled by darkness are lulled into a false sense of security. The tube of the pitcher has downward-pointing hairs in its depths, but no glands have been observed. This is interesting because the pitcher does produce fluid—without enzymes or wetting agents—and this fluid is even present in the developing but unopened pitcher (Austin 1875–1877). The fluid is entirely sterile until prey is captured. Hepburn et al. (1920) could detect no intrinsic digestive enzyme production by the pitcher, and these findings have not been challenged. In spite of the lack of known glands and enzyme production, pitcher liquid increases as prey items accumulate, this being first recorded by Austin (1875–1877; see also Hepburn et al. 1920). Austin even noted liquid increase when she fed pitchers fragments of meat with no insects present, so the liquid must come from the plant. At present, exactly how the seemingly inactive liquid is exuded into the pitcher cavity is unknown. As mentioned, the sterile pitcher liquid has no wetting action, but once prey begins to accumulate, supernatant liquid from the pitcher then seems to have a wetting action on additional prey (Austin 1875–1877).

Darlingtonia has a red flower, and, as one might expect, an anthocyanin-free population has been discovered (Elder 1994; Meyers-Rice 1997). Meyers-Rice (1998) named selected plants of this horticultural variety 'Othello'. Other than having yellow flowers and entirely green or yellowish green foliage, the plants are morphologically identical to the red-pigmented ones and apparently are able to catch prey as well.

Like *Sarracenia*, there are several insect associates of *Darlingtonia californica*, only a few of which will be reviewed here because studies on their relationship with the plant are ongoing and require confirmation (Austin 1875–1877; Jones 1916; Fashing 1981; Nielsen 1990). So far, between twenty and twenty-five associated species have been proposed. Rebecca Austin was the first to record dipteran larvae feeding on pitcher prey, describing larvae surrounding first catches of the season as having the "appearance of a wet ball of cotton larger than a pea." These were likely larvae of *Metrocnemus edwardsi* (recall the description of these larvae, which surround and bore through chitinous exoskeletons of insects, in the *Sarracenia* chapter). This is the most frequent larva, although Jones (1916) also noted the dipteran *Botanobia darlingtoniae*. In his review, Fashing (1981) confirmed the presence of both *M. edwardsi* and *B. darlingtoniae*. The spider *Eperigone trilobata* forms webs around and in the flowers, but also sometimes within pitchers. Some other species of mite larvae apparently feed on plant tissue above the water line (Fashing 1981).

An interesting feature of all this is Austin's insistence that she found "worms" (dipteran larvae) within pitchers prior to their opening. The worms apparently were found most often in pitchers growing in full sun that had red pigment developing. Closer examination disclosed small "dots" in the lower pitchers that may have been resealed punctures, the implication being that flies and/or midges used their ovipositors to pierce the unopened pitchers and deposit larvae within. If so, there is nothing similar to this reported in other members of the family Sarraceniaceae. No researchers since Austin have been able to confirm or disprove this

A flower of *Darlingtonia californica* 'Othello'. This is a red-pigment-free form with yellow flower petals. Photograph by Barry Meyers-Rice.

hypothesis. This is one of several observations by the determined and innately skillful Rebecca Austin that Jones (1950) acknowledged missing in his two-month stay in *Darlingtonia* country.

Cultivation Notes

Darlingtonia californica has proven to be one of the most difficult carnivorous plants to cultivate successfully. Apparently, the plant's requirements for cool root and rhizome temperatures with running water are very difficult to meet. Except in a few instances on the northern California and Oregon Coasts, the plant cannot simply be potted and expected to grow. In the Southeast, many of us have nearly reached an impasse because of very warm summer temperatures. The plant's aerial parts are able to do well in warm air temperatures, because these can be quite high in their native areas, but the habitats' cool seep and stream waters running over the roots and rhizomes appear to save them.

I have seen plants doing well in George Newman's collection in New Hampshire, and he has been able to raise seedlings as well. Even though days can be very warm there in the summer, the cool nights and carryover of these temperatures into the morning may be factors in his success. In North Wales, there is a report of *Darlingtonia* growing well outdoors, even surviving a freezing winter where the aerial temperature near ground level reached −7°C (Johnson 1929). Johnson grew his plants in wet loam near water, where they produced many pitchers but never flowered. He then moved them to "slightly" higher ground with better drainage consisting of stones and rotted vegetable refuse, and the plants promptly flowered every season thereafter. Johnson's success is difficult to explain in light of a majority of failures, and his methods seem so casual. Curiously, however, he also noted dipteran larvae in his pitchers grown in Wales.

There have been several ideas about how to grow *Darlingtonia* in North America away from its native sites. Someone proposed acquiring an old soft-drink cooler—the kind with a sliding, clear glass or plastic door over the top and into which you reached down to get a drink. That individual planned to place *Sphagnum* in the cooler and fluorescent lights banks over the clear doors and plug it all in. I never heard if the experiment was ever tried, let alone successful.

I have had very modest success in the oppressive summertime warmth of the Southeast by using a wooden slat basket, the sort that orchid growers use. I pack this with live *Sphagnum*, plant my *Darlingtonia*, and place the plants under the bench near the front edge, where there is bright shade but protection from the full effects of the sun. I then water the basket through at least twice daily, especially in the warm season. The use of the slat basket along with comparatively porous *Sphagnum* results in a great deal of evaporative cooling of the rhizome and roots; the frequent watering both replaces lost water and cools the plant. Using this technique, I am able to get the plants to grow, including putting out pitchers during the season, stolon formation with young plants coming out between the slats of the baskets, and even spring flowering on occasion. However, the pitchers are never very tall and I do have losses.

Seeds must be fresh or stored in a dry container in the refrigerator. They are not difficult to germinate in indoor terrarium conditions in any medium, but after true leaves begin to emerge, the usual difficulties with growing adult plants ensue and there are losses. The seeds need not be stratified, although I think they germinate more promptly if they are sown and then cooled before placing them out to germinate.

SUNDEWS

Drosera

WITH THEIR GLANDULAR leaves glistening in the sun, sundews are certainly the jewels of the carnivorous plant world. There are an estimated 135 species of sundew in the world (Schlauer 1996), with seven of these living in North America. This number is an estimate because new species are being discovered yearly, particularly in Australia, and others are being repositioned at various subgeneric levels. The world's *Drosera* species range in size from the pygmy sundews of Australia, the rosettes of which barely exceed 1.5 cm in diameter, to the giant *Drosera regia* of South Africa, which has leaves ranging to 1 m in length. We need not be reticent about our seven species, however, because they offer a remarkable variation in leaf form and have a beauty all their own.

Description

This genus description for *Drosera* Linnaeus will be short on many details such as measurements, leaf shapes and sizes, and other features that will be described more exactly in each species discussion. *Drosera* plants are annual or perennial herbs in the form of a rosette; roots fibrous; stems very short in all species but *D. intermedia*; leaves mostly with prominent petioles, blades with considerable variation in form but all with mucilaginous stalked and sessile glands most heavily concentrated on the upper and lateral surfaces with a few beneath; scape tall and slender (*D. brevifolia* glandular); inflorescence a scorpioid raceme with unopened flower buds nodding at the top; raceme rarely bifid or trifid near the top; flowers actinomorphic and mostly with parts in fives; five sepals; five petals varying from white to rosy pink depending largely on species; sepals and petals persistent; five stamens ringed around superior green ovary; three styles deeply divided to near the bases so they superficially appear to be six; stigmas 0.5 mm and bulbous; seed capsules valvate; seeds minute but with

A fine stand of the thread-leaf sundew, *Drosera filiformis* variety *tracyi*, in southern Alabama. The glandular, elongate leaves glisten in the early morning sun (hence the name sundew). Note the bare areas between clumps of bunchgrass, which allow these large sundews to grow with minimum competition for space.

species-specific surface patterns and shapes under microscope; no particular flower fragrance noted. Chromosome number $2n = 20$, except in *Drosera anglica* $2n = 40$.

Synonyms, Common Names, and Etymology

There are no synonyms for the genus *Drosera*, which seems to have enjoyed a rather stable nomenclatural history compared to some other carnivorous plant genera. Common names include sundew and catch-fly for the genus as a whole, but there are particular common names for some of the species to be discussed. The origin of the common name sundew is obvious, particularly on a dewy morning with some residual background haze. The generic epithet is from the Greek *droseros*, meaning glistening in the sun.

Habitat

Depending on species and location, in the North *Drosera* species grow in *Sphagnum* bogs, and in the mountains and in the South in savannas and seeps and along stream and bay margins. I always think of the sundew as the last-ditch carnivorous plant in terms of site evaluation. Sundews usually grow in great numbers with various other carnivorous plant species. But sometimes the bog has become so depauperate that only sundews are found. If the location does not at least support sundews, other carnivorous plants are not likely to be there.

Pollination

The *Drosera* inflorescence is a raceme with a tall scape and multiple flowers attached by short pedicels at the nodding tip. The number of flowers varies by species, but ranges on average from five to twenty. One by one, the flowers open in order from the bottom up, with anthesis usually beginning at about 9:00 or 10:00 A.M. and flowers closing at about 2:00 P.M. The flowers only open fully in bright sunlight, and each flower remains open only for about five hours on one day, although occasionally a flower will open for a second day. If two adjacent flowers are seen open at once, the lowermost is likely in its second day.

Nothing is known about *Drosera* pollinators, although there is one mention of *Agapostemon radiatus* and *Bombus* as pollinating agents of *D. filiformis* variety *tracyi* in Florida, but with no references or further explanation (Wilson 1994). That pollinators exist is evident by the frequent presence of *Drosera* hybrids where more than one species grow at a site. However, to insure seed production even at the cost of missing the benefits of crossing, self-pollination does occur when the flower closes at the end of its brief anthesis. Therefore, cultivated plants that have flowered in a closed terrarium will usually yield seed.

Among plants, in general, pollen grains are often coated by a substance called pollenkitt, a mixture of oil and protein. Oil production is relatively metabolically expensive in plants, so the production of this substance likely serves a purpose. Although the value of pollenkitt is not known for certain, theories indicate that the substance might be involved in the pollination process as a lure for pollinators, as an adhesive so that the pollen grains will stick to pollinator bodies, or both. Pollenkitt has also been shown by extraction and liquid chromatography experiments to often have a fragrance of its own, usually different from any nectar fragrance of

the flower. This fragrance may serve as an additional attractant. Incidentally, the allergenic properties of most spe-

Flowers of *Drosera filiformis* variety *tracyi*. Two flowers are open simultaneously, so the lower is likely in its second day. This species has rosy pink petals. The five short stamens with their relatively large anthers and yellow pollen are evident. There are three longer, narrower styles, but each is deeply divided so they appear superficially to be six. Note that many of the small, knoblike stigmas have pollen on them. The three divided styles tend to array on the corolla of one-half of the flower. The buds below are already spent (note pink corolla tips protruding) and a few remaining unopened buds are behind the flowers.

cies' pollen grains have been shown to lie in their pollenkitts (Faegri and van der Pijl 1979).

While studying pollen grain viability in *Drosera* hybrids, I examined freshly stained wet mounts of pollen and noticed rather large quantities of yellow or golden oil droplets of varying size. Some very small ones are within the grains, which is not unusual in many species. But the numbers of larger and free-floating droplets was striking. The sheer volume was greater than any pollenkitt that might have eluted and aggregated from grain surfaces into droplets. Oil is produced in place of nectar in some species' flowers, but these are nearly all in the Southern Hemisphere (Faegri and van der Pijl 1979). In North American sundews, the oil production is by the anthers, not nectar glands.

One of the effects of pollenkitt is to aggregate pollen grains into clumps (Faegri and van der Pijl 1979), and such clumps are too large to be carried aloft for wind pollination, so the presence of anther oils and pollen clumping speaks for a living pollinating agent. Also, plants that produce relatively fewer pollen grains per flower have more pollenkitt and pollen grain clumping (Faegri and van der Pijl 1979). Indeed, in my investigations I have been impressed with the relatively small numbers of pollen grains produced by *Drosera* flowers.

In conclusion, although *Drosera* flowers are capable of self-pollination at the end of their brief anthesis, the presence of an unknown pollinator is clearly indicated by the evidence cited above. The intriguing production of relatively large quantities of metabolically expensive oil by *Drosera* anthers requires further study. Seeds are probably dispersed on the feet of birds or by floating on water.

Comments

In seedlings, the leaves of nearly all *Drosera* species have round or nearly round leaf blades, even in the species as *D. filiformis* and *D. linearis*, which have such divergent adult leaves. Depending on the species, nearly half a growing season may pass before the adult leaf morphology appears in newly emergent leaves.

Important taxonomic features of sundews include the presence or absence of scale-like stipules at the bases of petioles. If present, the form and attachment (or lack thereof) to the petiole are also important features. However, the seven North American species are not difficult to identify, so I will concentrate on more easily visible structures.

The length of the petiole (leaf stalk) varies depending on species, and the petiole lacks glands. It leads to the leaf blade, which varies from nearly round to filiform (threadlike), again depending on species. The blade is modified to behave as a trap. Stalked glands are located around the margins and base of the blade (and occasionally sparsely on the undersurface), with the stalk being prominently elongate and narrow. At the tip is a small, knobby gland usually colored red and covered with a secretion of sticky mucilage. A dense group of glands is present in the more central portion of the upper blade, with those glands around the edges of the group having very short stalks and those in the center being stalkless (ses-

A leaf blade of *Drosera intermedia*. Note the long tentacles with red glandular tips and, in this case, red stalks around the margins of the blade. In the center are additional glands with short or no stalks. At the top near the tip of the leaf blade, some stalked glands can be seen bent toward the blade center with a very small insect; here we view the nearly completed rapid phase of movement.

sile). These central glands also have usually smaller, glandular knobs that are bright red and have mucilage covering the surface.

Prey, usually small insects, either land on or crawl over the leaf blade surface. Several ideas have been proposed concerning what might lure prey to the leaves, including the red color of the glandular tips, a fragrance, or glistening of the mucilaginous tips in the sunlight. In some cases, there may be no allurement: a flying insect seeking rest may incidentally land on the leaf. In either event, the prey quickly becomes mired in the sticky mucilage. During attempts to escape, the prey contacts additional glands whose mucilage aggregates with that already encumbering the prey, until finally it is covered in the sticky secretion and presumably suffocates when its spiracles are plugged.

Meanwhile, the leaf is moving—movements that may not seem as dramatic as those in *Dionaea*, but still remarkable. As a result of stimulation and a small electrical discharge (Williams and Spanswick 1972; Williams 1976; Williams and Pickard 1979), the primary long, glandular, marginal tentacles attached to the prey by the sticky mucilage begin to bend inward toward the center of the leaf. Instead of the sensitive point being near the trichome base, as in *Dionaea*, in *Drosera* the point is along the narrowest part of the stalk in its upper end. This bending movement is termed the rapid phase, which Darwin (1875) noted to take three to twenty minutes depending on such factors as temperature and the general condition of the leaf and plant. After bending of the primary long tentacles begins, two slow-phase movements also occur. In the first, additional long, marginal tentacles not originally attached to the prey also begin to bend inward toward the center of the leaf blade, eventually joining mucilage with the first glands. In the second slow movement, which does not occur in all species, the leaf blade itself begins to bend upward, with the crease halfway along the blade so that it folds over the prey, similar to closing all the fingers of one hand together over the palm. At least the second of the slow movements (leaf bending) and to some extent the first (additional stalked gland bending) have been shown to be an actual growth event mediated by plant hormones (Bopp and Weber 1981). The hormone auxin (indoleacetic acid) builds up in the tip of the leaf as a result of the capture stimulus and then flows internally halfway toward the base of the blade, where cells of the lower layer of the blade are stimulated to grow rapidly and thus fold the leaf upward and over the prey.

At this point digestion can begin. The stalked marginal glands produce digestive juices with protease, esterase, and acid phosphatase (Parkes 1980). Thus, these glands serve a dual purpose: mucilage production for trapping and then digestive enzyme production. Digestion occurs on the leaf surface. Darwin (1875) showed that application of certain chemicals increased digestive juice secretion to the extent that it actually dripped or ran from the leaf blade in his conditions. Chandler (1978) showed that resident bacteria on the leaf also produce enzymes that assist plant enzymes with digestion. Absorption presumably occurs through the shorter (sessile) central blade glands. The physiology of *Drosera* has not been studied as intensively as *Dionaea*, and more work needs to be done.

There is only one well-understood insect associate of North American sundews, although others will most certainly be found. The caterpillar of the plume moth (*Trichoptilus parvulus*) feeds on *Drosera capillaris* only at night, being concealed beneath the leaf during the day. First discovered in Florida, the minute (1.5 mm in early instars) larva eats the stalked glands of the leaf blades and then consumes the leaf and any trapped prey. The larva begins by eating the mucilaginous glandular knob and then eats the remainder of the tentacle. Finding partially denuded *Drosera* leaves with fecal remains during the day would be a clue to the larva's presence. Initially, the larva seems to avoid entrapment by means of its tiny size and gland-by-gland approach to the job; later in development, bristles projecting from its body are easily withdrawn from globs of mucilage. Pupation usually occurs near the tips of the tall *D. capillaris* inflorescences (Eisner and Shepherd 1965).

Many species of North American *Drosera*, particularly those that grow in the North, form winter buds called hibernacula. As summer draws into autumn, newly arising leaf primordia remain dwarfed and form a tightly compacted spherule in the center of the plant. Sometimes the hibernacula are covered in hairs as further protection. When autumn deepens into winter, older leaves shrivel and turn black, but the hibernacula remain deep green and firm. In spring, each hibernaculum gives rise to a new plant. In a few *Drosera* species and hybrids, I have noticed that the hibernacula tend to bud into secondary hibernacula, each sprouting into plants in the spring.

Frances Wynne (1944) did some interesting work on the morphology of North American *Drosera* seeds. Wynne provided drawings showing a particular and consistent shape and surface morphology for each species, these being easily visible under a low-power dissecting microscope. Wynne's illustrations were reproduced in Gleason (1952). I have found the drawings to be very helpful in doing taxonomic and other work with *Drosera* species.

Cultivation Notes

Except for one or two species, North American sundews are relatively easy to grow. The peculiarities of each species will be mentioned in their respective sections.

Live *Sphagnum* seems to overwhelm most sundews, so I prefer to grow them in Canadian peat or a mixture of peat with silica sand. For continuous moisture, the pots should be placed in a saucer of water, and bright light is best. *Drosera* species lend themselves very nicely to growing in terraria because there is not much vertical growth, except in *Drosera filiformis*,

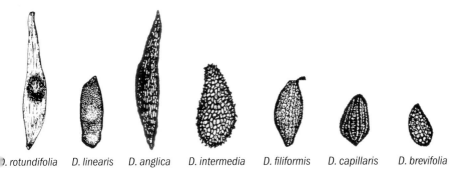

). rotundifolia   D. linearis   D. anglica   D. intermedia   D. filiformis   D. capillaris   D. brevifolia

A comparison drawing of seeds of the North American *Drosera* species. Adapted from Wynne (1944). (Used with permission.)

but even these plants seem to do well. If not exposed to insects, sundews benefit from a light monthly misting of fertilizer solution during the growing season, as described in the Introduction. If hibernacula-forming species are being grown, cool the plants for the winter. The hibernacula of *Drosera intermedia* develop at the tops of the tall central stems and should be pushed gently down so they set on the soil surface.

In cultivation, propagation will often occur on its own, with spent leaves giving rise to plant buds or fallen seed sprouting in the medium. Individual growing leaves can be cut and induced to bud using the method described in the Introduction. Recall that flowers of North American sundews self-pollinate as the flowers close each day. Seed can be harvested from the dry capsules and stored dry in the refrigerator or sown over the medium or into pots of fresh soil.

Drosera rotundifolia Linnaeus

Synonyms
Drosera septentrionalis, *Drosera rotundifolia* variety *comosa*

Common Name
Drosera rotundifolia is commonly known as the round-leaved sundew.

Description
More or less flat rosette when growing in the open, to 15 cm across. Petioles to 5 cm long, leaf blade suborbicular to 1.5 cm across, wider than long. Flower scapes glabrous, to 20 cm; corolla white, occasionally with pink veins, to 8 mm across; no fragrance. Prominent, hairless hibernacula form in the autumn.

Flowering Season
June to September

Distribution
The species' range is generally northern, extending into the Maritime Provinces (see Map 12). There is a break in the Midwest, and then *Drosera*

A cultivated *Drosera rotundifolia* in flower.

rotundifolia is more common in the Northwest. With further exploration, the broken areas of distribution in northern Canada into Alaska may prove to be larger and contiguous.

Habitat

Drosera rotundifolia is most frequently found growing in sphagnous bogs, often in the *Sphagnum* itself but also in adjacent patches of peat. The largest plants grow in the wettest locations. The species seems to survive being nearly half buried by exuberantly growing *Sphagnum* with no problems.

Map 12. Historical distribution of *Drosera rotundifolia*.

Comments

Drosera rotundifolia is probably the most studied sundew. Charles Darwin's book *Inectivorous Plants* (1875) was devoted almost entirely to his extensive experimentation with the species. In the carnivorous plant field, Darwin is most commonly recalled for his comments on the wonders of *Dionaea*, but the Venus flytrap and pitcher plants actually had much less space than *Drosera* in the book.

Due to its habit of growing in or closely adjacent to very acidic *Sphagnum*, sometimes *Drosera rotundifolia* appears only as the glistening leaf blades poking up between the strands of moss, or perhaps the prominent flower scape will be visible. As well as growing in Europe, the species is very common throughout boreal and montane bogs in North America.

Identification of *Drosera rotundifolia* is not difficult. While some early-season or young leaves may be nearly round, most often adult leaves are wider than long, a feature not shared with any other North American *Drosera*.

Leaves of *Drosera rotundifolia*. Note that the leaf blades are wider than long. The blade on the left contains the residual chitinous remains of prey.

Cultivation Notes

Cultivation of *Drosera rotundifolia* is relatively easy. The species grows equally well in a peat, sand-peat mix, or in live *Sphagnum*, if you do not mind your plants being partially buried in the *Sphagnum* as the moss grows. This can be prevented to some degree by using one of the smaller, closely clumping *Sphagnum* species as opposed to one of the coarse ramblers. The plants do best if quite wet. In autumn, a firm, dark green hibernaculum will form and will easily carry over to the next growing season. During winter, keep your plants cooler. Because this sundew is a low-growing rosette, the species lends itself nicely to terrarium growth, but you would have to cool the hibernacula during winter using one of the techniques discussed in the Introduction.

Drosera linearis Goldie

Common Name

Drosera linearis is commonly known as the linear-leaved sundew.

Description

Leaves erect, petioles 2–4 cm and flattened, leaf blades linear with strictly parallel sides when mature, 3–7 cm. Flower scape glabrous, 5–12 cm; petals white, rarely with pale pink tips; anthers and pollen orange; no flower fragrance; winter hibernaculum present.

Flowering Season

June into August

Distribution

Map 13 indicates the very limited, boreal distribution of *Drosera linearis*. Many of the shaded areas actually encompass relatively few good remaining marl fens with the plants, some of these with limited populations. The general regions are the lower eastern Maritime Provinces just into Maine and around the northern Great Lakes. Populations in Maine and some in Minnesota have been found relatively recently.

Habitat

The habitat of *Drosera linearis* is nearly restricted to marl fens, the character of which has been discussed in the Introduction (for additional information with particular emphasis on *Drosera linearis*, see Schnell 1980a, 1982b). Geological studies suggest that marl fens were once far more common and very large, particularly in the Great Lakes area, but natural evolution of landforms has severely reduced their numbers (Schwintzer 1978). In addition, since the arrival of Europeans and particularly in the past century, drainage of such areas for construction has increased.

Drosera linearis grows directly in the wet, basic marl, often in a centimeter or so of water. Plants tend to grow spaced: they rarely clump and even more rarely mass. The plants sometimes ascend onto hummocks if these are supporting nonsphagnous mosses or consist of marly peat and sand stacks. I have seen plants growing in the crevices of fallen logs lying about some fens. Similar to the situation with so many carnivorous plants, the pH and particular mineral content of this marl fen habitat seem less a requirement than an opportunity to grow with minimum competition.

Map 13. Historical distribution of *Drosera linearis*.

Comments

In any marl fen where *Drosera linearis* is present, it is often accompanied by two other sundew species, *D. anglica* and *D. rotundifolia*, but there is ecological stratification. *Drosera linearis*, as mentioned, grows in the open marl areas up to the bases of sphagnous hummocks and bog margins, only ascending those hummocks composed of marly sand or covered in nonsphagnous mosses. *Drosera rotundifolia*, in contrast, favors the surfaces of sphagnous hummocks and fen margins. *Drosera anglica* has a somewhat intermediate position often described as "one foot in and one foot out of the marl," growing around the bases of hummocks and sphagnous fen margins.

I have noticed an interesting positioning of *Drosera linearis* in most fens, particularly those close to or on the shore of one of the Great Lakes. The plants almost always grow in the landward half to third of small or medium fens, rarely in the area toward the lake. In very large, multi-

Drosera linearis looking unusually dewy on a dull, wet June morning in Michigan. The parallel leaf blade sides are visible. A few of the leaves are partially bent as a slow response to prey capture. The white petal tips are still folded in their buds on this cloudy day—they will likely not open at all.

A leaf of *Drosera linearis* in cultivation. The sides of the blade are always parallel and usually at least seven times longer than wide.

hectare fens, the species favors the eastern portion. The reasons for this are a mystery, unless the phenomenon is related to winds. *Drosera linearis* forms winter hibernacula, which are not closely bound to the loose, soupy marl. Prevailing, heavy autumn and winter winds may dislocate any hibernacula from western or lakeward sides and push them inland or east, depending on the fen size. This movement would have to occur prior to freezing of the fen water and snow cover.

Cultivation Notes

In my experience, *Drosera linearis* is the most difficult North American sundew to maintain consistently in cultivation. The problem lies with handling the smaller hibernacula and their tendency to sprout too early in the spring—or late winter—in greenhouse or terrarium cultivation. Generally, plants grown in Canadian peat kept quite wet and with the pots in the open do well the first season. Robust flowers yield quantities of viable seed. *Drosera linearis* seed stores well under dry refrigeration and germinates readily after stratification because the seeds mature in the autumn in nature.

Even in the cool greenhouse and terrarium (just above freezing), innate (obligate) dormancy seems to be finished by late winter here in Virginia. As longer, warmer days approach in March, the hibernacula promptly begin growing. Consequently, the cultivated plants have grown, flowered, set seed (due to self-pollination), and reformed another hibernaculum by June, when the plants are just getting started in nature. In a few weeks to a month, a second, shorter innate period of dormancy has passed, and the plants promptly resprout into smaller plants with weaker leaves and no flowers. If left alone, the plants linger in this state the remainder of the summer and early autumn and then reform smaller winter hibernacula for the winter here. I have found that allowing the plants to go through there double growth period is the best policy rather than trying to refrigerate hibernacula until May because there is loss by fungus attack in the refrigerator. But using the laissez faire approach results in some hibernacula loss over the second and ensuing winters anyway. The plants are then replaced by seed germination.

Drosera anglica Hudson

Synonyms
Drosera longifolia

Common Name
The common name of *Drosera anglica* is the great sundew.

Description
Petioles 3–7 cm, glabrous (smooth) to sparsely hairy-glandular; blades obovate-spatulate to linear-spatulate, 3–7 mm wide by 15–35 mm long. Flower scape glabrous, 5–25 cm long; flowers 8–10 mm wide; petals white; no fragrance; forms winter hibernacula.

Drosera anglica growing on the Bruce Peninsula in Ontario. The leaf blades are elongate, similar to *D. linearis*, but the sides are not parallel and are somewhat wider at the midpoint.

Flowering Season
June to August

Distribution
The range of *Drosera anglica* is somewhat broken across northern North America (see Map 14), but the species may be discovered in additional locations as exploration proceeds. The species tends to grow within the broad range of *Drosera rotundifolia*, although not in as many sites. Curiously, the distribution also includes Hawaii (see Comment below).

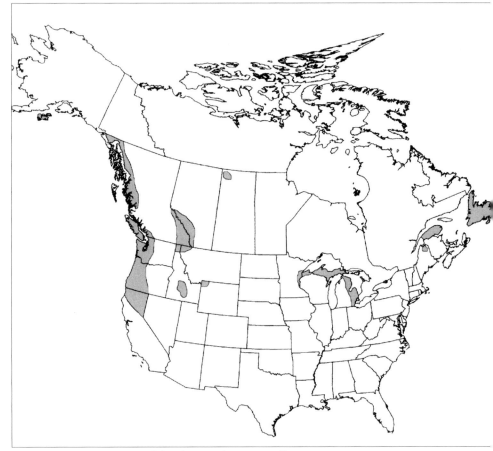

Map 14. Historical distribution of *Drosera anglica*.

Habitat

As discussed in the *Drosera linearis* section, *D. anglica* may grow with that species and *D. rotundifolia* in marl fens in the East, usually in a habitat intermediate between the open marl and any *Sphagnum* hummocks or fen margins. The species is also found in sphagnous bogs, often associated with *D. rotundifolia*.

Comments

Sites in the Alakai Swamp located on the island of Kauai in the Hawaiian archipelago are not shown on the North American distribution map for *Drosera anglica* (Map 14). These sites are of interest because the species is generally considered cool temperate or boreal. However, because Alakai Swamp is at 1500–2000 m elevation, temperatures are quite moderate.

A closer view of *Drosera anglica* in cultivation. Note that the mature blades widen gradually from the petiole end upward until about 65–70% of the blade length is reached. The blades remain at this width for about 20% of their length and then narrow acutely near the leaf tip.

There are never freezing temperatures, but night temperatures frequently drop to just above freezing and days are often cooler than the tropical lowlands. Within the continental ranges, winters are cold and hibernacula form, but hibernacula never form in the Hawaiian plants, even when they are grown from seed in North American areas. The plants of Alakai are generally smaller than in North America, and this characteristic carries through in plants grown on the continent. Instead of hibernacula, during winter or shortened photoperiods on Kauai, new leaves become progressively shorter until only a small winter rosette remains. As the seasonal photoperiod increases, newer leaves lengthen (Mazrimas 1987; Gon 1994; George Newman, personal correspondence). I have grown the Alakai plants from seed and find their lifespan shorter than continental plants. The Alakai Swamp is a nature preserve with several long trails, one of which has a boardwalk over a *Drosera anglica* site where the plants can be seen and photographed easily.

In 1955, Wood published a paper making a strong argument for the hybrid origin of *Drosera anglica*. Working mainly in northern Michigan, he first noted that the chromosome count for *D. anglica* is $2n = 40$, whereas all other North American sundews are $2n = 20$. Again, the hybrids of North American *Drosera* species are sterile, unlike, for example, the situation with *Sarracenia* species, where hybrids are interfertile (Wynne 1944; Wood 1955; Cheek 1993; Schnell 1995b). Very frequently when plant hybrids are sterile, doubling of the chromosome numbers allows them to become interfertile; such plants are often named as species.

During meiosis (reduction division), plants produce ova and pollen tube sperm nuclei with half the somatic chromosome number, so that their union produces another plant with the same somatic number. In some hybrids, however, chromosomes of the two parent plants are unable to match up properly, and sexual reproduction is thus impossible in the sterile hybrid. But if the chromosome number in the hybrid doubles, usually due to an aberrant arrest in meiosis caused by some external environmental stimulus, then the two sets of parent chromosomes are able to match up with each other when the pollen tube sperm nucleus unites with the ovum. Such hybrid chromosome doubling is called either allopolyploidy or, more commonly, amphiploidy. More details of this process can be found in standard college-level biology or botany textbooks. Estimates of plants of amphiploid origin generally range from as few as 25% (Rosenzweig 1995) to as many as 70–80% (Barrett 1989).

With his hybrid hypothesis in mind, Wood (1955) noted that *Drosera anglica* frequently grew in the same bogs as *D. linearis* and *D. rotundifolia.* The intermediacy in the appearance of hybrid plants when compared to the two parents (as in *Sarracenia*) indicated that *D. anglica* was likely the product of a union of its two companion sundews. By doing chromosome counts of plants identified as *D. anglica,* Wood also noted that some of the sterile plants (those that never set seed) had counts of $2n = 20$, indicating that they were sterile hybrids and not the amphiploid species, whereas other plants set abundant, viable seed; were $2n = 40$; and were the amphiploid species. Thus, not unexpectedly, hybridization was occurring on a regular basis.

Wood's (1955) next discovery was particularly fascinating. After examining many fens, he noted that some of the bogs had rather large numbers of *Drosera anglica* in them, whereas other fens great distances away had but a few individuals that were difficult to find, but proven to be the species. All the while, he ran across the sterile hybrid, *D. ×anglica.* His exciting conclusion was that speciation was still occurring in multiple bogs (polytopy).

In general, Wood (1955) was unable to discern *Drosera anglica* from *D. ×anglica* in the field, although in one place in his paper he did mention that the hybrid usually had shorter, more rounded leaf blades (similar to the hybrid *D. ×obovata* [*D. anglica* × *D. rotundifolia*]). For his studies, Wood used more exacting methods of chromosome counts and planimetry (two-dimensional measurement) of leaf surface cells and guard cells of stomata—such cells were definitely larger in the species than the hybrid, presumably due to doubled genetic material. However, differentiating *D. anglica* from *D. ×anglica* by simple inspection in the field is so difficult that a recent Michigan flora (Voss 1985) suggested referring to all such plants as the hybrid in the Great Lakes region.

After many years studying *Drosera anglica* and *D. ×anglica* in the field and in cultivation, I believe I can tell the two apart by means other than chromosome counting, measuring leaf surface cells, or examining pollen for viability under the microscope. The process involves three observations (Schnell 1999): (1) If plants produce viable seed, they are the species. *Drosera* hybrids do not produce viable seed and are unable to cross with each other or with species. (2) If you see plants in flower and have a millimeter ruler handy, the flowers of the species, *Drosera anglica*, are larger than those of the hybrid. The species' flowers average 8–10 mm across, whereas the hybrid's are 6–7 mm across. (3) The scapes, or flower stalks, of the species are thicker (1.5–2.0 mm average) than scapes of the hybrid (1.0–1.2 mm average).

When in the field in the growing season, at least two of the above characters should be present to evaluate in any plant. After awhile, you can dispense of the ruler. As with all measurements and sorting in biology, there are overlapping exceptions to the above criteria, but these minor

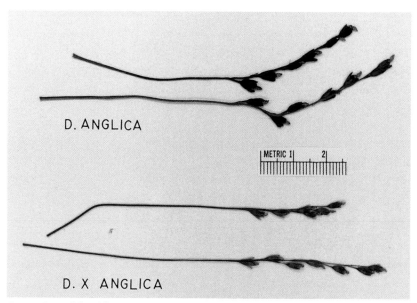

Comparison of dried flower stalks of *Drosera anglica* and *D. ×anglica* late in the season. Note that the scape of the species is thicker than that of the hybrid. Of course, with maturing seed, the dried flowers of the species are larger.

exceptions can be circumvented by making multiple examinations of the characters in the plant. The most consistent character is, of course, the presence or absence of viable seed production.

Dispersal Questions

Examining the distribution maps for *Drosera linearis* (Map 13) and *D. anglica* (Map 14), you may wonder how *D. anglica* became so widely distributed when *D. linearis* is so localized. Besides North America, *D. anglica* extends across northern Europe and even into the mountains of southern Europe. Except for small sites in the Northeast, *D. linearis* is largely confined to the Great Lakes region.

Dispersal to Kauai in the Hawaiian archipelago is most likely explained by carriage of seeds in mud on the feet of migrating plovers from Alaska. As often happens in island dispersal, there is a bottleneck, or founder effect, in which the limited genetic material may exhibit previously hidden variations that will be predominantly expressed in the new habitat, in this case smaller individuals and no hibernacula in plants in the Alakai Swamp.

But the continental differences in dispersal are more difficult to explain. As understood today, bird migration routes do not seem to work, nor does water flow. However, we do know that marl fens were once far larger and more common than today. Perhaps *Drosera linearis*, with its strict habitat requirements, is suffering from range reduction, while *D. anglica*, with more liberal habitat requirements, is able to maintain itself in what may have been a much larger range for both. Because *D. rotundifolia* often grows with *D. anglica* anywhere, and continuing species formation is apparently ongoing and polytopic (Wood 1955; and thus it is likely early in the species' evolutionary history as well), a distribution reduction for *D. linearis* is a possibility. But, in the end, we do not know for certain.

Cultivation Notes

Drosera anglica has about the same cultivation requirements as *D. rotundifolia* and is far easier to grow than *D. linearis*. It can be grown in Canadian peat or a small species of slow-growing *Sphagnum* that will not overwhelm the plants. Grow *D. anglica* in a wet medium and in bright light. The winter hibernaculum is about as sturdy as *D. rotundifolia*'s and certainly not as fussy as that of *D. linearis*. Seed is readily germinated and responds best to stratification. Seeds may be stored dry for several years in the refrigerator.

Drosera intermedia Hayne

Drosera intermedia is distinctive among the North American sundews in that the stem is lengthened and plants can be found growing to 20 cm tall. In side view, the growing rosette at the top of the stem forms a hemisphere.

Synonyms
Drosera longifolia, D. americana, D. foliosa, D. intermedia forma *corymbosa*

Common Name
Drosera intermedia is commonly known as the oblong-leaved sundew.

Description
In mature plants, stems elongate up to 20 cm in the South; leaves with glabrous petioles three to four times as long as blades; blades spatulate to obovate, to 5 mm wide and 15 mm long; leaves in hemispherical rosette. Flower scapes arise not centrally but from stem between leaves, arching at base upward; petals usually white, with occasional pink tinge; no fragrance; winter hibernacula present.

Flowering Season
June to August

Distribution
As indicated on Map 15, the species' distribution is limited to the East but is rather broken. Sites are chiefly concentrated in the Maritime Provinces and New England, around the Great Lakes, and in the Atlantic and Gulf coastal plains.

Habitat
Drosera intermedia prefers an extremely wet habitat, often growing in floating debris in open water. In the North, plants are equally at home in

Sphagnum and wet peat lake, stream, and aqueous blowout margins or mats. In the South, the species does grow in pine savannas, but it is most robust adjacent to streams; ponds; and low, very wet areas, particularly on the margins of bays.

Comments

Generally, *Drosera intermedia* plants are smaller in the North than in the South. This characteristic tends to remain constant in cultivation. The largest plants I have seen (to 20 cm in height) are around the margins of the Carolina Bays in the Carolinas. These plants grow in shallow, acidic water and receive partial shading during parts of the day, but are not etiolated, having good color and sturdy tissue.

Distinguishing *Drosera intermedia* from other species is not difficult. In northern sites, there might be some initial confusion with *D. anglica*. The leaves, particularly the blades, of *D. intermedia* are much smaller than those of *D. anglica*. The flower scapes of North American sundews arise from the center of the rosette and grow straight up, with the exception of *D. intermedia*, where the scapes arise from the stems between leaves and therefore grow out at an angle initially and then become vertical, resulting in a somewhat offset appearance. Finally, the hemispherical pattern of the rosette of *D. intermedia* is unique.

The flowers of *Drosera intermedia* often exhibit vegetative apomixes, with plantlets appearing in place of flower parts in the flower. These plantlets can be rooted (see Introduction).

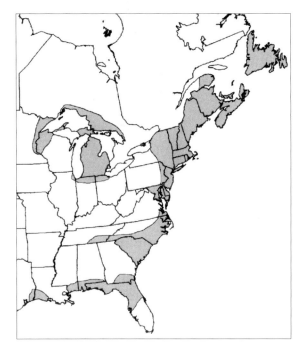

Map 15. Historical distribution of *Drosera intermedia*.

Drosera intermedia in Columbus County, North Carolina. The hemispherical rosette is raised off the ground by the stem. Note the flower scapes arching out from between the leaves below and then ascending.

Plants of *Drosera intermedia* form prominent hibernacula in the autumn. These grow in the center of the rosette at the top of the stem. Some stems remain erect over the winter and support the hibernacula in the air, but most bend to adverse weather and fall to the ground or into the water and sprout the following spring.

Cultivation Notes

Drosera intermedia is easy to grow, whether in terraria, greenhouses, or outdoor bogs. Due to the long stem, which is able to lift the rosette above the growing moss, this species grows well in *Sphagnum* as well as peat. The plants should be grown in very wet medium under bright light. I have even grown *D. intermedia* directly in the water and debris of drain trays, where the plants come up between pots. The hibernaculum is sturdy and easily managed, but it is better to push it straight down against the peat surface for best rooting in the spring. There is abundant seed set from self-pollination, and the seeds store well for years in a dry, refrigerated vial. Seeds sprout readily and vigorously when sown on the surface of peat.

Drosera filiformis Rafinesque

Drosera filiformis, with its unique filiform leaves and rosy pink flowers, is easily identified and stands out at a distance on a dewy morning.

Synonyms

Drosera tenuifolia, Drosera tracyi (in part)

Common Names

Two common names for *Drosera filiformis* are thread-leaf sundew and dew-thread.

Description

Leaves erect, petiole 1.0–2.0 cm, blends into 25–50-cm filiform blade; glands red or green depending on variety. Flower scape glabrous, sometimes partially suffused with red, and slightly taller than leaves; flower rosy pink, 1.0–2.0 cm in diameter depending on variety; no flower fragrance; large, hirsute hibernaculum.

Flowering Season
May to June

Distribution
Map 16 indicates the distribution of the species. The darker gray, mostly in the Northeast and mid-Atlantic, represents the distribution of *Drosera filiformis* variety *filiformis*, with the small dot off the coast of Maine representing a colony found in Nova Scotia. Note that there is also an area in the Florida Panhandle. The lighter gray along the Gulf Coast represents the distribution for *Drosera filiformis* variety *tracyi*. There is anecdotal evidence of a site in South Carolina, but no information on it was ever published, there is no herbarium sheet, and the species has never been found during Natural Heritage surveys.

Habitat
This species grows in damp savannas, sandy seeps, and margins of slow streams and shallow bays, frequently accompanying other carnivorous plants. *Drosera filiformis* does not grow in *Sphagnum*.

Comments
Drosera filiformis was described by the colorful naturalist Constantine Samuel Rafinesque (1808 in

Map 16. Historical distribution of *Drosera filiformis*. The darker gray areas, predominantly in the Northeast and mid-Atlantic and including a site in Nova Scotia and locations in the Florida Panhandle, represent variety *filiformis*. The lighter gray areas along the Gulf Coast represent variety *tracyi*.

Diels 1906). Because he listed the plant as a North American boreal with red glands, Rafinesque clearly was describing the northern expression of the species. Nearly a century later in the Droseraceae section of *Das Pflanzenreich*, Diels (1906) dealt with *Drosera filiformis* and then described variety *tracyi*, the green southern expression. After the epithet, Diels inserted the Latin phrase "*Macfarlane msc. sub titulo speciei*," which translates as "Macfarlane in manuscript(?) under the title species." If the abbreviation *msc.* indeed means "manuscript," this would suggest a prepared manuscript somewhere with the species *Drosera tracyi* appropriately described. Such a work was never found, published or unpublished. Publication of the species *D. tracyi* is usually ascribed to Macfarlane's chapter in Bailey's (1914) *Standard Cyclopedia of Horticulture* in which he referred to the red plants as *D. filiformis* and the green as *D. tracyi*. However, the section in Bailey, which is so often used as a reference for the combination *D. tracyi*, does not constitute effective publication of the species originally (it was preceded by variety *tracyi* in Diels 1906) or as a new combination. Therefore, *D. tracyi* seems to be essentially a *nomen nudum* and is illegitimate.

So, what of the *msc.*, the possible manuscript? In a 1995 letter to me, Peter Taylor seems to have solved the mystery. He mentioned that a frequent practice in those days was to write the newly intended species on the herbarium sheet, thus *handwritten* or *manuscript*, abbreviated *msc.* Actual publication never was accomplished. This explanation would seem to lay to rest the concept of *Drosera tracyi* as a species, unless someone would wish to publish it now. But, beyond that, I believe there are important biological features indicating that the red northern and green southern expressions of *Drosera filiformis* are in fact one species (see Schnell 1995).

Among the features indicating one species with two infraspecies is the identity of the seeds from the two varieties. They have exactly the same appearance, including size, as described and pictured by Wynne (1944). Seed morphology in North American sundews is distinct for each species (Wynne 1944; Wood 1966; personal observations).

Another argument for a single species arises from the study of hybrids.

As mentioned in the section covering *Drosera anglica*, hybrids of North American *Drosera* species are not difficult to produce (several occur naturally), but they are entirely sterile with nonviable pollen and no viable seed production. Mazrimas produced a hybrid between *D. filiformis* variety *filiformis* and variety *tracyi* and published it as the cultivar 'California Sunset' (see Variety *tracyi* Diels section). Mazrimas kindly provided me with pollen samples and dried, season's end flowers from his cultivars. Studies indicated that the pollen was viable and the dried flowers contained viable seeds with *D. filiformis* morphology. When the seeds were sown, healthy seedlings grew. Therefore, we have completely the opposite of what we would expect if cultivar 'California Sunset' was a hybrid between two North American *Drosera* species, thus strongly supporting the concept of two infraspecies, varieties *filiformis* and *tracyi* of the species *D. filiformis*.

A variation of *Drosera filiformis* variety *tracyi* with white flowers and lack of red pigment suffusion of the leaf petioles has been found in Alabama. This interesting form maintains its character in cultivation. Although not yet reported, I fully expect an anthocyanin-free form of variety *filiformis* to turn up one day. There would be some difficulty in discerning such a plant from a disjunct variety *tracyi*, but variety *filiformis* is smaller and has a unique anther feature. Under magnification, one can see that the anthers of about 75–80% of variety *tracyi* are separated into two lobes by the connective at the tip of the stamen filament. In addition to being smaller, the anther lobes of variety *filiformis* are nearly always joined at their distal ends.

The flowers of *Drosera filiformis* seem to be compass flowers to some degree. Plants studied at a site in Florida all opened facing just south of east, never west, and they did not turn during the day (Wilson 1994). It would be interesting to see if this is true of other *Drosera* species and whether digging up the plants, potting them, and turning them 180° would affect the direction flowers faced when they opened. In the greenhouse, the flowers also open facing east.

The hibernacula of *Drosera filiformis* are large and hardy. They are covered with a rather dense mat of hairs compared to other sundews with hibernacula, those of variety *filiformis* being most dense. In the spring, expanding leaves cause the mat to part.

There are disjunct populations of *Drosera filiformis* variety *filiformis* in Bay and Washington Counties north of Panama City, Florida. We are faced with the same possible explanations as for presence of *Dionaea* in the Apalachicola National Forest east of there: (1) they may have been planted there by someone; (2) the populations may be remnants of a once wider distribution, or (3) they may have arisen from propagules carried there by some natural activity. I think we can eliminate the first possibility with some certainty because there are too many sites and the nature of the sites—seeps on the margins of lime sinkholes—are so consistent. Rather than being remnant populations, there are several factors suggesting natural movement to the sites. As with *Dionaea*, these include the populations being directly under a branch of the Atlantic bird migration

A hibernaculum of *Drosera filiformis* variety *tracyi* in early spring in cultivation. The blackened stumps of last year's leaves ring the structure. Emergent green spring leaves are opening the hair mat.

flyway and the uniform appearance of the variety *filiformis* plants, which are somewhat smaller than those in northern populations and a deeper red. The relative size, deep red glands, and pigment suffusion into the leaf blades are maintained in cultivation and are in striking contrast to plants from the mid-Atlantic sites.

Infraspecies and Cultivar
I recognize two infraspecies, acknowledging two schools of thought: one for the infraspecies and another for two species. Opinion seems about evenly split in various floras and papers in the literature.

Variety *filiformis*
This is the autonymic variety (varietal and species epithet the same). Wynne's (1944) use of variety *typica* is not acceptable. This is the smaller variety, which grows in the northeast, mid-Atlantic, and Bay and Washington Counties, Florida, where it can be found in seeps around the shores of a large series of lime sinkholes, sometimes in company with variety *tracyi* (Anderson 1991). The leaves range to 25–30 cm in length and have prominent red glands, sometimes with red pigment suffused in the blade tissue, particularly strongly in the Florida sites. The flowers measure from 1.0 to 1.3 cm across.

Variety *tracyi* Diels
This is the larger variety, which grows along the Gulf Coast. The longer leaves range to 50 cm and are entirely green (except for occasional infusion of red in petiole bases) with colorless glands, although some believe them to be a very pale orange. The larger flowers are 2.0 cm across.

Drosera filiformis 'California Sunset'
Hybrids have yet to be found where the two varieties grow together around a few lime sinkholes north of Panama City, Florida, although I would not be surprised if they were found one day. To date, there are no observations on possibly differing flowering periods for the two varieties there. However, hybrids are easily produced in cultivation, and one produced by J. A. Mazrimas in 1973 has been registered as a cultivar, *Drosera filiformis* 'California Sunset' (Robinson 1981a). The hybrid cultivar is

nearly intermediate in all characters, particularly leaf color. Heterosis (hybrid vigor) is indicated by the leaves being nearly as long as in variety *tracyi*, and the hibernaculum frequently buds. The anther lobes of the cultivar are separate and the stamen filament green, as is often the case with variety *tracyi*.

Cultivation Notes

Drosera filiformis in its two varieties is another easily grown sundew. Both lend themselves to growth in a terrarium, although variety *filiformis* might be more suitable because of its smaller size. The plants do nicely in Canadian peat kept uniformly damp. The leaves seem particularly adept at capturing fungus gnats and small fruit flies. The winter hibernaculum

Drosera filiformis variety *filiformis* in Columbus County, North Carolina. Notice the red gland tips and general reddish aspect to the plants.

Drosera filiformis variety *tracyi* in Alabama. Except for some suffused red pigment in the petioles, the leaves are green and the glands colorless. The bright rosy pink flowers are easily spotted in the field.

is heavy and sturdy, but is subject to rot if kept too warm. The wet, dense hair mat covering the bud may give an illusion of the structure having rotted, but touching discloses that it is quite firm when intact.

Drosera capillaris Poiret

Synonyms
Drosera rotundifolia variety *capillaris, Drosera minor, Drosera brevifolia* variety *major*

Common Name
Drosera capillaris is commonly known as the pink sundew.

Description
Leaves in flattened rosette averaging 3.5–4.0 cm across; petioles sparsely glandular-pilose, 1.0–3.0 cm long; blades spatulate, 0.5–1.0 cm long by 3–5 mm wide. Flower scape glabrous; flowers to 1.0 cm in diameter; petals white to pale pink; no fragrance; no hibernaculum.

Flowering Season
May to August

Distribution
Drosera capillaris is very common in the coastal plain from southeastern Virginia down to eastern Texas (see Map 17). There is a disjunct population in south-central Tennessee.

Habitat
Drosera capillaris grows in the sandy, peaty soils of savannas, along bay margins, and on the edges of shallow bodies of water. The species may be associated with *Sphagnum* but does not usually grow in it.

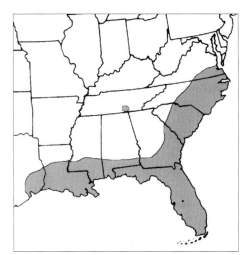

Map 17. Historical distribution of *Drosera capillaris*.

Comments

Although *Drosera capillaris* is commonly called the pink sundew, its flowers are not always pink; they are often white. Flower color cannot be used as an absolute to differentiate the species from *D. rotundifolia*. Other factors such as habitat (*capillaris* in sand or peat versus *rotundifolia* in *Sphagnum*), leaf blade shape (longer than wide versus wider than long), and hibernaculum (absence or presence) are better characters to tell one species from the other.

Drosera capillaris is undoubtedly the most ubiquitous sundew in the Southeast, often being the only carnivorous plant in a habitat accompanied by the bladderwort, *Utricularia gibba*. If a habitat in the southeastern coastal plain does not support this sundew, it will probably not support any carnivorous plants.

A *Drosera capillaris* growing in Brunswick County, North Carolina. The spatulate leaf is shaped much like *Drosera intermedia*, but *D. capillaris* does not grow a long stem, is smaller when mature, and the flower scape arises straight up from the center of the rosette.

In the southern extremes of its distribution, rather large examples of *Drosera capillaris* are frequently found with rosettes measuring up to 6–7 cm. These may grow as an entire colony of large plants or interspersed among more typically sized plants. Such large plants tend to maintain their size in cultivation and often have more leaves per rosette than the usual plants. These require further study and may indeed be hybrids in some instances.

Cultivation Notes
Drosera capillaris is easy to grow. It has no hibernaculum; the plant is a perennial and will continue growing new leaves throughout the winter if kept in a warm, bright place; therefore, this sundew is ideal for terrarium growing. The species does well in peat or peat-sand mix, which should be kept continuously damp. The flowers set seed readily and the seed may be sown for more plants or stored dry in the refrigerator.

Drosera brevifolia Pursh

This sundew is the smallest of our North American species. *Drosera brevifolia* would be difficult to see in the field if it were not for its occasional massing and its disproportionately larger flower.

Synonyms
Drosera annua, Drosera leucantha, Drosera pusilla

Common Names
Drosera brevifolia is commonly known as shortleaf sundew and dwarf sundew.

Description
Annual or biennial flat rosette to 2.0 cm across; short, scarcely petiolate-cuneate (wedge-shaped) leaves with slightly curved to flattened free ends. Flower scape, pedicels, and calyces markedly glandular; flowers 1.0–1.6 cm across; petals white to pale pink; no fragrance. There is no hibernaculum.

Flowering Season
April to May

Distribution
Drosera brevifolia closely hugs the arc of the Atlantic to Gulf coastal plain from eastern Virginia into eastern Texas, with a break in south-central Louisiana (see Map 18; Murry and Urbatsch 1979). There are also several disjunct locations, as indicated on the map.

Habitat
Drosera brevifolia is generally found in savannas and along seeps, but also in clay areas in its inland sites. The species appears capable of withstanding a drier habitat than most sundews. Sometimes the plants are intermingled among other carnivorous plants, whereas in other locations they may mass on an embankment or shallow ditch margin.

Comments
In the 1960s there was a small taxonomic tempest concerning *Drosera brevifolia*. It seemed to begin when Wood (1960) of Harvard published his chapters on *Drosera* and *Sarracenia* species of the Southeast "toward a generic flora of that region." Wood felt that the epithet *brevifolia* was valid and that *D. annua* was an unnecessary synonym. In 1962, Shinners published his paper on *Drosera* of the Southeast, eliminating *D. brevifolia* and replacing it with two species, *D. annua* Reed and *D. leucantha* Shinners. In the paper, Shinners decried Wood and the Harvard generic flora project in no uncertain terms and called into question Wood's methods. Shinners (1962) did offer the reasoning for his taxonomic choices, but it contained some questionable

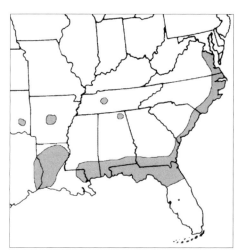

Map 18. Historical distribution of *Drosera brevifolia*.

Drosera brevifolia in Columbus County, North Carolina. Note the very short petioles that are more or less continuous with the leaf blade expansion. The wedge-shaped blades have blunted tips. If exposed to bright light all day, the plants are frequently deep red.

A flowering scape of *Drosera brevifolia*. The most striking feature, unique among North American sundews, is the glandular nature of the scape, pedicels, and calyces (sepal groups), which may require a hand lens to appreciate. The entire plant rosette may be no more than 2.0 cm across, yet the flower is 1.0–1.6 cm across—another striking feature. The petals may be white or pink, as in this example.

logic and relied heavily on such things as flower color. Wood (1966) replied, remarking that Shinners's paper was "unnecessarily ill-humored," and laid out his careful reasoning for the one species, *D. brevifolia*. Wood included a cogent review of herbarium sheets, history, and the identity of the seeds of the herbarium specimens, with seed morphology having been established by Wynne (1944). Unfortunately, during the four-year lapse, several floras were completed using Shinners's nomenclature (such as Radford et al. 1968).

According to Shinners (1962), *Drosera leucantha*, with white flowers, supposedly predominated along the Atlantic Coast. *Drosera annua*, with pink flowers, was most prominent in the western part of the range and inland. However, Shinners admitted much intermingling in between, where the two purported taxa often grew in the same site. Now that the dust has settled on this argument, most taxonomists and I concur on one species, *D. brevifolia*, with variation.

Identifying *Drosera brevifolia* depends on recognizing the very short, wedge-shaped leaves in a small rosette. Younger plants of the common *D. capillaris* can be distinguished from *D. brevifolia* adults of the same size rosette by noting leaf shape and petiole length. Of course, if *D. brevifolia* is in flower, one will note the larger flower in proportion to the small rosette, and magnification discloses the unique glandular scape, pedicels, and calyces. Also, from experience I have learned that when *D. brevifolia* plants grow in light colored, sandy soil in full sunlight, they have a distinctive, very deep red coloration that is different from the brighter red of *D. capillaris*.

Cultivation Notes

Drosera brevifolia is a determinate plant in horticultural terms; that is, after growing vegetatively for one or two years, the plant flowers and then dies at the end of the season, relying on seed for continuation of the colony. This causes some problems in cultivation because the grower must be certain to spread seed over the surface of the soil in the old pot or a new one to ensure having plants the next spring.

Other than this determinate nature, the plant grows as easily as *Drosera capillaris* in peat or peat-sand mix kept moist and placed in good light. There are no problems with seed germination, which does not require stratification. *Drosera brevifolia* grows well in a terrarium, as long as the plant is not subjected to standing water on its leaves. I do notice more rot with *D. brevifolia*, but this can be prevented by not having the soil as wet and keeping water droplets off the leaves. Cold wetness in cultivation is not good, and you may wish to hold over the late summer seed for spring germination.

Drosera Hybrids

As I have mentioned several times, North American sundews hybridize rather easily and some hybrids can be found in nature. However, the hybrids are sterile and cannot cross with each other or back into parent species. As is the case with *Sarracenia* hybrids, *Drosera* hybrids' characters are intermediate between the parent species. The hybrid *Drosera* ×*anglica* was discussed in the *D. anglica* section, and the artificial hybrid cultivar *D. filiformis* 'California Sunset' is covered under *D. filiformis*.

Drosera ×*obovata* Mertens and Koch

Drosera ×*obovata* is a relatively common hybrid wherever *D. anglica* and *D. rotundifolia* are found growing together. The hybrid can be seen most prominently in the Great Lakes region and in the bogs of northern California and western Oregon, but is also occasionally found in southeastern Canada and New England.

The plant's characteristics are intermediate between the parents' and are best identified by the leaf, which is not as rounded as *Drosera rotundifolia* and not as long as *D. anglica*. Of course, the hybrid has a hibernaculum. The most difficult identification problems are in some Great Lakes bogs where *D. anglica*, *D. rotundifolia*, and *D. linearis* may be found together. As mentioned in the section on *D. anglica*, the hybrid between *D. linearis* and *D. rotundifolia* (*D.* ×*anglica*) may look very much like *D.*

×*obovata* and experience is required to separate the two. Of course, both have nonviable pollen and seeds. Comparatively, the leaf blade of *D.* ×*obovata* is shorter and more rounded than the blade of *D.* ×*anglica*.

Drosera ×hybrida Macfarlane

Macfarlane (1899) identified this hybrid in a New Jersey bog among an abundance of *Drosera filiformis* variety *filiformis* and *D. intermedia*. He noted the intermediate characteristics of the plant, saw that seed was nonviable, and did extensive microscopic anatomical studies to demonstrate the intermediacy of various cell sizes and shapes. To the eye in the field, the hybrid tends more toward *D. filiformis* variety *filiformis*, although Macfarlane felt that his anatomical studies showed characters that in sum leaned a bit more toward *D. intermedia*. The hybrid's flower is intermediate in diameter, but is usually whiter, as in *D. intermedia*. The leaves of *D.* ×*hybrida* are shorter than in *D. filiformis* variety *filiformis*, being up to 9.0 cm in length as compared to 25 cm. Also, the hybrid leaf widens ever so slightly at its midpoint along its course. Without experience and flowers, however, one would have a difficult time distinguishing the hybrid from a young plant of *D. filiformis* variety *filiformis*.

Several years ago, Richard Sivertsen kindly showed me the type location for *Drosera* ×*hybrida*, now in Bass River State Forest. The original bog had been dammed into a shallow lake, and an artificial, small sand beach had been installed for recreational bathers. Just adjacent to one end of the sand was a few-meter remnant of the original location, where the plants were readily found. Since then, the beach was widened and the site has been destroyed. However, Sivertsen has since found a few other locations for the hybrid in New Jersey. It is nowhere common, and I have not seen it outside of New Jersey, even in the few locations where the parent sundews grow together, such as southeastern North Carolina or in northern Florida north of Panama City.

Drosera anglica × D. linearis

I first saw and studied this hybrid in Chippewa County, Michigan (Schnell 1995a). What roused my attention were patches of massing sundews that were a deep red and appeared initially to be *Drosera anglica* growing on low hummocks. Such clustering and coloration of that species is unusual. On closer examination, I wondered if the plants might actually be *D. linearis*, however, again the clustering and coloring is unusual for that species. Typical *D. linearis* and *D. anglica* plants were also plentiful in the fen. Further examination and observation of plants in cultivation disclosed nonviable pollen and seeds. The plants were morphologically intermediate between *D. anglica* and *D. linearis*, and I concluded that the plants were hybrids with remarkable heterosis. Since the initial work, I have found similar populations of this hybrid elsewhere in northern Michigan, where they always grow in vigorously dense stands with the parent species.

Drosera capillaris × *D. intermedia*

Although discovered in Pender County, North Carolina, in 1984 (Sheridan 1987), this purported hybrid apparently has not been studied further because there are no additional reports from the author. Growing in a wet seep adjacent to a pasture with *Drosera brevifolia, D. capillaris*, and *D. intermedia*, the suspected hybrid seemed most allied with *D. capillaris* and *D. intermedia*. The plants were described as having a stem like *D. intermedia*, although not as long, and broader petioles and larger leaf blades as in *D. capillaris*. The scape curved outward and then vertically as in *D. intermedia*. Examination of a withered flower microscopically disclosed presumably aborted seeds, but Sheridan was to check for viability. There is no mention of pollen viability studies on fresh flowers. There were very few examples of the suspected hybrid at the location.

I viewed the plants at the reported location in 1989 and agree that they have characteristics strongly suggestive of hybrid origin. Being so few, I did not remove plants for further study. Other pressing activities pushed my interest in this site to the background and I have not been back since. During my field activities, I watch for similar hybrids in other areas where the possible parents are abundant, but have not seen others, although such a hybrid is clearly possible.

BUTTERWORTS

Pinguicula

A LONG WITH BLADDERWORTS (*Utricularia*), butterworts (*Pinguicula* Linnaeus) are members of the family Lentibulariaceae. At first glance, the butterworts seem a bit plain compared to other carnivorous plants, such as *Dionaea* with its gaping, toothed jaws; the prominent, graceful pitchers of *Sarracenia* and *Darlingtonia*; and the glistening, almost bejeweled sundews. But you will see that butterworts have their own subtle beauty and complexities, both in their carnivorous leaves and unusual flower structure. Indeed, some find butterworts so attractive that the International *Pinguicula* Study Group has been formed to research and share information about these plants. Based in Europe, the group publishes an informative, occasional newsletter.

Description

Terrestrial, usually perennial herbs with rosettes and fibrous roots; stem less than 5 mm; leaves decumbent (or nearly so), elliptic to oblong with upwardly recurved margins, glandular upper surfaces, short (2–3 mm) or no petiole, leaf tips bluntly pointed; flower scapes 3–20 cm, arising from between leaves at plant axis, lightly glandular (densely hirsute in *P. villosa*), one to many scapes per plant; flower nodding and zygomorphic; calyx five partially fused sepals and bilobed, with three upper, partially fused sepals and two lower, lightly glandular; corolla with two partially fused petals in upper lip and three partially fused petals in lower lip, opening of corolla with prominent glandular hairy palate of lower lobe, a cylindrical short tubular portion of the corolla lined by glandular hairs and containing the stamens and pistil, ending in a spur of variable length; two stamens with stout filaments curved around the ovary; anthers beneath the stigma lobe and having abundant yellow pollen; pistil with apronlike stigma overlying the anthers; short, stout style and spherical, glandular ovary between the stamen filaments; seed capsule to 6 mm, spherical to slightly pear shaped, brown, two valved upon opening; seeds dark brown and minute. Chromosome numbers vary among the species.

The butterwort *Pinguicula vulgaris* Linnaeus growing on the border of a Michigan fen. The bright green rosettes with their nodding purple flowers stand out like little stars among other plants.

Habitat

In the North and West, butterworts grow in wet places, including fens, cobbles, and seeping rocks and slopes. In the South, the plants grow in wet areas in savannas, along bays and stream margins, and in ditches.

Pollination

In contrast to the actinomorphic flowers of sundews, pitcher plants, and the Venus flytrap, the flowers of the family Lentibulariaceae are zygomorphic. Actinomorphic flowers are radially symmetrical—one can make an infinite number of cuts through the center of the flower to get two equal halves. Zygomorphic flowers are bilaterally symmetrical, that is, the flower can only be halved through one plane. Zygomorphic flowers are common in the plant world and always indicate that an animal pollinator works the flower. The bilateral symmetry of the flower helps properly line up the insect, bat, or bird in its approach to the flower, much like guidance systems on an airport runway. The pollinator is aided in its choice of the flower by fragrance; experience with similar flowers; and, for insects, color patterns that reflect "bee color" light in blues, violets, and ultraviolet (Kevan 1978, 1979).

The corolla of *Pinguicula* flowers is composed of five partially fused petals with free petal tips: two petals fused into an upper lip and three into a lower lip. The free petal tips result in the corolla being lobed to varying degrees. As you look at the nodding flower head on, there is an opening in the center of the corolla and a hairy, usually yellow, tonguelike structure (the palate) that most often is protruding. A ridge of glandular hairs is located inside the cylindrical tube and behind the palate, with additional hairs on the inner tube walls. Studies of these three sets of glandular hairs indicate that their morphology is species specific (Wood and Godfrey 1957; Godfrey and Stripling 1961; Casper 1966; Godfrey and Wooten 1981). To see these sets of hairs, you must dissect the flower and observe the hairs with a dissecting microscope.

Because the flower is nodding, the stamens and pistil are inverted and are attached inside the tube to the receptacle on the scape, at what is the top of the flower in the living plant. At the extreme end of the flower tube, the corolla narrows into a nectar-collecting spur.

Cultivated plants of *Pinguicula primuliflora* Wood & Godfrey. Note the decumbent, elliptic leaves with recurved (rolled) margins and leaf surfaces prominently dotted with glands. The younger leaves arising from the plant's central axis are erect but become decumbent as they mature.

Pinguicula's internal flower structure and arrangement of stamens and ovary encourages cross-pollination. Prior to the first edition of this book (Schnell 1976), I had worked out the probable mechanism of pollination based on flower structure, although mechanisms of butterwort pollination have not been reported in the literature to date. The pollinator, likely a small, native bee, would be lured to the flower and alight on the lower lip of the corolla, then work its way into the tube, over the palate and the ridge behind it, to get at the nectar pooled in the lower tube and spur. As the bee entered the tight tube cylinder, any pollen on the bee from another flower would be smeared over the apronlike outer receptive surface of the stigma. As the bee withdrew from the close confines of the tube, friction would cause the flaplike stigma to be pulled upward, thus exposing the anthers. Fresh pollen would then be deposited on the bee, and any pollen that might be smeared against the nonreceptive undersurface of the stigma would not be important.

Field botanists doing floristic studies often quickly collect specimens for their plant presses. There is a record (unfortunately, I cannot find the reference) of a flower of *Pinguicula lutea* in a major herbarium with a small native bee inside the flower, pressed for posterity. In 1997, long after my hypothetical analysis of *Pinguicula* pollination, I visited the Harvard Botanical Museum in Cambridge, Massachusetts, for the first time. I particularly wanted to see the famed "Glass Flowers" exhibit, a large series of truly remarkable panels and sculptures executed in colored glass between 1887 and 1936 by the Blaschkas of Dresden, Ger-

An angled view of the flower of *Pinguicula ionantha* Godfrey. Note the upper lip with two partially incised petal tips, or lobes, and the lower lip with three lobes. The exserted, yellow palate is clearly visible. At the base of the corolla and to the left is the short, cylindrical tube with purple pigment; the blunt but prominent spur extends downward.

many. This work was commissioned by Professor George Goodale of Harvard (Schultes and Davis 1982). I perused the several hundred enchanting and very accurate exhibits, pleased to see several carnivorous plants represented. I was startled, however, when I came across a panel showing a *Pinguicula* flower series: one sculpture showed a bee entering the flower and a second illustrated the bee exiting, lifting the stigma apron as it did so. As far as I know, Professor Goodale never published this information nor does it seem to have been published by anyone back then, but the process was faithfully executed.

Following pollination, the usually spherical or sometimes pear-shaped seed capsules mature over a period of six to eight weeks. The capsules turn brown as they dry and dehisce in a bivalved fashion, releasing quantities of dusty seed.

No natural hybrids of U.S. or Canadian butterworts have been described, and so far attempts at artificial crossings have failed. Such is not the case among the numerous Mexican *Pinguicula* species, however, which seem to hybridize readily in cultivation. A few hybrids of northern species (including *P. vulgaris*, which is represented in our area as well) in northern and central Europe have been reported (Casper 1966).

Comments

Although there are only nine species of butterwort in the United States and Canada, identifying them can be quite difficult. In the field, location will be somewhat helpful: there is only one species in

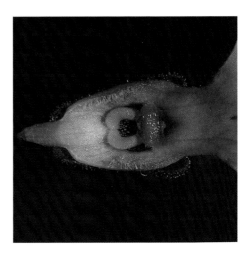

A dissected flower of *Pinguicula planifolia* showing the stamens and pistil. Note the portion of the upper lobe of the corolla (right) and the spur (left). The two stout stamen filaments (white in the photograph) curve around the brown, glandular ovary. The brownish red, apronlike stigma is like a flap lying over the anthers; yellow pollen grains are visible at the left edge of the stigma flap.

the Northeast and three in the West, but six grow in the Southeast. But for the beginner, identification is most readily achieved with flower characters, particularly color patterns. Degree of lobe incision in the corolla is also helpful. Corolla hairs, as mentioned above, are very useful for species in the Southeast, in particular, but investigating these hairs requires flower dissection and microscopy. In the Southeast, *Pinguicula planifolia* usually has beefy red leaves and *P. primuliflora* commonly reproduces by vegetative budding from the leaf tips. When not in flower, however, identification of most butterworts is problematic. For instance, when trying to separate *Pinguicula lutea* Walter and *P. caerulea* Walter, which have the same distribution in the Southeast, I have often waited for them to come into flower.

The butterworts of the North and West form winter buds, or hibernacula. As autumn deepens, the leaves begin to dry and die back, leaving a tight, bulblike winter bud in the plant's axis that is still imbedded in the substrate. Frequently numerous, smaller daughter buds, or gemmae, ring the main winter bud at about the soil surface level. Along with the main hibernaculum, each gemma is capable of growing into a new plant in the spring. The hibernacula and gemmae may be loosened by severe winter or early spring storms and sometimes will be found floating in the Great Lakes shallows, the buds thus serving to distribute the plant. Hibernacula are not produced by the southeastern species.

Thus far, only two practical human uses for butterworts have been described, these being nicely reviewed in Lloyd (1942). Butterwort leaves and plant sap have been used to "rope" milk by the Nordic peoples as well as in Wales and the Italian Alps. A single or combination of substances in the leaves causes milk to coagulate into a ropy mass that some liken to the production of the dessert junket by rennet. No whey is produced, so it is difficult to ascribe the process to changes in the milk protein casein only. The product has been described as tough and hardly palatable by some, but tender and edible by others, there apparently being some vagaries in the usefulness of the process. Leaf surface bacteria may participate in some way. The other practical use is application of butterwort leaves to sores on the udders of stock animals, and there appears to be some real efficacy in that process.

Prey Capture, Digestion, and Absorption

The rather bland-appearing butterworts have complexities first studied and largely elucidated by Darwin (1875). Since his seminal studies, our understanding of the processes of trapping prey, digestion, and absorption has only been fine-tuned.

The plants of most *Pinguicula* species have a musty, mushroomlike odor, which may serve to attract prey. The usual victims are quite small, consisting mainly of gnats and the occasional smaller mosquito or midge, which are about all the tiny glands on the leaf surface can manage. Examination under the dissecting microscope discloses two kinds of intermingled, minute glands: stalked and unstalked (sessile) glands.

The stalked glands secrete mucilaginous material at their tips, which ensnares the prey in ropy strands. Although the leaf margins of most butterworts are curled somewhat to begin with, prey capture stimulates more inward curling, which Darwin thought would bring the prey on the margins into closer contact with glands. This may be the case for marginal catches, but Lloyd (1942) has also suggested that the marginal curvature results in a central flat dish formation in which digestion and absorption can take place. This curving activity is slow, taking place in as little as one and a half hours up to three and a half hours (Darwin 1875; Lloyd 1942). As with other carnivorous plants, this curving may be caused by cell growth. Various inorganic and organic nitrogenous mixtures can stimulate movement, although slower movements can even be stimulated by ground glass particles (Darwin 1875).

The stalked glands are capable of releasing amylase, but it is the sessile glands that release the all-important protease for organic nitrogen digestion. Acid phosphatase, esterase, and ribonuclease activity are detectable in both types of glands (Heslop-Harrison and Knox 1971). The digestive fluids cover the leaf surfaces within an hour after stimulation, just as the margins are curling up to form the lip of the dish. Radiocarbon studies show that digestion products begin entering the leaf tissue in as little as two hours after stimulation, and movement of absorbate from the leaf begins in twelve hours. Autoradiographs indicate that absorption apparently occurs around the bases of the sessile glands (Heslop-Harrison and Knox 1971).

Within one to three days, the leaf surface is again dry and the margins resume their normal degree of curvature (Darwin 1875; Lloyd 1942). As mentioned in the Introduction, studies show that substances absorbed with the digested prey (probably phosphates) seem to stimulate or enable butterworts' roots to absorb more of what nutrients may be present in the soil (Aldenius et al. 1983).

Pinguicula vulgaris Linnaeus

Pinguicula vulgaris is our most widespread butterwort, its distribution sweeping across eastern Canada, through the Great Lakes region, then into the great Northwest and Alaska. This species is rather easily located in appropriate habitat and is frequently found by the hundreds crowded together. This little plant is a delight, especially in flower.

Synonyms
Because *Pinguicula vulgaris* has a nearly worldwide boreal and Old World montane distribution, it is inundated with synonyms too numerous to list here. A few pertinent examples, including actual species with which it is confused in other areas, are *Pinguicula alpina*, *P. arctica*, *P. grandiflora*, *P. leptoceras*, *P. villosa*, and *P. norica*.

Common Names
Pinguicula vulgaris is commonly known as butterwort and northern butterwort.

Description
Perennial, green rosettes to 8 cm; scape to 18 cm; corolla pale to dark purple with lighter

A flower of *Pinguicula vulgaris* in northern Michigan. The corolla is generally purple, but with a light center. Note that the lobes of the lower lip are widely separated and the center lobe is longer. The glandular hairs of the palate are loosely arranged compared to the palates of species in the Southeast.

to white center having patches of yellow; palate thin and loose; lobes of lower lip widely separated; central lobe longer and somewhat rhomboid; spur 3–8 mm; no detectable fragrance. Chromosome number $2n = 64$.

Flowering Season
June to August

Distribution
Map 19 shows the approximate distribution of *Pinguicula vulgaris*. As might be expected, distribution margins are less well known in the North and West.

Pinguicula vulgaris in flower in eastern Ontario. Note the trapped gnats and some debris on the leaf surfaces. The flower has a scape with few glands, a purple corolla with a white center, and a prominent spur. There is also a maturing seed capsule with the yellowish tan remnant of the stigma on top.

Habitat

Pinguicula vulgaris grows in fens; damp, sandy swales between Great Lakes dunes; cobbles; and to some extent *Sphagnum* around pools (in the tundra particularly). In the East, the species is also found on wet, seeping cliffs, such as the beginnings of the Niagara escarpment on the Bruce Peninsula in Ontario.

Comments

Pinguicula vulgaris is one of two or three species in this region that produce winter buds, or hibernacula (see the genus section at the beginning of the chapter). These winter buds are frequently ringed with ancillary buds, or gemmae.

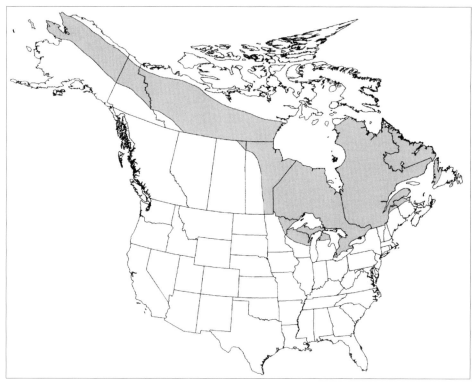

Map 19. Approximate historical distribution of *Pinguicula vulgaris*. The margins in the North and in Alaska particularly require clarification.

White-flowered variants of *Pinguicula vulgaris* have been informally noted on occasion, but thus far have not been named. The white variants have been confused with *Pinguicula alpina,* but that butterwort does not grow in the United States or Canada.

Uprooted hibernacula of *Pinguicula vulgaris*. These are ringed round the base by smaller ancillary buds, or gemmae. All are capable of growing into plants in the spring.

Cultivation Notes

Generally *Pinguicula vulgaris* plants grow well in a mix of Canadian peat and silica sand or simply plain peat. In cultivation, they do better in open shade than full sunlight. The pots should be placed in a saucer of pure water. Difficulties come during the winter bud stage, when rot frequently sets into cultivated material. For minimum loss, keep the pots drier and cool at this time. Some growers prefer to uproot the buds, clean and dry them, and dust them lightly with sulfur as a fungicide. The buds are then stored in a plastic bag in the refrigerator and set out again in the spring. Still, losses are high with all hibernaculum-forming species.

Steiger (1975) has an elaborate but very workable system for growing the northern and montane butterworts, which require cooler temperatures. The system uses cool artificial lighting, refrigeration, and flowing water; it works well with *Pinguicula vulgaris, P. macroceras,* and *P. villosa.*

Hand-pollination is achieved by tearing down the lower flower lip until the pistil and stamens are exposed. Using a toothpick, sweep one end up between the two anthers under the stigma apron, then gently deposit the yellow pollen on the external surface of the stigma. If the timing is right, seed capsules should mature.

Pinguicula macroceras Link

In the first edition of this book (Schnell 1976), I mentioned under the heading of *Pinguicula vulgaris* the proposed species of *P. macroceras* in the West. Since then, little work has been done except for defining one more subspecies of the entity. The basic problem boils down to whether *P. macroceras* is indeed a separate, well-defined species or simply a variant or series of variants of *P. vulgaris.* The plants and flowers are very similar, and there is considerable overlap in the characters that appear to weakly differentiate them. With an individual plant and flower in hand, it is usually difficult to identify the plant to species. The differential characters have been defined largely on the basis of populations of plants; but, when graphed, the quantified characters show a wide overlap of the curve bases with two weakly defined separate peaks (such as in Casper 1962). Quite frankly, as a pathologist, if I were confronted with a diagnostic test with such broad overlap, I would promptly throw the test out. However, variation is generally the norm in biology, and here we are simply trying to decide identity. But do we have enough information?

In this edition, I have separated the discussion of *Pinguicula macroceras* from *P. vulgaris* to examine the problem on its own merit. I will present the available information in the usual species format and then discuss any merits.

Synonyms
Pinguicula vulgaris subspecies *macroceras*, *Pinguicula vulgaris* variety *macroceras*, *Pinguicula microceras* (most prominently)

Common Name
The common name for *Pinguicula macroceras* is butterwort.

Description
Perennial, green rosette similar in character and size to *Pinguicula vulgaris*; yellowish green leaves but sometimes reddish to reddish brown; scape to 15 cm; lower two synsepalous calyx lobes incised for half their length (cf. two-thirds length for *P. vulgaris*); corolla usually light to dark purple with white center occasionally having yellow patches; palate not compact but glandular hairs separated; lobes of corolla lips in one subspecies large and usually overlapping; spur blunt and 6–9 mm (cf. 3–8 mm in *P. vulgaris*); corolla length from tip of spur to lips 18–27 mm (cf. 14–21 mm for *P. vulgaris*); no noted flower fragrance. Chromosome number $2n = 64$.

Flowering Season
As early as late April, but most commonly from May through July

Distribution
The rough historic distribution of *Pinguicula macroceras* is shown on Map 20. The distribution is more definite in California, Oregon, and Washington largely due to the efforts of Rondeau (1995), who has tirelessly

searched for carnivorous plant sites in these three states and plans to do so in Canada and Alaska. Comparison of Maps 19 and 20 indicates an area of uncertain overlap with *Pinguicula vulgaris*. This area, largely in the Yukon and northern Alaska, requires thorough botanical exploration to help clarify the status of *P. macroceras*.

Habitat

Pinguicula macroceras grows mostly in seeps along road cuts and ditches, banks of streams, and in rocky seepages, particularly in serpentine soils along the California-Oregon border. The species seems to prefer north-facing locations and partial or complete shade.

Infraspecies

To complicate matters in this incompletely studied group of plants, several infraspecies have been published or proposed for *Pinguicula macroceras*.

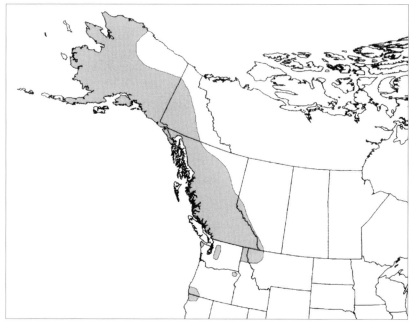

Map 20. Approximate historical distribution of *Pinguicula macroceras*. See text for discussion.

Variety *macroceras*

According to ICBN rules, this is an autonymic variety by virtue of other published infraspecies. Plants of this variety have typical species characters; large flowers with touching or overlapping lower lip lobes; a long, blunt spur; and characteristic lower lobe calyx changes (see measurements in Description above). Occasionally, white-flowered forms of this variety are seen. Unfortunately, the plants are not available in large numbers from exactly known locations and are found mainly in western Canada and Alaska.

Subspecies *nortensis* Steiger and Rondeau (1997)

This subspecies is limited to the area of the California-Oregon border (see Map 20), where you are most likely to find the occasional red-leafed variant. The face of the corolla is very much like *Pinguicula vulgaris* with smaller, elongate, widely separated lower lip lobes, but the spur is elongate.

Cultivated plants of *Pinguicula macroceras* subspecies *nortensis* from Del Norte County, California. The leaves here are pale green and the rosette is generally nonspecific. Glandular leaf surfaces are visible.

The spur is rarely blunt, however; most examples I have seen have an acute spur. Chromosome number $2n = 64$.

Variety *microceras* (Chamisso) Casper
This infraspecies seems to be confined to the Aleutian Islands and is peculiar in that the spur is relatively short, 1–3 mm on average. The lobes of the lower lip of the calyx are described as entirely separated (Casper 1962), but I do not find comments on the lobes of the lower lip of the small flower. Casper included this taxon in a key in his 1962 paper, but diminished the importance of the plants as a separate entity in his 1966 monograph, apparently feeling that spur variations may be subject to environmental effects. Populations of these plants near the distribution juncture of *Pinguicula vulgaris* and variety *macroceras* certainly deserve intense field study.

An Unnamed Variety
Rondeau (1995) mentions another group of *Pinguicula macroceras* between Mount Rainier and Mount Baker in the Cascades of Washington.

Flowers of *Pinguicula macroceras* subspecies *nortensis*. The flowers have a striking resemblance to those of *P. vulgaris* (see photographs in the preceding section) except for the slightly longer spur, which is clearly acute as in *P. vulgaris*. The lower lip lobes are narrow and not touching or overlapping.

These plants have smaller flowers (< 20 mm), short scapes (< 7 cm), and smaller rosettes. There is no mention of overlap of the petal lower lip lobe or the character of the spur. This variant is presently unnamed.

Comments

In different variants of *Pinguicula macroceras*, variation exists in the shapes of the overlapping lower lip lobes and in whether they are separate or overlapping. It is also extremely difficult to determine the degree of separation of calyx lobes. Finally, overall flower size includes the spur in the measurement (without the spurs, there is an average of only 1.0–1.5 mm difference in flower length between *Pinguicula vulgaris* and *P. macroceras* variants with long spurs). Thus, we are left with spur length as the final arbiter in distinguishing *P. macroceras* from *P. vulgaris*. However, we also must consider variety *microceras*.

Casper (1962) presented both a table of comparative corolla and spur length measurements and line graphs to show peaks of *Pinguicula vulgaris* and *P. macroceras*. Each taxon was represented by several hundred individuals in his study. One set of data included the problematic variety *microceras* and one did not. Both tables and graphs showed a great degree of overlap, as I mentioned in the introduction to this section, although there were separate, blunt peaks in the graphs. Using the data with variety *microceras* (which Casper diminished in his 1966 monograph), we see that the spur length of *P. vulgaris* has a modal peak at 5 mm (not in the center of its 3–6 mm range given by Casper, but toward the long end), and *P. macroceras* peaks modally at 7–8 mm (again, not at the center of the length range, but near the short end). Individuals from both taxa have spur lengths within the range of 1–10 mm. Upon closer examination of these data, one might conclude that spur length is useful as a secondary character, but certainly not a primary one.

Corolla glandular hairs can be used to distinguish the southeastern butterworts, but this is not the case when comparing *Pinguicula vulgaris* and *P. macroceras*. Casper (1962) provided several nice plates of corolla hair drawings with some minor differences between the two taxa in question, but Rondeau (1995) and Steiger and Rondeau (1997) found that the drawings did not match their examples of subspecies *nortensis*. (Although these authors described their observations, drawings would have been more useful.)

The degree of incision of the lower calyx lip is very difficult to judge in *Pinguicula macroceras* due to its size and the rounded shapes of the lobes. Further, there seems to be some confusion in that one authority describes the incision of the lower calyx lip as two-thirds of its length, whereas another source says the lobes are united for two-thirds of their length.

Both taxa have the same uniquely high chromosome number of $2n = 64$. So, what are we left with? Spur length in plants whose corollas look very much alike (even in Steiger 1982). Casper (1962, 1966), Rondeau (1995), and Steiger and Rondeau (1997) presented determined cases for separate species, and in the end they may be right. A *nortensis*-like plant is abundant in Japan, and Komiya (1972) prefers to think of them as *Pinguicula vulgaris*—the spur be damned, apparently. In Alaska and Canadian environs, Hulten (1968) listed the *macroceras* plants as a subspecies of *P. vulgaris* and was quoted by Casper (1962) as saying he often could not tell one from the other. However, Casper criticized Hulten for comparing these plants with European *P. vulgaris*, believing that there is a clearer distinction between the two taxa as they approach each other's ranges (character displacement).

Clearly, more work is needed beyond measuring spurs and flowers. Except for field exploration, over the past thirty or forty years there has been a strange lull in new types of research on this species question. First, more fieldwork needs to be done. Rondeau (1995), in particular, addressed this factor in an aggressive manner in northern California, Oregon, and Washington, but now it is time to get into the vast Canadian and Alaskan areas, with special emphasis in the area of apparent range juncture of *Pinguicula vulgaris* and *P. macroceras* in Alaska and the Yukon. Second, reciprocal transplants and critical, large-volume greenhouse experiments, growing all variants side by side, are needed to address potential relationships between spur length and environment. Third, additional chromosome counts must be done beyond variety *nortensis* within *P. macroceras*. Finally, DNA and molecular biology studies should

Are these plants *Pinguicula macroceras* variety *macroceras?* The flowers have large over-lapping lower lip lobes and long, blunt (not acute) spurs. However, these plants were growing in Upper Michigan and most assuredly are polymorphic variants of *P. vulgaris.* Migration of these plants (or seed) into a new and unstable area might have given rise to a *macroceras*-like colony.

be applied to a broad array of samples of variations and locations in both species.

Throughout this discussion, for convenience I have treated the West Coast plants as a species, *Pinguicula macroceras*. However, speciation has not been established. If the suggested further studies prove to be not practical or at all possible, at this point I would favor subspecies rank for the *macroceras* plants in *P. vulgaris*, but I will withhold final judgment in case these questions are addressed.

One hypothesis is worth presenting: perhaps plants of *Pinguicula vulgaris* passed across the northern end of the Continental Divide in northern Alaska and then examples of them drifted south, establishing small colonies at scattered points into northern California. Due to founder effects and genetic bottlenecks, polymorphic variants of the *P. vulgaris* plants may have established and bred in incompletely differentiated enclaves. As populations, these groups may display the small variations from the general parent species but occasionally be found as individuals in stands of *P. vulgaris*. Plants might also have spread via the Aleutian land bridge into Japan. This would be one—but only one—possible explanation for the variations in distant locations in present-day northern California, Oregon, and Washington. As studies proceed further north, additional variants may also be found.

Cultivation Notes
The same methods as used for *Pinguicula vulgaris* are applicable here. I have found *P. macroceras* to be somewhat easier to grow.

Pinguicula villosa Linnaeus

Very little work has been done on this relatively lesser-known, small northern species, probably because its habitat is far north and relatively inaccessible. Also, *Pinguicula villosa* is difficult to maintain in cultivation.

Synonyms
Pinguicula involuta, P. acutifolia

Common Name

Pinguicula villosa is commonly known as the northern butterwort, a name shared with *Pinguicula vulgaris*.

Description

Compact rosettes 1.0–2.0 cm; markedly recurved leaves with slightly more prominent, hirsute petiole; leaves green to slightly copper at times in full sun; scapes 3.0–6.0 cm and markedly glandular-hirsute; corollas 0.5–1.0 cm, purple with light centers streaked with yellow and darker veins; no fragrance noted; seed capsules rare with sparse seed; forms a winter hibernaculum. Chromosome number $2n = 16$.

A composite figure of *Pinguicula villosa*. In the two photographs of flowers (left), note the densely and prominently glandular-hirsute scape, the very small flowers, and the stocky spur. The tiny leaf rosettes (right) have intensely recurved leaf margins and slightly more prominent hirsute petioles.

Flowering Season
June into July

Distribution
Distribution of *Pinguicula villosa* (Map 21) is poorly known because generally it grows in the far north in regions that are difficult to access. Also, due to the small size of the plant and flower, it is difficult to find the species in the field.

Habitat
Pinguicula villosa grows mostly in northern *Sphagnum* bogs in openings of black spruce (*Picea mariana*) forests. The plants usually grow on the

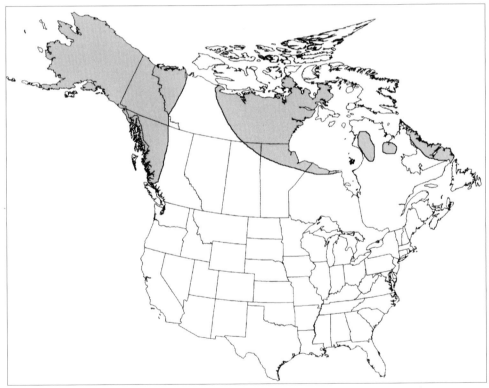

Map 21. Approximate historical distribution of *Pinguicula villosa*. Further exploration may result in a more continuous range in the North.

tops and sides of hummocks composed of compact *Sphagnum* species, which do not overwhelm the small rosettes.

Comments

Lamb (1991) summarized the known natural history and biology of this species, which may become better known with further exploration, and mapped several locations. Due to the inconspicuous size of the rosette and flower, the plants are best found by first noting a likely habitat site then looking more closely for the plants. Even compact *Sphagnum* can be nearly overwhelming, and Lamb described sometimes seeing only individual leaves protruding above the moss "like tiny gaping green mouths."

In addition to the small size of the rosettes and their rather unique leaves, *Pinguicula villosa* is easily identified by the flower. The scape is prominently glandular-hirsute, and the corolla is less than 1.0 cm in length with a prominent, stocky spur.

Cultivation Notes

In general, *Pinguicula villosa* can be grown using the methods for *Pinguicula vulgaris*, although I confess that this is the most difficult North American butterwort I have attempted to grow. Lamb (1991) indicated that if natural light is used (such as a greenhouse or window-sill terrarium), it is beneficial to keep the winter hibernacula under refrigeration until the usual growing season. During the growing season, which usually begins in May, higher temperatures do not seem to be important in spite of the species' northern habitat. However, keeping the winter hibernacula continuously warm (as in more southerly summers and autumn) can be fatal to the plant.

Pinguicula lutea Walter

With *Pinguicula lutea*, I begin the discussion of the last six species of butterwort in our area, all of which are native to the southeastern United States. These are all perennial in habit, although *P. pumila* is likely short lived. None produce winter hibernacula, and they are found in various parts of the coastal plain. I present a composite figure of the corolla hairs of these six species (derived from Godfrey and Stripling 1961); the corolla hair characters are very specific and useful in identifying the southeastern butterworts. I will refer to this figure in later species sections of this chapter.

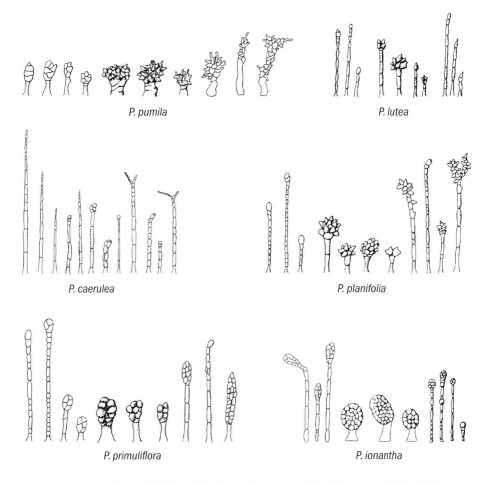

P. pumila

P. lutea

P. caerulea

P. planifolia

P. primuliflora

P. ionantha

Drawings of the corolla hairs of the six southeastern species of butterwort. These hairs may be observed with the aid of a dissecting microscope. There are three groups of hairs for each species, with each group representing (from left to right): the palate, a ridge on the corolla immediately behind the palate, and the inner wall of the corolla tube. Adapted from Godfrey and Stripling (1961). (Used with permission.)

Pinguicula lutea is one of the more common and easily seen of the southeastern species. This butterwort is a welcome sign of early spring as its tiny, bright yellow flowers bob in the breezes of the savannas, where the plant sometimes grows in tight colonies of hundreds of individuals.

Synonyms
Pinguicula campanulata, P. edentula, Isoloba recurva

Common Name
The common name for *Pinguicula lutea* is the yellow butterwort.

Description
Perennial, green rosettes 5–10 cm across; leaves markedly recurved upward, narrow, sharp tip; scapes to 20 cm, only lightly glandular; corollas bright yellow, 2.0–3.0 cm across, lips lobed; palate yellow and strongly exserted; no fragrance. Chromosome number $2n = 32$.

Flowering Season
February to May

Distribution
Pinguicula lutea is rather widely distributed in savannas along the arc of the coastal plain from southeastern North Carolina into Louisiana (Map 22).

Habitat
In many savannas, *Pinguicula lutea* can usually be found as large colonies growing in sandy peat in either full sun or light shade. The soil is often constantly damp but with no standing water. The plants may be difficult to spot when not in flower because they may be hidden beneath bunchgrass.

Comments
There is some occasional variation in *Pinguicula lutea* flower color. Plants having pale, straw-colored flowers were noted

Map 22. Historical distribution of *Pinguicula lutea*.

west of Tallahassee, Florida (Landon T. Ross, personal correspondence; mentioned in Schnell 1980d). In Liberty County, Florida, north of Wilma, Folkerts and Freeman (1989) found a colony of *Pinguicula lutea* with entirely white flowers, which they described as forma *alba*. They note that herbarium specimens of the white-flowered form, even when properly

Pinguicula lutea in cultivation. Note the bright yellow flower with strongly exserted palate and the markedly recurved leaves.

dried, assume a pale tan color. The search of other herbarium specimens for white forms may be difficult because the yellow flowers also dry as tan. In the white-flowered form, the corolla hairs are still specific for *P. lutea*.

Pinguicula lutea locations in the western part of the range, especially in the area of the Alabama-Mississippi border, have particularly large specimens with larger flowers. These larger plants remain consistent in cultivation.

Cultivation Notes

Pinguicula lutea is relatively easy to grow, although I confess that it and *P. pumila* can be short lived in cultivation. This butterwort can be grown in either Canadian peat or a mix of peat and sand or peat and perlite, with the pots placed in shallow water in a tray. This species grows well in a terrarium and can be managed in the greenhouse. Bright light is best, and in the terrarium this should be achieved with fluorescent lights rather than sunny window light. The difficulty with cultivating this species is keeping it in cold (but not freezing), wet conditions over the winter, such as the greenhouse kept quite cool for *Sarracenia* pitcher plants during dormancy. Under the stress of cultivation, these butterworts do not seem to do well in temperatures below 15°C, although they are exposed to greater cold and wetness in nature.

Propagation may be achieved with seed, which can be produced as described under *Pinguicula vulgaris*. The seed requires no stratification and germinates promptly on the same medium used for growing plants.

Pinguicula caerulea Walter

This species, with its small but strikingly beautiful flower, grows in much of the same range as *Pinguicula lutea* and largely in the same conditions, but the two species are never intermingled and colonies rarely abut one another. Similar to the yellow butterwort, colonies of *P. caerulea* may contain hundreds of plants, but are difficult to spot when not in flower.

Synonyms

Pinguicula elatior, Isoloba elatior

Common Name

Pinguicula caerulea is commonly known as violet butterwort, in reference to the flower color.

Description

Perennial, green rosettes 5–10 cm across; leaves markedly recurved upward, narrow, sharp tip; scapes to 25 cm, only lightly glandular but slightly hirsute near the base; corolla violet, usually prominent violet veins, may be darker or lighter, 2.0–3.0 cm across; lips lobed; palate exserted and usually cream colored; no fragrance. Chromosome number $2n = 32$.

Flowering Season

February to May

Distribution

Pinguicula caerulea grows in colonies in some savannas along the Atlantic coastal plain, extending into peninsular Florida (Map 23).

Habitat

Pinguicula caerulea grows in sites similar to *Pinguicula lutea*: in sandy, damp savannas in either full sun or light shade, not associated with standing water. This butterwort may be difficult to spot when not in flower and growing beneath overarching leaves of bunchgrass.

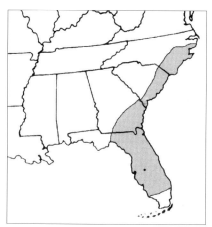

Map 23. Historical distribution of *Pinguicula caerulea*.

Comments

As noted by Barnhart (1933) and Walter (quoted in Barnhart), when not in flower, the plants of *Pinguicula caerulea* and *P. lutea* appear nearly if not entirely identical. One usually must wait for the plants to come into flower for positive identification. Some long-term growers claim to be able to tell the vegetative aspects of the plants apart by highly subjective means that defy description. However, once a colony of either species is identified, you can be nearly assured that examples of the other species will not grow in that colony. The question of why species with similar vegetative appearance and nearly identical habitat requirements do not intermix still awaits field research. I am able to grow the two intermingled in the same tray in cultivation, so there does not appear to be allelopathy. The distribution is also very similar, except that *P. caerulea* does not grow as far west as *P. lutea*.

There is some corolla color variation within *Pinguicula caerulea*, the usual flower being pale violet with prominent veins. Some flowers are deep violet, with the venation obliterated by the violet base pigment. Color also varies in the other direction to white-flowered specimens (such as Barnhart 1933), which have been described as forma *leucantha* Schnell (1980d). This form grows scattered through some colonies of *Pinguicula caerulea* and remains consistent in cultivation. There are intermediates in such colonies, suggesting interform hybridization. The plants

Flower of *Pinguicula caerulea* growing in South Carolina. Note the lighter violet color with prominent deep violet veins, although some examples lack the veins and are a deeper violet. The exserted palate is a cream color. The stigma apron can be seen just above and behind the palate.

A flower of *Pinguicula caerulea* forma *leucantha* in Brunswick County, North Carolina. The corolla lacks all violet pigment.

can be differentiated from the white-flowered plants of *P. pumila* by the size of the flower and plant (much smaller in *P. pumila*) and by corolla hairs (see drawings in *P. lutea* section).

Cultivation Notes
Cultivation is essentially identical with *Pinguicula lutea*, except that for some reason *P. caerulea* lends itself to long-term cultivation much more readily. The plants seem more capable of surviving colder, wet winters in a *Sarracenia* greenhouse.

Pinguicula planifolia Chapman

This southeastern butterwort is probably the most easily identified due to the red leaf color and generally large plant size. *Pinguicula planifolia* has a very small distribution and is being considered for endangered species status.

Common Name
The common name for *Pinguicula planifolia* is Chapman's butterwort.

Description
Perennial rosette to 15 cm; leaves flatter and margins slightly recurved upward; usually colored a beefy to bright red in full sun; scape cream to reddish green, to 30 cm; corolla pale purple with a darker purple center; palate yellow and strongly exserted; lip lobes notched one-third to one-half their length; corolla hairs are illustrated in the *P. lutea* section; flower has a sweet, honeylike fragrance. Chromosome number $2n = 32$.

Flowering Season
March to April

Distribution
Pinguicula planifolia has a very narrow distribution from Liberty and Leon Counties in Florida to the Louisiana line and barely north into Alabama (Map 24).

A plant of *Pinguicula planifolia* in Liberty County, Florida. In this example, note the beefy red leaves (some plants are brighter red), the flatter mature leaves with slightly rolled edges, and prominent leaf surface glands.

Flower of *Pinguicula planifolia* in Florida. The flower is pale purple with a darker purple center, the lobes are incised about half their length, and the yellow palate is strongly exserted.

Habitat

Pinguicula planifolia usually grows in the open in rather large, prominent colonies. The soil is peaty to sandy peat and usually quite wet, often with a few millimeters of standing water on the surface.

Comments

Pinguicula planifolia is a particularly fascinating butterwort, and large, open colonies are quite striking in the field. The plants are almost always a beefy to bright red color, making identification easy. Plants shaded out by shrub or herbaceous growth may be more green with less to no red pigment, but these can generally be identified by the company they keep.

The flower is also unique with its deeply incised lobes, pale pinkish purple color, and dark centers. In some flowers, the base color appears nearly white, but the darker center and red leaves seem to be constant in plants I have seen. The next species to be discussed, *Pinguicula ionantha*, frequently grows near, immediately adjacent to, and even partially admixed with *P. planifolia* colonies. However, the flower of *P. ionantha* is white with a dark center, the leaves are green, and the corolla lip lobes are just notched.

Pinguicula planifolia lives in a wetter habitat than *P. caerulea*, often growing in shallow, wet seeps or the margins of ponds or ephemeral pools. If the site dries as the season passes into deep summer, the plant survives but newer leaves are shorter and more prominently recurved.

Map 24. Historical distribution of *Pinguicula planifolia*.

Cultivation Notes

Generally, *Pinguicula planifolia* can be grown as is *Pinguicula lutea*, but the medium can be kept quite wet, often with a millimeter or so of water on the soil surface. It is very difficult to maintain the deep leaf color in cultivation unless warmth, bright light, and a very acidic soil are provided. Even if growing conditions are suboptimal, the leaves will at least be partially suffused in red and flower characters will remain constant.

Pinguicula ionantha Godfrey

This Gulf Coast butterwort has an extremely limited distribution and is federally endangered, mainly due to the small range and its susceptibility to habitat drainage. Only described in 1961, this attractive species is retreating from easy viewing due to habitat destruction.

Synonyms
Pinguicula primuliflora

Common Name
Pinguicula ionantha is commonly known as Godfrey's butterwort.

Description
Perennial, green rosettes to 10 cm; leaves generally flatter than *Pinguicula lutea* or *P. caerulea* with moderately upward recurved margins; scape 10–15 cm tall, green; corolla most often 2 cm across; lobes shallowly notched (not more than one-quarter length of lobe); base color white with a purple throat; palate bright yellow and strongly exserted; corolla hairs are illustrated in the *P. lutea* section; flower fragrance sweet and honeylike. Chromosome number $2n = 22$.

Flowering Season
February to April

Distribution
Pinguicula ionantha is limited to a small area in the central Florida Panhandle (Map 25).

Habitat
Similar to *Pinguicula planifolia*, *P. ionantha* thrives in open peat or sandy peat in very wet areas, sometimes even being submerged for several days after a heavy rain.

Map 25. Historical distribution of *Pinguicula ionantha*.

Comments

Because *Pinguicula ionantha* may grow alongside and even with *P. planifolia*, differentiation is important (see *P. planifolia* section for details). If both are in flower, the flower details noted in the captions of the *P. planifolia* and *P. ionantha* illustrations are consistent, except for the occasional white flowered *P. planifolia*. Even so, the degree of incision of the corolla lobes is telling. Also, *P. planifolia* usually has red in its leaves, which *P. ionantha* never does.

Godfrey's butterwort lives in a very wet habitat, and, although its colonies are relatively few compared to other southern butterworts, any one colony may have several hundred plants. The species is quite sensitive to consistent drying of the habitat. The plants seem to have sought refuge in drainage ditches as pools and ponds were drained, but now ditches are being revised to improve drainage and even this reserve habitat is being lost. Unfortunately, even colonies in federally owned national forest land are not exempt from drainage.

Flower of *Pinguicula ionantha* in Liberty County, Florida. The corolla is white with a purple center, the yellow palate is strongly exserted, and the notches of the lobes are shallow.

Cultivation Notes

Pinguicula ionantha is as easy to grow as *P. planifolia* and may be cultivated and propagated with the same methods under the same conditions. When grown in the greenhouse, the lengthening photoperiod as early as January causes flowering, a bright feature in the doldrums of winter. Because this species is endangered, plants must not be collected in the wild. The keen grower may be able to obtain seed or an extra plant or two from another grower, but this material cannot cross state lines without a federal permit.

Pinguicula primuliflora Wood & Godfrey

This large, southern butterwort has a clustering habit. The plant is particularly attractive in bloom and has a flower that looks superficially like a primrose (hence the specific epithet).

Common Names

There is no recorded common name for *Pinguicula primuliflora*. But, at the risk of seeming to support common names over scientific, I propose budding butterwort, reflecting the plant's common growth habit.

Description

Perennial, green rosette to 15–20 cm; leaves flattened with moderate upward recurved margins; plantlets frequently bud from leaf tips and decaying older leaves; scape cream to green, to 15 cm tall; corolla to 2 cm across, pale purple to pinkish with white center; palate yellow and exserted; external surface of tube and spur bright yellow; corolla hairs are illustrated in the *P. lutea* section; no fragrance. Chromosome number $2n = 32$.

Flowering Season

February to April

Distribution

The relatively narrow distribution of *Pinguicula primuliflora* extends from the western Florida Panhandle across southern Alabama and southern Mississippi into Louisiana (Map 26). One disjunct population has been described from Autauga County, Alabama.

Habitat

Pinguicula primuliflora prefers a very wet habitat and is frequently seen growing on the shores of slow streams, ponds, and pools, often extending onto the

Map 26. Historical distribution of *Pinguicula primuliflora*.

Pinguicula primuliflora in cultivation. Note that the pinkish purple flower has a white center. The palate is bright yellow and strongly exserted.

water surface as a mat. This species may be found in somewhat drier but damp savanna locations, where the leaves are shorter and more recurved.

Comments

Pinguicula primuliflora has the interesting habit of budding plantlets from leaf tips and decaying older leaves. This vegetative reproduction results in the plants tending to grow in clusters of plants of varying age. The budding also results in a mat of plants that may extend out from margins of streams into the open water.

Every time I travel the Gulf Coast, I stop at an unnamed stream on the edge of Eglin Air Force Base in western Florida to visit old friends—a stand of *Pinguicula primuliflora*. Shrubby overgrowth is thick, but the kilometer or so hike is worthwhile. I have been able to follow this particular stand for many years because no one else is likely to find and disturb it. As a bonus, there are nice examples of *Sarracenia rubra* subspecies *gulfensis* here also (with no other *Sarracenia* species nearby, so there is no introgression). The water flows gently most of the time, and the strong

Leaves of a cultivated *Pinguicula primuliflora* with plantlets budding from the leaf tips and older decaying leaves.

clumps of butterwort along the shores grow nicely out onto the surface of the water in large mats. During several years there were heavy spring rains, and the little stream became a torrent, washing the mats somewhere downstream. The plants in the soil on the shores held, though, and in a few years the mats reformed due to leaf budding. No spring torrent has been strong enough to wash away the base plants on the shoreline.

Leaf budding is not entirely unique to *Pinguicula primuliflora* and can be seen occasionally—but only occasionally—in *P. planifolia* and *P. ionantha*. However, budding is only found regularly in *P. primuliflora*, and only this species exhibits the cluster growth habit in prime habitat.

A disjunct location for *Pinguicula primuliflora* has been found in Autauga County, Alabama, just north of Montgomery, in *Sarracenia rubra*

A clump of plants of *Pinguicula primuliflora* growing on Eglin Air Force Base in western Florida. Note the cluster habit of growth and the variation in plant size due to leaf budding.

subspecies *alabamensis* country. In fact, the butterworts were discovered in a stand of the pitcher plants during a floristic survey (Murphy and Boyd 1999).

Cultivation Notes

I have found *Pinguicula primuliflora* very easy to grow in the greenhouse, and I believe it would make a good terrarium subject. The very early spring flowers (January in cultivation here in southwestern Virginia) along with those of *P. ionantha* and *P. planifolia* are a welcome sight in the hump of winter. Smaller species of clumping *Sphagnum* are an ideal medium for cultivation. I grow the plants in very wet *Sphagnum* in large, flat trays to accommodate the leaf budding habit, although the trays fill very rapidly with progeny. Bright open shade is the ideal light.

In general, cultivated butterworts rot when exposed to repeated, direct applications of water on their leaves. I water from the side by plunging a pot with drain holes into a corner of the tray and filling the pot with water daily or making drain holes in the growing tray and placing it into a larger tray of water. Unfortunately, I soon run out of trays large enough. Pots work well for a season or two, but *Pinguicula primuliflora* clusters will soon overgrow the average pot. I hate to throw out excess healthy carnivorous plants, and in a hurry I will carelessly stick some plants tumbling over the margins of their trays into *Sphagnum*-topped pots of Sarracenia plants. The butterworts can soon cover an entire tray of pitcher plant pots. If I were to suggest an American butterwort for the new, inexperienced grower to start with, it would be *P. primuliflora*. Only the blackest thumb would not be rewarded, and the plants always produce beautiful flowers in the spring.

Pinguicula pumila Michaux

This tiny butterwort (the plants average about half the size of *Pinguicula lutea* and *P. caerulea*) has a wide variety of flower colors, which might cause confusion; however, the species is smaller in all respects, including flower size.

Plants of *Pinguicula pumila* in Collier County, Florida. These rosettes are only about 3.0 cm across.

Plants of *Pinguicula pumila* in Collier County, Florida, with uncommon red venation of the leaves. There is also some slight suffusion of red pigment into the leaf tissue.

Synonyms
Pinguicula australis, Isoloba pumila, P. floridensis, P. violacea

Description
Short-lived, perennial rosette to 3.5 cm across; leaves mostly green but occasionally red veined near the center with slight suffusion of red pigment, strong upward recurved margins; scape green, to about 10 cm tall; corolla to 1.5 cm across, variably white, purple, or yellow; palate white to cream, not exserted; corolla hairs are illustrated in the *P. lutea* section; no flower fragrance. Chromosome number $2n = 22$.

Flowering Season
April to May, sometimes also autumn through January in southern Florida

Distribution
Pinguicula pumila grows along the coastal plain from central North Carolina down to the Louisiana line and throughout Florida. Colonies of the plants are rare in the Carolinas, but become more common along the Gulf Coast and into peninsular Florida (Map 27).

Habitat
Pinguicula pumila favors pine savannas with damp, sandy or sand-peat soils, usually in the open. In southern Florida, colonies are found on the edges of sandy hammocks among the marly fens of the Everglades and Big Cypress Swamp.

Comments
Due to their small size, *Pinguicula pumila* plants are more easily seen when in flower, but even then the flowers themselves are small. Colonies are scarce in the Carolinas, but are more readily found in the Gulf Coast area, particular in peninsular Florida.

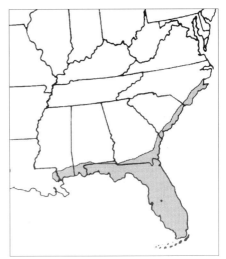

Map 27. Historical distribution of *Pinguicula pumila.*

Yellow, purple, and white flowers of *Pinguicula pumila*.

Flower color varies from yellow to purple to white, and single colonies often have plants with all these flower colors, resulting in a rather unique visual effect. Moldenke (1934) described the yellow-flowered variant as variety *buswellii* Moldenke, feeling that plants with yellow flowers were quite rare and deserving of varietal status. In the 1960s I was fortunate to find Moldenke's type location in Lee County, Florida, still extant. The colony at the site was unique in that all the specimens there had only yellow flowers. Since then, the site has been destroyed for a building project. Moldenke (1934) mentioned that several botanists familiar with *Pinguicula pumila*, including Barnhart, regarded these yellow-flowered plants as simply part of the species spectrum and they had seen such plants mixed with purple- and white-flowered plants in many other locations. I have also commonly seen yellow-flowered plants in many locations in Big Cypress Swamp. Like Barnhart, I consider all three flower colors as a normal part of the flower color spectrum in this species.

Considering the small size of the plant and flower and the usual presence of mixed flower colors in a colony, there should be little difficulty identifying *Pinguicula pumila* in the field. Until one gains experience with the genus overall, the only confusion might be with the yellow-flowered variant and *P. lutea*.

Cultivation Notes

Pinguicula pumila appears to be a short-lived perennial that depends on reseeding for continuation of the colony. Therefore, it is difficult to keep the plant for any period of time, and I find the species to have the same difficulties as *P. lutea* in cultivation. I would suggest using the same media and techniques as with *P. lutea*, being certain not to keep the medium too wet and cold in winter and avoiding splashing water on the leaves. To ensure keeping this plant in your collection, attempt to pollinate flowers and sow seed (hand-pollination is discussed in the Cultivation Notes of *P. vulgaris*).

BLADDERWORTS

I F THE VENUS flytrap and pitcher plants are the flamboyant members of the carnivorous plant world, sundews the jewels, and butterworts the shy trappers, bladderworts are probably the silent service. Hardly noticeable out of flower unless searched for and with submersed traps no more than a few millimeters across at most, these plants seem to be minor players. However, aside from the magnificent spectacle when in flower, the tiny traps of this genus are actually the most complex of the carnivorous plants.

Utricularia

Utricularia Linnaeus species are members of the family Lentibulariaceae, as are the butterworts. This brotherhood is engendered mainly by the flower structure, because their vegetative aspects could not be more different. Furthermore, bladderworts are something of renegades among plants. They do not obey the rules. They are dicotyledons, but have no cotyledons. They do not have roots, but have stolons that sometimes behave as roots. Of the 214 bladderwort species in the world, three or four have rudimentary stems, but the rest have stolons in their place. The leaves of *Utricularia* are usually branched, filiform structures, but are also often present as more typical leaflike structures. Furthermore, although the plants have evolved to function as aquatic trappers, many are terrestrial species with their unique traps buried in the moist depths of the soil.

Description

Annual or perennial, herbaceous aquatic, semiterrestrial, or terrestrial; rootless; North American species stemless but with variably long, branching, stemlike stolons, the latter in some aquatic species often with winter hibernacula (turions) at their tips in autumn; leaves elongate, branching, filiform structures bearing bladderlike traps below water or ground level, sometimes leaves are aerial and are short and linear or paddle shaped around base of the peduncle; peduncles aerial to 50 cm tall with scales and sometimes floats or radially arranged foxtail, dissected, leaflike

Mass stand of the bladderwort *Utricularia cornuta* Michaux in Brunswick County, North Carolina. When not in flower, the stand would be hardly noticed.

branches; one to twenty flowers in raceme, opening consecutively, bracts and bracteoles present, pedicels to 3 cm long; calyx bilobed; corolla zygomorphic with upper and lower lips representing two and three fused petals, respectively; lips often lobed in some species; palate on lower lip at corolla opening raised, ridged, often colored with white or red streaks, only lightly glandular, no or very small tube ending in spur lined by nectar glands; two stamens short, curved, thick, and arching around globose ovary; pollen yellow and sticky; pistil with bilabiate stigma, one labia rudimentary, the other hanging apronlike over anthers with receptive surface external; some flowers cleistogamous in some species; seed capsules brown, papery, globose; seeds 0.5 mm and usually many.

Habitat

Bladderworts are typically aquatic or semiaquatic plants found in ponds and slowly meandering streams usually associated with bogs of one sort or another. They are most easily found in the regions of northern and western bogs and southeastern savannas, but have been found in vernal pools in the Arizona mountains as well as manmade ditches. In addition, some species are adapted to a terrestrial habitat, albeit a usually moist one. The terrestrial species are often subjected to flooding after heavy rains and spring thaws, but when the ground surface is dry, the stolons and bladders are in deeper, moister levels.

Near the end of summer, the northern aquatic species produce a series of hibernacula at the ends of stolon branches. In water plants these structures are known as turions and consist of a short length of stolon with a tightly compacted series of leaves wrapped into a tight ball. As winter comes on and the stolons of the plants begin to die, the freed turions sink to the bottoms of pools or streams, where they become winter resting bodies. Turions are also highly resistant to desiccation. In spring, as the waters warm and lengthening daylight penetrates to the pond bottoms, the turions activate, with increasing respiration and photosynthesis causing the structures to now float to the surface, where they sprout into plants for the new season. Studies have indicated that turion dormancy time can be divided into two phases: obligate and facultative. The obligate phase is apparently genetically set and remains in effect regardless of light and temperature changes. Obligate dormancy periods are frequently shorter than actual dormancy in nature, and healthy plant growth can be induced in the laboratory under the correct temperature and light conditions. In nature, cold, dark winter days extend dormancy into the facultative period imposed by low temperatures and lack of light. Turion activity seems to be directly mediated by inherent plant hormone levels (Winston and Gorham 1979a, 1979b; Juniper et al. 1989).

Pollination

In the United States and Canada, *Utricularia* species generally flower through the temperate growing season from as early as March or April in the South through August and even into September. Exceptions are the disjunct tropical species *U. simulans* and *U. amethystina* in extreme

Two branches of the aquatic species *Utricularia macrorhiza*. The branching, stemlike stolons are apparent. Arrayed along the stolons are the utricles, or bladder traps. Beyond these, divided filiform leaves are seen. The left end of the upper stolon has a bulbous hibernaculum (called a turion in water plants) in this late-summer example.

southern Florida, which generally flower from late October through January, and specimens of *U. foliosa*, which flower into November.

The flowers are similar in structure to *Pinguicula* species, except that the tube found in butterwort flowers is rudimentary to absent in bladderworts, with the stamens and pistil being largely concealed by the juncture of the two corolla lips rather than in a tube. I would expect the same pollination mechanisms and encouragement of cross-pollination as in *Pinguicula* species, but pollinators have not been observed in bladderworts to date. Most *Utricularia* species are undoubtedly capable of self-pollination, as evidenced by some species having both open (chasmogamous) and closed (cleistogamous) corollas simultaneously or at different times of the season and still being able to produce seed. Cleistogamous flowers have incompletely developed corollas and are much smaller with no apparent opening to the anthers and pistil. Other noncarnivorous plants have cleistogamous flowers as well, such as some violets (*Viola*) and the cultivated annual velvet flower (or painted tongue, *Salpiglossis sinuata*). Studies of *S. sinuata* have shown that pollen produced by the flower is able to germinate in the dark, moist confines of the anthers in the closed corollas; tips of pollen tubes then penetrate the anther walls, enter the stigmas, and grow down the styles to the ovaries (Lee et al. 1979). In some bladderworts, the cleistogamous flower phase has caused confusion and early on resulted in two species designations for the open and closed corolla phase of the same plant. The once recognized *Utricularia cleistogama* is simply a cleistogamous phase of *U. subulata*.

There are no proven instances of hybridization among *Utricularia* species, especially in the United States and Canada. Taylor (1989) and others have seen suspicious cases elsewhere, but these were never studied.

The Trap

The little traps, which range from 0.1 to 0.5 cm on average (some tropical species to 1.0 cm or more), are suspended from the stolons, or leaf branches, by short stalks. In other carnivorous plant species the traps are clearly modified leaves, but this is less clear in bladderworts. The traps can branch from the stolon in place of finely divided, filiform leaves, which are then found branching off beyond the traps.

The bladder, or trap, is attached to the stolon branch by a stalk that may be in the nearly basal position at the very end opposite the trap opening or anywhere along the base, depending on the species. The trap itself is a baglike structure with an opening at one end. The opening is complex and surrounded by appendages and bristles, some of these known as antennae. At the very mouth, there are some small, stalked glands that have been shown to produce mucilage, but so far the usefulness of this material, so important in adhesive traps of sundews and butterworts, has not been demonstrated (Juniper et al. 1989). Small prey do not appear to get stuck to the glands or entangled in their secretions.

The trap mouth is subtended by a shelf upon which is a raised structure called the threshold. Suspended from the top of the bladder mouth is a trapdoor, which in the closed position rests tightly against the thresh-

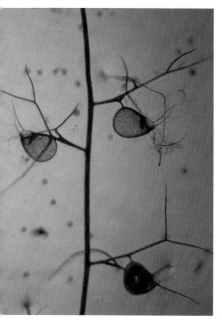

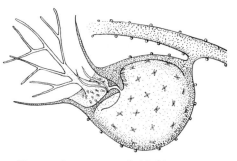

The complex structure of a bladderwort trap. See text for a description of the structure. Drawing by David Kutt.

Left: A portion of stolon of *Utricularia striata*, a common, fixed, aquatic species. In this case each stolon branch has one trap and a divided filiform leaf. At this magnification, you can see bristles and appendages arising from the narrow, mouth end of the trap.

old to form a seal. Specialized trigger hairs that activate movement are located in the area of the trapdoor and are often attached to it.

There are other glands in addition to the mucilaginous glands in the external mouth area. The surfaces of the trap and sometimes the stolon have glands similar to those lining the trap. Whether these glands serve as an allurement has not been determined. The interior of the trap has short-stalked glands with four arms; these are referred to as quadrifid glands, or quadrifids. Nearer the mouth in the area of the shelf supporting the threshold, the glands become two-armed, or bifid. The function(s) of these interior glands are also controversial. Some assume they produce digestive enzymes, but this has not been proven beyond doubt. The interior glands do absorb digested nutrients, and they seem to participate in water resorption to reset the trap (see below).

The exact shapes and configuration of the quadrifid glands have some taxonomic value, but not in the genus as a whole due to the limits of discernable variation among the 214 species. The quadrifid glands are most useful when trying to distinguish two or three difficult species in certain regions, as outlined and reviewed by Taylor (1989). Variations mainly revolve around the relative lengths of the arms on either side of the attachment point as well as the angle of divergence (or noting the arms to be parallel); indeed, some workers have gone to the extreme of measuring the angles in degrees. Considering the variation of angles that I and others have noted in single traps or multiple traps of the same species, this practice seems excessive and unreliable. Taylor (1989) presented fine drawings of quadrifid traps of several species.

For those with a steady hand and access to microscopes, quadrifid glands may be seen rather easily. With a finely pointed forceps, remove a trap from its stolon and place it on a glass slide on the stage of a dissecting microscope. Under low power and using a fresh, single-edge razor blade, half the trap from top to bottom, using the forceps to hold the tissue in place with gentle pressure. Flip the top half up so the trap interior is now visible and move your slide to a compound microscope. Glands can be seen at 200–430× magnification.

Sometimes, fine strands of algae become entangled in the bristles and appendages of the traps, but these do not seem to interfere with trap function. Tiny, multicellular water animals called ιotifers (due to the wheel-like movement of bristles around their mouths as they filter feed) attach themselves to a substrate by means of a foot structure. At least one species (*Ptygura beauchampi*) has been found to attach to the bristles and appendages of *Utricularia macrorhiza*. The rotifers do not attach to the traps of four other temperate, sympatric species, however, and they are not prey. What causes the rotifers to attach to this particular bladderwort species is not known, but it is postulated to be chemical in nature (Wallace 1978).

Trap Function

Darwin (1875) believed that the prey forced its way by the trapdoor into the trap and was retained by a one-way valve effect of the door. He admit-

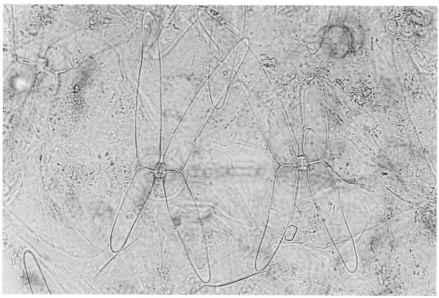

A microscopic view of quadrifid glands of *Utricularia ochroleuca*, prepared as described in the text. Note that the two glands here are in an X shape created by the four arms diverging from the central attachment point. Note also that one pair of arms is shorter than the other.

ted some dissatisfaction with this explanation, however, because it did not explain the entrance of smaller, seemingly weaker prey into the trap. Darwin also felt that the antennae and bristles acted in concert as sort of a funnel to guide the prey toward the opening. According to Meyers and Strickler (1979), he was more likely correct in this assumption.

We now know that the trapping and resetting process is extremely complex. In fact, many of the bladderworts' secrets are yet to be revealed. For many years, researchers felt that small water animals simply blun-

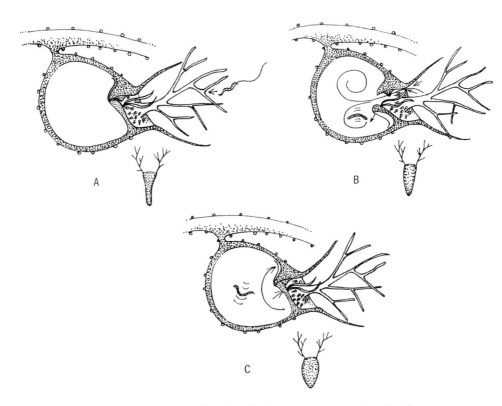

Profiles of *Utricularia* traps from the side (large image, top) and top (small image, bottom) during closure. In (A), a small prey approaches the bristles near the trapdoor, resulting in (B) the door opening and water and the prey rushing into the trap, after which (C) the door recloses. Note the changes in trap profile, which indicate changes in internal pressure, as discussed in the text. Drawings by David Kutt.

dered up to the traps, followed the funneling device, and ultimately triggered the trap. Given the large numbers of organisms living in aquatic environments and the large numbers of bladderwort traps, trapping may be somewhat haphazard. However, there is evidence of attraction as well, possibly by the mysterious mucilaginous material secreted by the glands on the brink of the trap mouth. Rather than ensnaring prey as mucilage does in terrestrial carnivorous plants, some or all of the secretion may be attractive (Joel 1982).

The traps of bladderworts always contain liquid, but in the set trap there is less liquid than could be held in the trap, resulting in a negative pressure on the inside that causes the flexible walls to pinch inward. If a small defect should exist in the trap wall at this set stage, water would rush into the interior due to the negative pressure. The trapdoor is held tightly against and sealed to the threshold, although the nature of this sealing process is not known. The trap is ready.

As a small aquatic animal approaches the trap mouth, it enters the bristle and antennae funnel. The animal gets closer to the door and contacts the trigger hairs associated with it. Then the door flies open and the negative interior pressure sucks water into the mouth along with the hapless prey. The trapdoor settles back to the threshold and the animal is trapped within. Because there is no longer a negative pressure within the trap, its sides are now straight or may bulge outward slightly.

The mechanism of how the door operates is not known. There are currently two different theories (see Juniper et al. 1989). One is that the trigger hair acts as a mechanical handle that jars the door just loose enough at a portion of its seal to allow the inward rush of water to begin, with the pressure of water coming in causing the door to open the rest of the way (which is close to Darwin's concept). The second theory is that the trigger hair movement is excitatory, similar to trigger hairs in *Dionaea*, and that an electrical discharge changes the door turgor so that it opens. To date, however, no electrical activity has been recorded. Attempts to get the trap to fire with external electrodes applied to either side of the trap have met with mixed results. Regardless of the mechanism, the trapdoor movement is the most rapid known among plants (with the possible exception of the movement of stamens in the triggerplants, *Stylidium*), being on the order of 0.02 seconds (Joel 1982).

Resetting the Trap

In *Utricularia*, resetting the trap involves resealing the trapdoor and absorbing and excreting fluid from the interior so negative pressure again develops. Studies indicate that water is absorbed by the internal bifid glands near the trap mouth and that the fluid exits the trap through the pavement epithelium of the trapdoor threshold (Sydenham and Findlay 1975; Sasago and Sibaoka 1985a, 1985b). Fineran (1985) suggested that some of the water absorbed by internal glands exits via external surface glands on the trap as well. Again, there is no definite information on the nature of trapdoor sealing, which may involve an increase in the door's turgor that makes it more rigid.

The process of resetting the trap takes about twenty to forty minutes on average (Darwin 1875). However, a temperature decrease can slow resetting to as much as several hours. The process requires energy as evidenced by increased respiratory activity (Sydenham and Findlay 1975; Sasago and Sibaoka 1985a, 1985b).

Digestion and Absorption

The question of digestion in *Utricularia* comes down to the usual one: Is it bacterial or inherently enzymatic? Parkes (1980) reported that the quadrifid glands contain esterases, acid phosphatase, and protease, with the enzymes varying among species. Sterile axenic cultures of various bladderworts have shown that the traps are able to digest *Paramecium* species from equally sterile axenic cultures, so intrinsic enzyme production plays at least some role (Pringsheim and Pringsheim 1962). The possible additive effects of microbial activity in the plants' natural environment, however, have not been entirely ruled out.

Prey and organic nutrients contribute to the vigor of bladderwort plants. Sorenson and Jackson (1968) fed *Paramecium* to *Utricularia gibba* plants in a nearly optimal artificial culture medium and noted no increased growth. However, when *U. gibba* growing in incomplete media (more nearly representing native habitat) were fed paramecia, growth and bladder production were enhanced. Pringsheim and Pringsheim (1962) noted that sterile axenic cultures of *U. exoleta* in an inorganic nutrient solution produced good vegetative growth but flowered only if sterile organic beef extract was added. Thus, bladderworts appear to benefit from entrapped prey.

Some organisms are able to survive entrapment by bladderworts and to even thrive. Lloyd (1942) noted *Euglena* and some diatoms within bladders, where they lived and reproduced. Roberts (1972) observed the novelty of the tiny aquatic seed plant *Wolffia* (duckweed, water meal) in traps of *Utricularia macrorhiza* in a bay in Lake Erie. The traps did not appear to digest the plants. Duckweed grows on the surface of still waters, often very thickly, and Roberts postulated that disturbances fired the traps, which incidentally caught the *Wolffia*.

Introduction to the Species

With the *Utricularia* species, I will depart from the format of the preceding chapters for several reasons. There are nineteen species of bladderworts in the United States and Canada, and several, particularly among the yellow-flowered species, are difficult for the novice to identify. In fact, in some of the following sections, I will discuss more than one species at a time to contrast differences between seemingly similar taxa. As a result of the superb monograph by Taylor (1989), synonymy will be largely restricted to recently changed epithet designations. Many older field guides and floras may have other binomials for a particular plant. Only one or two of the bladderworts have common names, so these will be merely mentioned. There will be no distribution maps because many of the species occur in spotty fashion throughout the United States and Canada. There has also been some confusion among experienced field botanists concerning identification of what they have collected and labeled for herbariums, thereby compromising exact range delineation in some cases. Thus, I will mention distribution in broader terms. Chromosome counts are also conflicting and incomplete for North American bladderworts. The chromosomes are very tiny, and there is evidence of autopolyploidy in some species. Those wishing to review various attempts to count chromosomes are referred to Taylor (1989). Descriptions of species will be in a more narrative fashion, but of sufficient detail to identify the plant, particularly in flower.

Botanists and advanced amateurs use keys to quickly identify related groups of plants. A key is composed of couplets of contrasting characters in which the reader makes an either-or choice and then is directed to another couplet, which ultimately leads to an identification. There have been many keys devised for *Utricularia*—as many as there are regional floras—but most involve a combination of flower and vegetative features. Vegetative keys for the bladderworts are extremely complex, even if one were designed pictorially, because details are technical and subtle; also, low-power microscopy is often required. The best key for U.S. and Canadian *Utricularia* that I have seen is one commissioned for a special edition of *Carnivorous Plant Newsletter* by Peter Taylor (1991), to whom the issue was dedicated. It is actually two keys in one: a vegetative key for the advanced student and a floral key more useful to the beginner. Because most bladderworts are noticed in the field when in flower, some sort of floral identification system along with a few other easily observed characters seems most useful.

The key that I have designed for this book is by no means a natural system, as most botanists might prefer. I make no apologies, however, if this tool serves its purpose. I have numbered the species so that as you move through the key, you can easily locate the species discussions. In addition to heavy reliance on flower color, the key refers to growth habit. For purposes of discussion here, U.S. and Canadian bladderworts have three usual growth habits: two aquatic and one terrestrial. In the first aquatic habit, the plant is free-floating with no attachment; in the second, some of the stolons affix the plant to the pond bottom, with the buried stolons having traps attached. Lifting the plant from the water will usually immediately disclose whether it was affixed. Taylor (1989) noted that one can often examine terrestrial bladderworts "dry-shod." The substrate is usually a sandy peat that is quite damp above to very wet below the surface, but the area may frequently be inundated by shallow water after rain or snowmelt. In any event, there are no floating stolons or filiform leaves in the terrestrial bladderworts.

To identify a bladderwort using this key, compare the plant's characters to the key beginning with A. If the characters match the description, the species is identified; if they do not match, move to B. If the plant's characters match the B description, move successively through the BB entries until a species is identified. If the plant's characters do not match, move to C, and so on until the species is identified. Species and species pairs are discussed in the text that follows the key.

Key to Species and Species Groups of U.S. and Canadian *Utricularia*

A. White flowers that are minute (2.0–2.5 mm)
      1. *U. olivacea*
B. Flowers usually pink, rose, or light purple
   BB. free-floating, aquatic
      2. *U. purpurea*
   BB. affixed in mud
      3. *U. resupinata*
   BB. terrestrial, restricted to southern Florida
      4. *U. amethystine*
C. Flowers yellow, aquatic, free-floating
   CC. stolon flattened in cross-section, no peduncle floats
      5. *U. foliosa*
   CC. stem round, no peduncle floats
      6. *U. geminiscapa*
      7. *U. macrorhiza*
      (10. *U. gibba* occasionally free-floating)
   CC. stolon round; peduncle with radial, spokelike floats
      8. *U. inflata*
      9. *U. radiata*

D. Flowers yellow, aquatic, affixed to bottom of pool
> 10. *U. gibba*
> 11. *U. floridana*
> 12. *U. striata*
> 13. *U. minor*
> 14. *U. intermedia*
> 15. *U. ochroleuca*

E. Flowers yellow, terrestrial
> EE. peduncle and flower with fimbriated (fringed) scales, bracts, and calyces, restricted to southern Florida
> > 16. *U. simulans*
>
> EE. peduncle and flower without fimbriated scales, bracts, and calyces
> > 17. *U. cornuta*
> > 18. *U. juncea*
> > 19. *U. subulata*

1. *Utricularia olivacea* Wright ex Griesbach

Utricularia olivacea is considered by many to be the smallest by weight of any flowering plant in the world. The stolons are threadlike, less than 1.0 mm in thickness. Because these aquatic, annual plants are often intertwined among other species of *Utricularia* in the same location, identifying them in the vegetative state is nearly impossible. However, if you are exploring bladderwort shallows of the coastal plain in August or September, you may see the minute (1.0–2.5 mm) white flowers peppering the surface.

Utricularia olivacea grows in suitable locations in New Jersey, North and South Carolina, Georgia, and Florida, but the plant's small size and limited flowering period may have precluded identification in more locations and states. The stolons do not have divided or aerial leaves, only the traps, which measure 1.0 mm or less. The pedicels are up to 1.0 cm in length. In Florida, flowering may occur from November through March.

Biovularia olivacea is an important synonym that you may come across

A small stand of *Utricularia olivacea* in Brunswick County, North Carolina. For size comparison, the stolon of *U. purpurea* running across the upper left corner is 1.5 mm in thickness. *Utricularia olivacea*'s minute white flowers and their buds on slender pedicels pepper the surface.

A closer view of *Utricularia olivacea* flowers. A magnifying glass is helpful in appreciating these flowers in the field.

in older literature. This name reflects an interesting feature of the species: the carpel has only two ovules (biovulate) and appears to bear one seed, although Taylor (1989) is not certain whether this conclusion is based on a seedpod rather than the supposed single seed. The margins of the calyx are smooth when the plant is in flower, but as the seedpod matures, the margins become coarsely and irregularly toothed. Flowers in dried herbarium specimens tend to turn yellowish tan, thus the mistaken notion among some previous students that the flowers were yellow rather than white. In addition to Taylor (1989), other informative papers include Beal and Quay (1968) and Cooper (1977). A pollination study of the small flowers would be interesting, but they may also be self-pollinating. In the field, I have seen the flowers visited by small midges and gnatlike flying insects, but, of course, further proof is required to indicate these visitors as pollinators.

I have not had long-term success in cultivating *Utricularia olivacea*, probably due to its annual character and preference for growing among other bladderworts and water plants. I have managed to keep it through two flowering seasons, so apparently seeds of the original collection germinated. I always grew it in single culture and have not tried cultures mixed with other *Utricularia* species, which may be more successful. A sandy or sand-peat medium with an overlying few centimeters of pure water is worth trying initially.

2. *Utricularia purpurea* Walter

Utricularia purpurea is a free-floating, aquatic perennial up to about 1 m in length, found in shallow to moderately deep ponds or slowly running bog waters. The vegetative plant parts usually have a pale brown to reddish brown color, and the growth tips are often bright red. A key feature in this free-floating bladderwort is the bright pink to pinkish violet flowers.

The round (terete) stolons are 0.5–2.0 mm across and have whorls (verticillate) of branching capillary segments. The stolons have a spongy feel when squeezed. Even though the distribution of *Utricularia purpurea* extends into eastern Canada, no turions are formed. The peduncle is 3–20 cm tall and 0.5–1.0 mm thick in the aerial portion but widening gradually to a thickness of up to 3.0 mm at the water line and below. The advantage of this widening to the plant is not known.

The flowers are from 1.0 to 2.0 cm long and there may be two or three per peduncle. A very clear characteristic of the corolla is that the lower lip is divided into three lobes; the two lateral lobes are saccate (pouch shaped) and the middle lobe is longer and somewhat quadrate (square cornered). The spur is quite short and cone shaped.

Utricularia purpurea has a rather wide distribution in the East and can be found in suitable waters from Ontario, Quebec, New Brunswick, and

Utricularia purpurea nearly filling a pond in Collier County, Florida. An immediate identification can be made by noting that this is an aquatic bladderwort with pink to pinkish violet flowers.

A *Utricularia purpurea* flower. Note particularly that the two lateral lobes of the lower lip are inflated and pouch shaped, whereas the middle lobe is flattened and longer.

Nova Scotia (Hay et al. 1990) down through the coastal plan from Maine to Texas, extending inland to Michigan, Illinois, and Indiana. Additional isolated sites may well be found in other states.

A white-flowered form of *Utricularia purpurea* has been found in a lake in New Hampshire and described as forma *alba* (Hellquist 1974). In all other respects, this form is much like the plants that produce pinkish violet flowers.

Utricularia purpurea is difficult to transport. If in a vessel or shipment for more than a day or two, it tends to undergo fragmentation, or autolysis, from which it will not recover. I have never grown this bladderwort successfully. For those determined to try, a suitable established pond to which chemicals are not added would be the best bet, especially if located in or near the general distribution of the plant.

3. *Utricularia resupinata* Greene ex Bigelow

This fixed, semiaquatic perennial has some stolons that behave as rhizoids, which tend to fix the matted plant into underlying mud. The stolons are up to 10 cm long and up to 1.5 mm thick. *Utricularia resupinata* does not produce turions. Grasslike, aerial leaves emanate from the bases of the peduncles; these are rounded, filiform, and up to 5 cm in length. A unique feature is that the distal one-fourth to one-third or so of the leaves is articulated (jointed). The lower parts of the aerial leaves frequently have bladders. Taylor (1989) was able to identify the plant out of flower in Florida because of the long, peculiarly articulated aerial leaves.

The flower is rosy pink, stands upright, and is marked by an especially prominent, cylindrical spur so that the flower appears C shaped in side view. The palate is coarsely wrinkled. The 4–20-cm peduncle has an interesting tubular bract near the top, with the bract tending to surround the stem. The specific epithet indicates resupinate, or upside down, which this species is not. It only seems so because of the prominent spur and side profile of the corolla.

Utricularia resupinata has an extensive range including eastern Canada, down the coastal plain from Maine to Georgia and Florida, and westward into Michigan, Indiana, and Wisconsin. It was most recently found in Minnesota (Ownbey and Smith 1988). The species tends to grow in shallow water with very mucky substrates; in the Great Lakes area *U. resupinata* has been found in false-bottomed lakes (see Introduction). For a long time this bladderwort was thought to be absent in Virginia and the Carolinas. However, in the 1990s, T. L. Mellichamp (personal correspondence) found *U. resupinata* in Columbus County, North Carolina,

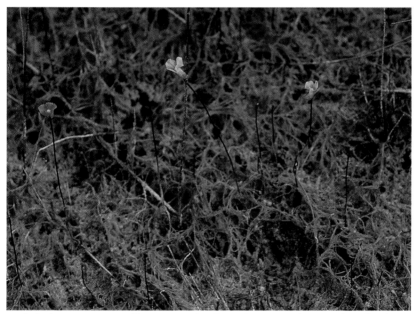

Utricularia resupinata in Collier County, Florida. In these examples, note the red peduncles; the rosy pink flower with a large, prominent spur; and the grasslike, aerial leaves.

along the shore of an aquatic Carolina Bay, Lake Waccamaw. A drought lasting several years had caused the lake margin to recede, leaving a muddy swath along several shores. *Utricularia resupinata* apparently had been growing vegetatively beneath the water surface in the mud and only became clearly visible when the water receded and the plants flowered. I would expect the species to turn up elsewhere in the mid-Atlantic coastal plain. Gates (1929, 1939) studied *Utricularia resupinata* in Michigan and noticed that it only flowered in lowering water levels and in temperatures slightly increased over normal, as apparently occurred in the Lake Waccamaw population discovered by Mellichamp.

Several others and I have been able to keep *Utricularia resupinata* in cultivation, although it is shy to flower. I grow the stolon mat in a shallow tray with drain holes, the substrate being peat or peaty sand. I place the tray into another one without drain holes and fill the bottom tray with water so that the level is just above the soil surface, resulting in a slurry muck. The plant is not visible throughout most of the year in the greenhouse, but every spring, the green aerial leaves appear with a few flowers. I would imagine that the species would be a good terrarium subject as well. Because this bladderwort lacks turions, Taylor (1989) surmises that it may survive over the winter as seeds in the North.

Two flowers of *Utricularia resupinata*. Again, note the large spur and C-shaped profile of the corolla. About one-third of the way down the peduncle, tubular bracts can be seen. Tubular bracts are present only in one other bladderwort species, the South American *U. spruceana* (Taylor 1989).

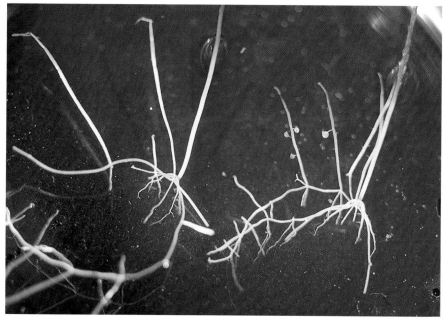

A mat of *Utricularia resupinata* washed free of soil and floated in water in a dish. The green-tipped, aerial leaves are visible; note that the distal one-third or so has a crease or articulation (joint). On the right, the lower parts of the aerial leaves have bladders attached.

4. *Utricularia amethystina* Salzmann ex Saint-Hilaire & Girard

Utricularia amethystina is a tropical, probably perennial species found rather widely in the neotropics, but is recorded from only two collections in extreme southern peninsular Florida. Jeanette P. Standley first found the species in a location described vaguely as "east of Fort Meyers in Lee County." Based on Standley's specimens, Barnhart described the collections as *Calpidisca standleyae*. Rickett changed the genus to *Utricularia standleyae*, but his publication was never valid (see history in Taylor 1989). All of this is moot, however, because Taylor has determined that the plants are the same as the tropical *Utricularia amethystina*, which takes precedence.

Len Brass made a second collection of this bladderwort in 1946, this time in Collier County, Florida. His location description was somewhat more exacting. Unfortunately, the site that matches his description has been severely disturbed; recently, with construction of Interstate 75 across southern Florida, the site has been turned into a borrow pit. Before that construction, I scouted the area for several years during different possible flowering seasons and never found the species. I even engaged others who were going to southern Florida for one reason or another (Larry Mellichamp kindly gave up a day or two of a Christmas vacation in the search), but to date we have not found examples of *Utricularia amethystina*. The species is likely somewhere else on the eastern edge of Big Cypress Swamp. I anticipate that one day I or someone else will again find this

A composite figure of *Utricularia amethystina*; this specimen is material grown by me from a collection in Venezuela. Note the prominent rosette of paddle-shaped, aerial leaves around the bases of the peduncles (right) and additional small leaves arising from stolons beneath the mud surface. The small flower (left) has a very small upper lip, a more prominent lower lip with a yellow spot near the base, and a prominent spur extending out from beneath the lower lip.

bladderwort in southern Florida, but right now it remains as an excuse for us to spend some time in Naples, Florida, every now and then either in late October or, better yet, January.

Throughout its neotropical range, *Utricularia amethystina* is a rather polymorphous species, particularly in such factors as flower size and color. In tropical Florida, however, the old herbarium collections have been of smaller plants growing in damp sand to peaty soil, usually in the open but more tolerant of shade than most bladderworts. When in flower, prominent aerial leaves form a rosette around the base of the peduncle, the leaves having obovate blades and short, narrow petioles and measuring to 1.5 cm long overall. The flower is mauve to rosy pink and measures to 1.5 cm in length. It has a small upper lip, and the longer lower lip has a prominent yellow dot at the throat. The spur is up to twice as long as the lower lip.

Utricularia amethystina showed up in my collection as a volunteer among some *Drosera* plants from Venezuela. I did not know I had this bladderwort until it flowered among the sundews. Peter Taylor confirmed the identity during a visit to my greenhouse. It continues to appear yearly, growing among other plants in Canadian peat, but disappears completely after a flowering episode.

5. *Utricularia foliosa* Linnaeus

Utricularia foliosa is a large, rank, free-floating perennial found in still or slowly moving clear waters of ponds, lakes, streams, and ditches of the Southeast. The range extends from North Carolina (where it is not common) down to eastern Texas, but this bladderwort is strangely absent so far from South Carolina and Georgia, where it may yet be found. The plant reaches its zenith in Florida, and everywhere it has been confused with *U. macrorhiza* (called *U. vulgaris* at times), although the latter grows much farther north.

This bladderwort may be several meters in length with large stolons up to 5 mm wide. The stolons are flattened rather than round, a feature unique in the genus. Plumes of three kinds of finely divided leaves branch from the stolons, these being best described by Godfrey and Wooten (1981). One kind is especially finely divided and extends horizontally in the water. These lateral branches have fewer traps near their bases. A second kind is more elongate and bushy and extends deeply into the water. These deep branches contain the most traps. Finally, there is a branch nearly devoid of plumose proliferation, which is located near the water surface and rarely has traps.

The flowers of *Utricularia foliosa* number from three to twenty on a peduncle 7–45 cm long, but averaging 25–30 cm. Pedicels are delicate and rather long and arching as the flower ages into fruit. The yellow flowers are up to 2.0 cm long. The upper lip is smaller than the lower, but still

Utricularia foliosa in a roadside ditch in Collier County, Florida. A curving, large, main stolon is seen in the lower center, from which the plumose, foxtail branches fill the water. The yellow flowers on large peduncles are clearly seen.

quite prominent and semicircular in outline. The lower lip has a very prominent palate that is often colored a deeper, almost golden yellow compared to the rest of the corolla. The spur of the lower lip is conical and always shorter. Seedpods are dark purple and somewhat like berries. These pods float on the water, whereas the seeds within sink.

Surprisingly, I have had some success in growing this rather huge plant in the confines of the greenhouse. It does not have space to attain full size, but it does manage to flower for several years. Most of my *Sarracenia* plants are in round pots in deep trays of the sort used to collect dishes in restaurants. There is sufficient watery space between the pots to support *Utricularia foliosa* nicely. It is worth trying to grow this bladderwort in southeastern ponds or ponds in conservatories, and it may even do well in large plastic tubs in good light. Even though the plants survive in lakes that become quite cold in the winter in eastern North Carolina, I am not certain that keeping it outdoors in tubs in such climes and further north would be successful.

A flowering peduncle of *Utricularia foliosa*. Note the slightly longer lower lip, the deeper yellow palate with some fine red streaking, and the arching pedicels with berrylike fruit.

Right: Close-up of *Utricularia foliosa* flowers. Note the very prominent palate with somewhat darker yellow color and the longer lower lip. Between the two flowers is a dark, maturing seedpod.

6. *Utricularia geminiscapa* Benjamin
7. *Utricularia macrorhiza* Le Conte

Although these two free-floating, aquatic perennials are not related, they share the same distribution in eastern Canada and the northeastern United States, where *Utricularia geminiscapa* is restricted (with the exception of one herbarium collection in a roadside ditch in Beaufort County, North Carolina). There may be some confusion in separating the two species, so I will discuss them together for comparison. In addition to the above distribution, *U. macrorhiza* is also found most commonly throughout Canada and portions of Alaska, down into northern California, and then generally throughout the United States in isolated areas, including the mountains of New Mexico and Arizona. *Utricularia macrorhiza* is usually not found in the Southeast, but occasionally sterile specimens are recorded from South Carolina and Florida, where individuals may have been carried on the feet of birds.

Both species form winter turions, those of *Utricularia geminiscapa* being smaller than in *U. macrorhiza*. *Utricularia geminiscapa* has no important synonyms, but *U. macrorhiza* has most frequently and until quite recently been thought of as the Old World *U. vulgaris*, sometimes as an infraspecies such as variety *americana*, subspecies *macrorhiza*, or even as the species *U. australis*. However, Taylor (1989) determined that the North American plants are sufficiently distinct to warrant separate species designation, *U. macrorhiza*, which should be reflected in newer floras. Both species are found in shallow to deep waters, acidic bog pools, lakes, and roadside ditches.

Utricularia geminiscapa has stolons to 60 cm long by 0.5 cm thick with narrowly branching, plumose, aquatic leaves. The species has two kinds of inflorescences: cleistogamous (closed) and chasmogamous (open). The inflorescences may arise simultaneously from the same node so that one or two cleistogamous, single pedicels with single flowers are bent into the water, while the more familiar chasmogamous inflorescence is aerial. The cleistogamous flowers look like small, closed buds, and early workers mistook them for turions. They are best seen by lifting the plant from the water and examining nodes from which open, aerial flowers arise. The aerial, chasmogamous flowers are on a 5–25-cm peduncle and are up to 1.0 cm long. The yellow corollas have a prominent palatal area with red streaks; the spur is shorter than the lower lip and only slightly curved. The lower lip is always shallowly three lobed.

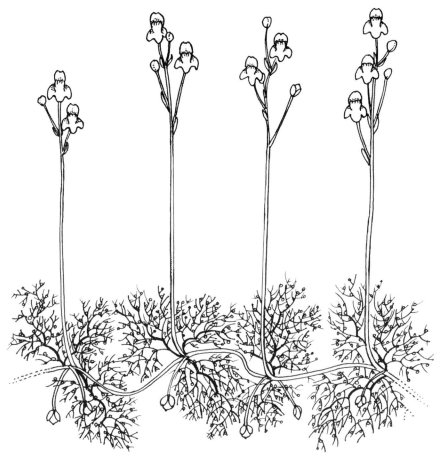

A composite drawing of characters of *Utricularia geminiscapa* in flower. Note the small, cleistogamous flowers dipping into the water at nodes with aerial, chasmogamous flowers. The lower lip of flowers of this species is always three lobed, as compared to the entire lip of *U. macrorhiza*, which has aerial, chasmogamous flowers only. Drawing by David Kutt.

Utricularia macrorhiza has vegetative dimensions that are similar to *U. geminiscapa*, but the leaves appear to be more widely plumose. This bladderwort does not produce cleistogamous aquatic flowers. The more robust peduncle is up 40 cm long, and the yellow flowers are larger than those of *U. geminiscapa*, to 2 cm. The spur is as long as the lower lip and is more prominently curved at the tip. The lower lip margin is entire, not lobed. More commonly, this species has deeply red (almost black), large traps to 3–4 mm.

If you wish to dissect traps to view quadrifid glands, the long arms of the glands of both species are nearly parallel, but the short arms of *Utricularia macrorhiza* are more divergent. This comparison should not be necessary if you note that *U. macrorhiza* is the more robust species with larger corollas, the differences in the lower lip margin and spur characters, and *U. geminiscapa* produces cleistogamous flowers (although these must be looked for below the water surface).

This frontal view of a *Utricularia macrorhiza* flower shows the free margin of the lower lip to be entire, not lobed.

Side view of the bright yellow flowers of *Utricularia macrorhiza* in Bruce County, Ontario. Note the thick peduncles and that the spur is prominently curved.

Both *Utricularia macrorhiza* and *U. geminiscapa* seem easy to grow anywhere in an outdoor pond, although there will be less flowering in warmer climes. Avoid toxic chemicals in the water. I simply have a large plastic tub sunk in the ground with a sandy peat substrate and the plants fill it each year. Turions form regularly in autumn and give rise to new plants in the spring. Overgrowth by algae does not seem to be a problem because the plants themselves are so vigorous. However, native species of snails found with the plants will also keep algae down. Beware of other species of snails that do not live with the plants in natural habitat (such as aquarium-shop purchases); these may eat the traps and leaves.

8. *Utricularia inflata* Walter
9. *Utricularia radiata* Small

These two species are closely related. Initially the novice may have difficulty telling them apart, so I will discuss them together for comparison. These bladderworts are the only two species in the United States and Canada with radial, inflated, spokelike floats about midway up the peduncle, which apparently hold the flowering raceme erect and above the water.

Utricularia inflata grows in Massachusetts (Sorrie 1992) and New York (Mitchell et al. 1994), but more commonly on the coastal plain from New Jersey to Texas, with some westward extension to Kentucky, Tennessee, and Arkansas and even a few sites in Washington. *Utricularia radiata* has a wider distribution: from eastern Canada through Maine, on the coastal plain south to Louisiana, and into Kentucky, Tennessee, and Arkansas. These distributions may expand with further exploration of suitable habitat at varying times in the growing season. The two species rarely grow together in the same water even where the distribution widely overlaps. Taylor (1989, 1991) has seen them together in Florida, however, where they are a study in contrasts.

Utricularia inflata and *U. radiata* grow in similar habitats: shallow to deep bog, pond, and lake waters or drainage ditches with slowly moving water. After flowering and seed set, which occur relatively early in the regional growing season, the characteristic floats begin to disintegrate along with the rest of the peduncle and only the rather nondescript aquatic components remain.

Some authorities had placed these two species into one with variants, such as *Utricularia inflata* variety *minor* or *U. inflata* variety *radiata* for *U. radiata*. However, Reinert and Godfrey (1962) and Taylor (1989) have satisfactorily demonstrated that these bladderworts are two separate species.

Utricularia inflata is a perennial and has the capacity to produce tubers (not turions) in challenging habitats. Most often noted when the water level is falling and the plants are marooned in very shallow water or muck, a specialized stolon will emerge from between two others and pro-

Utricularia inflata plants growing in a roadside ditch in northern Florida. The spokelike arrangement of air-filled floats keeps the peduncle erect and above water. Beneath the surface masses of stolons and leaves can be seen.

duce a small, starchy tuber at its terminus. Reinert and Godfrey (1962) showed in laboratory experiments that these tubers bud into new plants when placed in salubrious conditions. In contrast, *U. radiata* is largely an annual (although it may behave as a perennial in warm climes) and does not produce tubers. Taylor (1989) placed *U. radiata* plants into conditions that engendered tubers in *U. inflata* and saw no tuber production there, nor has it been seen in the wild or in herbarium specimens.

The two species are most readily diagnosed by differences in the inflorescences and their floats. The floats of *Utricularia inflata* are much larger, measuring to 25 cm across (more usually 15–20 cm with a rare tetraploid being up to twice that diameter) and the peduncles are 20–50 cm

A fine stand of flowering *Utricularia radiata* in a roadside ditch along Route 211 in Brunswick County, North Carolina. Improving drainage in roadside ditches throughout the South is making scenes such as this less common.

An inflorescence of *Utricularia inflata*. There are eight spokes, or arms, in the flotation disc in this example. Each arm tends to be widest at about two-thirds from the axis of the peduncle, gradually tapering to each end.

long, including the aquatic portion. There are five to ten spokes. *Utricularia radiata* has floats measuring 6–10 cm across, peduncles 7–25 cm long, and there are four to seven spokes. In all proportions, *U. radiata* is smaller.

Float characters may be used for identification. Besides differences in the size of floats and numbers of spokes, the float arms of *Utricularia inflata* are widest at a point about two-thirds out from the axis of the ped-

An inflorescence of *Utricularia radiata*. There are six spokes, or arms, in the flotation disc in this example. Each arm remains wider as it extends toward the peduncle axis, where it suddenly narrows.

uncle, narrowing gradually toward each end. The float arms of *U. radiata* are shorter and only narrow rather suddenly near the peduncle axis.

Wading into the water and securing a flower or two for close examination will reveal another helpful difference. The spurs of corollas of *Utricularia inflata* are nearly always notched to varying depths, whereas the spur of *U. radiata* usually is not. Examination of several flowers from several plants in the colony will provide a consensus on this point. For those interested in even finer details of differences between these two species, consult Reinert and Godfrey (1962) and Taylor (1989).

In cultivation, I have had no long-term success with *Utricularia radiata* because of its annual behavior. I have not been able to germinate seed to continue the culture. *Utricularia inflata* is more amenable to cultivation attempts, probably due to its perennial nature. It grows well in shallow or deeper pools of pure water over a substrate of sand or sandy peat. Even then, it keeps for only a few years and fades. Growers with access to boggy or acidic ponds or slow ditches on the coastal plain would likely have the greatest success in establishing either of these bladderworts.

A flower of *Utricularia inflata* viewed from the back. Note the notch at the tip of the spur. Spur notches in this species vary greatly in depth, but their presence is helpful in identification.

A flower of *Utricularia radiata* viewed from the back. The tip of the spur is not notched, the usual condition in this species.

10. *Utricularia gibba* Linnaeus

This little, generally affixed (but sometimes free-floating), aquatic, yellow-flowered bladderwort is probably the second most widespread *Utricularia* species in the world (after the terrestrial *U. subulata*) and one of the most complex taxonomically. This complexity is due to the marked variation in flower size as well as corresponding vegetative size throughout its range. The problem was completely discussed by Taylor (1989) as he recounted the difficult, often revisited decisions he made over the years. As a result, there is persistent taxonomic confusion in older and even some recent floras. A former species of the southern coastal plain, *Utricularia biflora*, has been taxonomically absorbed into *U. gibba* as a result of Taylor's studies, but I expect the name *U. biflora* to continue showing up now and then in future floras. To further complicate matters, there has always been confusion between the southern *U. biflora* and then *U. fibrosa*, now *U. striata* (see *U. striata* section). I will show differences between *U. striata* and the various expressions of *U. gibba* in the *U. striata* section.

Utricularia gibba in Michigan. The flower is less than 1 cm in length and the upper lip is slightly larger than the lower. Note the spur just protruding from beneath the lower lip. The peduncles are quite short.

Utricularia gibba is among a small set of yellow-flowered U.S. and Canadian species wherein the upper lip of the corolla is as large as or slightly larger than the lower lip. In *U. gibba* the upper lip is weakly but clearly three lobed. The spur is as long as or slightly longer than the lower

This smaller expression of *Utricularia gibba* was found in a pond adjacent to a stream in Columbus County, North Carolina. Note the weakly three-lobed appearance of the large upper lip and the very dense but finely threaded appearance of the aquatic vegetative portions of the plant. This example is very similar to the northern and western expression of this species.

lip. The peduncle is filamentous and up to 1.0 mm thick and 1–20 cm long. I will discuss the key features for identifying the three species of yellow-flowered, fixed, aquatic butterworts (*U. gibba, U. floridana,* and *U. striata*) near the end of the *U. striata* section.

The stolons of *Utricularia gibba* are 0.2–1.0 mm thick and to 20 cm long. Aquatic leaves are very finely divided. The combination of these characters results in a plant composed of fine threads, like very loosely interwoven strands of filamentous algae, but still a cohesive unit. I find that this rather subjective appearance aids in immediate recognition in northern bog waters, even when the plant is out of flower.

Utricularia gibba is widespread throughout the United States and Canada and absent only from the plains, the Rocky Mountain states and provinces, and Alaska. There is size variation, with the corolla varying from 0.8 to 1.5 cm. The plants may be affixed or free-floating, the latter rarely flowering because they are in deeper water. To flower, the plants

A comparison of flowers of the smaller, northernlike plant of *Utricularia gibba* (left) and the typical southern bifloral expression (right) from the same county in North Carolina.

The larger, two-flowered expression of *Utricularia gibba* (formerly *U. biflora*) in Columbus County, North Carolina. The flowers are usually in pairs, sometimes singles. In this region, these bladderworts are always affixed and growing in shallow water.

seem to require shallow water a few centimeters deep where they can affix to the bottom by rhizoids or suspend on other vegetative debris in the water. In the southeastern coastal plain, the usual expression of *U. gibba* is in the larger size range given above and almost always with no more than two flowers (hence the older epithet *biflora* for this set). In Columbus County, North Carolina, where the southeastern two-flowered expression of *U. gibba* abounds, I found in a small, side pond adjacent to a creek a stand of the species with typical northern expression of smaller, single flowers, the only such site I have seen in the South.

Utricularia gibba is the ideal aquatic bladderwort for cultivation; in fact, growers often describe it as a weed. It is a good subject for home ponds and aquaria, as long as the plant is not consumed by fish or snails or killed by toxic chemicals. I grow it between pots in shallow trays of water in the greenhouse, where the low water level is conducive to flowering.

11. *Utricularia floridana* Nash

This rather spectacular, large species, which is endemic to the southeastern United States, is closely related to *Utricularia gibba* and *U. striata*. All three have corolla upper lips as large as if not larger than the lower, and the upper lip is weakly three lobed. As the epithet indicates, *U. floridana* is most easily found in Florida, but is also reported from North and South Carolina, Georgia, and Alabama. Peter Taylor (1989) found the species in White Lake in Bladen County, North Carolina, in 1972 with no previous state record recorded. Apparently, he did not see the plants growing in the water, but washed up on shore.

Utricularia floridana reaches its best growth in water that is 1 m or deeper, although it has been seen in as little as 0.3 m of water. In Florida, it is found most prolifically in karst or lime sinkhole lakes, but the White Lake site suggests that more acidic waters are acceptable.

This rank perennial has stolons up to 50 cm long and 1 mm thick. The stolon branches strongly affixed into the sandy or silty lake bottom are generally without leaves, but have abundant traps. The main stolon ascending into the peduncle has numerous floating, finely divided, leafy branches that have been compared to foxtails or feather boas. The peduncle is up to 1.0 m long and 3 mm thick, and the yellow flowers are up to 2.0 cm in length. The lower lip has a prominent rugose swelling in the palate area.

I have not tried growing *Utricularia floridana* because it would require a rather large, deep tank or pond in a relatively warm clime for success. There might also be problems attaining proper water chemistry. How-

A nameless lime sinkhole in Washington County, Florida, with a nice stand of *Utricularia floridana*. Out from the shore, note the even line of plants growing in 1-m deep water. Floating vegetative debris extends out from the actual shoreline.

A closer view of *Utricularia floridana*. Note the finely dissected leaves, which resemble a foxtail or feather boa, floating in varying depths. These are attached to the 1-m long, ascending stolon and peduncle.

A close-up of a flower of *Utricularia floridana*. This plant could be *U. gibba* or *U. striata* as well, except these flowers are 2.0 cm in length. The upper lip is larger than the lower and weakly three lobed; in this example the lower lip is two lobed.

ever, those who own or have permission to access lime sinkholes in the Southeast might find some success if the plants could be transplanted.

12. *Utricularia striata* Le Conte ex Torrey

Known as *Utricularia fibrosa* in older floras and papers, this close rela-tive of *U. floridana* is also an endemic of the United States, being found in the coastal plain from Massachusetts to Texas and up to Oklahoma. *Utricularia striata* grows in shallow bog waters, marshes, and ditches as an affixed perennial, but is sometimes found in a slurry of *Sphagnum*.

A clump of *Utricularia striata* in Brunswick County, North Carolina, in early spring. Note that the flowers have an upper lip that is as large or larger than the lower lip.

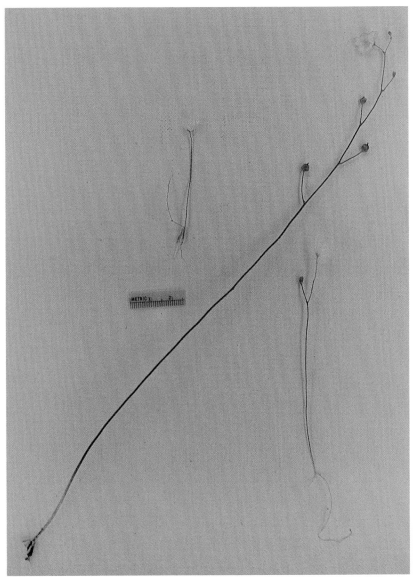

A comparison of inflorescences of *Utricularia gibba* and *U. striata*. A small example of *U. gibba* (above, left) found growing in a pond in Columbus County, North Carolina, but similar in proportions to northern and western examples. The more typical, southern bifloral form of *U. gibba* (below, right), found very near the other plant. *Utricularia striata* (diagonal) with its much longer and thicker peduncle.

Utricularia striata has a similar habit as *U. floridana*, but is much smaller. Again, stolons with large numbers of traps on them penetrate the sandy or silty bottoms of ponds or ditches. Immediately above in the water is a single whorl of stolons measuring 5–10 cm in length and up to 4 cm across with finely divided branches and leaves having fewer traps—a smaller foxtail. The peduncle is also much shorter than in *U. floridana*, measuring 10–40 cm and up to 2 mm in diameter. The yellow flowers to 2 cm in length are very similar to the other two members of this group, with the upper lip being as long as or longer than the lower and weakly three lobed.

The three species *Utricularia gibba*, *U. floridana*, and *U. striata* are closely related. All three are affixed, yellow-flowered aquatics, but are unique among other such bladderworts in the United States and Canada in that the upper lip of the corolla is as large or larger than the lower lip and appears weakly three lobed. *Utricularia floridana* is very easy to identify. This species is a large plant that grows in water 1 m or deeper; it has corollas 2 cm in length and large, foxtail-like, floating leaves up to 30 cm long and 5–8 cm across. The peduncle is 3 mm across. The smaller *U. striata* has smaller foxtails, 5–10 cm in length and to 4 cm across, with a peduncle only 10–40 cm long and up to 2 mm across. It grows in very shallow water (a few centimeters deep). Finally, the smallest member, *U. gibba* has no foxtails and a generally smaller flower of identical appearance. The filamentous peduncle is usually 1 mm or less.

Utricularia striata is relatively easy to grow. As with *U. gibba*, the plant does nicely between pots in shallow (8–10 cm) water trays and grows well in a tray of a slurry of *Sphagnum* and water in the greenhouse. Because this species extends as far north as the Massachusetts coastal plain, the plant should also survive in shallow, acidic ponds outdoors.

13. *Utricularia minor* Linnaeus

This perennial, affixed aquatic with a 2-mm turion in winter is closely related to the next two species, *Utricularia intermedia* and *U. ochroleuca*. This circumboreal species is found sporadically across Canada into

Alaska and down into the Pacific coastal states (see Ceska and Bell 1973; Rondeau 1995); into Nevada, Utah, Colorado, and some prairie states; around the Great Lakes; and into New England, Pennsylvania, and at least one location in New Jersey. There is also one known location in the northwestern mountains of North Carolina.

In the Great Lakes region, *Utricularia minor* (sometimes known by the common name, the lesser bladderwort) grows fairly commonly in fens and associated ponds and beach pools, usually in company with *U. intermedia*. In Canada and the West, the species is found generally in bog pools and shallow lake margins (Rondeau 1995). In the Great Lakes fens, *U. minor* reaches its best development in a few centimeters of water, but occasionally I have seen it in water to 35 cm deep.

Utricularia minor in an Upper Michigan fen. This photograph shows a green portion of a stolon with regularly arranged, palmately divided, somewhat filiform leaves along the stolon. The traps number only one per leaf. In three of the four corners of the photograph are segments of *U. intermedia*; compare the flatter, larger leaves with blunt ends in this species.

The fine, filiform stolons are up to 30 cm long and less than 1 mm wide. Portions of a single stolon may be buried shallowly in the substrate, these being generally colorless and frequently having traps. The aqueous sections of the single stolon are green and have fine, short (less than 1 cm), palmately divided leaves. Some leaves are rounded, whereas others, particularly in very shallow water, are flattened and at a glance often compared to minute crows' feet. The green, aqueous portions of the plant stolon have fewer traps, which tend to attach to the leaves.

The peduncle of *Utricularia minor* is filiform, 2.5–25.0 cm long (but averaging about 10–12 cm), and up to 1 mm thick. The corolla is a very pale, tannish yellow. The corolla is usually up to 1 cm long and appears quite narrow, being half as wide as long. The lower lip is much longer than the upper and often tends to have parallel sides due to some folding under of the margins. The raised palate is long rather than rounded. The spur is extremely short, barely a conical protrusion.

A stolon of *Utricularia minor* lifted from the substrate. Running across the upper left corner is a nearly white segment (the portion within the substrate) that has many traps. The green, aqueous segments have filiform leaves and few to no traps. When a *U. minor* stolon is pulled from the water and pond bottom, this alternating pattern of leaf and trap segments is typical.

Close-up side views of *Utricularia minor* flowers. The lateral folding down of the lower lip of the corolla makes the flower look narrow. At the base of the corolla abutting a reddish brown sepal, one can see the very small, conical to saccate spur protruding downward.

Utricularia minor in a beach pool along Lake Huron in Upper Michigan. Note the very narrow corollas, which are a very pale yellow to tannish yellow. Corollas are up to 1 cm long.

With some field experience, *Utricularia minor* is easily identified, usually at a glance, although you will want to pull a stolon from the water to examine the alternating pattern of leaf and trap segments and the finely palmate structure of the leaves.

Utricularia minor is very difficult to grow and keep from year to year, probably due to little understood environmental requirements. The tiny turion (2–3 mm) is also difficult to keep track of. I have kept the plant for about two years in shallow trays of water (2–3 cm deep) with an underlying substrate of sand, usually intermingled with *U. intermedia*.

14. *Utricularia intermedia* Hayne
15. *Utricularia ochroleuca* R. Hartman

I will discuss these two closely related, very similar species together to emphasize differentiation. Both species are affixed, aquatic perennials with winter turions that measure 5–7 mm across. Broadly speaking, they have a similar distribution as the one outlined for *Utricularia minor*, except that neither has been found as far south as New Jersey or into North Carolina. One important distributional difference, however, is that *U. ochroleuca* is uncommon, to the extent that new locations are noteworthy (such as Washington, Ceska and Bell 1973; Ontario, Riley and Walshe 1985; California, Rondeau 1998).

The habitat for both species is again similar to *Utricularia minor*. Where a shallow fen is not available, both *U. intermedia* and *U. ochroleuca* do well in shallows of lakes and bog ponds.

Unlike *Utricularia minor*, which has a stolon with an alternating pattern of leaf and trap segments, the green segment of the up to 30-cm stolon of both *U. intermedia* and *U. ochroleuca* rests on the substrate in a few centimeters of water and the trap-bearing segments are branches

Utricularia intermedia plants in a few centimeters of fen water in Presque Isle County, Michigan. Note the deep yellow flowers with a lower lip longer than the upper lip. Looking down at the water, you can also see leafy stolons resting on the bottom.

Leafy stolons of *Utricularia intermedia* on the silty substrate of a fen. The leaf segments are narrow but still broader than in *U. minor*. The somewhat overlapping, palmate leaves result in a unique appearance that is immediately recognizable as either *U. intermedia* or *U. ochroleuca*.

A *Utricularia intermedia* plant that has been pulled from the substrate and laid back into the water. On the right edge is the aquatic leafy portion that had rested on the bottom. Branching off to the left are stolon segments with traps and no leaves. *Utricularia minor* does not have such branches.

descending into the substrate, rather than a length of stolon. In both species, the aquatic stolon resting on the bottom has palmate branching leaves, without traps at all, and the segments of these leaves are flatter and wider than those in *U. minor.*

There are leaf differences between *Utricularia intermedia* and *U. ochroleuca.* In *U. intermedia* the tips of the leaf segments are slightly rounded (obtuse) and the lateral bristles, or setulae, do not rest on teeth. In *U. ochroleuca,* the leaf segment tips are sharp and narrower (acute) and the lateral setulae are on small, marginal teeth (dentate). These features must be examined closely with magnification because, if the water level is up due to heavy snowmelt or rains, the leaves of *U. intermedia* etiolate and superficially appear narrower with sharper tips as in *U. ochroleuca.*

Except for flower color (rather subjective unless compared side by side) and the spur, the flowers of *Utricularia intermedia* and *U. ochroleuca* are very similar. They occur on peduncles to 20 cm long and less than 1 mm in thickness. The corollas measure up to 1.6 cm in length and have longer lower lips compared to the upper lips. The spur in *Utricularia*

Front view of the deep yellow flower of *Utricularia intermedia.* Note that the lower lip is larger than the upper lip.

Back view of a *Utricularia intermedia* flower showing the spur, which is nearly as long as the lower lip. The spur of *U. ochroleuca* is half or less as long.

intermedia is narrow and nearly the length of the lower lip, whereas the spur of *U. ochroleuca* is only about half or less as long as the lower lip. The corolla of *U. intermedia* is deep yellow, whereas that of *U. ochroleuca* is pale yellow (hence the epithet, which translates as "yellowish white"). Interestingly, *U. ochroleuca* is completely sterile—viable seeds have never been reported. Taylor (1989) reported the pollen grains to be small and deformed. *Utricularia ochroleuca* apparently depends on vegetative dispersal, such as on the feet of birds.

The above description indicates significant differences between *Utricularia intermedia* and *U. ochroleuca*, particularly involving leafy segments (shape, no teeth versus teeth) and flowers (color intensity, character of spur, sterility of *U. ochroleuca*), which together allow easy separation in most cases. However, there are difficulties at times, such as in deep water, as mentioned above. Also, if you are up to trap dissection, the arms of the quadrifid glands in the traps of *U. intermedia* are parallel, whereas the arms of *U. ochroleuca* diverge to 45–70°. Taylor (1989) nicely outlined some difficulties in the study and identification of these two bladderworts.

There is also one other problem requiring further study: *Utricularia ochroleuca* may not be a species at all, but a sterile hybrid between *U. intermedia* and *U. minor*. Several authors strongly suggest this possibility (Rossbach 1939; Boivin 1966; Boche et al. 1968) and their reasoning is compelling. The narrow leaf segment shape of *U. ochroleuca* is intermediate between that of *U. minor*'s filiform segments and *U. intermedia*'s broader segments. *Utricularia ochroleuca* is a less robust plant than *U. intermedia*, being more like *U. minor*. The flower color of *U. ochroleuca* is lighter than in *U. intermedia*, tending toward *U. minor*. The spur of *U. ochroleuca* is also intermediate. The arms of the quadrifid glands of the traps of *U. ochroleuca* are moderately divergent, between the parallel arms of *U. intermedia* and the very widely divergent arms of *U. minor*. Finally, *U. ochroleuca* appears to be entirely sterile, with no viable seeds ever having been reported and with deformed pollen grains, as one would expect in a sterile hybrid.

I have only had experience in attempting to grow *Utricularia interme-*

dia, using the same methods and with the same outcome as in *U. minor* (see that section).

16. *Utricularia simulans* Pilger

Especially under low-power magnification, this is one of the most fascinating bladderworts in North America. Formerly referred to as *Utricularia fimbriata* in most floras and herbarium collections, Taylor (1989) determined that the plants best fit into the neotropical and African species *U. simulans*, reserving *U. fimbriata* for plants in the upper Orinoco in South America.

Utricularia simulans is restricted to the southern half of peninsular Florida, but is more readily found in the lower quarter subtropical and tropical reaches of the state. The plant grows in scattered but rather dense colonies on very sandy, damp, acidic soils low in organic matter and salts (Schnell 1980c). I have found the most plants on the western margins and areas of Big Cypress Swamp east of Naples, Florida, where they grow on slightly raised, white, sandy hummocks in areas of wetter, marly, more alkaline soils. The latter are dominated by *Taxodium ascendens* (pond cypress). The sandy, slightly raised areas are home to scattered *Pinus elliottii* variety *densa* (slash pine) and dense clumps of *Serenoa repens* (saw palmetto). *Utricularia simlans* may be found growing between these elements in slightly lower, damp, sandy areas.

Utricularia simulans is a probable perennial, terrestrial species with subterranean stolons a few centimeters long and less than 1 mm in diameter. Arising from these are peduncles surrounded at the base by a prominent ring of elongate, linear, aerial leaves about 1.0 cm long. In Florida, the peduncles are 4–12 cm tall and less than 1 mm thick. The most prominent character of this plant, best appreciated under slight magnification, is the presence of fimbriated scales, bracts, and calyces, with the scales and lower bracts looking like many-legged arthropods crawling up the peduncle. The yellow flowers are usually crowded into a tight raceme at the top of the peduncle. The corollas measure to 1.0 cm; the spurs are about as long as the lower lip and have a red tip.

A clump of *Utricularia simulans*. Note the white sand in the background. The flowers top the peduncle in a very tight raceme.

While the scattered, dense stands of these plants do favor sandy areas that dry out readily, a few single plants can be found here and there in the open marl of some areas between sandy hummocks. Colonies of *Utricularia simulans* are not common, but do tend to recur in the same place year after year. Flowering peak is at the end of October, which is also the usual end of the southern Florida summer rainy season, when some drying out begins for the winter. Taylor (1989) mentioned one author describing minute tubers in one *U. simulans* plant he examined,

Close-up of *Utricularia simulans* peduncles. Note the fringed scales, bracts, and calyces with red tips. Some say they look like arthropods ascending the peduncle.

A particularly crowded group of *Utricularia simulans* flowers. Such close racemes are common in this species and impart a unique aspect from a distance. Again, note the red fimbria of the calyces and the red tips of the spurs.

Rosettes of green, aerial leaves of *Utricularia simulans*. The bases of these sometimes have traps, as do the subterranean stolons.

but Taylor never saw these in all the specimens he studied nor have I yet come across them in the field. Such tubers would be organs of perennation during the dry season. After flowering and shedding their minute, brown, spherical seeds, the aerial portions of the plants dry up rather quickly and disappear until the following year.

I have had mixed success growing *Utricularia simulans*. I tried various sandy mixes, including native soil, and have not been able to keep them more than two years. They seem to do best in terrarium conditions, where I keep the soils barely damp. After flowering and dying back, the plants are nearly always promptly replaced by a fine stand of the terrestrial *U. cornuta*, which always seems to be intermingled with *U. simulans* but flowers at a later date. It is possible that the *U. cornuta* outcompetes the *U. simulans* in cultivation. I have had no success in germinating seeds of the species.

17. *Utricularia cornuta* Michaux
18. *Utricularia juncea* Vahl

Because they closely resemble one another, these two species will be discussed together to emphasize their differences. These perennial terrestrials have bright yellow flowers and grow in damp to wet sandy places that are frequently flooded by a few centimeters of water in particularly wet times. Both *Utricularia cornuta* and *U. juncea* may grow as impressive masses. Many early authorities felt that the two species were variants of one, but in a series of excellent systematic papers, Kondo (1971, 1972a, 1972b) showed them to be separate species, and Taylor (1989) concurred with this concept. *Utricularia cornuta* bears the common name of horned bladderwort, referring to the prominent vertical spur.

Utricularia cornuta has a wider distribution: from eastern Canada into Alberta and in Minnesota, Michigan, Wisconsin, Illinois, Arkansas, and all the eastern and Gulf states west to Texas. Washington was once included, but Taylor (1989, 1991) feels that a specimen labeled from there is an error. *Utricularia juncea*, in contrast, only grows in the eastern coastal plain of the United States from New Jersey to eastern Texas.

The distinction between these two bladderworts involves size and season of flowering. Both have a peduncle to 40 cm tall, but the flowers of *Utricularia cornuta* are up to 2.0 cm long and those of *U. juncea* only to 1.0 cm long. *Utricularia juncea* may have cleistogamous (closed) flowers in the colony or even on the same inflorescence along with chasmogamous (open) flowers, but *U. cornuta* only produces chasmogamous flowers. The flowers of both species have lower lips that are longer than the upper lips and the lateral edges fold down into a prominent, apronlike appearance. Both spurs are vertical and stand out away from the corolla lower lip. Kondo (1972a) noted that *U. juncea* has some purple coloration on the lower peduncles, whereas the same structures in *U. cornuta* are pale green. This is not always the case (Taylor 1989), however, and I have sometimes seen some purple on the peduncles of *U. cornuta* plants. Finally, in the usual temperate climates, *U. cornuta* flowers mainly in the spring, whereas *U. juncea* does so in late summer into autumn. The exception to this is in southern Florida, where *U. cornuta* has a second flowering season from November into January. In *U. cornuta* there is a definite flower fragrance that is pleasant and detectable in individual flowers. This fragrance is also quite noticeable when walking through a stand of the plants. I have noted no such fragrance in *U. juncea*. Both species have linear, grasslike, aerial leaves 1.0–2.0 cm long, these arising from subterranean stolons.

A colony of *Utricularia cornuta* occupying a tiny island on the solid granite bottom of a fast-moving mountain stream in Greenville County, South Carolina. The flowers tend to cluster at the tops of the peduncles and all are chasmogamous (open).

A stand of *Utricularia juncea* on the edge of a roadside ditch in eastern North Carolina in late summer.

Utricularia juncea in Collier County, Florida. Note the purple coloration of the lower portions of the peduncles. Most examples of this species have this peduncle coloration, but it is only occasionally seen in *U. cornuta*.

Close-up of *Utricularia cornuta* in flower. Note the prominent vertical spur, giving rise to the common name of horned bladderwort. The peduncle on the right bears some early maturing seedpods. The lateral edges of the lower lips are folded downward.

Close-ups of *Utricularia juncea* flowers. The flowers tend to be strung out more at the top of the peduncle. There is one chasmogamous (open) flower, and two cleistogamous (closed), the one with the spur being subcleistogamous.

In conclusion, the two species look very much alike, but *Utricularia cornuta* has generally larger, clustered flowers that are always chasmogamous and appear in the spring (except in southern Florida, where they also may flower November into January). This species only rarely has purple coloration of the lower peduncle. *Utricularia juncea* has smaller, more widely separated flowers, some of which may be cleistogamous (even on the same peduncle), that appear from late summer into autumn. This species usually has purple coloration of the lower peduncle.

Both species are very easy to grow in a sandy peat or pure peat medium kept constantly moist. They both do well in terrariums or the greenhouse and can be grown outdoors in suitable locations.

19. *Utricularia subulata* Linnaeus

This extremely common species is the smallest of our yellow-flowered, terrestrial bladderworts. *Utricularia subulata* is listed in some older floras as *Utricularia cleistogama* as well as *U. subulata,* having been mistaken for two separate species due to the presence of cleistogamous (closed) and chasmogamous (open) flowers. *Utricularia subulata* has been found in Nova Scotia, but is most common in the coastal plain from Massachusetts to eastern Texas, with sites in Tennessee and Arkansas also. The species grows in sand or sandy peat that is constantly moist and sometimes briefly inundated with water.

A stand of *Utricularia subulata* in eastern North Carolina. Even at this distance, the three-lobed lower lips are easily seen.

In North America, *Utricularia subulata* has subterranean stolons bearing 1.0–2.0-cm aerial leaves and peduncles to 10–15 cm. The wiry peduncles often have a zigzag pattern between flowering nodes. This is the only North American species with peltate bracts and scales; that is, the scales and bracts are attached to the peduncle at the centers of the tiny structures rather than at their ends. This diagnostic feature can be viewed with magnification. The bright yellow chasmogamous flowers are 0.5–1.0 cm

A small cluster of *Utricularia subulata*. Note the zigzag pattern of flowering on the peduncles.

long, and the raised palate tends to be a darker golden yellow. The lower lip is notched to three lobes. The spur may be shorter or longer than the lower lip, the tip often being minutely toothed. Cleistogamous flowers are less than 0.5 cm and are reddish to nearly white, thus the early confusion that the cleistogamous stage might represent a separate species or subspecies.

After a bit of experience, this species is easily identified at a glance and even at some distance in the field. Initially, look for yellow flowers 1 cm or less, a three-lobed lower lip, a dentate spur tip, a zigzag pattern of flower growth, and if necessary, use magnification to identify the peltate scales and bracts of the peduncle, which are unique in terrestrial North American bladderworts. If only cleistogamously flowering plants are seen, the peltate bracts and scales are still diagnostic.

I feel I hardly need to give growing instructions. Carnivorous plant growers know *Utricularia subulata* well as a vigorous grower, when put kindly, or even as a weed. The plant grows easily in all moist conditions and spreads readily by aerial seed distribution from pot to pot until it seems to be everywhere. I have even read a desperate plea in one of the carnivorous plant bulletins for help in "eradicating" the species from a collection, as though there would be some useful spray or other treatment. In spite of its proclivity to grow among all plants, this bladderwort is harmless and does not crowd out other species. Also, *U. subulata* is a pleasant sight to see flowering in very early spring in the greenhouse or terrarium.

Utricularia subulata in cultivation. The three-lobed lower lips are apparent along with the darker yellow palates. Note that the spur tips are toothed or slightly notched.

OTHER POSSIBLE
CARNIVOROUS SEED PLANTS

I

N THE PRECEDING chapters, I have discussed the usually accepted carnivorous plant genera and their species as they occur in the United
States and Canada. Some of these genera, including *Drosera*, *Pinguicula*, and *Utricularia*, have large numbers of species in other parts of the
world. In fact, these three genera are rather widely distributed. There are
also several other genera of carnivorous plants in the world with no representatives in North America. These carnivorous plants all contain the
basic kinds of traps discussed in the Introduction. For several generations we have discovered, collected, studied, grown, named, renamed, discussed, written, and read about these carnivorous genera.

However, several observers have at first timidly, then more boldly, suggested there may be other species having a carnivorous strategy that may
be somewhat off track of our standard concept of what constitutes a carnivorous plant. Several of the suggestions have been preliminary at best,
and the authors may have jumped to conclusions or made "an inductive
leap," as a mentor once said. For instance, a plant that is sticky (glandular)
and has insects stuck to it is not necessarily carnivorous, nor is a plant
that for some structural reason retains rainwater in little pools. Some may
be, however, and further study could be warranted.

One problem is that after initial announcements of a possible or
"clearly" new carnivorous plant are made, sophisticated studies are often
put off because they involve considerable time, expense, and scarce

resources, which are dedicated to other priorities. Many research methods, such as radioisotope tracer studies, were not available when some plants were proposed in the1920s and 1930s. Another problem is that once information gets into print (or on the Internet), it is often taken at face value, perhaps because it seems novel, exciting, and even a bit rebellious and new wave, whatever the wave is. Consequently, uncritical minds take up the flag even though original papers have not been consulted. The plants are then proudly listed among carnivorous plants in a particular growing collection, and then everyone wants to get on the bandwagon.

My intent is not to seem negative about new concepts of what constitutes a carnivorous plant; I would also be excited and intrigued as long as patience and appropriate study are applied. With so many plants in the world that remain undiscovered, as well as unknown properties of plants that have been right under our noses for hundreds of years, anyone would be foolish not to keep an open mind about the possibility of discovering new carnivorous plants.

Often, the problem is a matter of perspective. There are some who enthusiastically embrace a new, broader concept of what constitutes a carnivorous plant, and there are those who feel that the traditional carnivorous plant genera encompass all possible carnivorous traits. The latter claim the "new" plants do not fulfill all the criteria that have always been used. But, of course, concepts are products of their criteria. Two sets of criteria need not be divisive, but could be parallel, as long as the parallel nature is understood. To that extent, one day we may consider the terms *carnivorous* for the traditional genera and *paracarnivorous* for a more open, less strictly defined set of plants that derive benefits from small, trapped animals.

As an example, Spomer (1999) studied nineteen common "sticky" (glandular-leaved) weeds in the Pacific Northwest. He found that fifteen of these produced proteases, as determined by a gel film test, and two of these absorbed digested materials, as determined by radioisotope tracers. These plants deserve further study.

In this chapter, I discuss four species that grow in the United States and Canada that have been proposed as carnivorous plants, although they are not regularly listed among these. They are all in various stages of study—from being largely ignored since the original proposal to undergoing at least some additional work. At this writing, evaluation is far from complete for any of these plants, particularly for *Ibicella lutea* and *Dipsacus fullonum*, but all four are of some interest. If an enterprising student or researcher is looking for a good project, these species seem compelling.

Ibicella lutea (Lindley) Van Eseltine

Doing literature research on this plant is frustrating because family placement has changed, with *Ibicella* being the third genus applied to this species. Originally in the family Martyniaceae, *Ibicella lutea* was *Martynia lutea*. As of this writing, the family is Pedaliaceae and the genus has passed through *Proboscidea* to *Ibicella*, although there are still other species of *Proboscidea* in the family, as well as one *Martynia* (Kartesz 1994). Matters are more confusing when you consider that the original paper by Beal (1875) suggesting that this plant may be carnivorous simply mentioned it as *Martynia* with no reference to species. However, a paper by Mameli (1916) did mention then *Martynia lutea* as the subject of her studies, and this has been carried over by Juniper et al. (1989). Still, there is probably no reason to exclude other similar and closely related members of the family from consideration because they all have glandular hairs scattered among stiff, nonglandular trichomes.

Ibicella lutea is a 50–80 cm tall annual or perennial with lower mature leaves opposite, but alternating above. The leaves are nearly rounded, 10–20 cm across, and slightly lobed. The flowers are in a tight raceme, up to 6 cm long, and zygomorphic. Flowers are pale lavender to yellow to nearly white in different plants. Nearly the entire plant is covered in mixed glandular and nonglandular hairs, imparting a viscid quality to the surface. In or out of flower, there is a strong, rather foul-sweet fragrance. A unique feature of *I. lutea* and most other members of the family is the mature seedpod, which has long, curved, projecting horns that clasp onto the hooves and feet of animals. The animals then transport the seedpods, which disperse seeds as they go. This odd seed capsule is the source of the common names devil's claws and unicorn plant.

Ibicella lutea is commonly grown as a garden plant, largely to retrieve the seedpods in the autumn for use in ornamental dried arrangements. However, the powerful fragrance is often a deterrent to gardeners, and the plant frequently becomes weedy. Many species within Pedaliaceae are native to northern Mexico and the American Southwest, some having extended into the eastern United States. They tend to grow in sunny, dry, open areas.

What attracted Beal (1875) to the plant was the apparent entrapment of large numbers of small insects by the glandular hairs. He further noticed that the insect exoskeletons assumed a dry, empty appearance after several days. He applied small bits of beef to the glandular surface

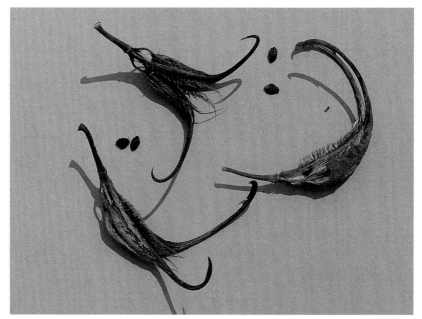

Seedpod and seeds of *Ibicella lutea*. Note the curved, projecting horns, which tend to ensnare the capsule around an animal's hoof or foot. The black to brown seeds measure to 0.8 cm.

and in some cases the fragments "disappeared." With these limited findings in hand, he drew the conclusion that the plant was carnivorous.

Mameli (1916), apparently not knowing of Beal's paper, did a rather thorough study for the time on *Ibicella lutea*. She made similar observations, using small blocks of hard-boiled egg white and observing dissolution and apparent absorption by the glandular surfaces of the plant. Since these two authors, nothing further was done until two reports appeared in *Carnivorous Plant Newsletter* in 1999.

Meyers-Rice (1999) and Wallace et al. (1999) independently did studies on the possibility of enzyme production by the surface glands of *Ibicella lutea*; Meyers-Rice extended the study to a few other members of the family as well. Both research teams used a screening method devised by Heslop-Harrison and Knox (1971). First, an aqueous yeast or bovine albumin mixture is applied to the plant's glandular surfaces as a "stimulating feed." To check for possible enzyme secretions, the gelatin/silver compound side of undeveloped black-and-white film is applied to the glandular surface and left in place for some time. If proteases are present, the gelatin is dissolved in those spots. Observation can be enhanced by then developing the film, which results in a black image with clear areas where there was protease activity. In *I. lutea*, the process was somewhat complicated by minute scratch marks caused by the stiff, nonglandular hairs intermingled among the glandular hairs, but ultimately both Meyers-Rice and Wallace et al. concluded that there was no inherent protease production by the glands.

Still, the apparently crude observations of Beal (1875) and Mameli (1916) cannot be entirely ignored. Although more expensive, autoradiographs could give a more definitive answer. Insects fed radiotracer-labeled food and given time to incorporate the material into their structures could be applied to the glandular areas of the plant, followed by timed autoradiographs of plant portions. Other studies may include tissue sections of plant glandular surfaces with special stains to indicate if any enzymes are present. In the meantime, the jury still seems to be out on this one, with the dissolution and apparent absorption of beef bits (Beal 1875) or egg albumin (Mameli 1916) and the apparent lack of proteases in the glands (Meyers-Rice 1999; Wallace et al. 1999) providing contradictory results at this point.

Ibicella lutea is an easy plant to grow, as are all members of the family Pedaliaceae. Seeds for some species (*Ibicella, Proboscidea,* or possibly *Martynia*) are available through garden catalogues, the attraction being the unique seedpods. (Because some seed companies understandably may be behind in proper genus nomenclature, look for all three in the catalogue indexes.) The seeds require some time to germinate, but this may be enhanced by either scarifying or pin-pricking the hard seed coat. Unlike most carnivorous plants, devil's claws grow nicely in ordinary potting soil or in the garden with full light and only modest moisture; fertilizer is desirable. The pollination mechanism is not yet understood. The green, immature seedpods may be cooked and eaten, although this would take some resolve because the plant overall has a very disagreeable odor.

Dipsacus fullonum Linnaeus

Dipsacus fullonum, the common teasel, is a member of the family Dipsacaceae. In the past, the plant has been referred to as *D. sylvestris* and may be listed as such in many floras. The epithet *sylvestris* is now relegated to a subspecies.

Teasel is found nearly throughout the United States and into southern Canada, where it is regarded as a weed in open spaces, reaching its strongest growth in low, damp, cooler areas. The species is a biennial with striated, hollow, and prickly stems that reach a height of 3.0 m, but most often to 1.0–1.5 m. The elongate, pointed leaves (lanceolate to elliptic) measure to 40 cm and are opposite. These lack petioles and are joined (connate) with the stem of the plant running up through them (perfoliate). The leaves have dentate, raised margins; as a result, a small basin is formed by the two opposite, joined leaves where the stem pierces them. The familiar inflorescences are in closely packed, bulbous spikes subtended by pointed, curved bracts that are often as long as the spikes. The small flowers are actinomorphic, pale pink to blue, and begin appearing in a rank in the middle of the spike, with succeeding ranks descending

A *Dipsacus fullonum* plant growing in a drainage ditch in Pulaski County, Virginia. The familiar bristled flower spikes with their prominent long, curved bracts are evident. The stem is prickly, and the opposite leaves join around the stem. The pink flowers begin blooming in the middle of the inflorescence, and flowering ascends and descends from there in ranks.

and ascending. The calyceal lobes are the familiar bristles of the teasel inflorescence. The points of the inflorescence bristles may be straight or curved. The common name teasel comes from the fact that the curved bristles of the inflorescence heads were once used to card wool.

After a rain, the cup-shaped union of the two opposite leaves around the perforating stem fills with water. This cup can hold up to 250 ml. The genus name, *Dipsacus*, is from the Greek word for thirst, an allusion to the water-holding leaf bases. The only liquid that seems to appear in these little basins is rainwater. There is often entrapped debris and the remains of insects in the watery leaf-base pools, which led Christy (1923) to believe that the teasel may be carnivorous. He also thought he saw protoplasmic filaments extending out into the pools, presumably to absorb nutrients. A more recent summary article by Masters (1967) described the pools more as phytotelms, little ponds on plants containing living water animals and algae as well as dead remains (see Introduction).

A pool of rainwater in the basin formed by the union of opposite leaves in *Dipsacus fullonum*. There is some debris in the water along with a few small, floating, dipterid corpses.

Christy (1923) did note that the fluid in the leaf basins has a lower surface tension than pure water, which enhances the ability of the liquid to drown any hapless insects that fall in. It remains to be seen whether insects are specifically attracted to the teasel basins and whether their remains break down by means of fermentation or digestive enzymes into usable components absorbed by the plants. No extensive work has been done in this area beyond Christy's initial proposals. At this stage, so much remains to be studied that *Dipsacus fullonum* would seem to be an intriguing project for careful professional or amateur investigations or even science fair projects.

The species is very easy to grow, thriving in gardens or low, wet areas with some partial shade during at least part of the day. Once established, however, colonies threaten to become weedy. Keeping in mind that teasel is a biennial, little will be accomplished by bringing fully flowering plants into the garden, unless flowering is quite early and the plants are able to become established to produce seed for next season's vegetative plants. Seed is available in some gardening seed catalogues, the attraction being material for dried arrangements. Pollination is accomplished by bumble bees, which are very active during flowering. The only practical use beyond dried arrangements may be the leaf pool liquid, which some rural folk believe to be a sure cure for warts (Masters 1967).

Catopsis berteroniana (J. A. and J. H. Schultes) Mez

Catopsis berteroniana is a member of Bromeliaceae, the pineapple family or bromeliads. In North America, the species is confined to tropical southern Florida, where it grows mostly on the tops of red mangrove trees (*Rhizophora mangle*), but also has been reported from other trees farther inland in hammocks (Craighead 1963). *Catopsis* is derived from the Greek word for view, a possible reference to the plants' high perches in trees. Many, if not most, bromeliads are epiphytes, or at least facultative epiphytes, and *C. berteroniana* fits this category.

Catopsis berteroniana is a perennial, epiphytic herb that may grow as tall as 40–45 cm. The plant is a pale, yellowish green in full sunlight. The leaves are shaped like long, narrow triangles with pointed free tips, the outer ones drooping slightly. The inner leaves form a narrow, somewhat tubular space known among bromeliads as a tank because rainwater collects in the deeper recesses of the central tube, as well as in the spaces formed by some of the outer leaves as they join the plant (leaf axils). There is a white, powdery wax covering the outer surfaces of the leaves near the bases, but this slippery material does not appear to be on the inner surfaces or the leaf tips. The inflorescence arises from the center of the tube and may reach 1 m in length. The inflorescence is a panicle with the flowers pointing out in all directions (polystichous). The small flowers have three white to pale yellow petals that barely protrude beyond the tips of the prominent green sepals.

In Florida, the species is considered endangered, although it can be readily seen in various areas of the Everglades and Big Cypress Swamp. Because *Catopsis berteroniana* prefers high, open tree branches, the plants are not very accessible. The pale, yellowish green, smooth leaves with white powdery wax on the lower portions allows for reliable identification in Florida.

The possibility that *Catopsis berteroniana* might be carnivorous was posited in a Ph.D. dissertation largely devoted to aquatic insect inhabitants of Florida bromeliads and was more or less mentioned as an aside (Fish 1976). The author noted accumulations of chitinous insect exoskeletons in the leaf axil pools of the plant. He removed some plants to campus, washed them out, and added fresh water. The

A *Catopsis berteroniana* plant in cultivation. The plant is pale green with pointed, elongate leaves forming a central, narrow tube. Note the powdery white wax on the lower, outer leaf surfaces.

plants readily accumulated more dead insects, and he noted that the waxy powder reflected ultraviolet light, which might serve as an insect attractant. Fish assumed the insects slipped on the outer, waxy surfaces of the preceding leaves above the axil pools and fell into the water. Based on these findings, he concluded that *C. berteroniana* is carnivorous.

In contrast, more detailed work has been done on the neotropical bromeliad *Brocchinea reducta*, which has also been proposed to be carnivorous. *Brocchinea reducta* is not native to the United States; has a more pronounced, taller, tighter tank; and produces the powdery white wax on the outer leaf surfaces. The plant is largely terrestrial, growing in open, sunny savannas or on flat-topped, mountainlike *tepuis*. The liquid in the tank has a sweet fragrance, which apparently lures insects, and it has a pH of 2.8–3.0. The plant apparently contributes these two factors, acidity and nectar fragrance, to rainwater. There is no evidence of secretions from the nonglandular trichomes found on the leaves, but they might in some way acidify the water and exude a fragrance. However, as the trapped insects decay, the plant is able to absorb amino acids through the trichomes (Givnish et al. 1984).

In the case of *Catopsis berteroniana*, no one has noted a fragrance or an acidification of tank fluid, nor has anyone specifically found that compounds from decaying insects are absorbed by the trichomes. I grow a small number of the plants and have noted no fragrance or significant change in the pH of the tank water.

Some peripheral published work may be pertinent to the problem, however. *Catopsis berteroniana* is a member of the *Tillandsia* group of bromeliads, which as a whole have no or weaker tanks. A study of absorption of water, calcium-45, and zinc-65 was undertaken in a group of bromeliads prior to the proposal that *C. berteroniana* might be carnivorous (Benzing and Burt 1970). *Catopsis berteroniana* happened to be in the group of twenty species tested, which included some other members of Tillandsioideae. The more xeric tillandsias absorbed far more water and isotopes than did *C. berteroniana*, which also had the least number of trichomes per square area of leaf. However, another study published in the same year as Fish's work (Benzing et al. 1976) found that *C. bertero-*

niana and other members of tankless Tillandsioideae absorbed radioisotope-tagged amino acids glycine and leucine administered foliarly.

Frank and O'Meara (1984) reported a study comparing the insect-trapping rate of *Catopsis berteroniana* with three other tank bromeliads from the Everglades. They strung out several potted examples of each on a metal rod in random fashion, washed out the tanks and leaf axils, and replaced the liquid with fresh water. When inspected at weekly intervals, they noted that *C. berteroniana* captured twelve times as many insects as the other three species. Clearly, there is an increased capture volume in this species. Frank and O'Meara also noted that two species of mosquito, *Wyeomyia vanduzeei* and *W. mitchellii*, bred in the tanks of *C. berteroniana* without harm, similar to *W. smithii* in *Sarracenia purpurea*.

In conclusion, *Catopsis berteroniana* has had more positive studies suggesting that it is a carnivorous plant than the first two species discussed in this chapter. Because digestive enzymes have not been found (there are no glands, but there are amino acid–absorptive trichomes), the soft tissues of prey are presumably reduced by bacterial action. The tanks and leaf axils of *C. berteroniana* do indeed gather more insects than other neighboring tank bromeliads. One of the requirements for evidence of carnivory in plants (as discussed in the Introduction) is that the activity ultimately results in more vigorous growth and reproduction, which has yet to be demonstrated in any of the species discussed so far in this chapter.

Catopsis berteroniana is relatively easy to grow, doing best in a greenhouse in more temperate climes, but it is adaptable to terrarium cultivation, if the terrarium is tall enough. The very long inflorescence would likely have to be cut off in a terrarium or just bent over. The species is an epiphyte, but it is quite responsive to a semiterrestrial existence in drained pots. Instead of soil or peat, use a mix of fir bark, peat, and perlite, a mix similar to that used for many orchids and available in larger garden centers already compounded. Keep water in the plants' tanks and leaf axils. The medium should be moist but not have standing water. In spite of this species' alleged carnivorous habit, the plants do best with regular fertilization administered similar to any potted bromeliad. After flowering, small buds arise in a rosette around the base of the plant. The original plant will eventually die after flowering, but the buds can be carefully separated after good roots have formed and potted up separately.

Capsella bursa-pastoris (Linnaeus) Medicus

Known commonly as shepherd's purse or pickpocket, this common lawn and garden weed throughout southern Canada and all of the United States is a member of the mustard family, Brassicaceae (formerly Cruciferae). Shepherd's purse was introduced from southern and eastern Europe and has become well established. *Capsella* means little box, *bursa* translates as purse, and *pastoris* means shepherd's, hence the common name shepherd's purse. This name refers to the 0.3–0.5-cm seed capsule, which is heart shaped like medieval purses. Interestingly, I will not be writing about proposed carnivorous properties of the plant itself, but of its seed.

Capsella bursa-pastoris is familiar to all gardeners and even those who just passively attend their lawns. The plant is a winter annual with a basal rosette of 4.0–10.0 cm long leaves having prominently and unevenly dissected or lobed margins. The leaves are up to1.0–2.0 cm wide. The flowering raceme, which measures up to 30 cm, arises from this rosette and bears smaller, lanceolate leaves. The white flowers are up to 1.0 cm across and have four white petals barely exceeding the sepals in length. The petals are in two pairs, the members of each pair being closer, resulting in a cross or X-shaped configuration of all four petals (hence the former family name Cruciferae). The mature seedpods contain 1-mm brown seeds.

The following material is largely adapted from an excellent summary article by Barber (1978), who participated in most of the definitive work. When exposed to water, the seeds of some plants develop a mucilaginous coat, the mucilage being secreted by the now-expanded seed capsule cells. When the seeds of *Capsella bursa-pastoris* are wetted and coated in their mucilage, they attract mosquito larvae, with up to twenty larvae attaching themselves by their heads to the mucilaginous surface. The larvae then die. It has been proven that the mucilage exudes a chemical attractant, and this chemical or a separate toxin is responsible for larval death. This work was initiated to study such activity for possible mosquito control.

Interest having been aroused, assays for proteolytic activity were undertaken and proteases were indeed found. Additional experiments disclosed that the seeds absorbed radioisotope-labeled amino acids. All of this is strong evidence of carnivory; however, shepherd's purse does not grow in water, the natural habitat of mosquito larvae. Experiments were then done on soil bacteria, nematodes, and protozoans, organisms more likely to be encountered by the rain-wetted seeds in soil prior to germination. While nematodes did not attach to the seeds as mosquito larvae had, they were attracted in greater numbers to the area of seeds, where most died. Likewise, protozoans placed in the crossbar of an H-shaped glass tube filled with water and with *Capsella* seeds in one side migrated from the crossbar into the seed side rather than the other side, as did certain bacteria. Clearly, these organisms were attracted to the seeds.

Thus, we have a very small seed with a mucilaginous coating that when moistened attracts small soil animals, kills them, secretes a protease, and absorbs amino acids. Apparently, the strategy is to supplement the tiny seed's limited food stores for satisfactory germination. But, does all of this actually invigorate germination and/or plant growth (at least in the seedling stage)? This bit of information is key in the story. Some would say the attraction and toxic activity is a mechanism to destroy possible seed or seedling predatory animals, particularly some species of nematodes. But this does not explain the protease production and amino acid absorption. If increased seedling viability can be proven, then we will have the strongest evidence for a carnivorous seed.

Shepherd's purse is very easily grown or simply observed in many gardens, lawns, pastures, and roadsides. The plant grows in any soil with moderate moisture and full sunlight. Fertilization is hardly necessary when potting or good garden soil is provided. If you wish to observe or experiment with the seeds, these may be easily recovered from the dried, brown seed capsules.

Conclusions

Considering what we know as of this writing, the strongest and best-assembled evidence for at least paracarnivory in the plants discussed here belongs to the seed of shepherd's purse, with *Catopsis* ranking a somewhat close second. There seems to be a break in active research at this point, but perhaps work will resume. The teasel is intriguing with its rain-filled pools at the conjoined leaf bases, but this is the only reliable observation of possible carnivory thus far. Finally, based on the film screening test, *Ibicella* apparently does not have any protease activity. However, dissolution of small bits of meat and egg albumin have been observed on its glandular surfaces, so carnivory cannot be dismissed at this point, although there is not much else to go on. The final point that must be made for any of these candidates is whether the results of the proposed carnivory actually lead to more vigorous plant growth and reproduction (or just seedling growth in the case of *Capsella*).

CONSERVATION ISSUES

It is one thing to identify causes of species extinction, quite another to provide remedies. Solutions to the problems demand political will, legislation, finance, education, and broad public support.

ROBERT J. WHITTAKER (1998)

W HAT WILL eventually happen to carnivorous plants? The quote from Whittaker implies that, today, species survival seems largely to depend on us. I am inclined to agree with him.

Fossil records indicate that there have been broad natural disasters in the past that have redesigned the pattern of life on Earth. Such forces work over millions of years, leaving much time for the evolution of many new species systems before the next cataclysm. However, within a few centuries humans have performed many seemingly small acts that in sum may equal the devastation of, say, an errant meteor. We humans have will and perspective. When asserting powers that lower water tables, destroy uncounted hectares of rain forest, or even seemingly affect weather patterns, will and perspective demand a sense of absolute responsibility, not the relative responsibility to the convenience of the moment. Since Europeans began to settle North America, 85% of forests and more than half of the grasslands and wetlands in the United States have been replaced or severely degraded (Stolzenburg 1999). Canadian destruction of natural areas has occurred most severely in southern and lower coastal population centers, although acid rain originating from industries in the United States is a concern even in less settled areas.

In this chapter, I present a highly personal view of carnivorous plants and conservation. I will mention a few numbers here and there, but most of those have been provided in volumes of conservation literature from highly technical expositions down to the daily newspaper and television news or nature programs. Yet, the irreversible destruction proceeds apace and even quickens. Are enough people paying attention? What are the priorities? Carnivorous plants are undoubtedly in trouble; I have hinted at this fact throughout the book. The ranges of pitcher plants and Venus flytraps would be the first to go, followed by the butterworts, sundews, and bladderworts, quite likely in that order. I do not pretend to have all the answers because even though the technical answers seem clear, a real answer requires political and public support. Also, conservation issues affect many groups of plants, from desert and mesic forests to sweeping grasslands, not to mention the interesting associates of carnivorous plants such as terrestrial orchids and, of course, all the animals associated with their ecosystems. We are quite capable of destroying any of these.

Snapshots

One year, I was asked to lead an amateur botanical club from the mountains of North Carolina on a tour of the southeastern North Carolina coastal plain. About midmorning, our little group of twenty or so people stopped at a small bay alongside a very busy, paved road that ran between two tourist towns. We were inspecting and photographing the superb stand of *Sarracenia rubra* subspecies *rubra* that I had been watching for many years. Beyond the small, open, pondlike bay there was a huge, dense shrub bog. After we had been there awhile, an official car pulled off the road and four men got out, all in uniforms varying from state game warden to deputy sheriff. One of the men approached, tipped his hat, and smiled.

"We saw you folks here and just wondered what you were seeing here."

One of the group explained that we were inspecting and photographing the pitcher plants, then said, "I bet you fellas keep an eye on these."

"Oh, yes," one of the officials replied, also smiling and implying that the site's botanical value was appreciated and watched over. They all tipped their hats, smiled, wished us well, got back into the car, and drove off.

The following year I passed by the site. The little bay was gone, the huge background shrub bog of several square kilometers was cleared to the ground. Within two years, a dense impenetrable stand of trees extended nearly to the road. The land was timber company property, not eligible for state protection after all. The pitcher plants were gone.

It was late spring in southeastern Georgia. We were driving back roads and stopped to look at a fine stand of several hectares of *Sarracenia flava* growing beyond a fence in a cow pasture. The cows were lazily chewing out the weeds between the pitcher plants. I was photographing the site when the landowner rushed down his driveway in his pickup truck and pulled up behind us, no doubt wondering what the out-of-state people were up to taking pictures of his pasture. We explained what we were doing.

"Oh, you're making pictures of those lilies," he said. Then he explained how he wished he could get rid of them so his pasture would be pure grass and not mostly pitcher plants. He mentioned how he had tried burning them out, but they came back stronger. Then he mowed them, but they still came back. He put his cows in, but the animals just ate anything but pitchers. All of this had been tried at the suggestions of the county agricultural agent, and, in fact, all of these ideas were perfect for furthering the pitcher plants. I was not about to tell him about drainage tiles and plowing. We just nodded sympathetically and left.

The once vast southeastern savannas are now reduced to less than 3% of the total area extant when Europeans arrived. Today these areas are mostly drained, mesic farms, pastures, and tree farms. In the Pacific Northwest, political pressures have made fewer lands available to timber companies, and there are increased demands on the Southeast for timber production. The drainage ditches along the edges of the roads became refuges for plants that populated the savannas by the millions or more—carnivorous plants, orchids, other fascinating savanna species, wildflowers. In many areas that I remember covered in natural drifts of plants only a few years before, the last available habitat is now the drainage ditches.

But as plants grow in the ditches, water flow slows, sometimes into little ponds packed with bladderworts. Because people are afraid that mosquitoes will breed or that the ditches will become filled with snakes, the state scrapes and clears the ditches so that water can flow. Consequently, the plants have lost their last refuges.

Not so long ago, you could stop your car on the shoulder of many roads in the Southeast, anywhere along some roads, and easily spend a whole day tromping through savannas and bays until you were out of sight of the car and the sound of traffic, just the on-shore breeze from the ocean a few kilometers away to the east. You could spend a whole season along just one road, moving the car ahead a few hundred meters, and strike out again. There was no running out of bays and savannas. Now those stands are lost to trees so close you cannot walk between them—that is all there is, the fast-growing pines for paper pulp.

Now you must drive off the previously fruitful roads and go many kilometers down timber tracks. Most often you just end up on another paved road. But occasionally a small copse of carnivorous plants greets your efforts. Perhaps these plants are too close to a stream for the timber companies to clear with their machinery.

Many people call or write me to ask for carnivorous plant locations, particularly in the Southeast, where they hope to make a grand tour of the arc of the coastal plain. I used to oblige, giving locations near main roads that are easily found, but not giving out sensitive location information on endangered species. These are sites that would have been seen by anyone if they had the time to travel the roads and come across them. These requests became so commonplace that I designed a grand tour that covered everything from eastern Texas into North Carolina. When anyone needed common location information, I simply printed out a copy and sent it to the inquiring carnivorous plant enthusiast.

That worked well for about a year, toward the end of which I began getting panicky phone calls from folks on the road wondering what errors they had made in the tour. Two years after initiating the process, I did a lot of fieldwork in the South and was greatly distressed to find that nearly half of the recommended roadside stops were now devoid of carnivorous plants. They had been destroyed in only two to three years' time. I erased the now useless tour from my computer and now do not give out information on locations.

I must finish the story I began in the Introduction of the central piedmont bog in North Carolina. I lived just a few kilometers from it for many years. It was a nice seep bog similar to the kind most often seen in the Appalachian Mountains some distance west. When first shown to me by a retired science teacher and local history buff, the bog seemed rather large for its kind and, after approaching it through dense shrubbery, very open. There was even a small bit of open water near the center. On several visits I even saw the now rare and endangered bog turtle (*Clemmys muhlenbergi*), which was considered more of a mountain inhabitant.

Within five years of finding the bog, the central open water had disappeared along with the bog turtles. In five more, when walking I noticed that I sank into the bog far less than originally, although I certainly had not lost weight. Also, the edges seemed to be closing in. The pitcher plants around the periphery were now less in the open and grew more between shrubs. This continued until my last year in the area, when the bog seemed to be gone suddenly, replaced by shrubs of varying height. The tree saplings I had watched on the edges were now sizable young trees. The pitcher plants became fewer and those that still bravely came up each year were terribly etiolated. The woods in which the fine little bog was located had never suffered fire in that time, which would have opened the habitat back up for carnivorous plants. More importantly, however, various county officials occasionally remarked for the newspaper that the water table in the county seemed to be falling.

One summer day, an experienced field botanist friend and I were exploring the Green Swamp in southeastern North Carolina. He wanted to finish the day by showing me what had always been a favorite location, one that he had not visited in a few years. After parking the car, we hopped the inevitable drainage ditches and were on the edge of what once had been a savanna. I glanced at him. My friend had an expression of completely crestfallen disorientation on his face. "Where have they all gone?" he asked. "You could always come here when you wanted to see sarracenias."

Long ago, when I lived in Atlanta, Georgia, I was corresponding with a teenage boy in Alabama who lived in *Sarracenia oreophila* country. He had been following the fortunes and misfortunes of those pitcher plants since he was a small boy. Just after he received his drivers' license, he came over for a visit and we headed out to see Gaither Plummer at the University of Georgia in Athens. On the way, we talked of the failing populations of his favorite pitcher plant. He mentioned one location that had been on a paved back road in some farmland. The bog was in the middle of a grass pasture. Whenever the boy stopped to see the pitcher plants, he spoke with the landowner about the plants and asked permission to go on the land, and the landowner always seemed pleasant about it. The boy even brought botanists to the location and seemed well received. One day he stopped by to see the plants and the little bog had been plowed under, a small blotch of raw earth in a grassy field. He tried to raise the owner, but no one would answer the door. My young friend felt that the isolated plowing of that one section in a field indicated that the landowner wanted to destroy the pitcher plants, which were then getting more and more attention and attracting more people.

In his later years, I was fortunate to engage in a lively correspondence with the botanist Edgar T. Wherry, whose name readers will find scattered in the *Sarracenia* chapter and bibliography. Even in his day, in the early third of the twentieth century, carnivorous plant locations were yielding to golf courses, factories, and farmland. Edgar once remarked in one of his letters, "Do not go back to a favorite location after twenty years. . . . It will almost always break your heart."

State Route 211 is a legendary road in southeastern North Carolina that runs through the Green Swamp. Old bog hands fondly remember the road as a premier field location. I remember when I first began traveling Route 211; every morning, there was a great deal of fresh roadkill, mostly wetland inhabitants—frogs, snakes, and turtles. One morning a couple of years ago as I traveled down the road, now lined by rows of silviculture in place of former savannas and bays, something suddenly hit me. Something that must have been happening slowly over the years, but just lit up that morning. The road was clean. There were no frogs, snakes, or turtles anymore, at least not enough to sacrifice excess to the rolling wheels each night. At lunchtime, at the old "free picnic table," as Rusty Kologiski used to call it, a gathering place next to a service station where our field groups used to assemble in a cool, gentle breeze beneath pine trees, I sat alone, eating, thinking, and remembering. Slowly, a relentless wave of undirected, deep sadness swept over me, my eyes moistened, a lump formed in my throat, and at first I had no idea what was going on. Then it occurred to me. I was mourning, grieving for the way it used to be and maybe could still be, at least in a few places.

Why Are Carnivorous Plant Locations Disappearing?

For millions of years, habitats and species have disappeared and new ones have risen due to various natural phenomena, be they volcanic activity, meteors, ice ages, continental drift, or even shifts in the Earth's magnetic poles. Many people may therefore wonder, "Why the concern now?" The concern now is that humans have entered the equation. We seem capable of unnaturally accelerating the pace of extinctions through our various activities and increasing numbers. Humans are literally throwing a monkey wrench into the delicate machinery of biodiversity and ecological balance and, in so doing, quite possibly endangering ourselves as well. It is not that the loss of carnivorous plants per se will cause us great harm, but they are a sensitive signal that something is seriously wrong, as are other losses, all possibly alerting us to pollution, loss of important habitats, and degradation of our water supplies. Let us look at some of the factors that have been suggested as primary causes of decreasing carnivorous plant populations.

Habitat Destruction

In my opinion and that of many others, habitat destruction is the primary reason for loss of carnivorous plants and their associated species. Habitat destruction may occur as a result of many activities. Some are direct, others are indirect but equally as lethal.

Habitat may be lost when land is needed and prepared for the many purposes other than wandering around and enjoying the wildlife (including plants). Ditching and drainage in the coastal plain converts a wetland habitat into a drier, mesic one so that tree farms may be established, urban areas expanded, massive housing and manufacturing facilities built, peat mining undertaken, or just to make more farmland available. Ditching and draining are very effective in the low, relatively flat areas of the coastal plain, with their sandy soils that allow rapid water drainage. In addition to losing abundant water, which is a primary requirement for carnivorous plants, mesic situations also encourage denser growths of grasses and other herbs, shrubs, and trees, which shade the floor of the savanna and crowd out all plants that are poor competitors.

Another important feature of habitat destruction, especially in the South, is prevention of fire. Savannas are fire-dependent ecosystems and many of the plants, including most carnivorous plants, depend on fire to open up the environment. Their buried rhizomes resist repeated, fast fires. However, wildfires are severe problems for nearby homes and communities; thus, they cannot be allowed except far out in the last remaining unsettled areas. We have all seen Smokey the Bear on signs, pamphlets, and television spots telling us that only we can prevent forest fires —meaning all fires in natural areas. Aside from the promotions missing the factor of lightning, people now find it very difficult to accept that a little fire is good for many ecosystems.

Rhizomatous carnivorous plants seem to have a great capacity for lying low when conditions are not satisfactory, particularly in densely crowded situations. In the Introduction, I described a small study where physical clearing, not burning, of brush in a large shrub bog in eastern North Carolina resulted in a great resurgence of pitcher plant growth the following year (Schnell 1982a). Unfortunately, the clearing was done to prepare the land for tree farming, and the site was also deeply ditched. The year after the pitcher plant resurgence, drainage was established. Although the former shrub bog was still relatively clear, dryness prevented pitcher plant growth. These observations underscore the importance of both adequate moisture and open space for pitcher plants.

In another situation, a couple from Maryland moved to southern Alabama with the intent of starting a horse farm. The land they purchased and built on had no evidence of carnivorous plants. In particular, they wanted to clear a large sloping area of heavy brush to make a pasture, so one autumn they burned it. The following spring they were amazed to see an open savanna flowering into dense stands of pitcher plants, orchids, lilies, and various other attractive savanna species. In fact, the couple was so impressed that they have given up on the pasture idea and are conserving the savanna through regular burns. They have even built a small boardwalk so visitors may wander through the wonders of this natural garden (Bender 1990).

At a place in the North Carolina sandhills region near Southern Pines, something similar happened. Weymouth Woods was willed to the care of North Carolina as a nature preserve. The preserve has a circular hiking path; as it descends to bottomland, there used to be a very dense shrub bog with nothing in particular to recommend it. One day, on a hunch, the director had the shrubs burned. Soon, there was an explosive growth of three species of pitcher plants and some sundews that had lay dormant for who knows how long.

In the northern and northwestern bogs, there seems to be less urgency to conserve habitat. In more populous areas, however, such as the Great Lakes shorelines, some fens on beaches are under threat by summer home and cottage development. But inland, other fens as well as sphagnous bogs are in provincial parks and national and state forests, where they seem safe from incursion. In the Pacific Northwest, bogs that are the homes of *Darlingtonia*, *Pinguicula*, and *Drosera* for the most part seem safe due to inaccessibility of many or their presence in national forests and a few preserves, although some bogs have been and are being destroyed.

Previous students of northern bogs (in the broad sense of the term) felt that all were ultimately doomed to proceed on individual timetables toward mesic woodland as kettles filled and fen margins crept in. However, this has been brought into question as the ultimate fate for all sphagnous bogs (see arguments summarized in Crum 1988). In the Southeast, the concept that carnivorous plants are destroying their own habitats by converting insects into ground fertilizer seems facile and is both unproven and empirically unlikely (see discussion of this point in the Introduction).

Falling Water Tables

In the previous section, I mentioned the effect of ditching on the water tables of the coastal plain. Also, in the *Darlingtonia* chapter I discussed the plight of Butterfly Valley in California, whose water table is dropping due to nearby housing development. Here, I am mainly concerned with piedmont and mountain bogs.

The disappearance of Appalachian Mountain bogs is a great concern (see Earley 1989). Even though peat core studies indicate that some bogs have been there for 11,000 years or more, during which time other bogs certainly dried up, in the past 50 years or so historically known and studied bogs have been degrading at a very rapid rate. Even in the relatively brief time I have been watching some of these bogs (about 40–45 years), my impression is that water levels in the bogs (or seeps feeding water to the sphagnous areas) are falling and the bogs are becoming smaller. The surrounding shrubs and trees are encroaching on them.

In this case, I believe a generalized lowering of the areas' water tables is a major part of the problem, which is at least partially due to local population increases and development as well as destruction of watershed forests. Periodic, multiyear droughts may also contribute. A secondary drying effect is created by marginal shrub and tree growth. These plants absorb and transpire enormous amounts of decreasingly available water from the seep and tend to invade the former bog as well. This may occur eventually anyway, but the process appears to be accelerated due to less water being available for seeps. Finally, fire suppression may play at least some part. Although fire in a sphagnous bog is not usual or as helpful as fire in a savanna, fires around the bogs may help suppress encroaching mesic shrubs and trees.

Damaging Effects of Introduced Exotics

Two vines introduced from Asia, kudzu (*Pueraria lobata* [Willdenow] Ohwi) and Japanese honeysuckle (*Lonicera japonica* Thunberg), have invaded the southeastern coastal plain and to a great extent the uplands as well. Brought into the country to control soil erosion in the 1930s, these vines have run completely out of control and have invaded many areas, including sphagnous bogs and savannas. Kudzu is known to grow 30 cm a day, and a season's growth has covered houses and parked cars. Of the two vines, honeysuckle is easier to eradicate from a local area, most safely by hand pulling if one wishes to avoid chemicals to preserve what native flora may remain. Kudzu, however, forms a huge taproot, useful as a source of starch in Asia, which makes eradication extremely difficult. *Lonicera japonica* is evergreen, whereas *Pueraria* is deciduous, dying back to an unsightly mass of brown, dead foliage each autumn, only to spring from the massive taproot and woody older branches each spring. The vines of kudzu are sometimes used as forage. Surprisingly, I still see *L. japonica* advertised yearly in a few nursery catalogues.

In the North, the perennial purple loosestrife (*Lythrum salicaria* Linnaeus) is running rampant and destroying marshes and bogs. A tall plant with cymes of admittedly attractive pale purple to pink flowers, loosestrife quickly forms dense colonies in its preferred wetland habitats. The species has been commonly offered in nursery catalogues as a plant for flower gardens and borders; in these drier conditions, the plant has somewhat more orderly behavior. Regardless of its attractiveness, cultivating the plant is strongly discouraged. Some nursery catalogues claim that their plants are sterile and unable to produce seeds and are therefore environmentally safe. However, there have been counterclaims to this. It is better to not grow the plant in gardens, from which seeds seem to readily escape to wetlands.

The worst offender among these exotics is melaleuca (*Melaleuca quinquenervia* [Cavanilles] Blake), which has become a severe problem in southern Florida. This white-and-black-barked tree was imported from Australia to dry up the Everglades for development and farming. The tree tends to quickly form dense colonies in subtropical and tropical Florida, and it does absorb prodigious amounts of water. Unfortunately, the tree has spread into huge plots of land, and its numbers are increasing long after its intended purpose has gone out of fashion. Melaleuca is crowding our native flora and destroying wetlands. Control is proving quite difficult, and to date no truly satisfactory methods have been devised.

Many other exotics have been imported purposefully or accidentally and show up in bogs and other desirable habitats as pests. In their original habitats on other continents there are natural controls such as disease, other plants, and insects that keep these plants sufficiently in check so that they are little problem in their homelands. However, across oceans, where their enemies do not reside, the plants are able to flourish if they encounter suitable habitat. Air travel has essentially eliminated geographic barriers as people travel the world and, one way or another, bring back plant novelties that may do untold damage. More troubling are the government agencies that encouraged such plants as kudzu for seemingly worthy and benign use, but did not pay attention to warnings at that time.

Mass Collections

Most people seem fascinated by carnivorous plants, some to the extent of wanting to grow a few, particularly *Dionaea* and some *Sarracenia* species. My rough estimate is that probably about 1% of growers are successful for at least a brief period of time, with the remainder losing or giving up their plants after a season or two. Lack of success then breeds disinterest and no further plants are collected or purchased by those who have failed. But there are enough growers who are successful or determined to try again and enough new growers fascinated by the plants that there has developed a considerable worldwide market in carnivorous plants, most of which will die prematurely.

To supply this market, nurseries with a sideline or specialty in carnivorous plants have sprung up in many countries. Clearly, these nurseries must obtain material from somewhere. The two obvious choices are widespread collection from the field involving thousands of plants at a time or trying to propagate material from initial collections. For commercial purposes, standard propagation methods are expensive because it takes time and special care to grow salable plants, and this time and care translate to many square meters of space in greenhouses that are expensive to operate, particularly if they do not generate product on nearly a yearly basis. The economic choices seemed obvious—until tissue culture.

By using a relatively small bit of tissue from the growth point of plants and separating the cells so that when placed on special media nearly each cell produces a new plant, thousands of offspring can be produced in more compact laboratories. Also, when the plantlets are adapted to soil and pots, they seem to grow faster than seedlings and are more predictable. Nearly all major groups of carnivorous plants have been cultured successfully from tissue to some degree. This technique clearly seems better than continuing mass collections, but unfortunately collecting continues.

There is a particularly large appetite for carnivorous plants in Europe, where people have a strong horticultural heritage. For years there was a huge flow of carnivorous plants from North America and other regions into wholesale nurseries in these countries, particularly the Netherlands. From these primary import nurseries, legitimate and sometimes illegitimate imports are dispersed throughout Europe to more localized secondary wholesalers or directly to large retail nurseries. I am certain that there are ethical wholesalers who do not participate in what are now questionable practices, but some still do so. In the mid-1990s I was assured by one European wholesale nursery owner that importation of Venus flytraps and *Sarracenia* species, in particular, was almost a thing of the past due to tissue culture, that all European material would come from that source. However, questionable and illegal exports continue, despite the rules and restrictions of the Convention on the International Trade of Endangered Species of Fauna and Flora and monitoring by Traffic, an arm of the World Wildlife Fund.

On morning, I was awakened by a ringing phone at 3:00 A.M., which is not unexpected in the medical profession; however, the purpose of the call turned out to be totally unexpected. Without any preliminary pleasantries, a voice announced, "I need 150,000 *Dionaea* right away!" Taken aback and still groggy from sleep, I managed a startled, "What?" The man repeated his demand, ever more urgently. I asked who he was. I never understood his name, although I did get that he was calling from the Netherlands. The fact that he had not properly accounted for time difference seemed to add to the man's agitation. I explained with equal curtness and perfect clarity that I never had, was not, and would never deal commercially in carnivorous plants. Without skipping a beat, he demanded I tell him of someone who could supply him with the plants. I said I knew of no one, and asked if he realized that it was illegal to collect the Venus flytrap in North Carolina—the only logical source of that many plants because it was before tissue culture had proven successful. He rudely, but thankfully, hung up.

Tissue culture still seems too slow for today's market. In 1998 ("Two Charged" 1998) an American collector and his Dutch contact were stopped at Baltimore-Washington International Airport with 12,000 *Dionaea* stuffed in a large suitcase. They were attempting to illegally export plants that had been illegally collected. Earley (1993) estimated that 500,000 Venus flytraps per year were being collected illegally from the wild. Both Earley and Stolzenberg (1993) gave fascinating accounts of carnivorous plant poaching, particularly in North Carolina, which has vast areas throughout the state preserved as game lands. These large areas are carefully monitored and are often kept closed except during certain hunting and fishing seasons. As a result of this lack of development as well as controlled burns, these lands, particularly in the southeastern part of the state, are refugia for carnivorous plants. Rangers patrol the game lands faithfully. They stand between the plants and another group of people who blacken their faces, put on fatigues, and belly-crawl through the game lands at night to poach for profit. There are running skirmishes between the poachers and rangers that read like high adventure in these articles. In one incident in full daylight, wildlife officers observed a young man riding a bicycle out of a savanna. In spite of it being a warm day, he was wearing a long-sleeved shirt buttoned at the neck and cuffs. The rider was stopped and questioned, and the officers noted a peculiar bulging in his shirt. The man had stuffed his shirt full of hundreds of *Dionaea* rhizomes.

One rather novel attack on carnivorous plants is the use of collected *Sarracenia* pitchers in flower arrangements. Although possibly in practice before then, I first became aware of it during the summer of 1961. I was seeing patients on rounds when I entered one room and immediately noticed that a flower arrangement had a single pitcher of *Sarracenia leucophylla* in it. The lid had been trimmed back, presumably because of drying, but the rest of the pitcher was in remarkably good condition. I immediately pointed this out to the uninterested patient, who had not particularly noticed it, and launched into an enthusiastic and what I thought was an enlightening exposition on pitcher plants, the patient all the while staring blandly at me and wondering why I had not asked about his postoperative pain and whether he was eating. When I was on break, I called the florist out of curiosity, but they did not seem to want to talk about it either.

Since then, the use of pitchers, particularly the white-topped pitcher plant, in floral arrangements has exploded—up to 4 million pitchers per year nationally and internationally in 1989 alone (Simpson 1994). The pitchers are shipped both fresh and dried for worldwide use. Recently I saw tied bunches of field-collected pitchers for sale in an upscale grocery store. Some collectors snip only one pitcher from a growth point, whereas others quickly clip everything from a rhizome. The pitchers are then washed clean of their catches and hung to drain. Good-sized, fresh pitchers with the fewest blemishes are then shipped out almost immediately as premium material. Others are dried and shipped for later use, as the ones I saw in the grocery store. Regular collectors insist that these pitchers are collected from private property with permission of the landowners, who usually get a small portion of the profit. Collectors also dig rhizomes from timber properties that are imminently threatened with drainage and development of silviculture, again with permission. These rhizomes are usually planted on the collectors' property for pitcher harvests. All interstate and export shipping is done with proper permits, although there is movement at this time to declare *Sarracenia leucophylla* endangered, largely as a result of habitat destruction and degradation.

The concern with collecting pitchers from living plants is what impact the activity will have on insect capture and photosynthesis in plants that have been deprived of one or more or perhaps all pitchers. Producing specialized trap leaves requires considerable energy; when produced as replacements out of the usual seasonal growth phases, there may be severe stress on stores in the rhizomes. This may result in growth setback and loss of efficiency for several seasons or may cause the plant to be more susceptible to disease. Research is in progress to investigate exactly what effect pitcher harvesting during spring and summer might have on the plants overall.

Collections of Carnivorous Plants by Individuals

Compared to habitat degradation and mass commercial collections, plant collecting by relatively few individuals would not seem to have much effect on carnivorous plant populations except in a few critical situations. These exceptions, however, are legitimately of great concern. Small, individual plant collections are usually made for personal horticultural purposes. The skill of the collector varies from the rank amateur who will try to put a few Venus flytraps into the flower border at home to individuals who are quite skilled at growing and propagating carnivorous plants.

Collecting can have a disastrous effect on a population if the individual collects from a site of an endangered species, such as *Sarracenia oreophila* or *S. rubra* subspecies *jonesii*, where a particular location may have only a dozen or fewer plants remaining. In this case, two or three plants may hold a large percentage of the genetic pool in that stand. The collector probably does not understand that removing the plants could adversely affect recovery or that decreased stability might result at the site. Such collecting has drastically different results than the removal of two or three plants from a stand of thousands of *S. flava* (unless location information is shared with another hobbyist who comes along and collects two or three plants, and so on).

One other potential problem with small, individual collections is that the collector is frequently interested in minor variations, such as an all-red pitcher plant, which may occur at a rate of less than 1% in a large stand. Removing this and/or other variants may reduce the level of total variation in the whole stand. Genetic variation within a group of plants can act as a sort of buffer against habitat changes that would adversely affect the majority of plants. Some of these variants are able to thrive under the new conditions, thus helping to sustain the colony.

In no instance should collections be undertaken from public properties such as parks, preserves, or government-administered forests. This may also include the edges of roadside ditches if the road right-of-way extends across the ditch. (Many states post intermittent signs mentioning the extent of right-of-way.) Collections from private properties should only be undertaken with the permission of the landowner. In most instances, endangered species may be collected from private property with the owner's permission, with no governmental permits being required, an unfortunate loophole in some cases. In the United States, however, federally endangered species cannot be transported across state lines or exported without special permits. Even with owner permission on private properties, it would be unethical to further put at risk a population of endangered species with rampant collection. Many experienced and skilled growers will select, for example, a pitcher plant rhizome with several growth points and only remove one of these with a few roots, leaving the main portion of the rhizome and its other growth points in place.

The beginner is better off learning how to grow and propagate carnivorous plants by purchasing material that has been propagated via tissue culture or excess plants given to him or her by another grower. The novice is then able to learn and modify the peculiarities of his or her own growing system using more or less expendable plants. Failures along this learn-ing curve will then not result in more plants being plucked from the field. Reasonably priced plants of several North American genera that have been propagated (they are mostly so labeled these days) are available from grocery and variety stores as well as local nurseries and some specialized carnivorous plant nurseries. Whenever I visit a grocery store, I always look for what I lightly call the "botany department," a corner where cut flowers and houseplants are sold. I am surprised at the carnivorous plant species that show up intermittently. Even in my eastern mountain county of 25,000 people, the grocery stores occasionally have propagated exam-ples of such exotic genera as *Nepenthes* and *Heliamphora* at very reason-able prices, not to mention the usual run of North American genera.

Conservation Efforts

I have no illusions about our ability to stop or massively reverse devel-opment in our retreating wetlands. Some remaining carnivorous plant locations that are not already under protection may be saved or recov-ered, but most will not be. To successfully save a freshwater wetland, a large area must be set aside so that peripheral drainage efforts for the development of surrounding private lands will not interfere with the lar-gest central portion of the preserve. In other words, a substantial buffer zone or watershed must also be set aside. The essential preserve should be hydrologically self-sustaining so there will be minimal interference with the water table as surrounding areas are drained. The possibility of use-ful diking and filling of existing ditches or seep slopes should be consid-ered. At best, we can only save a sample of remaining bog tracts.

There has been a subtle but useful change in conservation targets recently. Instead of simply focusing on endangered species, the paradigm has shifted to saving a diverse habitat with many plant representatives, including the threatened and endangered species, but also many associ-ated species within a single ecosystem. For example, an agency may have wished to conserve a site containing *Pinguicula ionantha*, and a team went out with tunnel vision looking for a large stand of this species.

Today, we instead search the region for a large area that contains many associated species as well as *Pinguicula ionantha*. Along the way, other species of concern as well as nonendangered plants and animals may be included in the preserve. Efforts and scarce funds are thus much better used.

Governmental Efforts

Some suitable bogs and savannas are conserved by their inclusion in provincial parks, national and state forests and parks, and wilderness areas. Funds for proper management and security are limited, and local and national political and economic concerns often drive politicians and bureaucrats in their decisions. Within government agencies, there is a fear that while much of the populace seems to cry out for timber harvest, water diversion, fire suppression, more access roads, and uses such as snowmobiles, all-terrain vehicles, and fast motorboats, seemingly small worries such as preserving carnivorous plants smack of elitism. From the government's perspective, all of these land uses are legitimate, and majority concerns tend to overwhelm minority ones most of the time.

Still, when wetlands are contained within a government preserve, it is imperative to bring conservational concerns to the attention of local officials and political figures and perhaps carry the case to capitals as well. Occasionally, these efforts are successful. Experts must be engaged to plea the case that sufficient areas be set aside, including the water buffer mentioned above. Simply putting a real or figurative fence around and a boardwalk across a bog most often will not suffice. It is disheartening to all concerned when wetland conservation attempts fail, perhaps due to largely preventable factors.

Private Efforts

I believe that private efforts will ultimately be the most useful in preserving the remaining natural habitats. Such organizations are free of the constraints of bureaucracy and elective politics, although admittedly there may be spirited discussion within the organizations on how to operate. Still, there is far less diffusion of aims and purposes, lands are purchased or received as donations outright or as conservation easements, and there is no confusion over the intent of setting aside the land. Whether the organization keeps the land to manage or turns it over to local, state, or provincial government for security and some management, the intended use of the tract is clear and unimpeachable.

Here, I mention two privately funded organizations that have been successful in land conservation efforts. These are certainly not the only conservation groups, and there are others who do as well. I do not intend to slight the others groups, but clearly there are space limitations here. Also, I have some familiarity with these organizations. The first is limited to state work, whereas the second deals with worldwide concerns.

The Michigan Nature Association is a statewide outgrowth of one county's nature organization that engaged in education and study. The small group became alarmed by the continuing destruction of natural areas in their county and began purchasing the remaining remnants of natural beauty. The group became particularly energized because they viewed local park authorities as destroying species' habitat that required protection. State agencies and conservation groups did not respond to their pleas. As a result, the county organization decided to expand into several counties in the greater Detroit area. The association was established in 1960 and soon became a statewide organization (Daubendiek and Newman 1988).

By 1994 the Michigan Nature Association had preserved 140 sanctuaries in 51 of Michigan's counties, for a total of approximately 3100 hectares of land. In 1986 the group botanist estimated that 82% of the state's plant species were represented in one or more of the preserves. Practically all endangered, threatened, or species of special concern in the state can be found in these areas (Holzman et al. 1994). Land is still being acquired, particularly in the targeted Oakland County area. With this many sanctuaries secured, however, focus is shifting to endowments to ensure administrative and maintenance costs in the coming years. Presently, most of the preserves are watched over by local volunteers.

The Michigan Nature Association publishes a guidebook to their projects (such as Holzman et al. 1994), and newer acquisitions are mentioned in their regular newsletter. Nearly all of the preserves are named and mentioned in the guidebook, which contains photographs, descriptions, and maps describing how to get to the sites. Most of the preserves are well marked with signs and many have maintained trails and boardwalks. These lands are open to the public, be they members or not. A few recently acquired, environmentally sensitive preserves (particularly some bogs and fens) do not have published maps, and those interested in visiting them are advised to contact the local monitor for a guided tour.

The Michigan Nature Association has done remarkably well with their sanctuaries, which represent all major ecosystems of the state and seem to be secure from secondary degradation due to activities in surrounding areas. The association continues to proclaim proudly that they have not used one cent of public money but have relied entirely on purchases or land donations. As you leaf through their guidebook or visit many of the preserves, you cannot help but admire the hard work that has gone into these projects.

In all fairness, however, the Michigan Nature Association is not the only group conserving land in Michigan. The state does have extensive state and national forestland, although the government agencies involved are not entirely focused on conservation. Still, many of these large areas have incidentally included tracts of natural diversity.

Started in 1953, the Nature Conservancy is not only a national organization, its scope is truly international. Today, the main and chapter offices, with more than 1000 employees and 10,000 volunteers, are likely to be staffed with real estate lawyers, MBAs, accountants, and tax lawyers working beside biologists and ecologists. By 1999 the Nature Conservancy had saved nearly 2.85 million hectares of land worldwide, 78% of which included so-called biologically significant sites with extensive biodiversity (Stolzenberg 1999). In eastern Virginia, the Nature Conservancy is working on reclaiming wetlands by filling ditches and diking low margins of properties to slow runoff. Where the coast of Alabama and Mississippi adjoins the Gulf of Mexico there is a 5700-hectare area of wet savannas known as Grand Bay. The Nature Conservancy is slowly aggregating this tract into probably the largest preserve of its kind, quite possibly one of the last extensive bastions of such savanna (Wilkinson 1999).

The Nature Conservancy started out by simply purchasing lands, but today the organization is extremely sophisticated. With more than $600 million to work with, the group often uses cash in a revolving manner. The Nature Conservancy has largely become an acquisition organization, preferring not to tie up needed funds by keeping lands. As soon as land is acquired outright, it is sold to states or provinces for maintenance. The Nature Conservancy's key strength is being able to act quickly when an opportunity arises, allowing slower government agencies to repay them in time. Some lands are acquired through donations, a practice that allows landowners to receive useful tax breaks. Often these lands are not suitable for preservation and the property is sold, thus providing the organization with more assets for its conservation work. Some lands are purchased from cash-strapped owners and then leased back to them with strict conservation restrictions. Other biologically valuable properties are adjacent to land that can be used for other purposes. Purchase of the whole package conserves the needed land, while sale of the adjacent lands to developers allows them to develop outside the buffer. The Nature Conservancy has also been known to work in concert with various government agencies and other conservation organizations, where its skills and quick action are welcome.

The Nature Conservancy has been extremely successful and will continue to grow with savvy management. One weakness, however, is that the county, state, province, or other entity that receives or purchases land from the Nature Conservancy may not always be capable of proper maintenance. This may be due to lack of biological expertise on the part of the government unit. Often, a biologist from a local university is paid to oversee the property, but he or she may not have experience in monitoring a wetland. I have seen a few good properties degrade as a result. Overall, these instances are comparatively few but may be important in certain areas where especially critical species are at stake.

Warehousing Carnivorous Plants

Many botanists and ecologists have viewed attempts to set aside and recover rapidly degrading wetlands and to save threatened species therein as a waste of time and a misdirection of efforts and money. They feel that once a system of species is spiraling downward, even if caused by human activity, that it should be let go. If thought through, such a spartan attitude can be understood, but most scientists would rather try to do something.

Many botanical gardens have begun programs to save threatened and rare species from areas under imminent development, often just ahead of the bulldozer. In addition to collecting threatened plants and growing them in their gardens, these organizations learn a great deal about the biology of the plants. It has been said that you never really know a plant until you grow and propagate it successfully. Seed banks are also established against future assaults on natural areas or for recovery efforts. Thus, far from simply warehousing plants, a great deal of knowledge is gained through these activities. Several botanical gardens have grouped together into a consortium in which each is designated certain species to study and propagate. There are criticisms of this activity, these involving the use of valued greenhouse space and funds and the observation that even a fairly good plant collection may not represent the genetic diversity necessary to reestablish plants successfully in the wild.

The North Carolina Botanical Garden, located on the campus of the University of North Carolina at Chapel Hill, participates in the endangered species consortium. The garden's focus is strictly native plants. The facility has successfully established artificial ecosystem gardens; maintains a large, natural woodland on the property; and participates in educational activities as well as research. The garden has even branched out a bit and has several critical natural properties throughout the state that have been turned over to its care.

North Carolina Botanical Garden engages in plant rescue missions that are governed by strict rules. When a critical area is about to fall to development, a recovery team from the garden gains permission from the developer and property owners to remove plant material from the site. If the numbers of recovered plants are too great for the garden to handle, some are released to knowledgeable native plant growers and other gardens. In my opinion, the good achieved and the positive spirit abounding in the North Carolina Botanical Garden far outweigh any criticism of their direction.

Recovery Efforts

Recovery efforts are attempts to reinvigorate a severely degraded habitat, such as an overgrown savanna. In this case, the recovery team attempts to clear overgrown brush and herbaceous plants, either manually or through controlled burns. Along with clearing, hydrologic concerns are addressed. Next, and often most controversially, there may be attempts to reintroduce lost species that have been recorded at the location, the transplants coming from other sites that are condemned by development or from botanical gardens that are rescuing and/or propagating such plants. The final phase is then to maintain any success with the project.

Replanting is controversial from several aspects. Many ecologists say replanting simply establishes a garden that in no way represents the original flora of the site. The genotypes of the transplants are clearly different from the original plants. Many other plants that were also native may not be transplanted along with, for example, several thousand pitcher plants, thus contributing to a garden effect. Also, the ages of the transplants may be relatively even instead of reflecting the differing ages and sizes of genets present in a natural site. There are other controversial aspects, but these are the most prominent.

Is replanting a viable option? Probably, as long as the limitations are understood and the recovery team is under no illusions that they may be establishing a field garden rather than an ecosystem. Much will depend on the individual characteristics of the location and its remaining flora. At the very least, if a replanting program is successful, examples of the species (one or more) being put back into the field may survive in something like an original environment rather than remaining always in a formal botanical garden.

At the other end of the recovery effort, the site may have examples of all recorded species remaining, but with certain critical and especially desirable species at very low levels. On the face of it, this would seem like a good project to at least seriously consider, but again there are controversies. The argument arises, unfortunately based on some experience with failures at recovery, that we are simply dealing with the "living dead" in such situations, that no attempts, no matter how intense, intelligent, and seemingly well placed, will save those critical plants at that site. The location may be cleared of competing brush and herbs by burning, hydrology seemingly addressed, and yet the critical plants continue to decrease and there is no evidence of seedling growth, a good measure of the health of a supposedly recovering location.

One problem related to recovery efforts is trying to discern what is the minimum number of genets required for a population to recover. For *Sarracenia* species, for example, the U.S. Fish and Wildlife Service has adopted the minimum number as 25 genets. Minimum viable populations are usually assayed in terms of trying to keep inbreeding below a 1% level. Looking at this from the other end, there should be enough individual genets so that cross-pollination is achieved yearly in at least 99% of them. Inbreeding often results in genetic depression and eventual failure of the population. How does this translate to real numbers? Twenty-five genets hardly seem enough. Some have proposed minimum numbers from 50 to 500 or even more (Whittaker 1998).

One reason for the large variation in the minimum viability number may lie in the total genetic constitution of the particular genus or species. *Sarracenia* species, for instance, with their thirteen pairs of chromosomes and history of rather prominent polymorphism and easy, viable hybridization, may have sufficient genetic variation to prevent the problems of inbreeding, at least for an undetermined period of time. Many genera and species are being studied to evaluate genetic variability and diversity in the laboratory (such as Godt and Hamrick 1998). Unfortunately, even if considerable variability is shown in a critical species in the laboratory, we may not yet know how to reasonably translate this to minimum viable numbers in the field.

Workers at the Atlanta Botanical Garden are engaged in an active bog recovery and maintenance program. In northern Georgia, they have cleared overgrown seepage sphagnous bogs and replaced *Sarracenia purpurea* subspecies *venosa* variety *montana* where necessary with material propagated at the garden. They are following survival and seedling activity closely. In Alabama, garden employees are working on maintenance and recovery by burning and weeding a sandy-clay hillside seep bog containing one of the largest remaining populations of *S. rubra* subspecies *alabamensis*. They are also propagating this subspecies at the garden.

There is an interesting story of how *Sarracenia purpurea* was established on a floating bog on a lake in Ohio—not quite a recovery effort but a de novo planting. Buckeye Lake is located just east of Columbus, Ohio, and was established as an impoundment in 1830 to further a projected statewide canal system. Surrounding the original stream prior to impoundment was an extensive sphagnous mat containing *Drosera rotundifolia* and some *Utricularia* species but no pitcher plants. As the lake filled in, the sphagnous areas were covered over. However, soon after, an 8-hectare segment of sphagnous mat literally popped to the surface as a floating bog mat. Due to the large number of cranberry plants present, it was dubbed Cranberry Island. In 1912 someone planted a single *Sarracenia purpurea* plant on the island, which today has expanded to about 157,000 plants. Even though all the pitcher plants originated from a single individual, there is certainly no inbreeding depression here. The island is now a preserve accessible only by boat, and a permit is required to visit (Risner 1987).

Closing Remarks

I do not propose that my views are the only or even the correct ones. Over time, the conservation methods mentioned here will be either proven successful or not (for a very detailed discussion of biodiversity and conservation problems, see Stein et al. 2000). This chapter has been necessarily brief. Conservation and recovery are complex, broad, constantly evolving disciplines, with new studies, ideas, and conclusions coming forth regularly. Interested readers may wish to peruse conservation and recovery titles at their local libraries or bookstores.

We have come full circle to Whittaker's quote at the beginning of this chapter. What will make a difference is how much cooperative effort, funding, time, and determination we are willing to invest in conservation. No amount of science or theory by itself can do it. We all have to decide whether carnivorous plants and their habitats are worth saving.

APPENDIX: Metric Conversions

TO CONVERT	MULTIPLY BY
kilometers to miles	0.62
miles to kilometers	1.60
meters to feet	3.27
feet to meters	0.30
centimeters to inches	0.39
inches to centimeters	2.54
millimeters to inches	0.04
inches to millimeters	25.40
square kilometers to square miles	0.39
square miles to square kilometers	2.59
square meters to square feet	10.80
square feet to square meters	0.09
hectares to acres	2.50
acres to hectares	0.40

$$°C = (°F - 32) \times 5/9$$
$$°F = (°C \times 9/5) + 32$$

GLOSSARY

abaxial pointing or facing away from the center (axis) of the plant

actinomorphic radially symmetrical

active trap carnivorous plant trap in which movement of plant parts takes place during the trapping process

adaxial pointing or facing toward the center (axis) of the plant

adnate fusion of unlike parts, such as stamens to petals

ala broad, bladelike expansion of the adaxial margin of a pitcher leaf

allelopathy whereby chemical secretions from a plant into the soil inhibit the growth of some other plants in the immediate vicinity

allochrony literally, different times; events such as flowering occur at different times in the season for two or more plant species or populations

allopolylpoidy *see* amphiploidy

amphiploidy process by which new species develop from a hybrid plant wherein the chromosome number of the hybrid doubles and the plant is then capable of maintaining its characteristics during sexual reproduction

anther tip portion of the stamen that produces pollen

anthesis period in which a flower expands, pollen is shed, and stigmas are receptive

apiculate having a sharp, fine, flexible point, such as the hood tips of several *Sarracenia*

apomixis *see* vegetative apomixis

areoles depigmented, windowlike areas of plant tissue, also known as fenestrations

asexual reproduction form of reproduction involving one parent plant with no exchange of genetic material, such as budding, cuttings, rhizome divisions

autonymic automatically established name as applied to a nominate subordinate taxon

autopolyploidy increasing an organism's own chromosome complement by multiples

axil acute angle between a stem and something attached to it, such as a petiole or a branch

backcrossing reproductive cross between a hybrid and one of its parent plants

beard confluence of plant hairs on the palate of a flower

bilabiate two-lipped

binomial nomenclature modern system of biological classification whereby each living organism bears a two-word name corresponding to its genus and species

biovulate condition wherein a flower ovary contains two ovules

bog in the broad sense, a freshwater, constantly moist or wet area dominated by mosses and herbaceous plants

bract small, modified leaf structure; in flowers, located below the calyx

bracteole small bract

calyx collective term for the sepals of a flower

carpel the pistil of the flower consisting of stigma, style, and ovary

chasmogamous flowers that open or expand fully during anthesis

cladophyl flattened stem that looks and functions like a leaf

cleistogamous flowers that open only partially or not at all during anthesis

clone in botany, a group of plants that all bear the same genetic composition, having been borne of one plant by repeated asexual reproduction

closing trap carnivorous plant trap in which essentially identical trap halves approximate and thus incarcerate the plant's prey

column in the context of pitcher leaves, the narrow structure supporting the lid, or hood

connate fusion of like parts of plants, such as petals to form a fused corolla (cf. adnate)

corolla collective term for all the petals of a flower

crestate abnormal growth wherein the growth point assumes a ridgelike structure (sometimes spelled cristate)

cross-pollination exchange of pollen in sexual reproduction between two different flowering plants

cuneate wedge shaped

cuticle water-impermeable, waxy coating of some plant surfaces

cymose terminal, broad, flat flower cluster with the center flowers opening first

ensiform sword shaped

enzyme chemical substance that speeds or enhances a chemical reaction without itself permanently changing or becoming a component of the reaction

etiolation soft, elongate, atypical growth in plants normally growing in full sunlight but placed in the shade

family closely related group of genera; a family may have only one genus, but classification is at the same level as other families with two or more genera

fenestrations depigmented, windowlike areas of plant tissue, also known as areoles

fertilization in seed-plant reproduction, the actual union of male and female elements

filiform threadlike

fimbriate feathery, or margin very finely divided

flypaper trap carnivorous plant trap in which the prey is ensnared by sticky, mucilaginous secretions

fusiform thickened in the middle but tapering smoothly toward each end

gemmae buds formed by vegetative reproduction in small, cuplike structures from which they are shed; term also applied to small, winter buds in *Pinguicula*

genus (pl. genera) biological classification ranking between the family and species level, comprising structurally or phylogenetically related species or an individual species exhibiting unusual differentiation

globose spherical

grass-sedge bog sandy bog dominated by grasses and sedges

heterosis hybrid vigor; the hybrid of two or more plants grows more vigorously than the parent(s)

hibernaculum (pl. hibernacula) winter bud from which plants will sprout with the return of proper growing conditions

hirsutism hairy

hood pitcher leaf appendage that usually (or derivatively) hangs over the pitcher opening; also called a lid

hybrid generally, a plant resulting from a cross between two or more taxa

inflorescence cluster of flowers on a single stalk (peduncle)

keel ridge on a plant part that is shaped roughly like the keel of a boat

kettlehole bog glacially scooped out kettle-shaped lake filling in with *Sphagnum*

lanceolate lance-shaped; longer than wide with one tip pointed and the other broadened

lid *see* hood

marl bog bog in which marl (calcium carbonate) is prominently present; usually a grass-sedge type

marsh tract of wetland, usually with fresh, salt, or brackish water to some depth, dominated by taller grasses and reeds

morphology in botany, the form and nonmicroscopic anatomy of plants

mucronate stout, sharp tip, usually on a small, raised cushion

obovate somewhat oval with one end narrower than the other; term applied to a leaf or petal that is attached at the narrow end with the broader end free

ovary lowermost portion of the pistil in which eggs develop; the ovary will become the seed capsule after fertilization

palate prominence on the lower lip of a sympetalous, usually zygomorphic flower

panduriform shaped like the contour of a fiddle or guitar

papillose bearing papilla, or protuberances

passive trap carnivorous plant trap in which no plant movement occurs as an integral part of the trapping process; for example, pitcher plants produce passive traps

pedicel stalk supporting a single flower of an inflorescence

peduncle main supporting stalk of one or several flowers

peltate broadly shaped plant structure (such as a leaf) with the stalk attached to the center instead of a margin

perfoliate state in which the base of a leaf or its petiole completely surround the stem

petal often colorful, form-giving, leaflike projections of a flower located above the calyx

petiole leaf stalk

phenolic in chemistry, a six-carbon hexagonal molecule with at least one –OH group attached, the compounds being frequently strongly scented

photosynthesis production of carbohydrates from carbon dioxide and water with the aid of chlorophyll and light

phyllodia usually flat, bladelike structures that are probably expanded or widened petioles

pilose bearing soft, long, and often shaggy plant hairs

pistil female reproductive part of a flower; sticky upper tip (stigma) receives pollen, which germinates and sends a pollen tube down the stalklike style to the ovary for fertilization of ova

pitfall trap carnivorous plant trap into which the prey falls and cannot exit

pollination physical application of pollen to a stigma, which may or may not result in fertilization

polymorphism variation of color or form within a taxon

polystichous leaves or other structures in vertical ranks

polytopy whereby a taxon of plants grows in two or more areas

primordia primitive or undeveloped structures antecedent to a mature structure

propagule any plant part capable of propagating a plant, such as seeds or stem fragments

protandrous plants wherein pollen ripens before the stigma of the flower is receptive

protogynous plants wherein the flower stigma is receptive prior to pollen ripening

quadrifid having four parts or branches

raceme type of inflorescence in which there is a central, unbranched stalk with flowers attached by pedicels

ramet branch of a plant clone capable of independent existence; for instance, branches of pitcher plant rhizomes that may be separated from the main plant and set out

reniform kidney shaped

resupinate upside down, or 180° from the usual orientation

reticulate netlike

rhizoid rootlike structures

rhizome elongate, rootlike underground stem filled with starchy reserves

rugose coarsely reticulate or wrinkled

saccate saclike

savanna sand-peat wetland dominated by short grasses, sedges, and widely scattered pines

scale thin, membranous, small, leaflike structure most often found on peduncles

scape long, naked peduncle, usually supporting a single flower or tight cluster of flowers at the top

scorpioid curved or coiled like a scorpion's tail

self-pollination pollination of a stigma with pollen from the same flower

sepal flower part situated just below the petals, usually green, but if the flower is technically without petals, the sepal may assume the form and color of a petal

sessile set immediately upon another structure without an intervening stalk, as a *sessile* leaf or gland

setulae minute bristles

sexual reproduction form of reproduction in which some genetic material is exchanged between two organisms

spatulate spoon shaped

species biological classification ranking below the genus or subgenus level, comprising related organisms or populations potentially capable of interbreeding

Sphagnum **bog** wetland dominated by *Sphagnum* mosses

spur in floral morphology, an elongate, closed appendage of the corolla of a sympetalous flower in which nectar is held or produced

stamen male reproductive structure of a flower, consisting of the pollen-producing anther at the tip of its supportive structure, the filament

stellate star shaped

stigma sticky, pollen-receptive, often knobby tip portion of the pistil

stolon runner, or any basal branch that may take root and give rise to an independent plant

stolonoid like a stem branch capable of forming a new plant

stratification in horticulture, the process whereby seeds require a period of damp, cold exposure before they will germinate

style often columnar structure that connects the stigma and ovary of a pistil

suborbicular nearly circular

swamp wetland with standing water to some depth that is dominated by trees

sympetalous having fused or joined petals

syngameon plant populations that are intermediate between the species level and extreme variants of the same species

synsepalous wherein the sepals of a flower are partially or wholly united

terete cylindrical; circular in cross-section

tetraploid an organism with twice the normal chromosome complement

threshold in *Utricularia*, the thickened surface of the trap opening against which the door rests

trapdoor in *Utricularia*, the veil of tissue that closes a trap opening

trapdoor trap carnivorous plant trap in which an appendage closes over an opening and incarcerates the plant's prey

trichome plant hair

trifid tip of a structure divided three ways nearly back to the middle

turgor distension of the protoplasmic layer and wall of a plant cell by the fluid contents

turion hibernaculum of a water plant, particularly *Utricularia* in this book

umbraculate umbrella shaped

vegetative apomixis form of asexual reproduction in which plantlets bud from flower parts

vegetative reproduction *see* asexual reproduction

velum in *Utricularia*, a membranous structure for secondary trap closure; this structure rests below the door against the threshold

verticillate whorled arrangement, such as whorls of flowers or stamens

zygomorphic bilaterally symmetrical

BIBLIOGRAPHY

Achterberg, C. van. 1973. A study about the Arthropoda caught by *Drosera* species. *Entomologischen Berichten* 33: 137–140.

Adamec, L. 1997. Mineral nutrition of carnivorous plants: a review. *Botanical Review* 63: 273–299.

Adamec, L., K. Dusakova, and M. Jonackovo. 1992. Growth effects of mineral nutrients applied to the substrate or on the leaves in four carnivorous plant species. *Carnivorous Plant Newsletter* 20: 18–24.

Addicott, J. F. 1974. Predation and prey community structure: an experimental study of the effect of mosquito larvae on the protozoan communities of pitcher plants. *Ecology* 55: 475–492.

Affolter, J. M., and R. F. Olivo. 1975. Action potentials in Venus's-flytraps: long-term observations following the capture of prey. *American Midland Naturalist* 93: 443–445.

Aldenius, J., B. Carlsson, and B. Karlsson. 1983. Effects of insect trapping on growth and nutrient content of *Pinguicula vulgaris* L. in relation to nutrient content of the substrate. *New Phytologist* 93: 53–59.

Anderson, L. C. 1991. Noteworthy plants from north Florida. V. *Sida* 14: 467–474.

Angerilli, N. P. D., and B. P. Beirne. 1974. Influence of some freshwater plants on the development and survival of mosquito larvae in British Columbia, Canada. *Canadian Journal of Zoology* 52: 813–815.

Angerilli, N. P. D., and B. P. Beirne. 1980. Influence of aquatic plants on colonization of artificial ponds by mosquitoes and their insect predators. *Canadian Entomologist* 112: 793–796.

Anonymous. 1984. Michel Sarrazin, 1659–1735. *Canadian Numismatic Journal* 29: 191.

Austin, R. M. 1875–1877. Excerpts of letters to Dr. W. M. Canby, Wilmington, Delaware, transcribed by F. M. Jones ca. 1920s. In B. E. Juniper, R. J. Robins, and D. M. Joel, eds. 1989. *The Carnivorous Plants*. New York: Academic Press. 311–313.

Baker, H. G., and I. Baker. 1973. Amino acids in nectar and their evolutionary significance. *Nature* 241: 543–545.

Barber, J. T. 1978. *Capsella bursa-pastoris* seeds: Are they "carnivorous"? *Carnivorous Plant Newsletter* 7: 39–42.

Barnhart, J. H. 1933. *Pinguicula caerulea. Addisonia* 18: 21–22, pl. 587.

Barrett, S. C. H. 1989. Mating system evolution and speciation in heterostylous plants. In D. Otte and J. A. Endler, eds. *Speciation and Its Consequences*. Sunderland, Mass.: Sinauer Associates. 257–283.

Bates, W. 1943. Control of somatic pain. *American Journal of Surgery* 59: 83.

Beal, E. O., and T. L. Quay. 1968. A review of *Utricularia olivacea* Wright ex Grisebach (Lentibulariaceae). *Journal of the Elisha Mitchell Society* 84: 462–466.

Beal, W. J. 1875. Carnivorous plants. *Journal of the American Association for the Advancement of Science* 1875B: 251–253.

Bell, C. R. 1949. A cytotaxonomic study of the Sarraceniaceae of North America. *Journal of the Elisha Mitchell Scientific Society* 65: 137–166.

Bell, C. R. 1952. Natural hybrids in the genus *Sarracenia*. I. History, distribution and taxonomy. *Journal of the Elisha Mitchell Society* 68: 55–80.

Bell, C. R. 1954. *Sarracenia leucophylla* Rafinesque. *Journal of the Elisha Mitchell Society* 70: 57–60.

Bell, C. R. 1967. *Plant Variation and Classification*. Belmont, Calif.: Wadsworth.

Bell, C. R., and F. W. Case. 1956. Natural hybrids in the genus *Sarracenia*. II. Current notes on distribution. *Journal of the Elisha Mitchell Society* 72: 142–152.

Bender, S. 1990. Beauty in the bog. *Southern Living* 25: 42–44.

Benolken, R. M., and S. L. Jacobsen. 1970. Response properties of sensory hairs excised from Venus's flytrap. *Journal of General Physiology* 56: 64–82.

Benzing, D. H., and K. M. Burt. 1970. Foliar permeability among twenty species of the Bromeliaceae. *Bulletin of the Torrey Botanical Club* 97: 269–279.

Benzing, D. H., K. Henderson, B. Kessel, and J. A. Sulak. 1976. The absorptive capacities of bromeliad trichomes. *American Journal of Botany* 63: 1009–1014.

Boche, T. W., K. Holbein, and K. Jacobsen. 1968. *The Flora of Greenland* (English edition). Copenhagen: P. Haase and Son.

Boivin, B. 1966. Enumeration des plantes du Canada. IV. Herbidees, 2° partie: Connaise. *Naturaliste Canada* 93: 989–1063.

Boldyreff, E. B. 1929. A study of the digestive secretion of *Sarracenia purpurea. Papers of the Michigan Academy of Science, Arts and Letters* (no volume): 55–64.

Bopp, M., and I. Weber. 1981. Hormonal regulation of the leaf blade movement of *Drosera capensis. Physiologia Plantarum* 53: 491–496.

Bradshaw, W. E. 1976. Geography of photoperiodic response in diapausing mosquito: control of dormancy in *Wyeomyia smithii. Nature* 262: 384–385.

Bradshaw, W. E. 1980. Blood-feeding and capacity for increase in the pitcher-plant mosquito *Wyeomyia smithii*. *Environmental Entomology* 9: 86–89.

Bradshaw, W. E. 1983. Interaction between the mosquito *Wyeomyia smithii*, the midge *Metriocnemus knabi*, and their carnivorous host *Sarracenia purpurea*. In J. H. Frank and L. P. Lounibos, eds. *Phytotelmata: Terrestrial Plants as Hosts for Aquatic Insect Communities*. Medford, N.J.: Plexus. 161–189.

Bradshaw, W. E., and L. P. Lounibos. 1977. Evolution of dormancy and its photoperiodic control in pitcher-plant mosquitoes. *Evolution* 31: 546–564.

Buffington, J. 1970. Ecological consideration of the cohabitation of pitcher plants by *Wyeomyia smithii* and *Metriocnemus knabi*. *Mosquito News* 30: 89–90.

Burdon Sanderson, J. S. 1873. Note on the electrical phenomena which accompany stimulation of the leaf of *Dionaea muscipula*. *Proceedings of the Royal Society* 21: 495–496.

Burdon Sanderson, J. S., and F. J. M. Page. 1876. On the mechanical effects and on the electrical disturbance consequent on excitation of the leaf of *Dionaea muscipula*. *Proceedings of the Royal Society* 25: 411–434.

Burr, C. A. 1979. The pollination ecology of *Sarracenia purpurea* in Cranberry Bog, Webridge, Vermont (Addison County). Masters thesis, Middlebury College, Middlebury, Vt.

Carow, T., and R. Furst. 1990. *Fleischfessende Pflanzen*. Nudlingen, Germany: Verlag Thomas Carow.

Case, F. W. 1956. Some Michigan records for *Sarracenia purpurea* forma *heterophylla*. *Rhodora* 58: 203–207.

Case, F. W., and R. B. Case. 1974. *Sarracenia alabamensis*, a newly recognized species from central Alabama. *Rhodora* 76: 650–665.

Case, F. W., and R. B. Case. 1976. The *Sarracenia rubra* complex. *Rhodora* 78: 270–325.

Casper, S. J. 1962. *Pinguicula macroceras* Link in North America. *Rhodora* 64: 212–221.

Casper, S. J. 1966. *Monographie der Gattung Pinguicula* L. Stuttgart: Bibliotheca Botanica.

Ceska, A., and M. A. M. Bell. 1973. *Utricularia* (Lentibulariaceae) in the Pacific Northwest. *Madroño* 22: 74–84.

Chandler, G. E. 1978. The uptake of digestion products by *Drosera*. *Carnivorous Plant Newsletter* 7: 51–54.

Chandler, G. E., and J. W. Anderson. 1976. Studies on the nutrition and growth of *Drosera* species with reference to the carnivorous habit. *New Phytologist* 76: 129–141.

Cheek, M. 1993. Notes on hybrids in *Drosera*. *Kew Magazine* 10: 138–144.

Christensen, N. L. 1976. The role of carnivory in *Sarracenia flava* L. with regard to specific nutrient deficiencies. *Journal of the Elisha Mitchell Society* 92: 144–147.

Christy, M. 1923. The common teazel as a carnivorous plant. *Journal of Botany* 61: 33–45.

Cooper, J. E. 1977. No. 76. *Utricularia olivacea. Endangered and Threatened Plants of North Carolina*. Raleigh: North Carolina State Museum.

Cooper-Driver, G. A. 1980. The role of flavanoids and related compounds in fern systematics. *Bulletin of the Torrey Botanical Club* 107: 116–127.

Craighead, F. C. 1963. *Orchids and Other Air Plants of the Everglades National Park*. Coral Gables, Fla.: University of Miami Press.

Crum, H. A. 1988. *A Focus on Peatlands and Peat Mosses*. Ann Arbor: University of Michigan Press.

D'Amato, P. 1998. *The Savage Garden*. Berkeley, Calif.: Ten Speed Press.

D'Amato, P. 1999. Dine on coniine and die. *Carnivorous Plant Newsletter* 28: 117–118.

Daniels, R. E. 1989. Adaptation and variation in bog mosses. *Plants Today* 2: 139–144.

Darwin, C. 1875. *Insectivorous Plants*. London: John Murray.

Darwin, F. 1878. Experiments on the nutrition of *Drosera rotundifolia*. *Journal of the Linnean Society of Botany* 17: 17–32.

Daubendiek, B. A., and E. S. Newman. 1988. *Michigan Nature Association in Retrospect*. Avoca, Mich.: Michigan Nature Association.

Daubenmire, R. F. 1974. *Plants and the Environment*: *A Textbook of Plant Autecology*. 3rd ed. New York: John Wiley.

DeBuhr, L. E. 1973. Distribution and reproductive biology of *Darlingtonia californica*. Master of Arts thesis, Claremont Graduate School, Claremont, Calif.

Deevey, E. S. 1958. Bogs. (*Scientific American* offprint.) San Francisco, Calif.: W. H. Freeman.

Degreef, J. D. 1988. The electrochemical mechanism of trap closure in *Dionaea muscipula*. *Carnivorous Plant Newsletter* 17: 80–83, 91–94.

Dennis, W. M. 1980. *Sarracenia oreophila* (Kearney) Wherry in the Blue Ridge province of northeastern Georgia. *Castanea* 45: 101–103.

Determann, R., and M. Groves. 1993. A new cultivar of *Sarracenia leucophylla* Raf. *Carnivorous Plant Newsletter* 22: 108–109.

Diels, L. 1906. No. 112. *Droseraceae*. In A. Engler, ed. *Das Pflanzenreich*. IV. Weinheim, Germany.

DiPalme, J. R., R. McMichael, and M. DiPalme. 1966. Touch receptor of the Venus flytrap, *Dionaea muscipula*. *Science* 152: 539–541.

Dodge, H. R. 1947. A new species of *Wyeomyia* from the pitcher-plant (Diptera: Culcidae). *Proceedings of the Entomological Society of Washington* 49: 117–122.

Drury, W. H. 1998. *Chance and Change*. Berkeley: University of California Press.

Earley, L. S. 1989. Wetlands in the highlands. *Wildlife in North Carolina* 53: 10–16.

Earley, L. S. 1993. Black market wildlife. *Wildlife in North Carolina* 57: 4–11.

Edwards, H. 1876. *Darlingtonia californica* Torrey. *Proceedings of the California Academy of Science* 6: 161–166.

Eisner, T., and J. Shepherd. 1965. Caterpillar feeding on a sundew plant. *Science* 150: 1608–1609.

Elder, C. L. 1994. Reproductive biology of the California pitcher plant (*Darlingtonia californica*). *Fremontia* 22: 29–30.

Eleuterius, L. N., and S. B. Jones. 1969. A floristic and ecological study of pitcher plant bogs in south Mississippi. *Rhodora* 71: 29–34.

Faegri, K., and L. van der Pijl. 1979. *The Principles of Pollination Ecology*. New York: Pergamon Press.

Fagerberg, W. R., and D. Allain. 1991. A quantitative study of tissue dynamics during closure in the traps of Venus's flytrap, *Dionaea muscipula* Ellis. *American Journal of Botany* 78: 647–657.

Fashing, N. J. 1981. Arthropod associates of the cobra lily (*Darlingtonia californica*). *Virginia Journal of Science* 32: 92.

Fineran, B. A. 1985. Glandular trichomes in *Utricularia*: a review of their structure and function. *Israel Journal of Botany* 34: 295–330.

Fish, D. 1976. Structure and composition of the aquatic invertebrate community inhabiting epiphytic bromeliads in south Florida and the discovery of an insectivorous bromeliad. Ph.D. diss., University of Florida, Gainesville.

Fish, D., and D. W. Hall. 1978. Succession and stratification of aquatic insects inhabiting the leaves of the insectivorous pitcher plant, *Sarracenia purpurea*. *American Midland Naturalist* 99: 172–183.

Folkerts, G. W. 1982. The Gulf Coast pitcher plant bogs. *American Scientist* 70: 260–267.

Folkerts, G. W. 1989. Facultative rhizome dimorphism in *Sarracenia psittacina* Michx. (Sarraceniaceae): an adaptation to deepening substrate. *Phytomorphology* 39: 285–289.

Folkerts, G. W., and D. R. Folkerts. 1989. Unique capsule dehiscence in *Sarracenia leucophylla* Raf. and a hypothesis concerning post-anthesis tilting in *Sarracenia* flowers. *Castanea* 54: 111–114.

Folkerts, G. W., and J. D. Freeman. 1989. *Pinguicula lutea* Walter f. *alba*, f. nova (Lentibulariaceae), a white-flowered form of the yellow butterwort. *Castanea* 54: 40–42.

Forman, R. T. T., ed. 1979. *Pine Barrens Ecosystem and Landscape*. New York: Academic Press.

Forsyth, A. B., and R. J. Robertson. 1975. K reproductive strategy and larval behavior of the pitcher-plant sarcophagid fly, *Blaesoxipha fletcheri*. *Canadian Journal of Zoology* 53: 174–179.

Frank, J. H., and L. P. Lounibos, eds. 1983. *Phytotelmata*: *Plants as Hosts for Aquatic Insect Communities*. Medford, N.J.: Plexus.

Frank, J. H., and G. F. O'Meara. 1984. The bromeliad *Catopsis berteroniana* traps terrestrial arthropods but harbors *Wyeomyia* larvae (Diptera: Culicidae). *Florida Entomologist* 67: 418–424.

Gagliardo, R. 1996. A new cultivar of *Dionaea muscipula* Ellis. *Carnivorous Plant Newsletter* 25: 50.

Gallie, D. R., and S. Chang. 1997. Signal transduction in the carnivorous plant *Sarracenia purpurea*. *Plant Physiology* 115: 1461–1471.

Gates, F. C. 1929. Heat and flowering of *Utricularia resupinata*. *Ecology* 10: 353-354.

Gates, F. C. 1939. Conditions for the flowering of *Utricularia resupinata*. *Contributions of the Department of Botany and Plant Pathology, Kansas* 397: 159–162.

Gibson, T. C. 1983. Competition, disturbance, and the carnivorous plant community in the southeastern United States. Ph.D. diss., University of Utah, Salt Lake City.

Gilliam, F. S. 1988. Interactions of fire with nutrients in the herbaceous layer of a nutrient-poor coastal plain forest. *Bulletin of the Torrey Botanical Club* 115: 265–271.

Givnish, T. J., E. L. Burkhardt, R. Hoppel, and I. Weintraub. 1984. Carnivory in the bromeliad *Brocchinea reducta*, with a cost/benefit model for the general restriction of carnivorous plants to sunny, moist, nutrient-poor habitats. *American Naturalist* 124: 479–497.

Gleason, H. A. 1952. *Britton and Brown Illustrated Flora of the United States and Adjacent Canada*. New York: New York Botanical Garden and Hafner Press.

Godfrey, R. K., and H. L. Stripling. 1961. A synopsis of *Pinguicula* (Lentibulariaceae) in the southeastern United States. *American Midland Naturalist* 66: 395–409.

Godfrey, R. K., and J. W. Wooten. 1981. *Aquatic and Wetland Plants of the Southeastern United States*: *Dicotyledons*. Athens: University of Georgia Press.

Godt, M. W., and J. L. Hamrick. 1998. Allozyme diversity in the endangered pitcher plant *Sarracenia rubra* subspecies *alabamensis* (Sarraceniaceae) and its close relative *S. rubra* subspecies *rubra*. *American Journal of Botany* 85: 802–810.

Godt, M. W., and J. L. Hamrick. 1999. Genetic divergence among infraspecific taxa of *Sarracenia purpurea*. *Systematic Botany* 23: 427–438.

Goins, A. E. 1977. Observations on the life history and ecology of the southern pitcher-plant mosquito, *Wyeomyia haynei* Dodge. Master of Science thesis, Auburn University, Auburn, Alabama.

Gon, S. 1994. The Hawaii population of *Drosera anglica*: a tropical twist on a temperate theme. *Carnivorous Plant Newsletter* 23: 68–69.

Govus, T. E. 1987. The occurrence of *Sarracenia oreophila* (Kearney) Wherry in the Blue Ridge province of southwestern North Carolina. *Castanea* 52: 310–311.

Grant, V. 1963. *Origins and Adaptations*. New York: Columbia University Press.

Hanrahan, R., and J. Miller. 1998. History of discovery: yellow-flowered *Sarracenia purpurea* L. subspecies *venosa* (Raf.) Wherry variety *burkii* Schnell. *Carnivorous Plant Newsletter* 27: 14–17.

Harder, R., and I. Zemlin. 1968. Blutenbildung von *Pinguicula lusitanica* in vitro durch futterung mit pollen. *Planta* 78: 72–78.

Harper, R. M. 1918. The American pitcher plants. *Journal of the Elisha Mitchell Scientific Society* 34: 110–125.

Harper, R. M. 1922. Some pine-barren bogs in central Alabama. *Torreya* 22: 57–59.

Harshberger, J. W. 1892. An abnormal development of inflorescence of *Dionaea*. *Contributions of the Botanical Laboratory of the University of Pennsylvania* 1: 45–49.

Harshberger, J. W. 1916. *The Vegetation of the New Jersey Pine-Barrens*. 1970. Reprint, New York: Dover.

Hay, S. G., A. Bouchand, and L. Brouilet. 1990. Additions to the flora of the island of Newfoundland. *Rhodora* 92: 277–293.

Heinrich, B. 1979. *Bumblebee Economics*. Cambridge, Mass.: Harvard University Press.

Hellquist, C. B. 1974. A white-flowered form of *Utricularia purpurea* from New Hampshire. *Rhodora* 76: 19.

Hepburn, J. S., and F. M. Jones. n.d. (ca. 1920s). Occurrence of anti-proteases in the larvae of the *Sarcophaga* associates of *Sarracenia flava*. *Contributions from the Botanical Laboratory of the University of Pennsylvania*. 4: 460–463.

Hepburn, J. S., E. Q. St. John, and F. M. Jones. 1920a. The absorption of nutrients and allied phenomena in the pitchers of Sarraceniaceae. *Journal of the Franklin Institute* (February): 147–184.

Hepburn, J. S., F. M. Jones, and E. Q. St. John. 1920b. The biochemistry of the American pitcher plants: biochemical studies of the North American Sarraceniaceae. *Transactions of the Wagner Free Institute of Science of Philadelphia* 11: 1–95.

Heslop-Harrison, Y., and R. B. Knox. 1971. A cytochemical study of the leaf-gland enzymes of insectivorous plants of the genus *Pinguicula*. *Planta* 96: 183–211.

Hilton, D. F. J. 1982. The biology of *Endothenia daeckeana* (Lepidoptera: Olethreutidae), an inhabitant of the ovaries of the northern pitcher plant, *Sarracenia purpurea purpurea* (Sarraceniaceae). *Canadian Entomology* 114: 269–274.

Holzman, R. W., B. A. Daubendiek, L. Rizor, and F. Sibley. 1994. *Nature Sanctuary Guidebook*. 7th ed. Avoca, Mich.: Michigan Nature Association.

Hooft, J. 1974. Vegetative reproduction in flytraps. *Carolina Tips* 37: 57–58.

Huggett, R. J. 1995. *Geoecology*: *An Evolutionary Approach*. London: Routledge.

Hulten, E. 1968. *Flora of Alaska and Neighboring Territories*. Stanford, Calif.: Stanford University Press.

Istock, C. A., K. Tanner, and H. Zimmer. 1983. Habitat selection by the pitcher plant mosquito, *Wyeomyia smithii*: behavioral and genetic aspects. In J. H. Frank and L. P. Lounibos, eds. *Phytotelmata*: *Terrestrial Plants as Hosts for Aquatic Insect Communities*. Medford, N.J.: Plexus.

Jennison, H. M. 1935. Notes on some plants of Tennessee. *Rhodora* 37: 309–323.

Joel, D. M. 1982. How the bladderwort captures its prey. *Israel Land and Nature* 8: 54–57.

Joel, D. M. 1986. Glandular structures in carnivorous plants: their role in mutual exploitation of insects. In B. E. Juniper and T. E. Southwood, eds. *Insects and the Plant Surface*. London: Edward Arnold.

Joel, D. M., P. A. Rea, and B. E. Juniper. 1983. The cuticle of *Dionaea muscipula* Ellis (Venus's flytrap) in relation to stimulation, secretion and absorption. *Protoplasma* 114: 44–51.

Joel, D. M., B. E. Juniper, and A. Dafni. 1985. Ultraviolet patterns in the traps of carnivorous plants. *New Phytologist* 101: 585–593.

Johnson, A. T. 1929. *Darlingtonia californica*. *Gardener's Chronicle* (14 September): 202–203.

Johnson, C. W. 1985. *Bogs of the Northeast*. Hanover, N.H.: University Press of New England.

Jones, F. M. 1904. Pitcher-plant insects. *Entomological News* 15: 14–17.

Jones, F. M. 1907. Pitcher-plant insects. II. *Entomological News* 18: 413–420.

Jones, F. M. 1908. Pitcher-plant insects. III. *Entomological News* 19: 150–156.

Jones, F. M. 1916. Two insect associates of the California pitcher-plant, *Darlingtonia californica*. *Entomological News* 27: 385–391.

Jones, F. M. 1918. *Dohniphora venusta* Coquillet (Dipt.) in *Sarracenia flava*. *Entomological News* 29: 299–302.

Jones, F. M. 1920. Another pitcher-plant insect (Diptera; Sciarinae). *Entomological News* 31: 91–94.

Jones, F. M. 1921. Pitcher plants and their moths. *Natural History* 21: 296–316.

Jones, F. M. 1923. The most wonderful plant in the world. *Natural History* 23: 589–596.

Jones, F. M. 1935. Pitcher plants and their insect associates. In M. V. Walcott. *Illustrations of North American Pitcher Plants*. Washington, D.C.: Smithsonian Institution.

Jones, F. M. 1950. Reminiscences of a Delaware naturalist. *Delaware Notes* 23: 13–35.

Juniper, B. E., A. J. Gilchrist, and R. J. Robins. 1977. Some features of secretory systems in plants. *Histochemical Journal* 9: 659–680.

Juniper, B. E., R. J. Robins, and D. M. Joel. 1989. *The Carnivorous Plants*. London: Academic Press.

Kartesz, J. T. 1994. *A Synonymized Checklist of the Vascular Flora of the United States, Canada, and Greenland*. 2d ed. 2 vols. Portland, Ore.: Timber Press.

Kearns, C. A., and D. W. Inouye. 1993. *Techniques for Pollination Biologists*. Niwot: University Press of Colorado.

Kevan, P. G. 1978. Floral coloration, its colorimetric analysis and significance in anthecology. In A. J. Richards, ed. *The Pollination of Flowers by Insects*. New York: Academic Press.

Kevan, P. G. 1979. Vegetation and floral colors revealed by ultraviolet light: interpretational difficulties for functional significance. *American Journal of Botany* 66: 749–751.

Kilham, P. 1982. The biogeochemistry of bog ecosystems and the chemical ecology of sphagnum. *Michigan Botanist* 21: 159–168.

Komiya, S. 1972. *Systematic Studies on the Lentibulariaceae*. Tokyo: Department of Biology, Nippon Dental College.

Kondo, K. 1971. Germination and developmental morphology of seeds in *Utricularia cornuta* Michx. and *Utricularia juncea* Vahl. *Rhodora* 73: 541–547.

Kondo, K. 1972a. A comparison of variability in *Utricularia cornuta* and *Utricularia juncea*. *American Journal of Botany* 59: 23–37.

Kondo, K. 1972b. A paper chromatographic comparison of *Utricularia cornuta* and *Utricularia juncea*. *Phyton* 30: 43–45.

Krajina, V. J. 1968. Sarraceniaceae, a new family for British Columbia. *Syesis* 1: 121–124.

Kruckeberg, A. R. 1954. The ecology of serpentine soils. III. Plant species in relation to serpentine soils. *Ecology* 35: 267–274.

Lamb, R. 1991. *Pinguicula villosa*, the northern butterwort. *Carnivorous Plant Newsletter* 20: 73–77.

Lambert, G. 1902. A l'etude de la pharmacologie du *Sarracenia purpurea*. *Annales de Hygeine et de Medecia Coloniale de Paris* 5: 652–662.

Larsen, J. A. 1982. *Ecology of the Northern Lowland Bogs and Coniferous Forests*. New York: Academic Press.

Lee, C. W., H. T. Erickson, and J. Janick. 1979. Cleistogamy in *Salpiglossis sinuata*. *American Journal of Botany* 66: 626–632.

Leonard, S. W. 1978. Venus' fly-trap in Florida: native or naturalized? *North Carolina Wild Flower Protection Society Newsletter* (Spring): 26–28.

Lichtner, F. T., and S. E. Williams. 1977. Prey capture and factors controlling trap narrowing in *Dionaea* (Droseraceae). *American Journal of Botany* 64: 881–886.

Lindquist, J. A. 1975. Bacteriological and ecological observations on the northern pitcher plant, *Sarracenia purpurea* L. Master of Science thesis, University of Wisconsin, Madison.

Line, L. 1999. An American original. *National Wildlife* 37: 18–27.

Lloyd, F. E. 1942. *The Carnivorous Plants*. Waltham, Mass.: Chronica Botanica.

Lounibos, L. P., and W. E. Bradshaw. 1975. A second diapause in *Wyeomyia smithii*: a seasonal incidence and maintenance by photoperiod. *Canadian Journal of Zoology* 53: 215–221.

Lounibos, L. P., C. Van Dover, and G. F. O'Meara. 1982. Fecundity, autogeny and larval environment of the pitcher-plant mosquito, *Wyeomyia smithii*. *Oecologia* (Berlin) 55: 160–164.

Lowry, B., D. Lee, and C. Hebant. 1980. The origin of land plants: a new look at an old problem. *Taxon* 29: 183–197.

Macfarlane, J. M. 1899. Observations on some hybrids between *Drosera filiformis* and *D. intermedia*. *Contributions of the Botanical Laboratory of the University of Pennsylvania* 2: 87–99.

Macfarlane, J. M. 1907. On the occurrence of natural hybrids in the genus *Sarracenia*. In *Report of the Conference on Genetics*. London. 1–4.

Macfarlane, J. M. 1908. No. 110 Sarraceniaceae. In A. Engler, ed. *Das Pflanzenreich*. IV. Weinheim, Germany. 1–39.

Macfarlane, J. M. 1914. Drosera. In L. H. Bailey, ed. *The Standard Cyclopedia of Horticulture*. Vol. 1. New York: Macmillan.

MacRoberts, M. H., and B. R. MacRoberts. 1991. The distribution of *Sarracenia* in Louisiana, with data on its abundance in the western part of the state. *Phytologia* 70: 119–125.

Maio, J. J. 1958. Predatory fungi. *Scientific American* 199: 67–71.

Maloney, A. B. 1945. A botanist on the road to Yerba Buena. *California Historical Society Quarterly* 24: 321–342.

Mameli, E. 1916. Ricerche anatomiche, fisiologiche e biologiche sulla *Martynia lutea* Lindl. *Atti del' Universita di Pavia* (Serie 2) 16: 137–188.

Mandossian, A. J. 1965. *Some Aspects of the Ecological Life History of Sarracenia purpurea*. Ph.D. diss., Michigan State University, East Lansing. No. 65-14245, Ann Arbor, Mich.: University Microfilms.

Masters, C. O. 1967. The biota of teasel waters as a science fair project. *Carolina Tips* 30: 21–22.

Masters, M. T. 1881a. *Gardeners' Chronicle*, 2d ser. 15: 817.

Masters, M. T. 1881b. *Gardeners' Chronicle*, 2d ser. 15: 628.

Masters, M. T. 1881c. *Gardeners' Chronicle*, 2d ser. 15: 11–12, 40–41.

Mazrimas, J. A. 1987. *Drosera anglica* from the Alakai Swamp, Kauai, Hawaii. *Carnivorous Plant Newsletter* 16: 21–22.

McCrea, K. D., and M. Levy. 1983. Photographic visualization of floral colors as perceived by honeybee pollinators. *American Journal of Botany* 70: 368–375.

McDaniel, S. T. 1966. *A Taxonomic Revision of Sarracenia (Sarraceniaceae)*. Ph.D. diss., Florida State University, Tallahassee. No. 67-345, Ann Arbor, Mich.: University Microfilms.

McQueen, C. B. 1990. *Field Guide to the Peat Mosses of Boreal North America*. Hanover, N.H.: University Press of New England.

Mellichamp, J. H. 1875. Notes on *Sarracenia variolaris*. In *Proceedings of the American Association for the Advancement of Science*. 23rd meeting. 113–133.

Mellichamp, T. L. 1978. Botanical history of carnivorous plants. II. *Darlingtonia*. *Carnivorous Plant Newsletter* 7: 82–85.

Merrill, E. D. 1948. Unlisted new names in Alphonso Wood's publications. *Rhodora* 50: 101–130.

Meyers, D. G., and J. R. Strickler. 1979. Capture enhancement in a carnivorous aquatic plant: function of antennae and bristles in *Utricularia vulgaris*. *Science* 203: 1022–1025.

Meyers-Rice, B. A. 1997. An anthocyanin-free variant of *Darlingtonia californica*: newly discovered and already imperiled. *Carnivorous Plant Newsletter* 27:129–132.

Meyers-Rice, B. A. 1998. *Darlingtonia californica* 'Othello'. *Carnivorous Plant Newsletter* 27: 40–42.

Meyers-Rice, B. A. 1999. Testing the appetites of *Ibicella* and *Drosophyllum*. *Carnivorous Plant Newsletter* 28: 40–43.

Mitchell, R. S., T. E. Maenza-Gmelch, and J. G. Barbour. 1994. *Utricularia inflata* Walt. (Lentibulariaceae), new to New York state. *Bulletin of the Torrey Botanical Club* 121: 295–297.

Mody, N. V., R. Henson, P. A. Hedin, V. Kokpol, and D. H. Miles. 1976. Isolation of the insect paralyzing agent coniine from *Sarracenia flava*. *Experimentia* 32: 829–830.

Mogi, M., and J. Mokry. 1980. Distribution of *Wyeomyia smithii* (Diptera: Culicidae) eggs in pitcher plants in Newfoundland, Canada. *Tropical Medicine* 22: 1–12.

Moldenke, H. N. 1934. Studies of new and noteworthy tropical American plants. *Phytologia* 1: 98–99.

Murphy, P. B., and R. S. Boyd. 1999. Population status and habitat characterization of the endangered plant, *Sarracenia rubra* subspecies *alabamensis*. *Castanea* 64: 101–113.

Murry, R. E., and L. E. Urbatsch. 1979. Preliminary reports on the flora of Louisiana. III. The families Droseraceae and Sarraceniaceae. *Castanea* 44: 24–38.

Naczi, R. F. C., E. M. Soper, F. W. Case, and R. B. Case. 1999. *Sarracenia rosea* (Sarraceniaceae), a new species of pitcher plant from the southeastern United States. *Sida* 18: 1183–1206.

Nelson, E. C. 1986. *Sarracenia* hybrids raised at Glasnevin Botanic Gardens, Ireland: nomenclature and typification. *Taxon* 35: 574–578.

Nelson, E. C. 1992. Carnivorous plants in Ireland. III. David Moore and *Sarracenia* × *moorei* at Glasnevin. *Carnivorous Plant Newsletter* 21: 95–98.

Nelson, E. C., and D. L. McKinley. 1990. *Aphrodite's Mousetrap*. Aberystwyth, Wales: Boethius Press.

Nielsen, D. W. 1990. Arthropod communities associated with *Darlingtonia californica*. *Annals of the Entomological Society of America* 83: 189–199.

Oliver, F. W. 1944. A mass catch of cabbage whites by sundews. *Proceedings of the Royal Entomological Society of London* 19: 5.

Ownbey, G. B., and W. R. Smith. 1988. New and noteworthy plant records for Minnesota. *Rhodora* 90: 369–377.

Paris, O. H., and C. E. Jenner. 1959. Photoperiodic control and diapause in the pitcher plant midge *Metriocnemus knabi*. In R. B. Withrow, ed. *Photoperiod and Related Phenomena in Plants and Animals*. Washington, D.C.: American Association for the Advancement of Science. 601–624.

Parkes, D. M. 1980. Adaptive mechanisms of surfaces and glands in some carnivorous plants. Master of Science thesis, Monash University, Clayton, Victoria, Australia.

Peterson, R. L., J. Nagawa, A. Vilmenay, A. Faust, and R. M. Duffield. 2000. An explanation for the absence of foreign mosquitoes in the leaves of *Sarracenia purpurea* L. Association of Southeastern Biologists, 61st Annual Meeting, University of Tennessee, Chattanooga.

Pickett, S. T. A., and P. S. White, eds. 1985. *The Ecology of Natural Disturbance and Patch Dynamics*. Orlando, Fla.: Academic Press.

Pietropaolo, J., and P. Pietropaolo. 1986. *Carnivorous Plants of the World*. Portland, Ore.: Timber Press.

Plummer, G. L. 1963. Soils of the pitcher plant habitats in the Georgia coastal plain. *Ecology* 44: 727–734.

Plummer, G. L., and J. B. Kethley. 1964. Foliar absorption of amino acids, peptides and other nutrients by the pitcher plant, *Sarracenia flava*. *Botanical Gazette* 125: 245–260.

Pramer, D. 1964. Nematode-trapping fungi. *Science* 144: 382–388.

Prankevicius, A. B., and D. M. Cameron. 1989. Free-living dinitrogen-fixing bacteria in the leaf of the northern pitcher plant (*Sarracenia purpurea* L.). *Naturaliste Canada* 116: 245–249.

Pringle, J. S. 1980. *An Introduction to Wetland Classification in the Great Lakes*

Region. Technical Bulletin no. 10. Hamilton, Ontario, Canada: Royal Botanic Gardens.

Pringsheim, E. G., and O. Pringsheim. 1962. Axenic culture of *Utricularia*. *American Journal of Botany* 49: 898–901.

Radford, A. E., H. E. Ahles, and C. R. Bell. 1968. *Manual of the Vascular Flora of the Carolinas*. Chapel Hill: University of North Carolina Press.

Reinert, G. W., and R. K. Godfrey. 1962. Reappraisal of *Utricularia inflata* and *U. radiata* (Lentibulariaceae). *American Journal of Botany* 49: 213–220.

Riley, J. L., and S. Walshe. 1985. New and interesting vascular plant records from northern Ontario. *Canadian Field Naturalist* 99: 30–33.

Richardson, C. J., ed. 1981. *Pocosin Wetlands*. Stroudsburg, Pa.: Hutchinson.

Risner, J. K. 1987. The floating isle of carnivorous plants. *Carnivorous Plant Newsletter* 16: 113–115.

Roberts, M. L. 1972. *Wolffia* in the bladders of *Utricularia*: an "herbivorous" plant. *Michigan Botanist* 11: 67–69.

Roberts, P. R., and H. J. Oosting. 1958. Responses of Venus fly trap (*Dionaea muscipula*) to factors involved in its endemism. *Ecological Monographs* 28: 193–218.

Robertson, A., and B. A. Roberts. 1982. Checklist of the alpine flora of the western Brook Pond and Deer Pond areas, Gros Marne National Park. *Rhodora* 84: 101–115.

Robins, R. J. 1976. The nature of the stimuli causing digestive juice secretion in *Dionaea muscipula* (Venus's flytrap). *Planta* 128: 263–265.

Robins, R. J., and B. E. Juniper. 1980. The secretory cycle of *Dionaea muscipula* Ellis. II. Storage and synthesis of the secretory proteins. *New Phytologist* 86: 297–311.

Robinson, A. G. 1972. A new species of aphid (Homoptera: Aphididae) from a pitcher-plant. *Canadian Entomologist* 104: 955–957.

Robinson, J. T. 1981a. New carnivorous plant cultivar received in 1980. *Carnivorous Plant Newsletter* 10: 95.

Robinson, J. T. 1981b. *Sarracenia purpurea* L. forma *heterophylla* (Eaton) Fernald: new to Connecticut. *Rhodora* 83: 156–157.

Romeo, J. T., J. D. Bacon, and T. J. Mabry. 1977. Ecological considerations of amino acids and flavanoids in *Sarracenia* species. *Biochemical Systematics and Ecology* 5: 117–120.

Rondeau, J. H. 1995. *Carnivorous Plants of the West*. Vol. II, *California, Oregon, and Washington*. Privately published by author.

Rondeau, J. H. 1998. *Utricularia ochroleuca* R. Hartman, Lentibulariaceae, new and noteworthy collections: California, Plumas County. *Madroño* 45: 184–185.

Rosenzweig, M. L. 1995. *Species Diversity in Space and Time*. Cambridge, England: Cambridge University Press.

Rossbach, G. B. 1939. Aquatic utricularias. *Rhodora* 41: 113–128.

Russell, A. M. 1918. The macroscopic and microscopic structure of some hybrid sarracenias compared with their parents. *Botanical Contributions of the University of Pennsylvania* 5: 3–41.

Rymal, D. E., and G. W. Folkerts. 1982. Insects associated with pitcher-plants (*Sarracenia*: Sarraceniaceae) and their relationship to pitcher-plant conservation. *Journal of the Alabama Academy of Science* 53: 131–151.

Sasago, A., and T. Sibaoka. 1985a. Water extrusion in the trap bladders of *Utricularia vulgaris*. I. A possible pathway of water across the bladder wall. *Botanical Magazine* (*Tokyo*) 98: 55–56.

Sasago, A., and T. Sibaoka. 1985b. Water extrusion in the trap bladders of *Utricularia vulgaris*. II. A possible mechanism of water outflow. *Botanical Magazine* (*Tokyo*) 98: 113–124.

Savage, H. 1982. *The Mysterious Carolina Bays*. Columbia: University of South Carolina Press.

Scala, J., K. Lott, D. W. Schwab, and F. E. Semersky. 1969. Digestive secretion of *Dionaea muscipula* (Venus's flytrap). *Plant Physiology* 44: 367–371.

Schlauer, J. 1996. A dichotomous key to the genus *Drosera* L. (Droseraceae). *Carnivorous Plant Newsletter* 25: 67–88.

Schnell, D. E. 1976. *Carnivorous Plants of the United States and Canada*. Winston-Salem, N.C.: John F. Blair.

Schnell, D. E. 1977. Infraspecific variation in *Sarracenia rubra* Walt.: some observations. *Castanea* 42: 149–170.

Schnell, D. E. 1978a. *Sarracenia* L. petal extract chromatography. *Castanea* 43: 107–115.

Schnell, D. E. 1978b. *Sarracenia flava* L.: infraspecific variation in eastern North Carolina. *Castanea* 43: 1–20.

Schnell, D. E. 1978c. *Sarracenia rubra* Walter: infraspecific nomenclatural corrections. *Castanea* 43: 260–261.

Schnell, D. E. 1978d. Systematic flower studies of *Sarracenia* L. *Castanea* 43: 211–220.

Schnell, D. E. 1979a. A critical review of published variants of *Sarracenia purpurea* L. *Castanea* 44: 47–59.

Schnell, D. E. 1979b. *Sarracenia rubra* Walter subspecies *gulfensis*: a new subspecies. *Castanea* 44: 217–223.

Schnell, D. E. 1980a. *Drosera linearis*. *Carnivorous Plant Newsletter* 9: 16–18.

Schnell, D. E. 1980b. Notes on the biology of *Sarracenia oreophila* (Kearney) Wherry. *Castanea* 45: 166–170.

Schnell, D. E. 1980c. Notes on *Utricularia simulans* Pilger (Lentibulariaceae) in southern Florida. *Castanea* 45: 270–276.

Schnell, D. E. 1980d. *Pinguicula caerulea* Walt. forma *leucantha*: a new form. *Castanea* 45: 56–60.

Schnell, D. E. 1981. *Sarracenia purpurea* L. subspecies *venosa* (Raf.) Wherry: variations in the Carolinas coastal plain. *Castanea* 46: 225–234.

Schnell, D. E. 1982a. Effects of simultaneous draining and brush cutting on a *Sarracenia* L. population in a southeastern North Carolina pocosin. *Castanea* 47: 248–260.

Schnell, D. E. 1982b. Notes on *Drosera linearis* Goldie in northeastern lower Michigan. *Castanea* 47: 313–328.

Schnell, D. E. 1982c. A photographic primer of variants of *Sarracenia rubra* Walt. *Carnivorous Plant Newsletter* 11: 41–45.

Schnell, D. E. 1983. Notes on the pollination of *Sarracenia flava* L. (Sarraceniaceae) in the piedmont province of North Carolina. *Rhodora* 85: 405–420.

Schnell, D. E. 1989. *Sarracenia alata* and *S. leucophylla* variations. *Carnivorous Plant Newsletter* 18: 79–84.

Schnell, D. E. 1993. *Sarracenia purpurea* L. subspecies *venosa* (Raf.) Wherry var. *burkii* Schnell (Sarraceniaceae): a new variety of the gulf coastal plain. *Rhodora* 95: 6–10.

Schnell, D. E. 1995a. *Drosera filiformis* Raf.: one species or two? *Carnivorous Plant Newsletter* 24: 11–15.

Schnell, D. E. 1995b. *Sarracenia flava* varieties: do we know what we are talking about? *Carnivorous Plant Newsletter* 24: 48–50.

Schnell, D. E. 1995c. A natural hybrid of *Drosera anglica* Huds. and *Drosera linearis* Goldie in Michigan. *Rhodora* 97: 164–170.

Schnell, D. E. 1998a. A pitcher key to the genus *Sarracenia* L. (Sarraceniaceae). *Castanea* 63: 489–492.

Schnell, D. E. 1998b. *Sarracenia flava* L. varieties. *Carnivorous Plant Newsletter* 27: 116–120.

Schnell, D. E. 1999. *Drosera anglica* Huds. vs. *Drosera × anglica*: what is the difference? *Carnivorous Plant Newsletter* 28: 107–115.

Schnell, D. E., and R. O. Determann. 1997. *Sarracenia purpurea* L. subspecies *venosa* (Raf.) Wherry variety *montana* Schnell & Determann (Sarraceniaceae): a new variety. *Castanea* 62: 60–62.

Schnell, D. E., and D. W. Krider. 1976. Cluster analysis of the genus *Sarracenia* L. in the southeastern United States. *Castanea* 41: 165–176.

Schuchert, C. 1955. *Atlas of Paleogeographic Maps of North America*. New York: John Wiley and Sons.

Schultes, R. E., and W. A. Davis. 1982. *The Glass Flowers at Harvard*. New York: E. P. Dutton.

Schwintzer, C. R. 1978. Vegetation and nutrient status of northern Michigan fens. *Canadian Journal of Botany* 56: 3044–3051.

Sharp, A. J., and A. Baker. 1964. First and interesting reports of flowering plants in Tennessee. *Castanea* 29: 178–185.

Sheridan, P. M. 1987. A preliminary report on *Drosera intermedia* × *D. capillaris*. *Carnivorous Plant Newsletter* 16: 71–73.

Sheridan, P. M. 1991. What is the identity of the west Gulf Coast pitcher plant, *Sarracenia alata* Wood? *Carnivorous Plant Newsletter* 20: 102–110.

Sheridan, P. M., and D. N. Karowe. 2000. Inbreeding, outbreeding, and heterosis in the yellow pitcher plant, *Sarracenia flava* (Sarraceniaceae), in Virginia. *American Journal of Botany* 87: 1628–1633.

Sheridan, P. M., and W. Scholl. 1993. Notes on some *Darlingtonia californica* Torrey bogs. *Carnivorous Plant Newsletter* 22: 70–75.

Shinners, L. H. 1962. *Drosera* (Droseraceae) in the southeastern United States: an interim report. *Sida* 1: 53–59.

Sibaoka, T. 1966. Action potentials in plant organs. *Symposium for the Society of Experimental Biology* 20: 49–74.

Simpson, R. B. 1994. *Pitchers in Trade*. Kew, England: Royal Botanic Gardens.

Slack, A. 1979. *Carnivorous Plants*. London: Ebury Press.

Slack, A. 1986. *Insect-Eating Plants and How to Grow Them*. Sherborne, England: Alphabooks.

Smith, J. B. 1902. Life history of *Aedes smithii*. *Journal of the New York Entomological Society* 10: 10–15.

Sorenson, D. R., and W. T. Jackson. 1968. The utilization of *Paramecia* by the carnivorous plant *Utricularia gibba*. *Planta* 83: 166–170.

Sorrie, B. A. 1992. *Utricularia inflata* Walter (Lentibulariaceae) in Massachusetts. *Rhodora* 94: 391–392.

Souben, P. 1996. Les plantes carnivores en philatelie. *Dionee* (No. 36): 10–19.

Spomer, G. C. 1999. Evidence of protocarnivorous capabilities in *Geranium viscosissimum* and *Potentilla arguta* and other sticky plants. *International Journal of Plant Science* 160: 98–101.

Stebbins, G. L. 1977. *Processes of Organic Evolution*. Englewood Cliffs, N.J.: Prentice-Hall.

Steiger, J. F. 1975. The *Pinguicula* species of the temperate growth type and their cultivation. *Carnivorous Plant Newsletter* 4: 8–18.

Steiger, J. F. 1982. Front and back cover photos of *Pinguicula macroceras* and *P. macroceras* subspecies *nortensis*, respectively. *Carnivorous Plant Newsletter* 11: 29, 52.

Steiger, J. F., and J. H. Rondeau. 1997. *Pinguicula macroceras* subspecies *nortensis*, a new subspecies of *Pinguicula* (Lentibulariaceae) from the California-Oregon border. *International Pinguicula Study Group Newsletter* 8: 3–8.

Stein, B. A., L. S. Kutner, and J. S. Adams, eds. 2000. *Precious Heritage*. New York: Oxford University Press.

Stewart, K. D., R. L. Petersen, and R. M. Duffield. 2000. Algal communities in *Sarracenia purpurea* L. leaves in the absence of midge and mosquito larvae. Association of Southeastern Biologists, 61st Annual Meeting, University of Tennessee, Chattanooga.

Stolzenberg, W. 1993. Busting plant poachers. *Nature Conservancy* 43: 16–23.

Stolzenberg, W. 1999. Greener acres. *Nature Conservancy* 49: 8.

Stoutamire, W. P. 1967. Sphagnum. *Cranbrook Institute of Science News Letter* 36: 98–104.

Stuhlman, O. 1948a. A mechanical analysis of the closure movements of Venus's flytrap. *Physical Review* 74: 1190.

Stuhlman, O. 1948b. A physical analysis of the opening and closing movements of the lobes of Venus's flytrap. *Bulletin of the Torrey Botanical Club* 75: 22–44.

Sydenham, P. H., and G. P. Findlay. 1975. Transport of solutes and water by resetting bladders of *Utricularia*. *Australian Journal of Plant Physiology* 2: 335–351.

Taylor, P. 1989. *The Genus Utricularia: A Taxonomic Monograph*. Kew Bulletin Additional Series, no. XIV. Kew, England: Royal Botanic Gardens.

Taylor, P. 1991. *Utricularia* in North America north of Mexico. *Carnivorous Plant Newsletter* 20: 8–20, 36–43.

"Two Charged with Smuggling Venus Flytraps." *Statesville Record and Landmark* (Statesville, N.C.), 8 May 1998.

Vogel, S. 1983. Ecophysiology and zoophilic pollination. In O. L. Lange, P. S. Nobel, C. B. Osmund, and C. B. Ziegler, eds. *Encyclopedia of Plant Physiology*. Vol. 12C. Berlin: Springer-Verlag.

Voss, E. G. 1985. *Michigan Flora*. Part II. Ann Arbor, Michigan: Cranbrook Institute of Science (Bulletin no. 59) and University of Michigan Herbarium.

Wallace, J., K. McGhee, and Biology Class. 1999. Testing for carnivory in *Ibicella lutea*. *Carnivorous Plant Newsletter* 28: 49–50.

Wallace, R. L. 1978. Substrate selection by larvae of the sessile rotifer *Ptygura beauchampii*. *Ecology* 59: 221–227.

Weakley, A. S., and M. P. Schafale. 1994. Non-alluvial wetlands of the southern Blue Ridge: diversity in a threatened ecosystem. *Water, Air and Soil Pollution* 77: 359–383.

Weiher, E. R., and C. W. Boylen. 1994. Alterations in aquatic plant community structure following liming of an acidic Adirondack lake. *Canadian Journal of Fishing and Aquatic Science* 51: 20–24.

Wells, B. W. 1932. *The Natural Gardens of North Carolina*. 1967. Reprint, Chapel Hill: University of North Carolina Press.

Wertheim, E. 1951. *Textbook of Organic Chemistry*. New York: Blakiston.

Wherry, E. T. 1929. Acidity relations of the Sarracenias. *Journal of the Washington Academy of Science* 19: 379–390.

Wherry, E. T. 1933a. The Appalachian relative of *Sarracenia flava*. *Bartonia* 15: 7–8.

Wherry, E. T. 1933b. The geographic relations of *Sarracenia purpurea*. *Bartonia* 15: 1–6.

Wherry, E. T. 1935. Descriptions and notes on distribution. In M. V. Walcott. *Illustrations of the North American Pitcherplants*. Washington, D.C.: Smithsonian Institution.

Wherry, E. T. 1972. Notes on *Sarracenia* subspecies. *Castanea* 37: 146–147.

Whittaker, R. J. 1998. *Island Biogeography*. Oxford, England: Oxford University Press.

Wilkinson, T. 1999. Stitching together Grand Bay. *Nature Conservancy* 49: 21–23.

Williams, R. M. 1966. Utilization of animal protein by the pitcher plant, *Sarracenia purpurea*. *Michigan Botanist* 5: 14–17.

Williams, S. E. 1973a. The "memory" of the Venus's flytrap. *Carnivorous Plant Newsletter* 2: 23–25.

Williams, S. E. 1973b. A salute to Sir John Burdon-Sanderson and Mr. Charles Darwin on the centennial of the discovery of nerve-like activity in the Venus's flytrap. *Carnivorous Plant Newsletter* 2: 41.

Williams, S. E. 1976. Comparative sensory physiology of the Droseraceae: the evolution of a plant sensory system. *Proceedings of the American Philosophical Society* 120: 187–204.

Williams, S. E. 1980. How venus's flytraps catch spiders and ants. *Carnivorous Plant Newsletter* 9: 65–78.

Williams, S. E., and A. B. Bennett. 1982. Leaf closure in the Venus flytrap and acid growth response. *Science* 218: 1120–1124.

Williams, S. E., and A. B. Bennett. 1983. Acid flux triggers the Venus's flytrap. *New Scientist* 97: 582.

Williams, S. E., and B. G. Pickard. 1979. The role of action potentials in the control of capture movements of *Drosera* and *Dionaea*. In *Tenth International Conference on Plant Growth Substances*, Madison, Wisconsin. 22–26.

Williams, S. E., and R. M. Spanswick. 1972. Intracellular recordings of the action potentials which mediate the thigmonastic movements of *Drosera*. *Plant Physiology* 49: 64.

Wilson, P. 1994. The east-facing flowers of *Drosera tracyi*. *American Midland Naturalist* 131: 366–369.

Winston, R. D., and P. R. Gorham. 1979a. Roles of endogenous and exogenous growth regulators in dormancy of *Utricularia vulgaris*. *Canadian Journal of Botany* 57: 2750–2759.

Winston, R. D., and P. R. Gorham. 1979b. Turions and dormancy states in *Utricularia vulgaris*. *Canadian Journal of Botany* 57: 2740–2749.

Wolfe, L. M. 1981. Feeding behavior of a plant: differential prey capture in old and new leaves of the pitcher plant (*Sarracenia purpurea*). *American Midland Naturalist* 106: 352–359.

Wood, C. E., Jr. 1955. Evidence for the hybrid origin of *Drosera anglica*. *Rhodora* 57: 105–130.

Wood, C. E., Jr. 1960. The genera of Sarraceniaceae and Droseraceae in the southeastern United States. *Journal of the Arnold Arboretum* 41: 152–156.

Wood, C. E., Jr. 1966. On the identity of *Drosera brevifolia*. *Journal of the Arnold Arboretum* 47: 89–99.

Wood, C. E., Jr., and R. K. Godfrey. 1957. *Pinguicula* (Lentibulariaceae) in the southeastern United States. *Rhodora* 59: 217–230.

Wray, D. L., and C. S. Brimley. 1943. The insect inquilines and victims of pitcher plants in North Carolina. *Annals of the Entomological Society of America* 36: 128–137.

Wynne, F. E. 1944. *Drosera* in eastern North America. *Bulletin of the Torrey Botanical Club* 71: 166–174.

INDEX OF PLANT NAMES

An *italicized* page number denotes a distribution map; **boldface** denotes an illustration or photograph.